Cătălin Gabriel Stănescu

Self-Help, Private Debt Collection and the Concomitant Risks

A Comparative Law Analysis

Springer

Cătălin Gabriel Stănescu
Legal Studies
Central European University
Budapest, Hungary

ISBN 978-3-319-37399-7 ISBN 978-3-319-21503-7 (eBook)
DOI 10.1007/978-3-319-21503-7

Springer Cham Heidelberg New York Dordrecht London

Softcover reprint of the hardcover 1st edition 2015

Printed on acid-free paper

Springer International Publishing AG Switzerland is part of Springer Science+Business Media (www.springer.com)

Mamei mele,
cu toată dragostea

Foreword

If sanctioned by law, self-help in private and commercial laws[1] is a fast, cheap and efficient alternative for court enforcement. It is also a quintessential tool for secured transactions law as evidenced by the early generation of US and Canadian laws or the latest generation examples from the CEE region and France. Treated with indulgency by the common law systems,[2] it has been always regarded upon with suspicion and has been limited to the minimum by civilian legal systems, including France and Germany, the two jurisdictions that have served as models for many other Continental European legal systems.

First, the book argues that self-help remedies and private debt collection are not only the trait of common law jurisdictions. The book researches the history of these institutions of law and argues that remnants of private enforcement can be found in civilian systems' contract law (focusing on several well-known examples from sales and service contracts). The reason for analyzing and identifying several types of self-help in contract law[3] is twofold. On the one hand, it proves that self-help is not incompatible with or unknown to civilian systems. On the other hand, it raises the question of why in civilian systems self-help is generally available for unsecured creditors in contract law, but particularly denied to secured creditors in secured transactions, when in fact, in common law systems, the secured creditors benefit from a larger protection, deriving logically from their secured status.

Second, the book claims and exemplifies that the twenty-first century brought with it a shift towards out-of-court enforcement and debt collection also in Continental Europe as was recognized, among others, by the drafters of the European Common Frame of Reference (DCFR), who have stressed the expectation of

[1] The distinction between private and commercial laws is relevant for dualist systems, such as Germany. Romania has recently become a monist system, by implementing a new Civil Code, which in fact is a code of private law, combining civil, commercial and family laws.

[2] Goode (2014), p. 135 at 151.

[3] The best known self-help device recognized by all chosen jurisdictions is the right to withhold performance. For details, see *infra*, Chap. 3, Sect. 3.4.

creditors for speedy and efficient enforcement in Book IX devoted to secured transactions law. The book contends that implementing and recognizing self-help remedies and private enforcement benefit the economies of civil law systems, where—similarly to the U.S. or other common law countries—the economic role of both business and consumer financing has increased drastically by the twenty-first century. In order to substantiate this claim, the book comes forward with examples of known and tested self-help forms and remedies to comparatively assess the efficiency and the intensity of the concomitant risks.

Third, the book argues that—despite their usefulness—self-help and private debt collection brought to the surface significant new risks, especially for consumer-debtors. Therefore, private enforcement needs to be paralleled by introducing tailor-made consumer-debtor protection regulation. The book uses the US Fair Debt Collection Practices Act as a benchmark and compares its unique panoply of tools with the kin regulatory frameworks offered by the other jurisdictions observed to find the most efficient solutions of prevention and deterrence of abuse to which the consumer-debtors might be subjected. A matrix of *de minimis* building blocks serves as the basis for finding the most suitable consumer protection tools for each.

Last but not least, specific attention is given to factoring, which functions in many instances as a form of pseudo-private debt collection and which has been exploited to bypass sector-specific consumer protection regulations.

Reference

Goode R (1998) The codification of commercial law. Monash Univ Law Rev 14

Acknowledgments

This book would not have been possible without the help and constant support of a large number of people to whom I wish to express my deep gratitude.

I would like to express my special appreciation and thanks to my supervisor, **Professor Tibor Tajti**, for being a tremendous mentor to me. He encouraged my research in the area of private debt collection and allowed me to grow as a researcher. His advice on my research is priceless.

I would also like to thank the other members of the International Business Law Branch of CEU Legal Studies Department: **Professor Stefan Messmann**, for encouraging me to engage in the S.J.D. endeavor, for believing in me and especially for his friendship, which means a lot to me; **Professor Tibor Varady**, for his constant support and advice; **Professor Caterina Sganga**, for the valuable comments concerning my work, for agreeing to serve as a committee member and for all the career advice she gave me. Last but not least, I would like to thank **Professor Gerard McCormack**, from the University of Leeds, for graciously accepting to serve as a member in my defense committee.

I express my warm thanks to **Mrs. Vera Varady**, for her friendship and support throughout the past 4 years; to **Ms. Vesna Milovic**, for being such a wonderful host during my research period in London; to **Mr. Robyn Bellers** (CEU Academic Writing Department), for all the time invested in my work and all the help provided for completing this project.

Many thanks go also to all the staff members of Central European University and to the Doctoral Research Support Grant Program, to Queen Mary School of Law (University of London), to the Institute for Advanced Legal Studies (London) and to the Max Planck Institute for Private Law (Hamburg) for facilitating the research conducted for this book and to my colleagues from NIS Petrol SRL, Romania, for their support and for their understanding regarding my dedication to the S.J.D. program I had started.

Very important was the contribution of my friends, who have incented and aided me to strive towards my goal. To all of them, a BIG "thank you": **Bogdan Timofti**, for all materials, moral support provided and most importantly his friendship, which means the world to me; **Simona Timofti**, for her kindness and understanding, as well as for her aid with the troublesome English; **Cosmin Andrei Artimof**, for believing in me and always being there; to **Asress Adimi Gikay**, for being such an amazing friend and companion through the struggles of the last five years; to **Cristian Enescu**, for his friendship and constant support; to **Tunde Szabo**, for the amazing times we had in Budapest; to **Cristiana Vrăbioiu**, for all the valuable translations from German; to **Matthias Ringer**, for being an amazing companion in London and for the German cases and legal clarifications sent; to **Alexandra and Oana Prodan**, for their friendship and support; and to my former associate **Alin Lucian Dumitrescu**, for all the materials concerning Romanian law that he made available.

I would like to express my appreciation to my dear girlfriend, **Nataliia Yevchuk**, for being such a strong motivation and for turning my life into a fairy tale.

A special thanks to my mother, **Stănescu Petruţa Anisia**. Words simply cannot express how grateful I am to her, for all the sacrifices she made on my behalf. Her prayers and understanding have sustained me this far. I hope I made her proud.

Abbreviations

ADR	Alternative Dispute Resolution
BFCP	Bureau for Financial Consumer Protection (the US)
BGB	Bürgerliches Gesetzbuch (German Civil Code)
CCA	Consumer Credit Act
CSA	Credit Services Association
CSA(s)	Consumer Sales Agreement(s)
DBSG	Debt Buyers and Sellers Group
DCFR	Draft Common Frame of Reference
EAST	Electronic Archive of Secured Transactions
ECJ	Court of Justice of the European Union
FCC	French Civil Code
FDCPA	Fair Debt Collection Practices Act
FLSA	Fair Labor Standards Act
FTC	Federal Trade Commission
HPA(s)	Hire-Purchase Agreement(s)
NACP	National Authority for Consumer Protection (Romania)
OFT	Office of Fair Trading (the UK)
RDG	The Law on Provision of Non-Judicial Legal Services (Germany)
RNCC	Romanian New Civil Code
ROT	Retention of Title
RSTL	Romanian Secured Transaction Law (Title VI of Law no 99/1999)
SGA	Sale of Goods Act
STL	Secured Transaction Law
UCC	Uniform Commercial Code
UCPD	Directive 2005/29/EC on Unfair Commercial Practices
UNCITRAL	United Nations Commission on International Trade Law

Contents

Chapter 1
Introduction

Access to credit, especially low cost credit, is essential to the growth of any economy, either emerging or established. Accessing credit is still of *critical* importance for consumers, small and medium-sized enterprises (SMEs) and large companies. Strongly connected to credit and collateral is the topic of enforcement, a Janus-faced problem, which deserves more attention and special treatment. On the one hand, efficient enforcement is of outmost importance to creditors, while on the other hand efficient protection against creditors' abuse is of utmost importance to consumer-debtors.[1] It is then relevant to bring forth into discussion the effectiveness of the traditional judicial methods of debt recovery as compared to alternative means, which are arguably better, cheaper and faster when considering the creditors' needs, as well as the efficiency of consumer-debtor protection mechanisms in place in the chosen jurisdictions, when considering the debtor's needs. Given the fact that the two are often intertwined, none of these aspects could and should be treated separately.

While analyzing the creditors' and debtors' needs in the context of access to credit, one can easily note that both constituencies prove equally vulnerable and have their own legitimate concerns. Lenders are more reluctant in extending credit that is considered risky, due to loss of confidence in the market and in debtors, be it businesses or consumers, but especially due to loss of confidence in the legal system, represented by courts, bailiffs and lack of (clear) substantive law.

[1] Business-debtors may also be subjected to abuse, but the magnitude of the abuse depends on the size and power of the business: the bigger the business the less likelihood for abuse. However, most of the chosen jurisdictions have decided to exclude business-debtors from the protections offered by the law and focus on consumers. It is for this reason that the book has decided to do the same. Hence, business-debtors will be addressed only where the relevant legal provisions analyzed have specifically mentioned them.

C.G. Stănescu, *Self-Help, Private Debt Collection and the Concomitant Risks*,
DOI 10.1007/978-3-319-21503-7_1

The rapidly changing economic climate showed just how exposed they are to shifting circumstances in the debtors' economic status and pushed for increased carefulness.[2]

From the borrowers' point of view, and particularly of SMEs', affordable credit is also critical for expanding business, which means that any increase in credit's price will be reflected in the financial possibilities, economic activity and even the actual existence of SMEs. If one takes into account that SMEs constitute a considerable percentage of many emerging and developed countries' economies,[3] any negative impact on the SMEs will have a negative impact on the entire national economy.[4] In other words, as the doctrine correctly emphasized, "the critical point in lack of access to finance is that inability to borrow reduces economic growth."[5] However, in order to gain access to credit, the lenders need to be sure not only of recovery of the collateral or of the debt, but also of *fast* and *efficient* recovery, both inside and outside the courts system but still within the boundaries of the law.

In the case of SMEs, receivables financing also plays a key role, especially when capital markets are underdeveloped; banks do not grant credit due to lack of SMEs' credit history or due to lack of trust in the newcomers. Hence, *factoring* became a suitable source of financing for SMEs. One of the main advantages of factoring is that receivables owed to an SME may be sold directly to a factoring company, for a discounted price, rather than using them as collateral. If one considers the empirical data existent at the EU level, which show that on average an SME has to wait between 20 and 100 days to get their invoices paid[6] (if at all), it becomes obvious why factoring companies grew so prolific and why the debt-buying industry (sometimes doubled by the debt collection industry) is in continuous expansion. Basically, creditors are happy either to sell their debts on a discount or to farm out their collection for a success fee, thus avoiding the risk of a larger loss and of lengthy, expensive court cases, while debt buyers or debt collectors, specialized in recoveries, are not only answering to a market demand but also making huge profits from their business.

In the light of the above, supplementing or amending the current legislation with instruments that aim to modernize the procedural laws for providing faster judicial proceedings and security globally seems to be a sound solution[7] but does not solve

---

[2] Orkun Akseli—Vulnerability and Access to Low Cost Credit in Devenney and Kenny (2012), p. 10.

[3] According to official information at EU level, in 2013, 99 % of businesses in Europe are SMEs. See http://ec.europa.eu/enterprise/policies/sme/facts-figures-analysis/index_en.htm, last visited 23.01.2015.

[4] For example, in the UK, statistics show that there are 4.7 million SMEs, with 13.5 million employees, and their contribution to the country's economy is more than half of turnover. Orkun Akseli—Vulnerability and Access to Low Cost Credit in Devenney and Kenny (2012), p. 18.

[5] Devenney and Kenny (2012), p. 11.

[6] Orkun Akseli—Vulnerability and Access to Low Cost Credit in Devenney and Kenny (2012), pp. 15–16, footnote 47.

[7] Kieninger (2004), pp. 7–8.

the problem of actual recovery. It is obviously beneficial for a creditor to obtain judgment against a defaulting debtor in 3 months instead of 3 years, but there is no guarantee that such judgment will be actually enforced. Therefore, private enforcement alternatives such as self-help, which have a long established tradition in the US and the UK, may prove to be a valuable source of inspiration for European developing countries,[8] such as Romania, and also for those with developed economies such as Germany and France.

It is generally accepted that secured lending reduces the risk of nonpayment and lowers the cost of access to credit.[9] But even so, a system that is entirely based on judicial enforcement will have serious efficiency issues. There are two possible justifications for excluding the state's involvement. One has to do with the state's incapacity to deal with all the issues that might arise from a business relationship. The second, which derived from the first, is that due to the risky and expensive nature of judicial proceedings,[10] a market for debt collection services has emerged and developed, and there are now many professional debt collection businesses available. One of the book's main claims is that the future of debt collection is shifting towards private enforcement;[11] hence, there is a need to address the concomitant risks deriving from it.

The most important element, which is common to all private collection practices, is the exclusion of the state's involvement. The collection is done by the creditor himself or through specialized private agents, without intervention from authorities: neither courts nor state bodies. Evidently, exclusion of *ex ante* judicial control and apparent lack of due process raises the issue of balancing between the interests of creditors and debtors and finding appropriate means to ensure enough protection against abuse from both sides while not affecting the efficiency of the debt collection itself.

At this point, the US model becomes relevant again since in the US resort to private debt collection is the usual practice,[12] notwithstanding whether the debt is secured or not. Obviously, in case of secured claims, a fast repossession of the

[8] One should also mention here the UNCITRAL Convention on the Assignment of Receivables, whose purpose was to establish a model for the modernization of domestic assignment law and as a first substantive step towards the overall harmonization of the law of assignment of receivables in international trade; the UNCITRAL Guide or the EBRD Model Law on Secured Transactions, which target the modernization of emerging markets' secured transactions regimes in which inefficient rules often prevent facilitation of secured credit; and last but not least, the UNIDROIT Convention on International Factoring, whose declared scope, although similar, is narrower than the one of UNCITRAL Convention on the Assignment of Receivables.

[9] Kieninger (2004), p. 7.

[10] Taylor (1998), pp. 847–850. Also King and Cook (1996), p. 7.

[11] The book's standing is not unique. Recently, the Draft Common Frame of Reference, representing the combined work of more than 250 European scholars and their current views, has emphasized the need to shift towards and encourage private enforcement. See von Bar and Clive (2010), p. 5614. For a similar view concerning the inevitability of channeling enforcement towards the out-of-court venue, see Tajti (2013), p. 13.

[12] Taylor (1998), p. 841; Gilmore (1999), p. 1212.

collateral enhances the position of the creditor and exerts additional pressure on the debtor to pay the debt. Moreover, in case of an unsuccessful private debt collection attempt, creditors enjoy the option to turn to formal court proceedings.[13] Parties can resort to state bodies at any time, which means that they are not deprived of their access to court and due process. This gives them a wider strategic advantage. One might argue that this right to choose the best avenue deemed appropriate is one of the reasons why the U.S. system proves to be so efficient.

1.1 Justification of Dealing with Private Enforcement

The need for simplicity, speed and the issue of costs borne by creditors has become a concern for states as well. At the European level, for example, this need led to the adoption of a European order for payment procedure and measures to simplify and speed up small claims litigation. The stated purpose was to make it easier to obtain, recognize and enforce court decisions throughout the Member States of the European Union.[14] However, these procedures remain judicial by nature and do not solve the issue of enforcement: creditors still need to resort to courts and go through the entire judicial process, pay judicial fees (even if they were reduced to a minimum), pay attorneys' fees, suffer the risk of losing the trial, while the debtor still has time to sell or hide the collateral and other assets.

The same need is the reason why this work is dedicated exclusively to nonjudicial enforcement and covers both theoretical and practical aspects of debt recovery. The topic is important since private enforcement is becoming a part of our day-to-day lives. The mere recognition of this fact should convince both practitioners and academics to dedicate more time to its research and understanding. At the same time, its study should enable practitioners to make correct use of it for the benefit of their clients.

This task is challenging since the topic does not fit easily within the canons of any area of private law. As the book will show, it touches upon commercial,

[13] "The US enforcement system is successful because it provides the secured party with an *option* entitling him to choose the best way of enforcing his security rights depending on the circumstances of each individual case. Thus, if for any reason self-help is not an acceptable alternative, the secured party may immediately turn to courts to protect his rights" Tajti (2002), p. 182. Also: Kieninger (2004), p. 60. This choice was maintained by the Revision of the UCC, and it is currently contained in Section 9-601(a)(1). In this regard: McCahey (2001), pp. 7–8.

[14] Recitals 3, 6, 7 and 8 of Regulation (EC) No. 861/2007 of the European Parliament and of the Council of 11 July 2007 establishing a European Small Claims Procedure, available online at http://eur-lex.europa.eu/legal-content/EN/ALL/;jsessionid=bDWtTW1LJ5yqYRGMSlvxpNPgp794JdJ2m51yFGsJ6xYgF5l4KKcx!847294412?uri=CELEX:32007R0861. Also Recitals 5, 6 and 9 of Regulation (EC) No 1896/2006 of the European Parliament and of the Council of 12 December 2006 creating a European order for payment procedure, available on line at http://eur-lex.europa.eu/legal-content/EN/ALL/?uri=CELEX:32006R1896, both last visited 22.01.2015.

contract and consumer protection laws. However, the topic's usefulness is beyond doubt if one considers the reform of secured transaction law based on the American model, which relies heavily on self-help devices and also due to the wide spread of private enforcement in continental jurisdictions.[15]

With respect to the author's domestic jurisdiction, Romania has adopted legislation that revolutionized (at least on paper) its secured transactions regime, however, without paralleling the spread of out-of-court enforcement with a requirement for licensing of private enforcers, sector-specific prudential and consumer protection regulations.[16] Although this aspect does not necessarily cause a backlash in resorting to private enforcement, it leaves most of it at (and outside) the boundaries of the law, which results in consumer-debtors being vulnerable to creditors' or third party collectors' abuse.[17]

In this regard, a comparative approach between the American benchmark and its chosen European counterparts proves useful in guiding legislators in finding the answers. The same comparison is also useful for practitioners who may easily learn and employ the experience of other legal systems in understanding and interpreting their own national legislation in the field.

Last, but not least, the book comes to fill in a literature gap. Although in the US one can find a large number of cases, articles and studies on the matter of self-help, to the extent of the author's research, at the time of writing the book there is no integrated work dedicated specifically to the issue of private enforcement. This situation is more visible in the chosen European jurisdictions where both literature and court cases are extremely scarce. No comparative work of this scale and depth has been identified either.

1.2 The Choice of US Law as Benchmark and the Choice of Jurisdictions

The book uses the private enforcement framework in the US as a benchmark for the analysis of the selected European jurisdictions: its justification, history, development, current status and future perspectives. Then it analyzes private collection in selected EU jurisdictions (UK, Germany and France) in the same way as it did with the US, where data and similar legislation are available. The UK is considered as a

[15] See *supra* footnote 8.

[16] "Prudential regulation [. . .], on the one hand, and market regulation and consumer protection regulation, on the other, serve different, if related, purposes. Prudential regulation is concerned with institutional and systemic stability. It has a particular focus on the management and regulation of risk and on the safety and soundness of institutions and the financial system. Consumer protection and market regulation are largely concerned with the conduct of market actors, whether retail, professional, or market infrastructures, and the protection of market confidence through the support of market efficiency, transparency and integrity." Ferran et al. (2012), p. 119.

[17] Tajti (2013), p. 13.

common law jurisdiction whose legislation is more intertwined with civil law systems due to its EU member status. Germany and France are the two jurisdictions that traditionally influenced greatly the Romanian legislation, until the reforms undertaken by the latter in late 1990s. Given the fact that France has also undertaken from 2006 on a multistep reform of secured transactions law, a look into it provides the necessary information on the new civil law trend in this area, despite that the reform has maintained the ban on self-help repossession, while Germany still retains an unreformed system. Finally, it includes a comparative analysis of the same practices in CEE—concentrating on the case of Romania, the author's home jurisdiction.

Romania is also an interesting and somehow peculiar case, since it introduced a secured transactions law in 1999, based on Article 9 of the UCC, and, on paper, it enjoyed one of the most modern secured transactions law in the EU. The draft proposal mentioned expressly the US as the source of inspiration for the Romanian law, and although Romania has just amended its Civil Code (Law no 71/2011 for the application of the New Civil Code repealed Title VI of Law 99/1999, by Art. 230, letter u)) based on the Quebec Civil Code,[18] a comparison with the US system and practice is still beneficial. The amendment maintained the US law as a model, but also provided for a more extensive judicial control, in order to bring the legal provisions in line with the decision of the Constitutional Court.[19]

However, Romania has failed to introduce a Fair Debt Collection Act,[20] and it is suffering right now from a legal void with respect to abuses to which debtors can be subjected. Once again, in this respect, the American and English experiences can both be beneficial. The third reason is the literature void. The issue of self-help practices and of repossession is almost completely ignored by Romanian authors. The book fills in this enormous gap and provides Romanian practitioners with an effective theoretical and practical apparatus in this area.

1.3 Central Category: Private Enforcement

As already mentioned, the goal of this work is to deliver a more practical than theoretical perspective. Where necessary, theory was employed to explain the practical implications and to justify the book's conclusions.

The principal reason for which creditors request access to private enforcement is to minimize the risk of nonrecovery with its accessory effects. There are multiple

---

[18] Iolanda Boti, *Influenta Codului Civil din Quebec asupra Noului Cod Civil din Romania* www.juridice.ro *at* http://www.juridice.ro/152502/influenta-codului-civil-din-quebec-asupra-noului-cod-civil-din-romania.html, p. 1.

[19] *Infra* Chap. 4, Sect. 4.1.3.3.

[20] An attempt to introduce such an act was rejected by the Romanian Parliament in 2012. See *infra* Chap. 6, Sect. 6.1.7.

explanations for this requirement, but beyond any discussion related to the economics and importance of credit, private enforcement proves to be of practical necessity. It is why even civilian jurisdictions, generally against any form of private justice, outside the judicial system imposed by the state, should recognize as such the covert self-help devices existent in their contract laws[21] and thus change their perception regarding self-help repossession and private enforcement altogether.

Of practical necessity is the matter of private enforcement to debtors as well as, and especially, to consumer-debtors. They need not only to be protected from abusive collection practices but also to be provided with adequate responses and incentives to determine them to act and defend themselves against abuse. At federal level,[22] the US has had a very effective tool in place—The Fair Debt Collection Practices Act—for the past 40 years, although this piece of legislation is in stringent need of update since it lags behind technological advancement. On the other hand, the UK and its 2014 Consumer Credit sourcebook cover for all modern abusive devices but lack the efficiency of their American counterpart due to the fact that their subjects can only resort to administrative enforcement. Both of them require similar attention and study since they prove to be valuable examples for those jurisdictions seeking a balance between creditor and debtor rights.

1.4 Limits of the Book

The topic is treated neither exhaustively nor in extensive detail, due to the inherent limitations of a monograph. The main concern was to identify, if possible, the idiosyncratic traits of private enforcement in the chosen jurisdictions and emphasize their practical aspects. This work is not a treatise of private enforcement, but it strives to become the starting point in this growing domain.

Usually in the area of secured transactions, the main focus is to ensure the creditor obtains recovery of his claim. However, in the narrower field of private enforcement, without minimizing the need to protect creditor's interests, the focus was on balancing these interests with the interests of the debtor. The special position held by the creditor when it comes to secured transactions must not become an excuse to allow him to resort to abuse in his relationship with the debtor. The book strives to make this position clear.

---

[21] Self-Help and Contract Law.

[22] The FDCPA has been used as a *de minimis* standard of protection against abusive debt collection practices, and the book refers mostly to this act. However, there is also FDCPA type of laws at state level in the US, most of them offering a higher degree of protection than the federal act. For details, see *infra* Chap. 6, Sect. 6.1.3.

1.5 Terminology: The Meaning of "Self-Help"

A terminology *caveat* is necessary at this point since, especially for those coming from a civil law jurisdiction, the term "self-help" might be puzzling or misleading. Not only that the term *per se* is obscured, but more importantly many from civilian systems might even confuse "self-help" with "self-defense."[23] Such confusion would somehow be justified by the common origin of self-help and self-defense, but the two are not the same. As it was rightfully pointed out, "the privilege of self-defense is perhaps the most notable form of self-help in criminal law. The privilege allows persons to use reasonable force against an aggressor to protect themselves against tortious or criminal attacks."[24]

However, these types of self-help, which are also recognized by civilian jurisdictions, are but a limited version and understanding of self-help. And they are not what this book is talking about. **For the purposes of this work, self-help must be understood as that "permissible conduct which individuals undertake, absent any legal obligation to do so, and without any assistance of a state official (the police, the bailiffs or the judiciary) in efforts to prevent or remedy a legal wrong."**[25] Self-help is therefore **a legally recognized extrajudicial alternative to traditional judicial remedies.**

1.6 Methodology

A practical approach to the topic may reflect and reveal different aspects than a purely theoretical one. The reasons lie not only in the different methodologies employed but also in the different interest and focus of a practitioner in comparison to those of an academic. However, there is a great deal of technicalities, which were employed for identifying issues and similarities between legal regimes, but always in the quest for a practical solution.

Speaking of methodology, the book analyzes and compares the chosen jurisdictions before reaching conclusions with respect to the future of self-help and private debt-collecting practices in the chosen European jurisdictions, by resorting to all three dimensions[26] of comparative law: empirical, analytical and normative.

---

[23] For example in BGB, Section 229, self-help is defined as an exception from the interdiction to exercise one's rights if they cause damage to the person or the things of another, and in Section 859 it is used to describe the right of a possessor to use force when defending himself against unlawful interference.

[24] Brandon et al. (1984), p. 878. On the delineation between self-help and self-defense in criminal law, see also Smith (2005), pp. 80–82.

[25] Brandon et al. (1984), p. 850.

[26] Rover (2007), p. 30.

The ***empirical*** dimension consists of a description of the different legal frameworks concerning private debt collection within the chosen jurisdictions, departing from the assumption that there are functionally equivalent institutions[27] in these different laws that can be compared with one another. The ***analytical*** dimension consists in providing the reader with an understanding of the notions and systems of the laws in force. Therefore, efforts have been made to provide the reader with a unified, adequate and (possible) neutral terminology as well as to identify and present only a set of relevant legal issues. Lastly, the ***normative*** dimension consists of a critical assessment of the different jurisdictions chosen, with a focus on domestic law. Therefore, where possible and needed, this work provides the reader with an answer to the question "which legal model solves the legal issues with which the book is concerned in the most appropriate way," together with a rational explanation for the chosen answer. The criteria employed were based on the solutions' practicality, economic rationale and risk-reducing function. In other words, the book tries to show which system answers best the challenges raised by self-help and private debt collection in the twenty-first century, which one places the smallest burden on the consumer and which one has the most deterrent effect on wrongdoers.

To comply with the abovementioned criteria and dimensions, several methods were combined and used together. Therefore, the method of ***legal families*** was employed in the comparison between the US and the UK, on the one side, and France, Germany and Romania, on the other side. The focus was on particular issues as they appear in all jurisdictions, with **the US** used **as a basis for comparison**: the first part of the book is dedicated to the definition and history of self-help, general self-help devices in contract law (broader approach) and especially self-help repossession (narrower approach); the second part deals with the specific issue of pseudo-debt collection, namely factoring and receivables financing, while the third part is dedicated to risk handling and consumer protection against unfair debt collection practices.

Where fitting and possible, the ***functional*** approach was used to evaluate the compared legal provisions (for example, in order to determine whether self-help repossession is justifiable or compatible and should or could be implemented as such by the civil law jurisdictions). ***Critical comparative law*** method was likewise

[27] Here the book considers one of the elements of the functional method as identified by Ralf Michaels, namely that "function itself serves as *tertium comparationis*. Institutions, both legal and non-legal, even doctrinally different ones, are comparable if functionally equivalent, if they fulfil similar functions in different legal systems." However, this work considers also the fourth element mentioned by Ralf Michaels, according to which functionality serves as a criteria for evaluation. "Functionalist comparative law [then] becomes a 'better-law comparison' – the better of several laws is that which fulfils its function better than the others." Michaels (2006), p. 342 (details at pp. 367–369). As with respect to concepts of functionality, the book combines classical functionalism with instrumentalism, focusing on the idea that "if law fulfills functions and meets societal needs, then the lawyer's job is to develop laws that perform these tasks [. . .], and comparative law can help compare the ability of different solutions to solve similar problems, and spur similar degrees of progress." Michaels (2006), p. 351.

employed in order to assess certain desired results of the comparison (such as the need for adopting and implementing a proper Fair Debt Collection Practices like act in Romania).

The analysis of the benchmark jurisdiction was done following a ***sequence of topics***. However, within the chapters, each topic was analyzed going ***country by country***. Attention is also given to unorthodox sources of law as newspaper articles, magazines, blogs and websites. This is needed because, in the absence of scholar studies, one has to look for information in the nonlegal area. However, this information was not used without a critical filter. Only those sources that could be corroborated with other sources and easily verified have been used for the purposes of this work. Hence, the reason for this type of comparison lied with the fact that unlike the American literature, the European one is rather scarce on the matter. Also, given the fact that in many European jurisdictions some nonjudicial practices (such as self-help repossession) are strictly forbidden by law (although they occur in practice), there were not any similar legal provisions to compare.

1.7 The Structure of the Book

The book is structured in three main parts. Each part deals with one specific facet of private enforcement, and together they strive to offer the reader a holistic and integrated picture of the topic, together with a multitude of practical implications. The normative proposals argue for a change in approach and perspective that would lead to the proper integration of private enforcement in the chosen jurisdictions and to solving the numerous existing legal issues.

The first part deals with the definition of self-help and its applications in the context of private and commercial law only. The *second chapter* offers the history and the legal background of private enforcement in the five jurisdictions chosen, while also analyzing the provisions of the DCFR, perceived as a glimpse into the future of the topic in Europe. The *third chapter* is dedicated to the analysis of three of the most employed self-help devices in sales law, which are common to all jurisdictions, in order to emphasize not only the existence of self-help devices across legal families but also their compatibility with both common law and civil law systems: the right to withhold performance, liquidated damages or penalty clauses and extrajudicial termination. However, as it is shown, in civilian systems these devices, which the book considers to be types of "passive self-help," are covert forms of self-help, widely used but not recognized as such. The *fourth chapter* deals solely with secured transactions law, namely self-help repossession and private administrative receivership, which the book considers as "active self-help."

The second part is dedicated to the special case of pseudo-debt collection under the coverage of factoring and receivables financing. Despite that factoring was used mostly in business relationships, nowadays it covers also business-to-consumer transactions; hence, this work could not have omitted it from its analysis.

The reasons are twofold: on the one hand, the US law, which is used as benchmark, established for factoring (i.e., sale of receivables) the same legal regime as for using receivables "only" as collateral. Therefore, since factoring in the US is covered by UCC Article 9 the distinction between business relationships and business–consumer relationships is not relevant for their legal regime. On the other hand, factoring has been employed in the European countries to cover for debt collection services, which led the book to the usage of the term "pseudo-factoring" or "pseudo-debt collection." A monograph dedicated to private enforcement would not be complete without the analysis of such quasi-debt collection practices, which is why the *fifth chapter* addresses them in detail.

The third part is dedicated to abusive debt collection practices and consumer-debtor protection. The *sixth* and *seventh chapters* cover the US federal FDCPA and its US state law counterparts as well as its kin legislation from the other chosen jurisdictions, where the case. They also propose a matrix of analysis of any antiabusive debt collection legislation, which should enable any interested party to assess the efficiency of such legislation.

References

Brandon DI, Cooper ML, Greshin JH, Harris AL, Head JM Jr, Jacques KR, Wiggins L (1984) SPECIAL PROJECT. Self-help: extrajudicial rights, privileges and remedies in contemporary American society. Vanderbilt Law Rev 37:845

Devenney J, Kenny M (2012) Consumer credit, debt and investment in Europe. Cambridge University Press, Cambridge

Ferran E, Moloney N, Hill J, Coffee JC Jr (2012) The regulatory aftermath of the global financial crisis. Cambridge University Press, Cambridge

Gilmore G (1999) Security interests in personal property. The Lawbook Exchange, LTD, Union, New Jersey

Kieninger E-M (2004) Security rights in movable property in European private law. Cambridge University Press, Cambridge

King LP, Cook ML (1996) Creditors' rights, debtors' protection, and bankruptcy. Mathew Bender, New York

McCahey JP (2001) Commentary on the enforcement of security interests under UCC Revised Article 9. Hahn & Hessen LLP, New York

Michaels R (2006) The functional method of comparative law. In: Reimann M, Zimmermann R (eds) The Oxford handbook of comparative law. Oxford University Press, Oxford

Rover J-H (2007) Secured lending in Eastern Europe. Comparative law of secured transactions and the EBRD Model Law. Oxford University Press, New York

Smith HE (2005) Self-help and the nature of property. J Law Econ Policy 1:69

Tajti T (2002) Comparative secured transactions law. Akadémiai Kiadó, Budapest

Tajti T (2013) Post-1990 secured transaction law reforms in central and eastern Europe. Szegedi Közjegyzői Közlöny II:1

Taylor CR (1998) Self-help in contract law: an exploration and proposal. Wake Forest Law Rev 33:839

von Bar C, Clive E (2010) Principles, definition and model rules of European private law. Draft Common Frame of Reference (DCFR). Oxford University Press, Oxford

Chapter 2
General Background and History of Self-Help and Private Enforcement

Self-help and debt collection are traced back to the beginning of trade in the history of mankind. Despite that self-help and debt collection receive more attention today, it would be a mistake to think they are new phenomena. In reality, they have been with us since the moment we started doing business—although in primitive form[1]—and they will continue to be with us in the future. Throughout our existence as a species, we have created methods to recover debts, both by private and public means, according to the conditions at hand.

As the book is dedicated to self-help, self-help repossession and other methods of private enforcement, it will not touch upon public means of collection. This should not be construed in the sense that they did not or do not exist. They most certainly do. As it will be shown, at various historic times, public means of enforcement have been the only ones permitted, while other times they coexisted with private means. Some might be surprised to learn, for example, how well developed and sophisticated private enforcement was before the fall of the Western Roman Empire. Some will be surprised to see how it reemerged after the Middle Ages when the local lords enjoyed absolute legal power.

What is certain is that self-help repossession and private debt collection methods are rampant in practice today in most legal systems, although not necessarily recognized by positive law. The lack of recognition raises concomitant risks, for any self-help method has a potential for abuse and only by acknowledging the problem can one find a solution. Therefore, a brief incursion within the history of self-help and private debt collection helps in understanding their development, functions and the rationale. This chapter also provides several theoretical explanations of the differences between the legal systems compared.

[1] Black and Baumgartner (1987), p. 33. "Historically, for instance, the degree of self-help has been highest in primitive societies, in bands and tribes, and has declined progressively with social evolution and the growth of law."

C.G. Stănescu, *Self-Help, Private Debt Collection and the Concomitant Risks*,
DOI 10.1007/978-3-319-21503-7_2

2.1 Why Should One Resort to Self-Help

One question to be answered before going into the history and analysis of private enforcement is "why does society or the commercial world need or resort to self-help?" Why do we not simply trust the power of the court systems and resort to the public means of enforcement,[2] given the level of advancement and sophistication of our legal systems?

In order to answer this question, one should consider what an action in court means and what kinds of problems it poses. In other words, the *first* issue is that the aggrieved party might not even know that there is a possibility to have his or her dispute settled by a court.[3] The *second* is represented by the language and procedural formalities in which the majority of people are not well versed in.[4] *Third*, depending on the jurisdiction or the state or national rule of procedure, prior communication and settlement attempts might be required before allowing a claim to be filed with the court. Such attempts must be documented; they are time consuming and might even involve expenses, all these factors having a deterring effect towards the party seeking reparation.[5] This is why many jurisdictions have tried to implement clearer provisions to ease the burden on certain categories of plaintiffs, such as consumers.[6] *Fourth*, the average duration of a court action is in itself discouraging since most European procedures take between 6 and 12 months to get a decision from the first instance court, the term being two or three times longer in case of an appeal or recourse filed against the previous judgments.[7] The *last* problems with public enforcement are represented by the risk of losing the trial and the expenses generated by the entire procedure.[8]

Costs of proceedings associated with the risk of losing might be the most important burden that the parties have to face when considering court action. They may include travel (and accommodation) expenses, judicial fees (required to start the procedure), attorney fees (for advice and representation), expenses generated by discovery (fees paid to experts, expenses of witnesses heard, administrative fees for obtaining official information from public authorities or copies from archives, etc.). Additionally, it should be kept in mind that all these expenses have to be paid when they occur and, despite the fact that generally the losing party will cover the winning party's expenses at the end of the trial (from the chosen

---

[2] Kronman (1985), pp. 24–25. The author emphasizes that although the existence of the state and its enforcement machinery would make reliance on self-help mechanisms unnecessary, in reality this is not the case, the reason being uncertainty of both parties: "The legal right to enforce a promise can reduce but never eliminate insecurity [. . .]."

[3] Brownsword et al. (2011), p. 491.

[4] Brownsword et al. (2011), pp. 492–493.

[5] Brownsword et al. (2011), p. 493.

[6] Brownsword et al. (2011), p. 494.

[7] Brownsword et al. (2011), pp. 494–495.

[8] Taylor (1998), p. 847.

jurisdictions the US is an exception in this regard[9]), many might not be able to cover them until then. Obviously, when a party cannot afford to address the court or defend itself in court due to high costs, access to justice is denied and any wrong or harm suffered cannot be remedied, repaired or compensated, as the case may be.[10]

Another important factor involved in the decision regarding addressing the court is the risk of losing the case entirely or failure to remedy the harms in full.[11] It is one of the reasons why, especially with respect to the collection of debts, creditors avoid addressing the courts before exhausting any other extrajudicial means available.[12]

The way in which self-help is perceived is another concern. The different understandings of this term might be what cause most of the continental European jurisdictions to react with mistrust and susceptibility when it comes to self-help and other forms of private enforcement. The reason is that in the continental perception, self-help is an "extra-legal action rather than [an] element of our legal network,"[13] "something at the borderline of criminal offense."[14] Since this position was expressed with respect to self-help employed by aggrieved consumers—victims of unfair traders—it can only mean that self-help employed by aggrieved creditors against their debtors (both natural and legal persons) will seem even more abusive and intrusive.

From the perspective of the common law jurisdictions, "although self-help is non-judicial, it is not extra-legal and does not lie outside the shadow of the law:"[15] it is a legitimate right—such as the right to refuse payment absent delivery or to stop delivery in the absence of payment,—it can be challenged by legal action and when employed without ill will or abuse, it has obvious advantages for the society and commercial relations.[16] In wide terms, self-help was defined as a **"legally permissible conduct that individuals undertake absent the compulsion of law and without the assistance of a government officials in efforts to prevent or remedy a legal wrong."**[17] For the purposes of this book, self-help shall be construed in the sense of the aforementioned definition.

[9] *Infra,* footnote 23 in Chap. 7.

[10] Brownsword et al. (2011), pp. 495–499.

[11] Kronman (1985), p. 26: "However broadly we define the class of compensable harms, any court-administered damages remedy carries with it a risk of undercompensation. No refinement of doctrine can eliminate this risk."

[12] Warren and Westbrook (2009), pp. 5–6. Also, Kronman (1985) p. 29, Brandon et al. (1984), p. 851.

[13] Taylor (1998), pp. 845–846.

[14] Brownsword et al. (2011), p. 488.

[15] Taylor (1998), p. 846. Also: Brandon et al. (1984), p. 850: "Self-help, [...], is a legally recognized alternative or substitute for a judicial remedy."

[16] Taylor (1998), p. 846. Also: Brandon et al. (1984), p. 850.

[17] Brandon et al. (1984), p. 850.

2.2 Self Help: History and Justification

Self-help is understood as the action taken, including use of force, in order to assert or protect one's rights, without the recourse to the formal legal procedure,[18] and its definition was not altered by the passage of time. It has a long history[19] that can be traced back to Jewish, Greek and Roman laws, and, despite a temporary ban during the late Middle Ages, it survived and was reactivated in modern days.

2.2.1 Self Help in Ancient Jewish, Greek and Roman Laws

Jewish law allowed self-help in a large number of situations, including recaption—the right to retake one's own property even by force and without legal process from another who was illegally possessing it.[20] The **Greek** state also looked upon self-help with benevolence: since the state did not enforce the judgments of its courts, a person who had obtained a judgment in a private lawsuit was supposed to enforce it by exercising self-help, even in an aggressive manner, to the point of breaching the peace and physically harm the debtor.[21] Since the Greek legal system recognized nonpossessory security devices (*hypothec* and sale subject to redemption by the debtor), the property that remained in the debtor's possession was correlated with the right of the creditor to take possession of the property upon the debtor's default by self-help. After repossession, the creditor was treated as the owner and he was under no duty of accounting to the debtor for any surplus, in case he decided to sell the property.[22]

The **Roman** law allowed self-help first in the law of the Twelve Tables with respect to criminal offenses.[23] Later, the civil actions of *manus injectio*, which allowed an aggrieved creditor to arrest the debtor on his own authority and action, as well as *pignoris capio* (distress) were seen as self-help methods of enforcing the debt.[24] The former was the original Roman mode of execution and the latter the first extrajudicial species of self-help.[25] *Pignoris capio* consisted in the taking of personal chattel without legal process from the possession of a wrongdoer into the hands of the party aggrieved, as a pledge for the redress of an injury, the

---

[18] Bannon (2000), p. 71. Also see: Brandon et al. (1984), p. 917, footnote 430; and St. John's Law Review (1974), p. 670.

[19] Taylor (1998), p. 844: "Prior to the existence of legal institutions to dictate rules of behavior and state authorities to enforce them, all social relations were a form of self-help."

[20] Ben-Menahem and Hecht (1993), p. 638.

[21] McCall (1973), p. 63.

[22] McCall (1973), pp. 63–64.

[23] McRobert (2012), p. 572.

[24] Whittuck (1904). Also: Bannon (2000), p. 81; and McCall (1973), p. 65.

[25] Street (2013), p. 17.

performance of a duty or the satisfaction of a demand.[26] Moreover, rather than resorting to public trials against private persons, the Roman state farmed-out tax and debt collection to public companies *societas publicanorum*, who purchased the state's claims and employed self-help methods to satisfy them,[27] a practice that is revived today.

Commentators have emphasized that, on the one hand, self-redress was, generally, merely tolerated in a time when the institutions of the Roman state were not yet consolidated[28] and was to be strictly banned by the constitution of the three emperors in 389 AC.[29] But on the other hand, creditors were entitled to arrest their debtors, with their own accord and with the observation of certain formalities, until a relatively late period.[30] Therefore, in time, *manus injectio* ceased to be an act of self-help and became a part of a statutory procedure (*legis action*) that took place before a magistrate of the state.[31]

Historians have considered the early recourse to self-help a "primitive custom" that became more and more restricted as the Roman state assumed the function of administering justice.[32] Unchecked self-help had obviously a great potential to produce violence and unfairness.[33] Therefore, with the growing consolidation of the Empire the tendency was to limit the sphere of self-help by providing adequate means to citizens for the redress of any injuries suffered, transferring the enforcement of rights from the individual to the state.[34] It was also contended that an explanation for the long disappearance of several legal concepts, including the use of self-help, is that they were banned or simply not incorporated in later codes, which led to their concealment for ages, until some of them were rediscovered in the course of the nineteenth century.[35]

Additionally, measures were taken to deter citizens from resorting to self-help means, i.e. during the reign of Emperor Valentinian I (364–375 AC), a person using force to recover his own goods from the possessor was deemed to have forfeited his property right to the possessor or was required to pay double the value if the repossessed property did not belong to him.[36] Here must lie the origin of the modern

---

[26] Street (2013), p. 278.

[27] Del Granado (2011), p. 322.

[28] Stein (1999), p. 4. Also see: Street (2013), p. 279.

[29] Whittuck (1904), Commentary to § 77 (online source, page unavailable).

[30] Whittuck (1904), Commentary (1) to § 77 (online source, page unavailable).

[31] Whittuck (1904), Commentary (2) to § 77 (online source, page unavailable).

[32] Morey (1884), p. 402.

[33] Taylor (1998), p. 844.

[34] Morey (1884), p. 403. Also: Stein (1999), p. 4: "The Twelve Tables show, however, a *determination to institutionalize* such cases and keep them *within strict limits*" (emphasis added). For details on how *pignoris capio* switched from being an extrajudicial to a judicial method of enforcement: Street (2013), p. 281.

[35] Kieninger (2004), p 38.

[36] Ben-Menahem and Hecht (1993), p. 648. Also: Morey (1884), p. 403.

day requirement that any repossession through self-help must take place *without the breach of peace*.

After the fall of the Western Empire, the Roman legislation that survived in the East kept a similar approach: whoever took anything through the use of self-help was to return the goods and pay damages, no matter if the repossession was justifiable or not.[37] Legislation implemented under Justinian I (527–565 AC) contained rules with respect to what today would qualify as fair debt collection practices, forbidding creditors to engage in any kind of abuse against their debtors or their families (i.e., disturbing funerals for the purpose of extracting the debt) and imposing a monetary fine or a physical correction on them in case of breach.[38]

According to Jewish, Greek and Roman laws, the recourse to self-help was based on the doctrine of necessity.[39] As long as the state was unable to provide the adequate methods of redress or defense, citizens were allowed to help themselves as they could and saw fit. It is the main reason why even today there is a general agreement that self-defense is a valid response against a threat in criminal law[40] as long as certain conditions are met. But where there is a judicial response, the position of the state is that the citizen should make use of the court venue. This is the view that survived in most of the civil law states today. The question is, are the judicial means offered by the state always adequate and proper to ensure a speedy and satisfactory redress? And if not, what then?

2.2.2 Self-Help from Middle Ages Until Today

With the disappearance of the Western Empire and the emergence of the feudal order, a new legal system arose and, hence, the need to restrain the use of violent kinds of self-help in order to protect the weak parties.[41] The result was a total ban[42] of informal self-help during the twelfth and thirteenth centuries.[43] The process was, however, similar to the one seen in ancient societies. At the outset of the Middle Ages, self-help remedies became heavily relied upon.[44] Since the law was not as sophisticated anymore, it became hard to differentiate between nonviolent permissible actions and violent, prohibited ones. Reliance on self-help gave the strongest members of society a disproportionate advantage compared to the other members.

[37] Ben-Menahem and Hecht (1993), p. 648.

[38] Ben-Menahem and Hecht (1993), p. 648.

[39] Ben-Menahem and Hecht (1993), pp. 648–649.

[40] Bannon (2000), p. 72. These self-help methods were also allowed in ancient Rome.

[41] Pollock and Maitland (1898), pp. 31 and 471.

[42] The process was slow and took place in stages, not all of a sudden. For details: Street (2013), p. 289.

[43] Pollock and Maitland (1898), p. 395. Also: McCall (1973), p. 67.

[44] Brandon et al. (1984), p. 852.

Such reality led to concerns and desire of the rulers to centralize economic and judicial power, by (re)establishing a system of courts.[45] Therefore, self-help was regarded as an enemy of law, a contempt to the king and his courts.[46] Complete prohibition of all self-help means was the only measure that could be taken to constrain such unwanted activities,[47] together with delegation to the local lords of power to adjudicate and enforce law on their territory.

However, similar to what happened in ancient Rome with *manus injectio* or *pignoris capio*, the legal ban did not stop self-help from happening;[48] it simply sent it to the underground as individuals continued to seek to avoid and correct incurred injuries as quickly and directly as possible.[49] As the legal system evolved again, in modern times the society had to confront the reality that self-help was common.[50] Law became more permissive towards self-help, which was no longer seen as a primitive method located outside the boundaries of law,[51] but as a rational and effective solution to disputes,[52] as long as it was conducted in a fair and nonviolent manner.[53]

With respect to rediscovery of rules and techniques developed in the past, Roy Goode observed that [commercial] law was and is "about problem-solving, about fashioning the contract structures and other legal tools by which the legitimate needs of the market can be met."[54] Following his logic, it would not be wrong to conclude that rediscovery of self-help by sophisticated legal systems does not necessarily mean return to primitivism but a response to the inability of the states to provide adequate, speedy and less costly methods needed for the development of credit and business in modern-day economies. By recognizing and incorporating an increasing number of nonviolent self-help actions into its legal framework as rational and effective solutions to disputes,[55] common law systems seem to have answered positively the question above and there are indications that civilian systems will follow.

---

[45] Brandon et al. (1984), pp. 852–853.

[46] Street (2013), pp. 286–287.

[47] Taylor (1998), p. 844.

[48] An American scholar compared the results of banning self-help with the results of banning alcohol during the Prohibition. See Taylor (1998), p. 845; and Brandon et al. (1984), p. 853.

[49] Taylor (1998), pp. 844–845.

[50] Taylor (1998), p. 845; and Brandon et al. (1984), p. 853. "The inability of medieval courts to stop all forms of self-help and the judicial realization that some self-help was preferable to formal legal redress spurred the development of indistinct guidelines for permissible self-help. As early as 1768 Blackstone recited rules to govern self-help privileges of self-defense, recapture of property, and summary abatement of nuisance."

[51] Taylor (1998), p. 845. Also: McCall (1973), pp. 67–68.

[52] On the Roman origin of distress in common law as self-help species intended as a speedy and effective means of getting security for the performance of a duty: Street (2013), p. 282.

[53] McCall (1973), p. 67.

[54] Goode (1988); Goode (1998), p. 4.

[55] Taylor (1998), p. 845. Also McCall (1973), pp. 72–74.

2.3 Same Purposes, Different Paths

Private debt collection and especially self-help repossession are strongly intertwined with secured credit (lending). Because of this, understanding their evolution requires also understanding the history of secured transactions; the two hardly could be separated. This applies especially to continental Europe where this branch of law is yet to develop into a comprehensive system similar to the one enshrined in UCC Article 9 encompassing also self-help.[56] These systems are yet to realize how close the linkages are. Therefore, a brief overview of secured transactions in the jurisdictions in question is provided below.

Since the book does not deal with secured transactions as such, the ensuing elaboration does not aim to be an exhaustive treatment of all the building blocks of this branch of law either. Rather, the focus will be limited to enforcement of security interests and the differences that exist between the selected laws. Thus, their main focus will be on how the existing secured transactions laws in place view and treat private enforcement.

As far as this work is concerned, secured transactions in personal property[57] is the center of analysis. This is not to imply that, and it should not be construed to mean that, self-help repossession and recourse to private enforcement do not exist with respect to real property, or what the civilian systems refer to as immovable goods. But in the area of real property, rules are stricter and less harmonized, real property is harder to hide, demolish or otherwise misappropriate given the requirement for strict formalities to be followed.[58] Additionally, since this work deals strictly with collection of personal property, enforcement of security interests on real property (i.e., mortgages) will be left aside.

[56] Tajti (2002a), p. 187; and Tajti (2012a), pp. 116–118.

[57] Given that US law is the benchmark of this analysis, the book opted to use the common law terminology, which includes both tangible (choses in possession) and intangible (choses in action) property. However, due to the nature of the topic, in dealing with civilian systems references shall be made to their own concepts, namely movables and intangibles. For a detailed discussion on terminology caveats: McKendrick (2010), p. 32.

[58] On the differences between real property and personal property and the distinguishing characters of personal property: McKendrick (2010), pp. 32–34. Goode emphasizes that "the term personal property is used as the antithesis of real property" and explains the differences in applicable legal regimes. In the case of real property, for example, he notices that land is immovable and permanent, which makes it harder to transfer or use (via restrictions) but also allows multiple interests for longer periods of time. Additionally, its identity can be easily established for the title is likely to be registered.

2.3.1 *Common Law Jurisdictions*

Although the book uses US law as benchmark, the following presentation comprises both common law jurisdictions covered, namely the US and the UK. As it will become evident, the fact that both the US and the UK laws belong to the same legal family does not mean their secured transactions laws are similar. On the contrary, the discrepancies[59] between them in the area of secured transactions are striking, besides the different naming in the latter—i.e., personal property security law.

2.3.1.1 US: The Revolutionary Model

The law of secured transactions in personal property has been unified in the US by way of a model law, Article 9 of the UCC, which extends to personal property, fixtures and sale of receivables.[60] Undoubtedly, through its success and influence, the UCC has been promoted as one of the great contributions to the field of law of American commercial law in the last century.[61] Since it is based on "a functional approach rather than on theoretical distinctions,"[62] and more and more countries are turning towards the UCC in redesigning their secured transactions law,[63] it made sense to use it as a benchmark for the purposes of this comparative analysis. However, in order to keep the things clear and simple, the following description will refer to five key elements:[64] (a) the unitary concept of security interests, (b) the unique enforcement system, (c) the role of attachment and perfection (filing system), (d) the system of priorities and (e) the floating lien concept.

---

[59] On the differences between English and US law and the underlying causes: Tajti (2002a), pp. 115–118.

[60] Rover (2007), p. 54 and McCall (1973), p. 75.

[61] It should be mentioned from the outset that Article 9 is not an applicable statute in itself. Secured transaction law is state law and not a federal law in the US. It was designed as a model law in order to bring a greater level of uniformity between the various state laws. Hence, despite the fact that now all states, including District Columbia, have adopted it, these adopted versions are not identical in all aspects. They do share though most of the features that characterize its general thrust of the codification. See: Rover (2007), pp. 54–55.

[62] Kieninger (2004), p. 57. The European theoretical approach was also described as "dogmatic (or systemic) thinking," due to the fact that classes of assets are still defined by "their natural or ideal features, completely disregarding that such classification is insufficient for and causes problems in business life." Tajti (2012b), p. 125.

[63] Rover (2007), pp. 56–58. Also: Kieninger (2004), p. 54.

[64] For the first attempt to explain UCC Article 9 to non-Americans by reducing the system to its core elements, "building blocks," see: Tajti (2002a), p. 141. The reason is that according to the mentioned author, these five elements will be *sine qua non* requirements of any nonrudimentary security system. However, Tajti uses a slightly different order than the one employed by this work. The reason for changing it has to do with the purposes of the book, which focus more on the issue on enforcement and not on explaining the system as a whole.

Two things should be mentioned from the outset: first, these "innovative" provisions were not invented by the drafters of the Code; they were not their original creation. In reality, the drafters relied heavily on the already existing body of precode personal security laws.[65] The large number of commercial laws that covered the separately existing "independent security devices" was put together carefully in a "mosaic where each of the constituent-stones is based on a more or less differing subset of rules."[66] Second, UCC Article 9 must be read and understood from a functional point of view since it introduced a "unitary" approach of security devices,[67] meaning that the Code replaced the former devices with a single one, governed by a single body of rules and a unified terminology.[68]

This unitary concept has simplified the rules of security rights since every transaction with which the parties intend to create a security interest is covered by the UCC regime of Article 9, notwithstanding the previous traditional distinction among security devices, which was mostly based on form.[69] Each of the security devices rested on a peculiar "industry" that had been in existence for decades if not a century, which means that at the time when Article 9 appeared these industries strongly relied on mature business with the appropriate know-how.[70] However, the functional approach favored by the American drafters contrasts with that of the majority of European systems because for the former the title to the collateral is irrelevant[71] while for the latter it is not.[72]

As a result, Article 9 brings together and covers two kinds of property interests: on the one hand, the security interests in personal property and, on the other hand, the deemed security interests of those who purchased accounts or any other intangibles.[73] One question here would be why did the drafters of the UCC Article 9 decide to bring under the same umbrella discounting of receivables (purchase of receivables for less than their face value), also known as factoring? The answer lies with the fact that despite the conceptual differences between purchasing receivables and using them as security for a repayment obligation, in practice the distinction is hard to make. Even so, the assimilation did not set aside the need to distinguish a

[65] White and Summers (2010), p. 1148. At the same time, Article 9 made more sweeping changes in the law than any other article in the Code. See: McCall (1973), p. 75.

[66] Tibor Tajti—*Security Rights in Central and Eastern Europe* in Bussani and Werro (2009), p. 500. For an extensive history and context of the adoption of the UCC: Kieninger (2004), pp. 60–64.

[67] Rover (2007), p. 55.

[68] White and Summers (2010), p. 1149.

[69] It was pointed out though that this approach does not extinguish the question of whether or not a transaction is a secured transaction. The characterization is left to the decision of the courts. Rover (2007), pp. 55–56. Also: Kieninger (2004), pp. 56–57; Tajti (2002a), p. 142.

[70] Tibor Tajti—*Security Rights in Central and Eastern Europe* in Bussani and Werro (2009), p. 501.

[71] Tajti (2002a), p. 142.

[72] Kieninger (2004), p. 57.

[73] Kieninger (2004), p. 56.

true sale from a secured loan, especially with respect to the determining of the destination of the surplus after the assignee has been paid.[74]

Obviously, the first step is to make sure that the security interest will be enforceable under the Article 9. Hence, the legal provisions describe in detail the steps that need to be taken in order for the security interest to come into existence and for the interest to *attach*[75] to the collateral,[76] which means that the security interest is enforceable against the other contracting party. However, the public must also be notified of the creation of the security interest, which is done through different methods established by the law (*filing* being the main one[77]), a process known as *perfection*. Through *perfection*, the security interest becomes enforceable against third parties.[78] After attachment and perfection, two most important consequences arise: the possibility of the creditor to foreclose or otherwise realize on the collateral to satisfy the claim against the defaulting debtor and also the enforceability against third parties.[79] Thus, in principle there must not be any intervention of a court in enforcement proceedings. The creditor is allowed recourse to self-help repossession and to a private sale of property taken as security.[80]

The priority system also has an effect on the security interest and its enforcement since it resolves the conflicts concerning situations in which several creditors have taken interests in the same collateral or situations in which additional purchasers of the collateral appear to have conflicting interests. These conflicts were resolved by what came to be known as *catch-all rule*,[81] which states that when there is more than one perfected security interest, they will rank according to the priority in time of perfection or filing (unless special rules dictate otherwise, e.g. PMSI). With respect to conflicting unperfected security interests, the priority will belong to the one who attaches first. This is not the end of the story, since additional special priority rules are to be found throughout the sections of Article 9. Therefore, anyone verifying priorities should make sure no special one applies, which situation—as it was pointed out[82]—might puzzle anyone coming from civil law jurisdictions. However, the issue of priority goes beyond the purposes of this work and will not be further analyzed.

---

[74] For details and terminological explanations concerning the interchangeably usage of receivable and accounts: Tajti (2002a), pp. 98–99 and footnote 289.

[75] For a detailed description of the necessary elements of attachment: Kieninger (2004), pp. 65–66. For distinctions between Article 9 attachment and attachment in civil procedure: Tajti (2002a), p. 38, footnote 37.

[76] Section 9-203 of the UCC.

[77] Tajti (2002a), pp. 144–158.

[78] On attachment and perfection and for an explanation concerning these North American concepts and the distinction between them, see: Tajti (2002a), pp. 37–40. On perfection and filing, see also: White and Summers (2007), pp. 44 and 54–82.

[79] White and Summers (2010), p. 1185.

[80] Rover (2007), p. 56.

[81] Section 9-322 of the UCC.

[82] Tajti (2002a), p. 165.

The final key element of Article 9 is the concept of floating lien. US law does not have a "floating charge" in the sense that it exists in English law, but it recognizes the "floating lien," which is a way of taking security in accounts, inventory or equipment, present or future property, without being designated as such in Article 9.[83] In other words, the floating lien is a self-standing device stemming out of the fact that Article 9 is not a *numerus clausus* system[84] but a functional one (meaning that it is the security function and not the designation of the agreement that matters).[85] Both the US and the English categories fulfill the same task: the encumbering of either the whole or a substantial part of the debtor's property, including present and future assets,[86] although they do not fit completely.[87] By allowing security interests in future (after acquired) property, in proceeds and for future advances under a secured debt, it means that it also recognizes the security interest to adapt to changes in collateral as well as in the secured debt.[88]

Obviously, a security interest law that provides for **a system of private enforcement has to make sure that no imbalance will occur between the interests of creditors and those of debtors**. Since in practice that is almost impossible, there is a need for the legislator to implement adequate protection rules to either deter or sanction any kind of abuses, especially with respect to consumer debtor cases.[89] The US is a good model in this regard since it provides for various defense lines. **First** line is provided by the provisions of Article 9 itself with the concomitant case law. **Second** comes the right to sue (punitive damages, conversion). **Third** line is represented by subject-specific consumer protection regulated on both federal level and state level. Individuals are encouraged to resort to litigation as "an extensive

[83] Section 9-204 of the UCC referring to "after-acquired property."

[84] In contrast, English security law is based on a number of nominated security devices, one of them being the floating charge.

[85] Tajti (2002a), p. 178.

[86] Tajti (2002a), pp. 178–179.

[87] There are two main differences between the English floating charge and the US floating lien. First, in the case of floating charge there is no priority until crystallization. Second, in the case of floating charge unfettered dominion is also common, which is important because English law defines the floating charge vis-à-vis the fixed charge, which is not the case with the US floating lien.

[88] Rover (2007), p. 56.

[89] Tajti (2012a), p. 117. Also: Tajti (2013), p. 126. The issue was discussed during the drafting of the UCC as well. However, the authors agreed that a reform of abusive practices in the field would be better attained by separate legislation rather by inserting protective rules in the UCC, which would be limited to transactions involving security interests. In the end, when Uniform Consumer Credit Code was adopted in 1968, it contained no provisions to regulate the right of a secured creditor to repossess upon default. Hence, repossession remained governed by the provisions of the UCC and it is also touched upon by the provisions of the FDCPA. See: McCall (1973), p. 78.

mechanism for public enforcement."[90] What is meant by this is that "individuals are incentivized to seek out and take action to rectify breaches of law (in the broadest sense) and in so doing to act often as 'private attorneys general' [. . .]."[91] The essential features of such protection mechanisms are availability of contingency fees, absence of cost shifting, strong procedural mechanisms of discovery, high damages for losses, statutory damages for breach of law and even punitive damages, and the possibility to resort to powerful administrative bodies that would impose different types of fines and penalties on wrongdoers. Therefore, the contrast with what is available in European states is striking.[92]

2.3.1.2 The UK: "Legislation from the Time of the Sewing Machine"[93]

Despite the fact that England takes pride in its capital city as one of the leading financial centers of the world, its principal commercial law statutes have remained in force and virtually unchanged for 100 years,[94] guided by the principle that if something is not broken then one should not fix it. Goode emphasizes that apart from the complex and old legislation governing chattel mortgages by individuals, the rules governing security interests in personal property, documents of title, performance and assignment of receivables were to be found almost exclusively in case law. Hence, it was the creativity and good sense of the judiciary combined with the ingenuity of businessmen and their attorneys that allowed the English system to do so well.[95] Therefore, if those drafting the law did not manage to keep up, the professionals using it did.

English law recognizes four types of consensual security interests: the pledge, the contractual lien, the mortgage and the equitable charge.[96] All of them require certain qualifications. The pledge is a possessory security interest, and its rules are

---

[90] Brownsword et al. (2011), p. 438.

[91] Brownsword et al. (2011), pp. 438–439.

[92] "Article 9's non-judicial enforcement scheme contrasts sharply with that typically found in Europe." Kieninger (2004), p. 79.

[93] Quirk (2008), p. 219.

[94] Goode (1988), p. 139.

[95] Goode (1988), p. 139. English law has been also characterized as a "compartmentalized but efficient model" and a "good example that alternatives (to the UCC model) exist." See: Tajti (2002a), p. 233.

[96] There are also authors who consider that there are only three: pledge, charge and mortgage. Kieninger (2004), p. 87.

almost identical in each of the jurisdictions, so the book will not dedicate more space to it. The contractual lien[97] is a mere contractual right of detention for goods that were delivered to the creditor for some other purpose than security and does not provide a right of sale.[98] The mortgage is a transfer of title to the creditor by way of security, upon an express or implied condition that once the sum secured has been repaid the good shall be returned to the mortgagor.[99] Since a delivery of possession is not a legal requirement for its creation, the mortgage is a true nonpossessory security interest. Depending on the circumstances, the mortgage may be legal or in equity, fixed or floating. Lastly, the equitable charge is an encumbrance that confers to the creditor a right to have a designated good of the charger appropriated as discharge of debtor's indebtedness. Similar to mortgages, they may be fixed or floating, but since they are mere encumbrances they will be only in equity (or by statute).[100] Goode called the floating charge "one of equity's most brilliant creations"[101] since it managed to "accommodate two competing requirements: that of the creditor for security and that of the debtor to be able to turn over his circulating assets freely in the ordinary course of business."[102] Although the floating charge is not of particular relevance to this work, the issue of private administrative receivers[103] cannot be analyzed in complete disregard of this device.

The difference between floating and fixed charges or mortgages is determined not by the way the charged property is described by the parties but by the chargor's power to sell the charged property.[104] The reforms in the field brought by The Enterprise Act 2002 have seriously weakened the creditor's protection given by

[97] It must be stressed that the concept of lien used here is different from the concept of lien used in the US. In the US, the term lien is broader than security interest because it comprises all claims, encumbrances or charges on property for the payment of any debt, obligation or duty, irrespective of the way they came into existence. For a detailed explanation of the US concept of lien: Tajti (2002a), pp. 40–41.

[98] Rover (2007), p. 50.

[99] Rover (2007), p. 50.

[100] Rover (2007), p. 50.

[101] Goode (1988), p. 146.

[102] Goode (1988), p. 147.

[103] An administrative receiver over the debtor's property may be privately appointed by creditors who took security over the debtor's property and stipulated in their contract of loan the power to appoint a receiver for the purpose of enforcing their security. McCormack (2008), p. 47. Given the purpose of this remedy and the fact that the appointment did not involve the judiciary, for the purposes of this work private administrative receivership is deemed a form of self-help. Hence, unless otherwise stated, hereinafter the term "receiver" shall refer to privately appointed receivers. For details, *infra* Chap. 4, Sect. 4.6.

[104] McKendrick (2010), p. 723. "The leading case is [...] in *Re Spectrum Plus Ltd* [...]. [T]he critical question to be asked relates to the control that is exercised over the assets that fall within the scope of the charge. While the courts were once willing to recognize that a charge could be fixed notwithstanding the fact that the charger retained an ability to remove the asset from the scope of the charge, it is now clear from *Spectrum* that the test to be applied is more restrictive one and that the ability to remove an asset from the scope of the charge will result in the conclusion that the charge is floating and not fixed." Also: Kieninger (2004), pp. 88–89.

floating charges or mortgages. The most significant changes were the loss of their right to appoint an administrative receiver in respect of floating charges[105] and the limitation of the value of the floating charge by creating a fund to be distributed to unsecured creditors from the realization of the assets subjected to a floating charge.[106] However, further changes to English security law concerning the implementation of a new notice filing system similar to the one implemented by the UCC or of a system based on the European Bank for Reconstruction and Development Model Law have been rejected as unfit, possibly creating considerable logistical hurdles.[107]

The real securities mentioned provide the creditor with several rights of enforcement, including right of pursuit, right of preference, retention or recovery of possession,[108] right of sale[109] and to sue for any deficiency,[110] right of foreclosure[111] or the right to ask for an order vesting legal title in the secured creditor. Additionally, the creditor may choose to appoint a receiver to take possession and sell the good(s) for him,[112] although due to recent changes, the effects of private administrative receivership have been seriously diminished as it is pointed out in Chap. 4.

Out of all the above, foreclosure of both real and personal property can be exercised only by an order of the court;[113] therefore, it is not a nonjudicial method of enforcement as in the US, while in the case of an equitable mortgage or a mere charge, there must be an express provision in the contract authorizing the creditor to take possession.[114] Additional restrictions were imposed by Consumer Credit Act (CCA) 1974 with respect to mandatory default notices where the agreement falls under its cover.[115] Last but not least, the creditor bears several duties with respect to the possession (to act in good faith, duty of care, manage, preserve and take reasonable care of the repossessed property)[116] and additional ones with respect

---

[105] Rover (2007), p. 51. For the role of administrative receivers in the UK and for its counterpart in Romanian law, see *infra*, Chap. 4, Sect. 4.6.

[106] Rover (2007), pp. 51–52.

[107] Rover (2007), p. 52. For details with respect to calls for reformation of the English law of security along the lines of Art 9: Kieninger (2004), pp. 90–93.

[108] Beale et al. (2012), pp. 574–578.

[109] Beale et al. (2012), pp. 578–584.

[110] Beale et al. (2012), p. 560.

[111] Although available, foreclosure is rarely pursued. See: Beale et al. (2012), pp. 568–570.

[112] There are several advantages in doing so, the most important one being the fact that the appointment of a receiver will insulate the secured creditor from any liability towards the debtor. For details: Beale et al. (2012), pp. 585–590.

[113] Beale et al. (2012), p. 568.

[114] Beale et al. (2012), p. 574.

[115] Beale et al. (2012), p. 575.

[116] Beale et al. (2012), pp. 576–577.

to the sale of the repossessed good (give notice, provide sufficient time to redeem, to dispose of the goods in a fair, proper and reasonable manner).[117] According to English law, the creditor is not entitled to sell the good to himself (personally or through agents) as it would amount to a breach of public policy concerning conflicts of interest.[118]

Besides the four mentioned types of consensual securities, English law recognizes other legal concepts that fulfill the function of creating a security for an obligation. These *quasi-securities* include reservation or retention of title (sometimes referred to as "Romalpa clauses") of a seller in a conditional sale agreement or the owner in a hire purchase agreement. Under such agreements, the title in the goods will not pass until the full price has been paid.[119] Apart from retention of title, a similar function was fulfilled by the assignment of receivables or of book debts by way of security. Under English law, assignments can take the form of either a legal assignment or an equitable one,[120] the difference being that in the case of the latter the rules are more lax and the assignment would only be effective between the assignor and assignee, regardless whether notice has been given to the debtor, while in the case of the former, the assignment requires written form signed by the assignor, it must be absolute, in total and notice must be given.[121] The aforementioned difference stems from the fact that—using the terminology of UCC Article 9 for comparison purposes—an equitable security is a security that has been only "attached" to the asset (and produces effect only between the contracting parties), while a legal one has been also "perfected," which would mean that it produces *erga omnes* effects. In addition, a legal interest has priority over an equitable one, according to English law priority rules.[122]

In the Romalpa case,[123] the reservation of title could be extended to all sums owed to the seller under prior or subsequent transactions, to the proceeds that resulted from subsales that were authorized by the buyer[124] and to any products made from the original goods and other materials that may belong to the buyer or a third party.[125] Since a reservation of title does not have to be registered in order to

[117] Beale et al. (2012), pp. 578–582.

[118] Beale et al. (2012), pp. 582–583.

[119] Rover (2007), p. 53.

[120] Rover (2007), p. 54.

[121] Tajti (2002a), p. 240.

[122] For more details concerning the differences between equitable and legal securities under English law: Tajti (2002a), pp. 238–240. The author emphasizes that equitable interests are more informal and somewhat a weaker kind of securities, otherwise said, "imperfect" securities, as opposed to legal securities, which imply that the registration requirements and formalities have been met and hence the security is a "perfect" one.

[123] *Aluminium Industrie Vaasen BV v. Romalpa Aluminium Ltd* [1976] 1 WLR 676.

[124] Rover (2007), p. 53.

[125] This extension has not passed the test of time in English courts, which later held that such an extension is in fact a charge. See Rover (2007), p. 53.

be created,[126] this raises concerns with respect to the risks employed by ostensible ownership.

The literature mentions several advantages of retention of title devices: the creditor has a personal right against the purchaser for breach of contract, also a statutory right of the unpaid seller, and real rights in goods. Thus, he can simply retake and resell the goods (or appoint a receiver to do it for him) and additionally he can claim any loss suffered as damages. But the reality is not so bright, since the goods rarely remain available for repossession and the debtors can pass good title to them to good-faith third parties. Unfortunately, the commentators do not go further than acknowledging this issue[127] and no solution is offered.

The distinction between security interests and *quasi securities* leads to differences in enforcement as well. Differences in regimes appear even between *quasi* securities themselves, depending on the way they are regarded: i.e., consumer sale agreements share common characteristics with the financial lease as originally they provided credit, while at the same time, financial leases share other characteristics with hire purchase agreements when the bailment character is taken into account.[128] The reason behind these differences lies with the fact that under English law, the financial lease is basically a hire contract.[129] Therefore, unlike conditional sale agreements or hire purchase agreements, it does not entail either the obligation or the option to buy the goods, but the one to return the collateral to the lessor or to deal with them, when the bailment expired, as the bailor directs.[130]

Generally, unlike in the case of security interests, in case of *quasi securities* the creditor does not owe an obligation to account for surplus or to sue for any deficiency.[131] Theoretically, there is also no equity of redemption[132] or any equity interests acquired. Therefore, even if the debtor paid out 90 % of the debt, the creditor can retake the asset. The question is more complicated in reality since the issue is debatable in the case of consumer sale agreements (where installments paid are considered part of the price of the good) and more problematic in the case of hire purchase agreements or financial leases (where they are considered rent or price for use).

Although the rights of the creditor should also be enhanced (since he is the owner of the goods), private enforcement is heavily limited, especially when it

126 Rover (2007), p. 53.

127 Beale et al. (2012), pp. 592–593.

128 Beale et al. (2012), p. 607.

129 McKendrick (2010), p. 767.

130 For details concerning quasi-securities in England: Tajti (2002a), pp. 254–256; and McKendrick (2010), pp. 751–779.

131 Beale et al. (2012), p. 591.

132 Beale et al. (2012), p. 607. Also: McCall (1973), p. 71.

comes to consumer goods (protected goods) or agreements regulated by the CCA.[133] Under a consumer sale agreement, the creditor must give notice of default, allow time for redemption and give another notice for enforcement.[134] He is barred from engaging in self-help repossession in case the buyer paid more than 1/3 of the total amount payable; otherwise, he might suffer severe consequences.[135] In the case of hire purchase agreements, the creditor's situation seems better only if he decides to terminate the hiring and not the agreement, since it will give him the right to repossess without notice.[136] Financial leases share with the conditional sale agreements the fact that goods may become protected (and therefore there is a ban on repossession)[137] and with hire purchase agreements the regime applicable to forfeiture of sums already paid.[138] All other CCA restrictions must be complied with.[139]

With respect to private enforcement and encouragement of self-help, Goode underlies that "in comparison to the continental legal systems the common law was **remarkably indulgent towards self-help** allowing acceleration clauses to be invoked, goods to be repossessed, receivers and managers appointed, all without the need for judicial approval, the only limiting factor being to refrain from any breach of peace."[140] The reasons are classic already: civilized self-help offered the speed, efficiency and flexibility needed for the smooth functioning of business life. That does not seem to be the case anymore, as the complicated regimes applicable to private enforcement described above demonstrate.

Moreover, another change in policy towards enforcement took place recently[141] in the UK concerning the regulation of corporate activities. The main idea behind the current policy is, according to the Financial Conduct Authority (FCA), twofold: making sure that firms put consumers at the heart of their business and that markets work well.[142] Therefore, the government adopted and implemented specific legislation—namely the Enforcement Guide—providing for new enforcement framework and powers in which the following three components were combined: first, the desire to maintain an open and cooperative relationship between the FCA and those it regulates; second, the duty of the regulatory body to observe principles such as

[133] Starting with 1st of April 2014, most of the CCA's provisions were included in the Consumer Credit sourcebook (CONC), available online at: http://media.fshandbook.info/content/full/CONC.pdf, last visited 12.12.2014.

[134] Beale et al. (2012), pp. 600–601.

[135] Beale et al. (2012), p. 601.

[136] Beale et al. (2012), p. 603.

[137] Beale et al. (2012), p. 612.

[138] Beale et al. (2012), p. 611.

[139] Beale et al. (2012), pp. 609 and 612.

[140] Goode (1988), pp. 151–152.

[141] The most recent change took place in 2014, starting with 1st of April, when the OFT was shut down and its attributions were partly given to the Financial Conduct Authority (FCA).

[142] http://www.fca.org.uk/about/what/enforcement, last visited 12.12.2014.

transparency, proportionality, responsiveness, consistency with its publicly stated policies and observance of fair treatment; third, the aim to change the conduct of the *person* who is the subject of its action by deterring future noncompliance, eliminating any financial gains or benefits from noncompliance and, where appropriate, remedying the harm caused by noncompliance.[143]

In matters related to consumer credit and debt collection, the abovementioned principles materialized in the Consumer Credit sourcebook. Specifically, Chap. 7—Arrears, default and recovery (including repossession—was adopted to comprise and amend all previous guidelines concerning unfair debt collection practices.[144] However, in these matters, the UK government maintained a model comprising three stages: the first is the encouragement of voluntary settlement (through alternative dispute resolution (ADR) methods such as mediation or noncourt bodies such as ombudsmen, tribunals, compensation schemes or business codes of conduct); the second is the regulatory assistance and oversight of agencies; and the third, as a measure of last resort, is the possibility to have judicial collective procedures, but only in cases where ADR proved unsuccessful and regulatory solutions were inappropriate.[145]

These recent reforms are meant to make the UK system more efficient, similar to its American counterpart. Since the transitory period expired in September 2014,[146] it remains to be seen how successful and effective these reforms will be. However, one may state that the previous regime, with its constant banning and limitation on the possibility of the aggrieved creditors in resorting to self-help repossession and other private enforcement means, may have affected the efficacy of private enforcement in the UK. Therefore, the search for a balance between the rights and expectations of creditors and those of debtors was considered somewhat unsuccessful and led to the current legislative changes.

2.3.2 Continental Europe

Before going into the presentation of the other chosen jurisdictions, some preliminary considerations are necessary. The legislators' focus on the continent has been mostly on "substance,"[147] in the sense of substantive rules and less on enforcement.

[143] Section 2.2 of The Enforcement Guide, into force from 1st of April 2014, available at: http://media.fshandbook.info/Handbook/EG_FCA_20140401.pdf, last visited 12.12.2014.

[144] Chapter 7 of the Consumer Credit sourcebook, available at: http://media.fshandbook.info/content/full/CONC.pdf, last visited 12.12.2014.

[145] Brownsword et al. (2011), p. 451.

[146] Most transitional provisions of Consumer Credit Handbook (CONC) applied until 30th of September 2014, i.e., Art. 7.17–7.19 of CONC related to Notice of sums in arrears or notice of default concerning sums under P2P agreements, available at: http://media.fshandbook.info/content/full/CONC.pdf, last visited 12.12.2014.

[147] Brownsword et al. (2011), p. 415.

As seen in the case of the US and the UK, the policy decisions of the legal and political systems on the balance that they seek to achieve between public and private enforcement are very important since depending on their decisions major consequences will occur.[148] It is because of these decisions that until now EU does not have a harmonized approach towards private enforcement and such a striking difference exists not only between the civil law jurisdictions covered (France, Germany, Romania) and the common law ones (the UK) but also between civil law jurisdictions themselves.

The three main problems stem from the different understanding of the term "private enforcement," a less important role of litigation and less judicial incentives for private action compared to the US. With respect to the first problem, European commentators read "private enforcement" as "the taking of action by private persons to vindicate their rights under private law, through the civil courts"[149] (emphasis added). Their understanding is not necessarily incorrect, but it is definitely too narrow given the fact that any adverted rights must be exercised through courts. Other differences in policy come from the remaining two problems such as the fact that litigation plays a less central role in European legal systems and the incentives designed to encourage citizens to resort to litigations are absent, unlike in the US. For example, cost shifting (the party that loses pays) is a universal principle of civil procedure law, success fees may be permitted but contingency fees are strictly banned, punitive damages, jury trials or collective actions are rare and are heavily opposed.[150]

A 2005 proposal,[151] meant to exempt a natural person (consumer) from the payment of the other party's attorney's fees in case he loses in the European Small Claims Procedure and he does not have legal representation, was declined on the ground that the successful party should not be disadvantaged. However, such a proposal could have eased the consumers' fear for additional expenses that they might have suffered in case their action or defense were unsuccessful. It might have also had a deterrent effect towards the other parties' decisions of engaging expensive legal action or defense where the chances of recovery were null.[152]

Regretfully, in the EU the lack of appropriate incentives granted to aggrieved consumers to determine them to take action and act on their own affects the enforceability of any consumer protection rules, including in the area of consumer credit and debt collection. For example, a study conducted in the Netherlands showed that from the total number of consumer complaints brought, only 7 % of them end in court or ADR proceedings, while 45 % of them go unresolved.[153] In the

---

148 Brownsword et al. (2011), p. 416.

149 Brownsword et al. (2011), p. 437.

150 Brownsword et al. (2011), p. 439. For details concerning the debate on whether to introduce collective redress, see also page 440.

151 Commission of the European Communities (2005).

152 Brownsword et al. (2011), p. 507.

153 Brownsword et al. (2011), p. 489.

light of empirical evidence such as this one, the strong focus at EU level to provide consumers with sufficient information will not cause any significant changes in the absence of incentives for private action similar to those available in the US.

That the American system places strong emphasis on private enforcement (both in the narrow and broader sense) is widely known in Europe, but it receives no critical analysis, only criticism and resistance.[154] The latter might come from lack of either understanding or desire to learn from the US.[155] At the same time, commentators have noted as relevant that after the fall of communism, the CEE states, confronted with the same policy decisions[156] in relation to their internal legal framework, were heavily affected by their communist legacy—paternalistic state, centralized control and destruction of private initiative. It seemed easier to adopt the traditional Western division between public and private enforcement than to shift radically towards the US private enforcement approach.[157] The reasons lay with the communality of property law features: the domination of the "unitary concept of ownership," the *numerus clausus* of property rights and the overall ban of self-help enforcement.[158] However, as was the case of Romania, some legislators decided to radically break from the past and step towards evolution, thus adopting and adapting the US model.[159]

Another serious obstacle against harmonization—despite the common origins of their civil legal systems—stems from the differences between the civil law countries themselves, differences that are simply becoming more and more profound.[160] At least with respect to the wide area of secured transactions (in which the issues of

[154] Taylor (1998), p. 845.

[155] Tibor Tajti—*Security Interests in Central and Eastern Europe* in Bussani and Werro (2009), pp. 497–498.

[156] Bussani and Werro (2009), p. 476. Tajti mentions two diverging policy concerns that collided at the time: on the one hand, the dogmatic requirements (such as finding an appropriate place in the system of the code) and, on the other hand, the need for new, efficient and pragmatic solutions.

[157] Brownsword et al. (2011), p. 441.

[158] Tibor Tajti—*Security Rights in Central and Eastern Europe* in Bussani and Werro (2009), p. 472.

[159] Stanescu and Timofti (2013), p. 176.

[160] For a detailed description of the origins of divergences between European jurisdictions themselves but also between the European jurisdictions and the US: Kieninger (2004), pp. 9–16. The author explains that historically, the industrial revolution brought a demand for credit in trade and industry, which could not be matched solely by security rights *in personam* and rights in immovable property, a challenge to which European jurisdictions answered differently. Some legislatures created special registered security rights based on the idea of pledge, where registration replaced actual possession of collateral (France, Romania). Others decided not to introduce any nonpossessory security rights, but for special registrable charges on ships, airplanes, agricultural inventory and overseas cables; hence, the courts had to compensate for the lack of innovation by validating contractual securities (Germany). Lastly, some went for innovations, such as the floating charge, which could be established over all or a part of a company's assets, hence providing a single security device where lenders in other jurisdictions had to resort to different kinds of rights for different kinds of assets (the UK). Another dividing line relates to the principle of publicity, which, although common to most jurisdictions, is enforced to different degrees.

self-help repossession and private debt collection are integrated), the European countries find themselves at very different levels of advancement and reform. If the UK is struggling with an old system in which it invested too much time to let go, France finally decided to take timid steps towards modernization, Germany is still indulging a nonreformed system and Romania has adopted what is probably one of the most modern secured transactions systems in Europe (at least on paper). Such levels will only deepen in time, making harmonization even harder to achieve, unless the EU member states will not turn towards documents such as the DCFR, which admittedly strive to find common acceptable answers to concrete legal issues.[161]

Finally, while officially most of the civil law jurisdictions have maintained their judicial enforcement systems, private enforcement agencies coexist in reality, many of them duly registered with company registries, and a private enforcement industry has begun to develop. After the fall of the Berlin wall, this industry became heavily present in the CEE region as well.[162] These agencies offer now a wide range of services that vary from private repossession of collateral to purchase and collection of receivables. If they were subjected to a functional legal framework that would ensure a sufficient number of mechanisms and safeguards to monitor their activities, there would be no problems[163] (the fact that they are needed is proven by the mere fact that they exist), but unfortunately this is not always the case. Especially in the CEE region, they have been inclined to deviate gradually towards organized crime and it is no wonder that whenever repossessors are mentioned, the recipient will imagine some sort of Mafia. Currently, these private enforcement services are still somewhere in the gray area between legality and illegality[164] as the book reveals.

2.3.2.1 France

The French secured transactions law was reformed in 2006 as a response to its current economic context.[165] Before the reform, the principle of multiplicity[166] was highly visible since numerous types of securities, most of them limited to specific

---

[161] Tajti (2013), p. 8.

[162] Tibor Tajti—*Security Rights in Central and Eastern Europe* in Bussani and Werro (2009), p. 494. Also: Tajti (2013), p. 127.

[163] Bussani and Werro (2009), p. 494.

[164] Bussani and Werro (2009), p. 495. Also Tajti (2012a), p. 117.

[165] Dahan and Simpson (2008), p. 259. The French secured transaction law was reformed by Ordinance of 23 March 2006, which has created a Book IV dedicated to security rights and guarantees in the Civil Code.

[166] Basically, the principle of multiplicity assumes that there are different types of security rights for each type of asset. The principle is still present in German law. See: Röver (2004), p. 46. It is generally assumed that shifting from the principle of multiplicity to a single method of creating security rights (as is the case now in the US) increases simplicity and efficiency in obtaining

industries, were created with their own particular regime.[167] Also, during the 1980s ownership rights were much favored by confirming retention of title clauses as effective in the event of debtor's insolvency. Loi Dailly enabled the transfer of the account receivables and has been widely used ever since[168] despite the fact that French assignment law remains more on the formal side and its procedures are cumbersome compared to their American counterparts.[169] Additional issues were caused by lack of transparency, due to the existence of multiple registries that affected the third parties by making the search extremely difficult or due to the fact that retention of title clauses and fiduciary transfers were not required to be registered.[170] All these examples proved only that the existing regime was inadequate to meet the economic demands and a reformation of the entire secured transaction system was necessary.[171]

Some of the most relevant changes were the extension of categories of assets that could be charged (including future ones) and the possibility to create nonpossessory security interests, which are now required to be registered in order to become opposable to third parties.[172] Another novelty concerns the perfection of the charge over receivables, which was much simplified by removing the prior requirement of serving a formal notification to the debtor. Currently, such notification is required only to make the charge opposable to the debtor but will not have any impact on the effects against third parties.[173]

Even so, in the area of enforcement, which is the most relevant part for the purposes of this work, the reform did not bring such serious changes. Strict foreclosure clauses are no longer prohibited, unless the secured debt is a consumer credit.[174] This means that French law recognizes the possibility of the parties to agree on strict foreclosure, as long as the value of the collateral was determined by an expert jointly appointed by the parties or by the court, unless the asset is listed on an organized market.[175] However, given the fact that insolvency law takes

---

security rights. See: International Trade Center (2010), p. 14. Hence, it is a main point of discussion concerning reforms of secured transaction laws. See: Calnan et al. (2012), pp. 8–9.

[167] Dahan and Simpson (2008), pp. 261.

[168] Dahan and Simpson (2008), p. 262.

[169] According to French law, for an assignment to be effective against third parties a notice of the assignment is to be served to the said third party. However, Loi Dailly tried to loosen the strictness of the notification rule by not requiring notification on the creation of the assignment, although as a matter of practice, notification via registered mail is still common. Tajti (2002a), p. 101.

[170] Dahan and Simpson (2008), p. 262.

[171] The reformation was successful only partially due to political interventions and policy issues. For a detailed description, Dahan and Simpson (2008), pp. 262–263.

[172] Dahan and Simpson (2008), pp. 264–265.

[173] Dahan and Simpson (2008), p. 266.

[174] French Civil Code, Art. 2348 and 2365.

[175] French Civil Code, Art. 2348.

precedence over secured transactions provisions, strict foreclosure clauses become ineffective in insolvency, when their benefit is probably needed most.[176] Additionally, the newly introduced nonpossessory pledge loses much of its interest to secured creditors because it does not grant them a right of retention and, hence, neither priority against unsecured creditors.[177]

The major downfall of the reform is that **judicial enforcement remains the rule**[178] with the notable exception of allowing *huissiers* to get involved in amicable (nonjudicial) debt collection.[179] In the view of the French legislators, the traditional view that realization of assets through a public auction based on a court order[180] is the only way to provide adequate protection to debtors remained in place. This is regrettable since public auctions are not always the best and fastest way to generate a high return from the sale of the assets. Additionally, since the realization of assets can only be performed via a court order, self-help repossession is obviously strictly banned under French law, which undermines the effectiveness of the new regime sought by the reform. However, contractual provisions allowing the secured creditor to take possession and appropriate the relevant asset are limitedly permitted by the law with respect to *certain* assets (emphasis added) such as cash or financial instruments.[181]

2.3.2.2 Germany

German security law, similar to English law, is characterized by the principle of multiplicity, meaning that there are available different types of security rights for each type of goods,[182] which may be legislated and also provided by case law or customary law.[183] The most relevant ones are the pledge of rights arising from a bank account, the security transfer of ownership in movable things and the retention of ownership, the security assignment of receivables and the land mortgage.

---

[176] Dahan and Simpson (2008), p. 268.

[177] Dahan and Simpson (2008), p. 268.

[178] Allan and Drobnig (1980), p. 632.

[179] Huissiers are in fact judicial officers empowered with the monopoly of servicing writs and enforcing judgments and writs of executions, similar to the bailiffs/sheriffs in the common law jurisdictions. However, in France they are also entitled to mediate, formulate legal findings, collect debts and perform public auction sales of movable goods. The most peculiar and significant (since it amounts to almost 20 % of their operations) aspect of their activity is that they can perform both judicial and nonjudicial debt collection. See: http://www.uihj.com/ressources/10148/54/france-en.pdf, last visited 22.01.2015. However, debt collection operations do not fall into the category of operations over which the huissiers enjoy monopoly. See: http://www.huissier-justice.fr/qui-est-il-127.aspx, last visited 22.01.2015.

[180] French Civil Code, Art. 2346.

[181] Hubert (2010), pp. 7–8.

[182] Rover (2007), p. 58.

[183] Rover (2007), p. 114.

Moreover, there is a prohibition on inventing new security devices on movables. This prohibition, established by the *numerus clausus* principle of German proprietary interests, has hindered economic and legal development[184] and also the possibility for the right of a proprietary character on the part of the provider of the security interest, comparable to the equity of redemption existing in English law.[185] This leaves the debtor with no more than a contractual right to claim the return of the pledged collateral, which puts the debtor in a very difficult position, especially in the case of creditor's bankruptcy.

Additionally, the legal requirement of possession impedes the creation of a security in movables that would allow the debtor to employ the secured good in his course of business, even dispose of it and shift the security interest to another, or that allows the creation of an ambulatory security interest that would become fixed on debtor's default, such as the floating charge.[186] Therefore, commentators have pointed out that the German Civil Code (BGB) does not really meet the need for effective and flexible securities in movable property required by commerce.[187] It is why the most flexible and widely employed security devices on personal property (kautelarische Sicherheiten) are not regulated by the BGB but are designed by contracts and validated by court decisions.[188]

The possessory pledge is the exception as it is regulated by the BGB, which allows for pledging in movable goods,[189] in receivables[190] and in other rights.[191] The group based on the notion of ownership is also covered by the BGB with respect to goods that are sold.[192] At the same time, the simple retention of ownership that was considered to be a transfer of ownership under the condition precedent that the sales price is paid[193] has been further developed by practice, legal doctrine and customary law[194] to cover other debts and future property.[195] The retention of ownership creates for the purchaser of the goods an expectancy right[196]

---

[184] Tajti (2002b), p. 106.

[185] Serick (1990), p. 2.

[186] Serick (1990), pp. 1–2 and 26.

[187] Serick (1990), pp. 1 and 15. Also: Tajti (2002b), p. 105.

[188] Tajti (2002b), pp. 106–107.

[189] German Civil Code (English Translation) (1896), Art 1204–1258. This has become obsolete in commercial practice. See: Rover (2007), p. 58.

[190] BGB, Art 1273, 1279–1290.

[191] BGB, Art 1291–1296.

[192] BGB, Art 455.

[193] BGB, Art 158 (1).

[194] Allan and Drobnig (1980), p. 619. Also: Serick (1990), p. 107, who calls it 'a matter of unwritten law,' 'a very sophisticated legal structure [. . .] constructed by jurists.'

[195] For details: Rover (2007), p. 59.

[196] This expectancy right is not to be found in the BGB, being a development of customary law. See: Rover (2007), p. 59.

since it will not hold full ownership in the purchased assets. This expectancy right is a right *in rem* that can be transferred separately to third parties.

Another type of security in movables based on the notion of ownership is the security transfer of ownership (*Sicherungsübereignung*), which has been created and developed by the practice and doctrine due to the limitations of the pledge (which was strictly possessory) and the impracticability of retention of ownership (limited in scope to securing payment in supply agreements).[197] Therefore, the security transfer took three different forms: in movable goods, in assignment of receivables and in other rights.[198] All of them are rights *in rem* and transfer in full a right to the new owner or holder, with the observation of respective rules of transfer appropriate to each asset in question.[199] Since the land mortgage is a security right in immovable goods, it will not be described and analyzed here.

From all chosen jurisdictions, the German system is the one completely unreformed despite calls for changes, asking either for "an efficient and elegant solution"[200] like the one adopted by the UCC Article 9, deemed to be as easy to implement in civil law countries as it was in common law ones, or for particular solutions to particular issues such as publicity or any other kind of registration in order to perfect the security. With regard to enforcement, the only route remains through courts, since German law does not allow self-help as the UCC Article 9 does.[201] However, private debt collection is known and widely employed,[202] as well as factoring,[203] yet they are not looked upon as forms of self-help.

2.3.2.3 Romania

At the time when communism fell, in 1989, Romania had a centralized, planned economy,[204] which did not rely on credit[205] and respective techniques to secure credit.[206] A general ban existed with respect to use of self-help as it was in the entire

[197] According to Tajti, these devices developed by businessmen and recognized by courts could be seen as proof that the *numerus clausus* principle employed by the German Civil Code does not suffice. See: Tibor Tajti—*Security Rights in Central and Eastern Europe* in Bussani and Werro (2009), pp. 472–473, footnote 18.

[198] Rover (2007), pp. 59–60.

[199] Rover (2007), p. 60.

[200] Allan and Drobnig (1980), p. 642. Also: Tajti (2002a), pp. 290–291.

[201] Franklin and Harms (2010), p. 131; Tajti (2002a), p. 285; Tajti (2012a), p. 116, footnote 50 and Tajti (2013), p. 135, footnote 332. The last source mentions that self-help repossession may be punishable under criminal law.

[202] Tajti (2013), pp. 132–133, specifically footnotes 325 and 327, pp. 135–136, footnote 332. Also: http://de.eos-solutions.com/leistungen/forderungsmanagement/inkasso/, last visited 10.12.2014.

[203] Serick (1990), p. 3 and Röver (2004), p. 48.

[204] On the issue of socialist legacy in all CEE area: Tibor Tajti—*Security Rights in Central and Eastern Europe* in Bussani and Werro (2009), pp. 479–481 and 490.

[205] de la Pena and Fleisig (2004), pp. 135–136.

[206] Rover (2007), p. 4.

CEE region.[207] As Romania desired to return to capitalism and join the market-based economy, a modern secured transaction law was required to serve that purpose and the need to attract credit and foreign investment. The fact that the existing legal regime of secured transaction had not been used for the past 50 years[208] proved to be more of an advantage, since, when the country started its individual reform process, it was basically able to start from scratch and choose the model that seemed to suit its interests best.[209]

As a matter of policy choice, Romania decided to go for a creditor-friendly approach,[210] while as a matter of model, it turned to the UCC Article 9, opting for a (mostly) functional approach.[211] This happened despite that the Anglo-American laws in general and the UCC in particular have a different understanding of property law than civil law jurisdictions, such as Romania, which shows in the distinctions of title and interest on the one hand and of attachment and perfection on the other.[212] Therefore, Romania became one of the few countries in Europe that

[207] Tibor Tajti—*Security Rights in Central and Eastern Europe* in Bussani and Werro (2009), p. 472.

[208] In 1999, the Romanian secured transaction law knew only two "big" institutions, contained in the Civil Code and the Commercial Code, both more than 100 years old: the hypothec (*ipotecă*) (used for real property) and the possessory pledge (*gajul*) (used for personal property). These two instruments were deemed insufficient and inadequate for the development of commercial credit, especially for those debtors who did not have any real property. Given that the possessory pledge meant that the personal property had to be taken from the debtor's possession and could not be used in his activity, it meant that the debtor's activity was brought to a halt as long as any merchandise acquired on credit had to go into the creditor's possession. More difficulties arose from the fact that the Commercial Code was not applied during communism to national contracts. Additionally, after the 1989 Revolution, the Supreme Court had to extend the interpretation of the provision governing exceptions to the possessory pledge in order to validate several nonpossessory pledges taken by several commercial banks. See: Rizoiu (2011), pp. 20–21.

[209] For an extensive discussion on how Romania chose its model law: de la Pena and Fleisig (2004), pp. 163–165.

[210] Office of the General Counsel (2012), p. 2. This approach, especially when it came to private enforcement, was not easily received by everyone. Rizoiu mentions two scholars: C. Rosu and G. Udrea, who not only feared the new secured transaction system, but actually supported the maintenance of the old one, or at least its intertwining with the general provisions requiring public enforcement through the norms established by the Civil Procedure Code. See: Rizoiu (2011), p. 567, footnotes 3 and 4.

[211] Romania opted for a formal approach but provided for certain common provisions for security rights and defined quasi-security transactions. This retained the formal classification of each transaction but specifically required their registration in the security register, which also led to harmonization of enforcement and other rules. Therefore, although the law applies to the outright creation of security rights, and it includes, in particular, assignment of receivables, conditional sales, leasing and rental contracts, it did not go as far as recharacterizing security devices as security rights. See Rover (2007), pp. 102 and 122.

[212] Rover (2007), p. 5.

decided to part with other civil law jurisdictions[213] and remained as such even after the adoption of the Romanian New Civil Code (RNCC) in 2011, which was heavily influenced by the Civil Code of Quebec.

Taking security on movable assets was initially governed by Title IV of Law 99/1999 regarding certain measures for speeding up the economic reform, which allowed for the creation of nonpossessory pledges,[214] subject to registration in the Electronic Archive of Security Interests in Personal Property.[215] The Law recognized that the bailiff system is inefficient, at least with respect to personal property, and hence it provided creditors with the option of private enforcement of their security interests, without judicial enforcement,[216] although such private enforcement could have been hampered by the deficient institutional framework and debtor's obstruction.[217] Even so, Romania was able to establish one of the most advanced regimes for secured transactions in CEE area,[218] maybe even going a bit too far for what the society was ready.

With the implementation of the RNCC, Romania has unified the formerly applicable enactments in the field of security interests and brought changes to the concept of security interest itself, and, according to an EBRD evaluation, it achieved a well-functioning legal regime regarding mortgages.[219] If the previous secured transaction law broke with the traditional approach and allowed for nonpossessory securities to be created, the new regime established by the RNCC has the ambition to reorganize the entire secured transaction system by implementing the mortgage over movables and create a "common framework" for all mortgages, with different rules depending only on the type of mortgaged goods: immovable or movables.[220]

The mortgage over movables (formerly known as *garanţie reală mobiliară*) is a nonpossessory security interest on a certain asset or a universality of assets (a floating security), which confers upon the secured creditor the possibility to

---

[213] Chaves et al. (2004), p. 4. Also: de la Pena and Fleisig (2004), p. 135: "This secured transactions law remains the only law with a fully functional approach [. . .] so far introduced in a developing country with a Civil Code tradition."

[214] de la Pena and Fleisig (2004), pp. 153–155.

[215] Office of the General Counsel (2012), p. 16.

[216] de la Pena and Fleisig (2004), pp. 165 and 202–212.

[217] A empirical survey of EBRD conducted 10 years ago showed that despite the presence of sound legal framework for secured transaction there were still issues with having and efficient enforcement mechanism in place in Romania. However, a recovery of at least 60 % of the market value of the collateralized asset was to be expected in 9 months or less. For details: Dahan et al. (2004), pp. 8 and 15.

[218] Office of the General Counsel (2012), p. 17.

[219] Office of the General Counsel (2012), p. 17.

[220] Thus, Romania seemed to have resolved, at least on paper, one of the fundamental issues affecting the countries in CEE region and not only the fact that many of the fields related to secured transactions are still scattered and subject to differing laws. See: Tibor Tajti—*Security Rights in Central and Eastern Europe* in Bussani and Werro (2009), p. 499.

satisfy its claim preferentially (directly or indirectly) and to pursue the collateral[221] irrespective of the person in whose hands it is (*in rem* right).[222] The mortgage over movables is purely contractual as opposed to the one over immovables, which can also derive from statutory provisions.[223]

Some limitations regard the mortgage over future assets or universality of assets. The parties must describe with sufficient precision the mortgaged goods or indicate the nature and content of the universality of goods mortgaged. Otherwise, a clause establishing a general mortgage over present and future goods will be considered imprecise and shall be deemed null and void.[224] Additionally, the RNCC provides that a mortgage over a universality of goods, present or future, tangible or intangible, can be acquired only with respect to the goods affected to an undertaking, being reserved only to the category of "professionals" and not to consumers.[225]

Mortgages over receivables are a special species of mortgages, established by an assignment of receivables. The new regime clarifies that the purpose of the assignment is not to transfer the claim from the assignor to the assignee but to grant it a security for the payment of a prior existing debt that the former had to the latter, which means that if the amount of the claim is smaller than the amount of the mortgaged receivables, the assignee will have to account to the assignor for the surplus.[226]

During the validity of the contract of mortgage over movables, the mortgagor is entitled to use and dispose in any legal way of the secured assets or its proceeds through whatever means they deem appropriate: leasing or sale.[227] Such acts of disposal over the mortgaged good are valid, even if the acquirer was aware of the contractual interdiction to dispose of the mortgaged good or the contractual provision declaring such disposal an event of default.[228] The reason lies with the intent of the legislator to ensure the free circulation of assets. Having the right to pursue the collateral, the creditor is secured even if the mortgagor has alienated it, as he can trace it in the hands of whoever possesses it.

The RNCC now provides for the private enforcement of mortgages over movables, while the Code of Civil Procedure still governs the judicial one. The secured creditor thus enjoys the three options that qualify as private enforcement: to sell the mortgaged asset, to keep it in satisfaction of the debt (full or partial strict

---

[221] This was meant to provide some additional protection to mortgagees since in case of movable property, secured creditors had to act promptly in case of default; otherwise, they would have faced the risk of the collateral being out of sight or unreachable. However, this protection remains more theoretical than practical.

[222] Vasilescu (2012), p. 175.

[223] Vasilescu (2012), p. 176.

[224] RNCC, Art 2391.

[225] RNCC, Art 2368.

[226] RNCC, Art 2408.

[227] RNCC, Art 2373.

[228] Such a provision is legal and will produce effects with respect to the triggering of the default, but it may not invalidate a potential transfer of the collateral to a third party. See: RNCC Art 2376.

foreclosure) or to administer it (close to the UK administrative receivership), but the latter is only available in the case of creditors holding a mortgage over the assets belonging to a commercial entity and only for a limited period of time (until full satisfaction of the secured debt).[229]

In order to set in practice the abovementioned possibilities, **the creditor is entitled to first take possession by his own means of the collateral,** together with all documentation attesting the ownership right of the mortgagor. However, **such takeover occurs only after a prior notification to the mortgagor and only if the mortgage agreement expressly provides such possibility.**[230] If privately conducted takeover is not possible, or the creditor does not wish to make use of it, then he will be entitled to ask for the support of the court for judicial enforcement.[231] All these will be developed in Chap. 4, which is dedicated to self-help repossession, strict foreclosure and administrative receivership.

With respect to possessory security interests, the RNCC decided to keep them under two forms: the pledge[232] and the retention right[233] (which existed before as a development of doctrine and court cases but was never legislated). The private enforcement rules applicable to the mortgages over movables will also apply to the possessory pledge once the debtor is in default.

Hence, Romania has a modern security interest regime, suitable to encourage and maintain access to credit, which is necessary for the development of market economy. Unlike France and Germany, Romanian law has managed to part with traditional legal principles and embraced innovations that improved, at least on paper, the conditions required for accessing fast and cheap credit. It also meant breaking up with its traditional models and opening towards efficient ones, which it sought to replicate in order to expand and make use of its economic potential. However, the existing legal framework and absence of relevant case law on the issue of self-help repossession should not be construed in the sense that there are no issues in practice.

2.4 DCFR: A Missed Opportunity

In order to have a glimpse into a possible future of private enforcement and self-help methods in the EU, one should read the DCFR, prepared by over 250 elite European scholars and professionals.[234] The document is meant to provide a

---

[229] RNCC, Art 2468. The last right resembles the UK administrative receivership. For more details and a comprehensive comparison, see *infra*, Chap. 4, Sect. 4.6.4.

[230] RNCC, Art 2440, Para 1.

[231] RNCC, Art 2442, Para 1.

[232] RNCC, Art 2480–2494.

[233] RNCC, Art 2495–2499.

[234] von Bar and Clive (2010), p. 1.

possible model for a Common Frame of Reference to be implemented or at least to be used as an inspiration for adequate solutions to private law questions[235] at EU level.

The entire Chapter 7 of Book IX (Proprietary security in movable assets) is dedicated to default and enforcement. The drafters clearly emphasize that rules contained in the chapter "essentially focus on the small sector of enforcement, namely extra-judicial enforcement."[236] The justification is that "in many European countries there is an increasing movement seeking an alternative to traditional methods of enforcing security rights because of its delays, costs and often disappointing results."[237] Since the starting point is the acknowledgment of the need for different rules of enforcement, one would have expected the document to deliver a revolutionary approach to the issue. Unfortunately, this is not the case as, probably due to the need for harmonization, the DCFR maintains four of the limitations already existing in the European legal frameworks: the ban of self-help methods, the separation between security interests and retention of ownership devices, the ban of prior agreed partial or full strict foreclosure and the prior notice requirement in case of consumer debtors.

The **first** and most disappointing limitation is the practical ban (although not explicitly expressed) of self-help methods[238] when it comes to the repossession of the collateral. Even though it may not seem so on paper, the requirement of an expressed consent from the debtor's side *at the time* of repossession renders self-help almost impossible in practice. It is hard to believe that any debtor, be it business or consumer, would relinquish the encumbered assets willingly. Moreover, in case the debtor or the person in possession of collateral refuses to deliver it or to provide access to the collateral to the secured creditor, the latter does not have the option of the American creditor to avoid lack of consent by either repossessing the collateral from public places or by avoiding the debtor's presence,[239] but he is obliged to immediately shift to court proceedings. Put otherwise, if the debtor does not expressly consent to repossession, the creditor is forced to shift from extrajudicial enforcement to judicial enforcement,[240] which is in contradiction of the initial premise of providing secured creditors with speedy and efficient alternatives to the traditional methods of enforcement.

[235] von Bar and Clive (2010), pp. 3–4.

[236] von Bar and Clive (2010), p. 5614.

[237] von Bar and Clive (2010), p. 5614.

[238] Art IX-7.201 and the following commentary C—Scope of Article and issue at stake. "The dilemma for the secured creditor arises if, as happens frequently, the security provider who is in possession of the encumbered assets and who may need them urgently for the continuation of its production or sales or other commercial activity, refuses or attempts to delay the transfer of possession. The Article is designed to solve this dilemma. Without saying so expressly, *self-help by the secured creditor is clearly excluded* (emphasis added)." von Bar and Clive (2010), pp. 5630–5632.

[239] Self-help repossession techniques in the US are analyzed in detail in Chap. 4, Sect. 4.1.4.

[240] Art IX-4.203 and the following commentaries. von Bar and Clive (2010), p. 5634.

The **second** limitation stems from the fact that the DCFR chooses to maintain the separation between security interests and retention of ownership devices, thus subjecting the two categories to different regimes of enforcement, an approach inherited from UK law. The reason is that, according to this separation, in the case of security interests one deals with encumbered assets that are owned by the security provider and, hence, his rights require respect and protection, while in the case of retention of ownership devices the enforcement is considered relatively easier since the owner is the creditor who merely needs to recover possession of the goods.[241] However, the latter also places the debtor in a worse position than the one of a US debtor, since the DCFR does not contain a rule similar to the 60 % rule[242] in US law or to the equity of redemption in US or UK law.

The contradiction between the need for fast, private enforcement methods and what is actually provided for is again striking. By distinguishing between proper security rights and retention of ownership devices in the fields of creation and enforcement,[243] the DCFR faces a serious issue of practicality: although the creditor is in fact the owner of the good, it does not necessarily mean repossession is actually guaranteed. On the contrary, the entire so-called extrajudicial regime established by the DCFR is likely to cause as much disappointment and frustration among the supporters of extrajudicial enforcement as many of the regimes into force, since the ban of self-help repossession devices and the mandatory judicial assistance allows sufficient time to the debtor to hinder the collection or to dispose of the good.

The **third** limitation is the ban of prior agreed strict/partial foreclosure[244] (unless the goods are fungible or a method of asset value determination was established). In the case of consumer goods, the ban is even wider, with the sole exception of fungible goods. Otherwise, any strict or partial foreclosure can take place by parties' agreement after default has occurred.[245] By providing so, debtors are empowered with a very useful tool that renders foreclosure almost useless since it is hard to believe that any debtor will ever agree to it.

Last, the DCFR imposed the requirement for the creditor to notify consumers whenever it intends to repossess the collateral with a minimum of 10 days before the actual repossession.[246] This requirement, combined with the ban of self-help methods, basically strips repossession of both the surprise element and the leverage factor since, on the one hand, the debtor is granted enough time to hide or estrange the goods and, on the other hand, in the absence of the debtor's consent, the creditor must resort to court proceedings. The drafters failed to balance the need to provide

[241] von Bar and Clive (2010), p. 5614.

[242] For details concerning the 60 % rule see *infra*, Chap. 4, Sect. 4.4.5.1.

[243] von Bar and Clive (2010), p. 5392.

[244] For a critical opinion on the *a priori* ban of agreements that allow the creditor to foreclose the collateral upon debtor's default: Veneziano (2008), pp. 94–95.

[245] Art IX-7.105 and the following comments. von Bar and Clive (2010), pp. 5621–5623.

[246] Art IX-7.201 (2) and the following comments. von Bar and Clive (2010), pp. 5631–5632.

adequate consumer protection with the secured creditor's expectancy of recovering its goods. The mere right to seek damages or assistance in court[247] does not even up the abovementioned imbalance.

On the positive side, one must mention the fact that the DCFR establishes a near functional approach to secured rights, the right of choice between extrajudicial and judicial enforcement[248] and even the possibility to shift from one to another, according to one's interests, thus taking the modern view already existent under the UCC Article 9 regime. Additionally, the DCFR takes the protective and legitimate view that "extra-judicial enforcement may not be used in order to harass the security provider,"[249] which is the starting point of any legislation aiming to protect debtors against unfair debt collection practices. However, despite this acknowledgment of inherent risks of abuse, the DCFR makes no reference about the need to implement sector-specific regulation against abuses (similar to the US FDCPA or the UK Consumer Credit sourcebook), nor does it contain any specific rules to hinder these unwanted effects.[250]

With respect to the realization of the encumbered assets, creditors are allowed to resort to several methods, including sales, leases, foreclosure or others (in the case of rights to payment).[251] The sale may take place in a private or public auction,[252] with or without the employment of a third party. In any way, it should be conducted in a commercially reasonable manner,[253] a standard that is left to the parties or the courts to be decided. Interestingly enough, for a chapter dedicated to the extrajudicial enforcement, the secured creditor seeking realization *via* a public auction may employ the supervision of a court officer.[254]

As pointed out already, the DCFR distinguishes between security rights *per se* and retention of ownership devices. Therefore, both of them have different governing regimes, even if they do share several common rules with respect to possession, immobilization and preservation.[255] Still, there are several specific provisions concerning retention of ownership devices with respect to the

[247] Art IX-7.104 and the following comments. von Bar and Clive (2010), pp. 5620–5621.

[248] "[T]he fact that the secured creditor may enforce its security right extra-judicially does not deprive the secured creditor of the possibility of invoking the assistance of the court or other competent authority [. . .]." See von Bar and Clive (2010), p. 5619.

[249] von Bar and Clive (2010), p. 5619. Unfortunately, this view corresponding to the same requirement found, for example, in US's FDCPA is not doubled of similar sanctions or defenses. The harassed security provider may only apply to the court against any such treatment and ask an injunction to stop it, together with damages, under the provisions of Art IX-7.104.

[250] Tajti (2013), p. 126.

[251] Art IX-7.207 and the following comments. von Bar and Clive (2010), pp. 5637–5641.

[252] Art IX-7.211 and the following comments. von Bar and Clive (2010), pp. 5645–5648.

[253] Art IX-7.212 and the following comments. von Bar and Clive (2010), pp. 5649–5650.

[254] Art IX-7.207 (3) and the comment B. Sale by public or private auction. von Bar and Clive (2010), p. 5637, respectively 5646.

[255] Art IX-7.302. von Bar and Clive (2010), p. 5667.

consequences of default that derive from the divergences in the regime of ownership applicable to the encumbered assets.[256]

Hence, since the creditor is also the owner of the goods, in order to exercise his ownership rights and seek possession, he must first terminate the contractual relationship between him and the debtor, notwithstanding if such relationship is qualified as a contract of sale, hire purchase, and financial leasing or consignment.[257] He also bears the risk that the debtor has passed valid title to a good-faith third party successor.[258] As a form of creditor protection, after repossession, in the case the creditor had sold or leased the goods he is entitled to any surplus if the resale/release price is higher than the initial price. The text is meant to ensure that the former buyer, hire purchaser, lessee or consignee will not benefit from his own default. The solution is fair under such a regime,[259] and the fact that it was specifically written down eliminates any risk of misunderstanding. Unfortunately, it is not enough. The drafters have failed to address the issue of creditor protection in the case where the debtor has passed valid title to the goods, thus transforming the owner of the goods into a mere unsecured creditor. Such a regime also fails to recognize any interest that the debtor might have acquired in the meantime (such as the 60 % rule in the US) and leaves open the question of unjust enrichment.[260]

In this book's opinion, despite the recognition of the need for extrajudicial enforcement, the DCFR fails to provide what is expected. If the DCFR is the future, then it is not a promising one. Just before the finalization of DCFR, Anna Veneziano, a scholar involved in the drafting of Book IX, criticized the maintenance of the separate regime for security interests and retention of ownership devices (the formalistic approach) and advocated the adoption of a unitary one, similar to Article 9 UCC. She claimed, not without merits, that the choice for a secured transactions regime will have implications on other key points such as publicity, priority or enforcement.[261] The previous discussion on the DFCR proves that her concerns were well founded.

Veneziano argued for the functional approach. She pointed out that maintaining a formalistic approach would cause serious issues, especially in the context of harmonization, since retention of title devices are usually governed by national, general and specific, contract law and are not subject to special requirements of ensuring publicity. She also stressed out the fact that many of the principles

[256] Art IX-7.301 and the following comments. von Bar and Clive (2010), pp. 5663–5666.

[257] von Bar and Clive (2010), p. 5664.

[258] von Bar and Clive (2010), p. 5665.

[259] It must be mentioned though that under the functional approach, the result would probably be different and the debtor's right to receive any difference between the value of the assets and the outstanding debt.

[260] Veneziano (2008), p. 95.

[261] Veneziano (2008), pp. 89–90.

governing them differ between the individual legal systems. Moreover, the applicable rules are not even the same for the different types of devices.[262] To complicate matters, some European jurisdictions have started to consider the security function of retention of title devices: France[263] and Romania are two such jurisdictions. Meanwhile, the international instruments dedicated to secured transactions (2001 Cape Town Convention on International Interests in Mobile Equipment and the draft UNCITRAL Legislative Guide on Secured Transactions) urge states to step out of traditional classifications and adopt a shifted paradigm under which all devices pursuing the same function should be treated alike, notwithstanding their structure or form.[264] Local calls for reform from UK practitioners point to the same direction.[265]

When it chose to stick to the traditional view with its rules of enforcement, the DCFR seems to have omitted the need of creditors for an efficient and predictable system, with clear and simple rules, that would enhance their trust in their enforcement rights and hence convince them to extend financing and access to cheaper credit.[266] Until now, their greatest obstacle has been the general procedural law, too linked to public policy concerns. Any imbalance between the creditors' and debtors' interests, towards any of them, would have a disruptive effect on the system itself.[267]

At this point, what raises the largest number of concerns is whether to empower the secured creditor to repossess the collateral without the involvement or authorization of a court, when the collateral is in the possession of the debtor. While common law jurisdictions and American-inspired regimes (such as the Romanian one) generally allow it—provided there is no breach of peace—**most of the European jurisdictions opt for an overprotective approach towards the debtor's rights, therefore banning self-help repossession and placing additional burden on the creditor.**[268] In these jurisdictions, self-help requires consent, either *a priori* or at the time of repossession, and observance of the no breach of peace standard, which expose the creditor to longer and costly procedures and to the risk that the debtor, once notified, will remove the collateral. However, the procreditor rules of ROT devices hardly provide any protections to the debtors. The latter view seems to have prevailed in the DCFR as well, and along with it the effort of harmonization in the field might be doomed before it actually started.

---

[262] Veneziano (2008), p. 90.

[263] According to Anna Veneziano's interpretation, the recent French reform of secured transactions law has integrated the *clause de reserve de la propriete*, thereby openly recognizing its character as a security. See: Veneziano (2008), p. 91.

[264] Veneziano (2008), p. 91.

[265] Calnan et al. (2012), p. 8, point 3.6.

[266] On the advantages and underlying reasons for self-help, see: Taylor (1998), pp. 847–850.

[267] Veneziano (2008), p. 92.

[268] Veneziano (2008), p. 94.

2.5 Conclusion

To sum up, it is clear from all the above that self-help devices and private enforcement have long been part of our legal systems, no matter if encouraged, banned or merely tolerated. They existed and continued to be employed because they were needed. They offer multiple advantages, especially when states fail to fulfill their function of offering sufficient, efficient and price-worthy judicial devices.

With respect to commercial relations, in the context of access to lending and low cost credit, creditors' access to self-help remedies remains a powerful incentive and a useful tool. The different perceptions on self-help arise from the different takes on secured transactions laws, different levels of reform, different concepts of ownership and different public policies (such as extensive protection to debtors or consumers). Therefore, **harmonization efforts come with a compromise at the expense of self-help devices.**

The issue is not purely theoretical, and it does not concern only the states themselves. The EU as a whole needs to determine soon what sort of enforcement system and practice is going to apply in case it plans to develop a single European civil justice system. Otherwise, documents such as DCFR make little sense[269] and absence of consensus with respect to what constitutes a general model of a civil justice system is definitely a serious obstacle against European harmonization. This does not necessarily mean that all European countries should rush now and adopt the American model, but since the UCC had also the effect of harmonizing different legal regimes of the federal states, a much more politically integrated Europe would definitely benefit from the American experience and example.[270]

The book contends that the functional approach and the regime applicable to self-help under the UCC Article 9 are the model to be followed and learn from. Therefore, the following chapters address in much detail passive forms of self-help in general (as methods employed in sales law notwithstanding the jurisdiction), which are available to all creditors (including unsecured ones); self-help repossession, administrative receivership and foreclosure in particular, which are available to secured creditors under UCC model laws or English law; factoring and debt collection; as well as protection against unfair debt collection practices. Throughout the ensuing analysis, US law is used as a benchmark in order to assess, by means of comparison, if there is a future and what is the future of private debt collection in the European jurisdictions chosen.

[269] For a detailed discussion on the policy choices and efforts for harmonization in the field of civil justice: Brownsword et al. (2011), pp. 448–450.

[270] Allan and Drobnig (1980), p. 642.

References

Allan DE, Drobnig U (1980) Secured credit in commercial insolvencies: a comparative analysis. Rabel J Comp Int Private Law 44:615

Bannon CJ (2000) Self-help and social status in Cicero's Pro Quinctio. Anc Soc 30:71

Beale H, Bridge M, Gullifer L, Lomnicka E (2012) The law of security and title-based financing. Oxford University Press, Oxford

Ben-Menahem H, Hecht NS (1993) Selected topics in Jewish law. The Open University of Israel Publishing House, Tel Aviv

Black D, Baumgartner MP (1987) On self-help in modern society. Dialect Anthropol 12:33

Brandon DI, Cooper ML, Greshin JH, Harris AL, Head JM Jr, Jacques KR, Wiggins L (1984) SPECIAL PROJECT. Self-help: extrajudicial rights, privileges and remedies in contemporary American society. Vanderbilt Law Rev 37

Brownsword R, Micklitz H-W, Niglia L, Weatherill S (2011) The foundations of European private law. Hart Publishing, Oxford/Portland, OR

Bussani M, Werro F (2009) European private law: a handbook. Stampfli Publishers Ltd Berne, Berne

Calnan R, Davies J, Dening M, Ereira D, Evans M, Gibbons K, Livingston D, Naccarato J, Roberts S, Swiss N, Tobin M, Yeowart G (2012) Discussion paper: secured transactions reform. The City of London Law Society, London

Chaves R, de la Pena N, Fleisig H (2004) Secured transactions reform: early results from Romania. CEAL ISSUES BRIEF. Center for Economic Analysis of Law, Washington, DC

Commission of the European Communities (2005) Proposal for a Regulation of the European Parliament and of the Council Establishing a European Small Claims Procedure

Dahan F, Simpson J (2008) Secured transactions reform and access to credit. Edward Elgar, Northampton/Cheltenham

Dahan F, Kutenicova E, Simpson J (2004) Enforcing secured transactions in central and eastern Europe: an empirical study. European Bank for Reconstruction and Development. www.ebrd.com/downloads/legal/secured/enf.pdf

de la Pena N, Fleisig HW (2004) Romania: law of security interests in personal property and commentaries. Rev Central East Eur Law 29(2)

Del Granado JJ (2011) The genius of Roman law from a law and economics perspective. San Diego Int Law J 13:301

Franklin D, Harms SA (2010) International commercial secured transactions. Carswell, Toronto

Goode R (1988) The codification of commercial law. Monash Univ Law Rev 14

Goode R (1998) Commercial law in the next millennium. In: Trust TH (ed) The Hamlyn lectures. Sweet & Maxwell, London

Hubert O (2010) Bank finance and regulation. Multi-jurisdictional survey. France. Enforcement of Security Interests in Banking Transactions. http://www.ibanet.org/LPD/Financial_Services_Section/Banking_Law/BankinglawSurveyApril2010.aspx. International Bar Association, pp 1–15

International Trade Center (2010) Increasing access to credit. Reforming secured transaction laws. International Trade Center, Geneva

Kieninger E-M (2004) Security rights in movable property in European private law. Cambridge University Press, Cambridge

Kronman AT (1985) Contract law and the state of nature. J Law Econ Organ 1:5

McCall JR (1973) The past as prologue: a history of the right to repossess. South Calif Law Rev 47

McCormack G (2008) Corporate rescue law – an Anglo-American perspective. Edward Elgar, Cheltenham

McKendrick E (2010) Goode on commercial law. Penguin, London

McRobert R (2012) Defining 'Breach of the Peace' in self-help repossessions. Wash Law Rev 87: 569

Morey WC (1884) Outlines of Roman law comprising its historical growth and general principles. G.P. Putnam's Sons, New York/London

Office of the General Counsel (2012) Commercial laws of Romania. An assessment by the EBRD. EBRD

Pollock SF, Maitland FW (1898) The history of English law. Before the time of Edward I. Cambridge University Press, Cambridge

Quirk P (2008) Whether Australian secured transactions laws will transition from the English System to the Personal Property Securities Act. Thomas Jefferson Law Rev 31:219

Rizoiu R (2011) Garantiile reale imobiliare. O abordare functionala - Analiza economica a dreptului garantiilor reale - Introducere in regimul juridic al ipotecilor mobiliare. Universul Juridic, Bucharest

Röver J-H (2004) Comparative principles of security interests: secured debt and charged property. King's College London

Rover J-H (2007) Secured lending in eastern Europe. Comparative law of secured transactions and the EBRD model law. Oxford University Press, New York

Serick R (1990) Securities in movables in German law: an outline. Kluwer Law and Taxation Publishers, Deventer

St. John's Law Review (1974) "Self-Help" remedies and due process. St. John's Law Rev 48:661

Stanescu C-G, Timofti BV (2013) Commercial and economic law of Romania. In: Stuyck PDJ, Terryn PE (eds) International encyclopaedia of laws. Kluwer Law International, The Netherlands

Stein P (1999) Roman law in European history. Cambridge University Press, Cambridge, UK

Street TA (2013) The foundations of legal liability. A presentation of the theory and development of the common law. Forgotten Books. www.ForgottenBooks.org

Tajti T (2002a) Comparative secured transactions law. Akadémiai Kiadó, Budapest

Tajti T (2002b) Viehweg's topics, Article 9 UCC, the "Kautelarische Sicherheiten" and the Hungarian secured transactions law reform. Vindobona J Int Commer Law Arbitration 6:93

Tajti T (2012a) When and why is the rubberstamp of the European Union insufficient? – Caveats to systems on the road towards the European Union. Zbornik. Pravnog Fakulteta U Zagrebu

Tajti T (2012b) Testing the equivalence of the new comprehensive Australian Personal Properties Securities Act, its Segmented European Equivalents and the Draft Common Frame of Reference. Bond Law Rev 24:85

Tajti T (2013) Post-1990 secured transaction law reforms in central and eastern Europe. Szegedi Közjegyzői Közlöny

Taylor CR (1998) Self-help in contract law: an exploration and proposal. Wake Forest Law Rev 33

Vasilescu P (2012) Drept civil. Obligatii - in reglementarea Noului Cod Civil. (Civil Law. Obligations - in the light of the New Civil Code. Hamangiu, Bucuresti

Veneziano A (2008) A secured transactions' regime for Europe. Treatment of Acquisition Finance Devices and Creditor's Enforcement Rights. Juridica Int Law Rev XIV:89

von Bar C, Clive E (2010) Principles, definitions and model rules of European private law. Draft Common Frame of Reference (DCFR). Oxford University Press, Oxford

Warren E, Westbrook JL (2009) The law of debtors and creditors: text, cases, and problems. Wolters Kluwer Law & Business, New York

White JJ, Summers RS (2007) Principles of secured transactions. Thomson & West, St. Paul

White JJ, Summers RS (2010) Uniform commercial code. In Practitioner treatise series. Thomson Reuters, USA

Whittuck EA (1904) Institutes of Roman Law (Gaii Institutiones by Gaius, with a Translation and Commentary by the late Edward Poste). Clarendon, Oxford

Chapter 3
Self-Help and Contract Law

As it was shown in the second chapter, self-help has been a useful and widely employed remedy in society since the outset of human kind. It allowed wronged parties to respond to their needs swiftly, to avoid expenses and delays caused by judicial proceedings.[1] Going from permission to ban, total ban, tolerance, permission again, tolerance and regulation,[2] self-help is now to be found on both sides of the Atlantic. The reason is that self-help came to be recognized as an efficient alternative to traditional judicial remedies and some of its forms are covert in several areas of law, such as commercial law, tort or criminal law.[3]

One aspect that went unnoticed is that **self-help remedies are and have been for a long time an integral part of contract law in all the jurisdictions selected and analyzed, in both common and civil laws, and they are employed in all stages of contract formation and enforcement.** The difference seems to be that, **while in the US they are recognized and employed as such,[4] the civilian systems**

---

[1] Taylor (1998), pp. 847–848.

[2] Tajti (2013a, b), pp. 135 (especially footnote 332) and 163: "The growing number of regulations trying to coral private enforcement in Europe is the proof of the recognition that things have radically changed by the 21st century."

[3] Dolly (2000), p. 671. For a detailed application of self-help in tort, criminal, commercial, landlord/tenant and family laws, see: Brandon et al. (1984), pp. 852–979.

[4] Self-help is defined as "a legally permissible conduct that individuals undertake absent the compulsion of law and without the assistance of a government official in efforts to *prevent* or *remedy* a legal wrong" (emphasis added). Brandon et al. (1984), p. 850, and Black and Baumgartner (1987), p. 33. A similar definition stated that "self-help refers to private actions taken by those interested in the controversy to *prevent* or *resolve* disputes without official assistance of a governmental official or disinterested third party." However, Taylor contends that self-help "may be defined more narrowly to include only steps available to parties after a contract has been made." See: Taylor (1998), p. 841 (footnote 5). Since the first quoted source has also referred to contractual remedies—such as liquidated damages—as self-help remedies and the US is the chosen benchmark for comparison, it made sense to use its approach for the comparison purposes of these remedies.

C.G. Stănescu, *Self-Help, Private Debt Collection and the Concomitant Risks*,
DOI 10.1007/978-3-319-21503-7_3

fail to acknowledge them as self-help means. This aspect is quintessential to this chapter for failure to perceive existing forms of self-help as self-help should not be construed in any way as lack of self-help remedies in civilian systems and the best way to exemplify it is by taking a look at contract law.

While in Europe nobody seems to notice any self-help remedies in contract law rules, in the US at least scholars did. Therefore, this chapter tries to theorize self-help remedies in contract law and then compare three important self-help remedies recognized in American law, to wit the right to withhold performance, liquidated damages and nonjudicial termination of contract with their equivalents available in the other jurisdictions. It will be shown why such contractual remedies were needed and how their importance is rising given the current trend of shifting towards extrajudicial enforcement. It also claims that the application of self-help remedies should be expanded and should be allowed to expand to all types of contracts and to the area of secured transactions where prompt private enforcement is more than a desired effect; it is a *sine qua non*.

In other words, this chapter shows that self-help remedies that are hidden in civilian systems' contract law are in fact available to unsecured creditors, which are free to employ them as they see fit. However, in most civilian systems private enforcement is still denied to secured creditors on grounds of public policy. This **factual contradiction** present in civilian systems cannot be justified. By proving that self-help remedies are neither incompatible with civilian systems nor unknown to them, this chapter argues that self-help remedies should be made available also to secured creditors, for they have been more careful when granting credit and hence deserve more protection than unsecured creditors.

3.1 Self-Help in Contract Law: An Introductory Case

Examples of how contractual self-help remedies are used in order to protect the contracting party's rights can be found not only in legal textbooks but also in historic sources that touch upon legal issues. A very interesting case is provided by Daniel Yergin,[5] who describes the initial events that led to the development of the oil industry in 1854. When prospective investors wanted to find out whether petroleum could have any practical properties, they have retained thereof the most renowned chemist of the time. The agreement provided for the payment of a fee for services amounting to 525 dollars, preconditioned on a down payment of 100. Since the amount was high for those times, they failed to make the down payment. Although displeased with their failure, the hired expert waived his right to the advance payment and went ahead to complete the work. However, upon completion, he made it expressly clear that unless they paid him in full he would withhold the result of his study. But although the report was deemed essential for setting off

[5] Yergin (2012), pp. 5–6.

and attracting additional capital, the initial investors were unable to produce the requested amount. Neither were they able to convince him to provide the report first. Only in early 1855, after one of the investors decided to pay on his own, was the report released and became what is considered to be the starting point of the petroleum business. But it is the successful application of a self-help remedy—enforcement of the contract without resort to judicial process—that made it all possible.

A simple look at the example reveals **four traits** of self-help remedies, starting with the obvious: first, *although they are not judicial, they are legal*. They are allowed by the law. Had it not been so, the chemist would have been forced by his clients to deliver the report in the absence of payment. But since the two obligations were interdependent, they had no possibility to sue for delivery of the report in the absence of their own performance. Second, allowance by law does not suffice; (most of the times) a contract must be in place. Third, it is not necessary, *per se*, for one of the parties to be in default before resorting to self-help, a threat of breach is sufficient.[6] The contract in the example did not specify a final term for delivery or payment, and the chemist waived his right to the down payment. Therefore, the parties had the opportunity to postpone the fulfillment of their obligations. In the end, upon completion of the report, the chemist used his own performance and the clients' interest in the result as leverage and withheld the report as a preemptive method of ensuring performance of the other contracting parties. Last but not least, given the date of the events described, it becomes obvious that self-help in contract law has been known in the US for more than 150 years.[7]

Notwithstanding the long history of self-help, there is still no coherent and single understanding of what self-help is or about its role in American commercial law.[8] Taylor points out that self-help, in the specific area of contract law, broadly includes "any action taken by either contracting party to limit the harm cause by defective performance, to attempt to preserve the contract and to prevent non-justified

[6] There are certain remedies designed only for the occurrence of default, such as the self-help repossession of collateral, but these specific remedies will be analyzed in the next chapter.

[7] An analogy with the right to withhold performance (and this case that illustrates it) can be made with another old self-help remedy, the right to stoppage *in transitu*. This right may be defined as "the right which the unpaid vendor has to repossess himself of his goods before they come into the actual or constructive possession of his solvent transferee," and it is considered "a necessary and equitable concomitant of a credit system." See: G. G. W. (1859), p. 577. According to the same article, most European countries recognized in attachment to this remedy a right to recover the goods even after they came into the possession of the buyer, provided that he could identify them, but such revendication right was heavily restricted and even removed after the implementation of the Napoleon Code and the laws that it inspired. G. G. W. (1859), pp. 579–580. The right of a seller of goods to regain possession of the goods may be exercised even if he had already parted with them under a contract for sale. Traditionally, this remedy applies when the goods were partly or wholly sold on credit and the buyer becomes bankrupt or insolvent before the goods arrive. Garner (2009), p. 1555.

[8] The lack of coherence might be caused by the fact that the rules governing self-help in US law are scattered across the fields of contract, restitution and equity. See Gergen (2009), p. 139.

termination of the contract"[9] and that self-help plays a vital part in contract law, although neither the Uniform Commercial Code (UCC) Article 2 nor the Restatement of Contracts—which does recognize resort to self-help—recommends it explicitly or provides a rationale for it.[10] For the purposes of this chapter, Taylor's position is further utilized as a benchmark, without any qualifications.

3.2 Attempts to Define the Role of Self-Help in American Contract Law

The fact that until now there is no unified theory of self-help in contract law can be explained. A theory of self-help in contract law would require the identification of the nonjudicial domain of contract behavior. However, it might seem difficult to identify such domain in the case of contractual disputes,[11] since most of the times the parties might be inclined to resort to judicial proceedings and ways of enforcement, which are backed up by the apparatus of the state. However, as this chapter proves, a wide range of behavior involving resolution of contractual disputes arise outside the coverage provided by the judiciary and one of these is self-help.[12] Moreover, this behavior is identifiable both in common law and civil law jurisdictions.

Employment of self-help in the nonjudicial domain of the contract is an intentional and conscious decision of the parties or of their counsel. Such efforts are spread throughout all contracting stages, be it drafting (use of standard terms, use of performance-orientated self-help clauses, use of dispute-orientated clauses, such as explicitly retaining the right to refuse delivery if buyer fails to pay), negotiation (self-help techniques in this area include hostage taking (placing a valuable asset

[9] Taylor (1998), pp. 842 and 845.

[10] Taylor (1998), p. 843. All American scholars touching upon the issue of self-help in contract law make references to the Second Restatement of Contracts. However, since the Restatement is not a binding legal document but a mere guideline, it shall not be a part of the analysis of this chapter.

[11] This is even more obvious in the case of civilian jurisdictions where the principle according to which no one is allowed do justice by himself is the backbone of their legal systems.

[12] Rubin (1995), pp. 108–109.

under the control of the other party),[13] taking collateral,[14] hand tying,[15] union[16] or asking for a compensating balance),[17] planning (such self-help strategies appear at the business executives' level who are developing plans in anticipation of future contractual relationships) or disputation (employing the right to self-help repossession of collateral or the right to exercise set-off), despite the fact that the line between them is not always as clear as it may seem.[18]

Taking into account all the above, it is clear that self-help does make a difference and therefore it becomes an important part of contract formation. However, since self-help is designed to *avoid* involvement of the judiciary, its actual importance and impact on contract law might not come from the study of judicial decisions. As it was rightfully emphasized, "the study of self-help strategies is essential for understanding the non-judicial life of contracts and broadens the role of the legal profession,"[19] especially when "the design, the negotiation and the execution of self-help strategies fall into the responsibilities of lawyers."[20] Private individuals might also resort to self-help more frequently, provided they become more informed about it.[21]

---

[13] By hostage taking, the creditor takes something of value to the other party and holds it until the contract is performed. In theory, the debtor will do his best to perform the contract in order to recover the hostage that will be lost otherwise. The most famous hostage-taking device is the pledge. For details and examples: Kronman (1985), pp. 12–15.

[14] By asking for collateral, the creditor demands from the other party something of value to it, rather than for the debtor to hold during the pendency of the contract. Although it does not ensure the exact performance of the contract, it guarantees that in case of nonperformance the value of the collateral will be delivered. Unlike hostage taking, the demand for collateral does not require possession of the collateral during the pendency of contract. The demand for collateral is commonly employed in secured transactions law. For details and examples: Kronman (1985), pp. 15–18.

[15] Hand tying involves a party taking action that will increase costs to it in case it breaches the contract. These costs attach upon breach, even if the other party takes no action. In other words, this mechanism functions by increasing the actual costs of nonperformance. For details, Kronman (1985), pp. 18–20. One example of hand tying is the provision for liquidated damages (in the US and the UK) or its equivalent—the penalty clause—in France, Germany or Romania.

[16] Union tries to ensure performance by supporting the development of sympathy, affection or love between parties. It is mostly found in communities that establish guiding norms of behavior on the presumption that by subordinating their own welfare to that of the community, everybody profits. Taylor (1998), p. 855. Also: Kronman (1985), pp. 20–24. For a theoretical explanation and the economic rationale behind each of these self-help techniques: Kronman (1985), pp. 12–24. Also: Taylor (1998), pp. 855–856.

[17] "The process of bargaining and agreeing upon terms of a contract is essentially a form of self-help that parties commonly employ in commercial transactions." See: Brandon et al. (1984), p. 911.

[18] For a detailed discussion on the self-help efforts in which stage of the contractual process: Rubin (1995), pp. 126–129.

[19] Brandon et al. (1984), p. 851.

[20] Rubin (1995), p. 130.

[21] Brandon et al. (1984), p. 851.

One last note, before going into the analysis of contractual self-help is needed: despite that as a rule contractual claims are judicially enforceable, parties still prefer to resort to self-help. The reason is that a mere possibility to enforce a contractual obligation *via* courts is never enough to completely eliminate the insecurity of nonperformance since no remedial system can eliminate completely the sources of contractual insecurity[22] and hence parties will rely on using their own devices.[23]

3.3 Typology of Self-Help Remedies: Passive v. Active Self-Help Remedies

Attempting to explain not only the legality of self-help repossession, but also the compatibility of self-help with the Romanian civil law system, a Romanian scholar[24] proposed a categorization of self-help remedies into passive v. active remedies, which makes it specifically relevant to this work. Rizoiu states that, despite the wish of civilian jurisdictions to completely eliminate self-help practices, remnants of self-help are still to be found in contract law, nominating, i.e., the right to withhold performance (*excepţia de neexecutare a contractului*) and the retention right (*dreptul de retenţie*). However, he emphasized that these are *passive* forms of self-help, in the sense that the party resorting to them refuses to fulfill an action, for example by denying the other party the access to an asset or a right under his control,[25] while the historical self-help, from which self-help repossession derives, is an *active* form of self-help, which implies an active involvement of the party exercising it: "pulling," "re-possessing" an asset from the breaching debtor.[26] It is this latter form of self-help that the continental systems have tried to ban completely, especially after the appearance of the French Civil Code.

Therefore, it should not come as a surprise that even nowadays all systems contain *passive* self-help remedies. Passive self-help is perceived as a form of defense, totally acceptable. A bigger question is whether the acceptance of such passive type remedies could change the perception of civilian systems with respect to the active type as well and whether the compatibility of civilian systems with passive self-help could be used to justify the compatibility with active self-help (namely self-help repossession). Being an exception from the civil law principle of judicial enforcement, active self-help would definitely require special legislation, with additional protection to prevent and deter abuse, but this aspect will be discussed in the following chapters.

---

[22] Kronman (1985), p. 29.

[23] Kronman (1985), p. 25.

[24] Rizoiu (2011), p. 581.

[25] Rizoiu (2011), p. 581.

[26] For a detailed history of self-help, see *supra* Chap. 2.

In the following pages, the book focuses on three passive self-help remedies available in contract law, namely the right to withhold performance, liquidated damages (and their civilian counterpart penalty clauses) and nonjudicial termination. The reason is that they are widely known and are covered by all chosen jurisdictions, which allows for a comprehensive comparative analysis. However, the choice should not be construed as exhaustive. Many other such remedies are available, especially in US and UK laws.[27] The purpose is not to present them all but to look across the boundaries of legal systems and jurisdictions for similarities and justifications. The analysis makes obvious that all chosen jurisdictions contain provisions that authorize, to a certain extent, the use of self-help in contractual relationships. It also emphasizes that the legal community is starting to recognize the importance of self-help, despite the fact that more steps forward are needed.[28]

3.4 Right to Withhold Performance as Contractual Self-Help Remedy

Besides repossession—which is thoroughly analyzed in Chap. 4—the principal self-help remedy is the power to withhold performance in response to breach. In common law jurisdictions, this remedy is usually employed in tandem with the power to refuse nonconforming performance[29] or with the right of stoppage in transit.[30] In civil law jurisdictions, it is connected to the retention right, considered to be just a particular form of the right to withhold performance.[31] Moreover, a

[27] For example in US law: the power to exit an informal or incomplete agreement (for details, Gergen (2009), pp. 1439–1448), UCC Section 2-717—deduction of damages (an extension of setoff rights), identification and recovery of the goods to the contract, revocation of acceptance, resale of goods in the buyer's possession upon rejection or justifiable revocation of acceptance (all covered by the UCC) (for details: Taylor (1998), pp. 870–871). In UK law, among self- remedies for breach of contract are mentioned retention of title, enforcement of securities, all monies clauses, proceeds of sale clause, setoff clauses and rights against the goods themselves (for details: Samantha Cotton, *Remedies for Breach of Contract* Practical Law PLC Magazine *at* http://uk.practicallaw.com/7-101-0603#, pp. 7–14). Other authors add to those already mentioned forfeiture of a deposit taken from the guilty party, stoppage in transit, rescission, resale and termination for breach. For details: McKendrick (2010), p. 123.

[28] Taylor (1998), p. 907, Gergen (2009), pp. 1399–1401. Also Brandon et al. (1984), p. 1040: "The self-help measures [. . .] illustrate the variation in the origins and development of existing self-help practices, and the diversity in the measures that the law recognizes as permissible and tolerable self-help conduct. Self-help, once the law of the land, gradually has been supplemented in many respects by the *increasing sophistication* of the organized criminal and civil justice which have become the hallmark of American society."

[29] Gergen (2009), p. 1398.

[30] G. G. W. (1859), pp. 577–578. Also: McKendrick (2010), p. 123.

[31] Rizoiu (2011), p. 573.

party may even use this power as a threat to extract concessions from the other party.[32]

3.4.1 The US

As mentioned above, the right to withhold performance is probably the main self-help remedy used in contract law. It is strongly related to the doctrine of material breach and substantial performance since any of the latter allows the aggrieved party to suspend performance, abandon the contract and make substitute arrangements or to recover in restitution for the reasonable value of any performance rendered. What is clear is that any party may withhold performance in response to a fundamental breach and may deny acceptance of any nonconforming performance in order to avoid loss that might not be adequately compensated, even if such a response would inflict a disproportionate loss on the defaulter.[33]

The power to exercise the right to withhold or refuse performance or threatening to do so in order to get concessions from the other party may be exercised also when one's rightful position is unclear.[34] In such case, in addition to the rules on mitigation and material breach, two new sets will be added in order to determine the consequences of exercising or not the nonperformance option. The application of each of them will depend on whether nonperformance is likely to have harmful consequences or not.[35] But generally speaking, a refusal or demand will be deemed honest if a right is uncertain.[36]

The voluntary payment doctrine is deemed to be a good example. Basically, the doctrine prohibits claims to recover overpayment by debtors who pay disputed debts. The purpose behind it is to make sure that those who have a legal right they wish to assert will do so as soon as it is possible. An ancillary effect of the doctrine is that a debtor will not pay more than he thinks he owes since he will be prevented from recovering the overpayment. First, the rules on accord and satisfaction empower the debtor to resolve a dispute on favorable terms. His leverage stems

---

[32] Narasimhan (1987) and Hillman (1990).

[33] Gergen (2009), pp. 1409–1411. The author recommends three factors for determining what can constitute fundamental breach: "1) whether the aggrieved party needs to withhold or refuse performance to avoid suffering a loss that will not be adequately compensated in damages, 2) the burden imposed on the defaulter by withholding or refusing performance and 3) whether the default was willful or in bad faith."

[34] Gergen (2009), pp. 1420–1421. Although the position of the party seeking to exercise its self-help remedy is unclear, the dispute itself must be honest.

[35] "One set [of rules] encourages the exercise of the nonperformance option to settle a dispute when nonperformance will not have harmful consequences. The other set, in conjunction with the rules on mitigation and material breach, discourages the exercise of nonperformance option to settle a dispute when nonperformance will have harmful consequences." Gergen (2009), p. 1420.

[36] Gergen (2009), p. 1422.

from the fact that his tendering of a partial payment carries with it an implied threat of total nonpayment, in the case where the creditor refuses the partial payment.[37] The second set of rules allows, and in certain situations it even demands, a party either to perform a disputed obligation or to accept performance of disputed sufficiency and after that to address a court to claim that less was owed or more was due.[38]

3.4.2 The UK

It was emphasized that English law is indulgent to self-help as a means of securing satisfaction in case of a contractual breach. The idea behind the law's positive encouragement of the innocent party to bypass the judicial process lied with the philosophy according to which diligence in the pursuit of remedies must be rewarded and not sanctioned.[39] Similar to the US, if one decides to construe the concept of self-help in a broader manner, then self-help becomes more visible and significant in practice.

According to English[40] law, performance may be lawfully withheld in cases where the other party neither has performed nor is ready and willing to perform, and that will constitute a valid self-help remedy.[41] The aforementioned cases[42] are

---

[37] UCC Section 1-207. The statute allows a party to reserve his right while accepting performance offered by the other party. However, although the statute established no specific exception, most of the courts have held the aforementioned provision not applicable in case of accord and satisfaction. For details concerning the different views taken by courts on whether the statute changed or not the common law doctrine concerning accord and satisfaction, see Gergen (2009), p. 1423, footnote 108.

[38] For details: Gergen (2009), pp. 1424–1427.

[39] McKendrick (2010), p. 123.

[40] The chosen jurisdiction is the UK. However, since Scottish law and the law of Northern Ireland are substantially different, when referring either to UK or English law, the two terms encompass the laws of England and Wales only. The reason is that UK law was employed as a common law jurisdiction for the purposes of this work. However, where idiosyncratic solutions from Scottish law resembled those of English law it will be specifically stated.

[41] Anthony Ogus, Remedies, English Report in Harris and Tallon (1989), p. 244. According to other authors, the right to withhold performance is also closely connected to termination for default since both remedies depend on the notion that the innocent party may not be under any obligation to render his performance until the party in breach has done something or is ready to do something. Beale et al. (2005), p. 546.

[42] Roy Goode mentions three other cases where the right to withhold performance may be exercised: where the contract so provides, where parties have agreed to suspend the contract or the party in breach has represented that it will not require performance and where the innocent party's performance is obstructed or made more difficult by the other party, whether by that party's failure in performance or the imposition of requirements outside the terms of the contract or by failure to provide the cooperation that the contract envisages as necessary for the innocent party's performance. See: McKendrick (2010), p. 143.

those where performance by one party is a condition precedent or concurrent for the obligation of the other party to perform.[43] Most of the times, parties will carefully draft their contracts in such way as to expressly provide for this effect, but they also have the possibility to address the court in order to obtain an appropriate characterization of their obligations.[44]

Theoretically speaking, courts should characterize the party's obligations based on their intentions. In practice, though, they seem to rely more on characterizations adopted by case law in relation to different types of contracts. The consequence is that in those situations where complete performance is required from one party, before the other is obliged to perform, the obligation is generally referred to as "entire": such is the case of building contracts where the work performed by the builder is considered to be a condition precedent for payment.[45] In contrast, one may find a severable obligation, where performance is divisible into units.[46] In this case, for each unit performed a similar obligation accrues on the other party to perform a corresponding part of its undertaking.[47]

The previous paragraph emphasizes the search for a flexible approach on the matter in English law. Since any failure to perform would give the right to the other party to refuse to perform, even breaches that caused little or no harm would have provided a valid excuse for nonperformance, which, in other words, amounts to abusing the self-help remedy. To respond to this abuse, qualifications in the form of a *de minimis* rule and certain exceptions were inserted in the Sale of Goods Act.[48] Courts went even further to create and classify contractual terms not within the

---

[43] Beale et al. (2005), pp. 547–551.

[44] *Kingston v. Preston* (1773) cited in Beale et al. (2005), p. 549.

[45] Harris and Tallon (1989), p. 244. The author makes reference to *Sumpter v. Hedges* [1898] 1 QB 673 (see footnote 7). The case is cited in Beale et al. (2005), p. 555. However, the authors show that the rule is too harsh and courts usually try to find the contract to be severable. They cite *Appleby v. Meyers* (1867) LR 2 CP 651, 660. They also state that in the case of lump sum building contracts, severability is impossible as there will be no way of apportioning the price over the various items of work. Therefore, they say, the doctrine of "substantial performance" was developed, in order to mitigate the unwanted and unfair results that nonseverability might cause. However, the substantial performance rule only allows the builder to recover the price if the defects are slight. The employer will not be obliged to pay if the work is not substantially complete, even if a lot of work has been done. See *Hoenig v. Isaacs* [1952] 2 All ER 176, Court of Appeal, and *Bolton v. Mahadeva* [1972] 1 WLR 1009 cited in Beale et al. (2005), pp. 556–558 respectively 559.

[46] Employment contracts are normally treated as severable so that the employee earns payment for the period served. It seems that at common law the contract is to be severable into units corresponding to the intervals at which the employee receives payment. *Taylor v. Laird* (1856) 1 H & N 266 25 LJ Ex 329 is cited as a relevant example. There the plaintiff was employed to command a steamer "for an exploring and trading voyage up the river Niger . . . at the rate of £ 50 per month." The plaintiff, however, did not complete the whole journey. The decision rendered was that the contract did not provide for the entire voyage since the phrase "per month" indicated that the plaintiff was entitled to be paid for each month he served. Beale et al. (2005), p. 553.

[47] Harris and Tallon (1989), p. 245.

[48] Beale et al. (2005), pp. 553, 562 and 596.

classic dichotomy of conditions and warranties but by adding, when deemed appropriate, a third category of "intermediate" or "innominate" terms.[49] The reason behind it is that if a contractual term cannot qualify as a condition, neither precedent nor concurrent, then it will not trigger the self-help remedy. Hence, parties must be cautious in their drafting with respect to the language that they will use, for a poorly drafted clause might preclude them from resorting to self-help.

3.4.3 France

Withholding of performance—"defense of unperformed contract" (*exception d'inexécution*, known under its Roman name of *exceptio non adimpleti contractus*)—together with its subsidiary, the retention right (*droit de retention*), is probably the clearest exception from the rejection of self-help and extrajudicial remedies in French law.[50] Although the term might be misleading in other languages, where exception is used to suggest a defense against a judicial action, the main trait of this remedy is that the party exercising it need not address the court (although it enjoys the choice to do so).

Similar to UCC Article 2 (and the Restatement of Contracts) and UK law, the remedy is only available in those cases where the duties of the parties are concurrent, and consists in the right of one party to refuse performance of its own obligation as long as the other party does not perform his. In the absence of a general text,[51] only starting with in the twentieth century have French courts decided to apply the remedy to all synallagmatic (bilateral)[52] contracts.[53]

---

[49] *Cehave NV v. Bremer Handelsgesellschaft mbH, the Hansa Nord* [1975] 3 All ER 739 cited in Beale et al. (2005), pp. 566–568.

[50] "There is also [. . .] a greater reluctance in French law than in the common law to allow recourse to self-help, this term being used in the wide sense, to include not only the exercise of physical force against the person or property of the debtor [. . .], but any remedy which is exercised without recourse to a court. [. . .] *To this rejection of self-help the only exception in the present context is the purely defensive withholding of performance* which goes under the name of *exceptio non adimpleti contractus* (under which can be subsumed the *droit de retention*)." Nicholas (1992), pp. 212–213. Also: Anthony Ogus in Harris and Tallon (1989), p. 244: "Indeed, in France the maxim *nul ne peut se faire justice à soi-même* conclusively prohibits this remedy [self-help]."

[51] There is no article in the Civil Code referring to *exceptio non adimpleti contractus* it is a creation of the jurisprudence. See: Marsh (1994), p. 324.

[52] Synallagmatic contracts are a typical civil law category, unknown to common law countries. The book opted to use the terminology of each legal family and, where necessary, has added the corresponding term or the closest equivalent from the other legal family.

[53] Nicholas (1992), pp. 213–214.

In France, withholding performance is founded on the doctrine of *causa*,[54] according to which, given the fact that each obligation is the cause of the other, the nonperformance of one will justify the nonperformance of the other. However, the remedy is a temporary one, since both the contract and the duty remain in force and the party employing it should be ready to perform as soon as the other party has done so.[55]

It seems the remedy is mainly a means of putting pressure on the debtor to perform. And because of this reason, it can easily turn into abuse in those cases where minor breaches of the other party are used as justification for nonperformance. Therefore, absent any precise rules, it is commonly accepted that the remedy must not be disproportionate to the wrong.[56]

As already mentioned, the withheld performance must be correlative to the obligation of the debtor and must arise from the same legal relationship. Therefore, in case the two obligations are not concurrent, one party will not be entitled to suspend its own performance in order to put pressure on the other party to perform.[57] The remedy will also not be available in cases where one party has agreed to a delay in performance from the other party or where it is obvious that—either from express language of the contract or based on common usage—the creditor's

---

[54] According to the doctrine of *causa* in the Napoleonic Code, the cause of the obligation of one party of a bilateral contract consists in the obligation assumed by the other. Also, in accordance with the French Civil Code, a contract is invalid if it has no cause or it has a false or an illicit one. See Nicholas (1992), p. 214. In contrast, consideration is viewed as the hallmark of a bargain. Anglo-American law has taken the decision to accept as legally enforceable only those agreements that constitute a bargain, unless they are entered into as a deed. See: Marsh (1994), pp. 103 and 324. Hence, the characteristics of the doctrine of consideration are the following: an agreement must be contained in a sealed instrument to be operative, unless it is supported by consideration; consideration may consist either in some benefit to the promisor or in some detriment to the promise; consideration is a fact that operates as one of the conventional causes or inducements of a promise; adequacy of consideration is not required. To put it in other words, the Anglo-American doctrine of consideration is narrower. That means that contracts that are not enforceable under the Anglo-American law requirement for consideration will still be enforced under the doctrine of *causa*. For example, an agreement without consideration in the Anglo-American sense would be enforceable in French law if it was a wholly gratuitous commission or an agreement to make a gift. For a detailed comparison between the two institutions: Lorenzen (1919), pp. 632–639. For cases when causa is narrower than consideration: Drake (1905), p. 23.

[55] This situation is most likely inconvenient to the creditor, especially in those cases where it does not wish to be tied up for long. But if the creditor wants to repudiate the contract and recover freedom of action, he is bound the provisions of Art 1184 of the French Civil Code, which requires a resolutory action brought in court. See: Nicholas (1992), p. 214.

[56] French courts have denied, for example, the right of a tenant to refuse payment in cases where the landlord's failure was relatively trivial or the right of an electricity supply company to cut off supply where the customer had disputed and refused to pay a small amount of the total sum claimed by the company. For a list of French decisions: Nicholas (1992), p. 215, footnote 19. Also: Marsh (1994), p. 324.

[57] For example, a shopkeeper tenant is not allowed to refuse payment of rent in order to pressure his landlord to pay for the goods he bought from the tenant's shop. See: Nicholas (1992), p. 215, footnote 215.

performance is expected to precede that of the debtor, even if the two obligations are intertwined.[58] However, in the case of a seller, the Civil Code established an exception that enables him to refrain from delivery even when a delay in payment of the price was granted, in the cases where the buyer has become insolvent and the seller is in imminent danger of losing the price. The buyer will be left with the option of giving security to pay at the due date,[59] or, evidently, he can choose to perform his obligation immediately. Such rules are common to all civil law jurisdictions.

The *exceptio* has an evident relationship with the *droit de retention* since they both serve the same purpose of pressuring the debtor by withholding from him that to which he is entitled by contract, and for this particular reason, the two remedies are often indistinguishable. However, the exception is much wider in its effects given that the creditor is not confined to retaining a specific asset to which the debtor is entitled. On the other hand, the retention right is not limited to synallagmatic contracts, being available for any type of contracts.[60]

Right to withhold performance was deemed highly useful in French law given the length of judicial proceedings.[61] It is a plain recognition of the fact that judicial remedies are not always fit to solve commercial matters. Notwithstanding that it is a temporary measure only,[62] suspending the contract and freezing the *status quo* until a final decision is reached, it offers a solid and swift protection to the creditor, at least in the area of sales and service contracts.

However, as it was stated in the beginning of this chapter, self-help remedies should be made available also to secured creditors who have already extended credit to nonperforming debtors. Unfortunately, secured creditors who are not in possession of the collateral do not enjoy the same swift and efficient solutions. Since its importance in practice cannot be denied[63] and since the above proves that self-help remedies are not necessarily incompatible to French law, the application of similar nonjudicial remedies in the area of secured transactions should be considered by the French academics and legislators.

---

[58] Nicholas (1992), p. 215. Also: Marsh (1994), p. 325.

[59] French Civil Code, Art 1613.

[60] Nicholas (1992), pp. 215–216.

[61] Harris and Tallon (1989), p. 294, and Marsh (1994), p. 325.

[62] It has been argued that the *exception d'inexécution* may lead, despite its temporary character, to irreversible results, the equivalent of a partial rescission, in the case of employment contracts. See Professor Ghestin's position cited Harris and Tallon (1989), p. 294.

[63] Marsh (1994), p. 325. "The important point about the *exceptio* is that it can be invoked by the party concerned *without the necessity of going to court* (emphasis added) and without even the need to issue a *mise en demeure*, even though in practice the giving of notice is advisable. Of course the other party has the right to go to court and claim that the *exceptio* has been incorrectly invoked and, if successful, to recover damages for the loss he had suffered."

3.4.4 Germany

Unlike its French counterpart, the right to withheld performance or literally the "defense of unperformed contract" (*Einrede des nicht erfüllten Vertrages*) has a statutory basis in Bürgerliches Gesetzbuch (BGB).[64] Similar to French law, it is applicable only if the obligations originate in a synallagmatic (bilateral) contract. Another similarity is that, in a wider sense, the *exceptio non adimpleti contractus* may be regarded as granting a right of retention (*Zurückbehaltungsrecht*), although it was emphasized[65] that the right to withhold performance must not be confused with the general right of retention (*allgemeines Zurückbehaltungsrecht*), which is laid down in BGB[66] and which is in the nature of a lien (known to common law jurisdictions as the workman's lien).

The *exceptio* stems from the BGB rule according to which unless the parties to a synallagmatic contract have agreed that one of them can perform later than the other, they have to exchange performances concurrently.[67] Hence, it would seem that in the case of synallagmatic obligations, the innocent party must frame its action so as to demand only contemporaneous performance (*Erfüllung Zug um Zug*).[68] However, the BGB has adopted a different method, since it only speaks of a "right" of the defendant to refuse performance of his own obligations until the plaintiff has performed his. In other words, the defense is not automatic, but it has to be pleaded by the defendant during a trial.

That the defense of the unperformed contract is not automatic proves it to be a self-help remedy, in line with the definition employed by this book. It is curious that no attention is dedicated to the fact that this remedy is not judicial, but it actually starts before any judicial action. However, the fact that this is not an automatic remedy has also procedural implications. Since the defense must be pleaded by the defendant, the judge may not take notice of it *ex officio*. By rejecting the involvement of the judiciary in the exercise of the defense, the German procedural law recognizes implicitly that the *exceptio* is a self-help remedy that can and must be raised solely by its beneficiary.

One may notice the practical importance of the application of this remedy in cases where defendants fail to appear in court and default judgments are entered against them, provided the plaintiffs have established their claim. The reason is that in such cases, the plaintiffs need not prove that they have performed their own

[64] BGB, Art 320.

[65] Markesinis et al. (2006), p. 351. Also: Marsh (1994), p. 340.

[66] BGB, Art 273.

[67] BGB, Art 320, para 1, reads as follows: "A person who is a party to a reciprocal contract may refuse his part of the performance until the other party renders consideration, *unless he is obliged to perform in advance* (emphasis added). If performance is to be made to more than one person, an individual person may be refused the part performance due to him until the complete consideration has been rendered."

[68] Marsh (1994), p. 339.

obligation since in judicial terms the defense has exactly that purpose. Once the defendant raises the *exceptio*, the burden of proof shifts to the plaintiff who has to show either that he performed his part or that the other party was, according to the contract, obliged to perform first.[69] However, from the above, it results that although the remedy is exercised tacitly outside and before any judicial action, the person exercising it must also make a clear statement thereof in front of the court as well, in order to validate it during *ex post* judicial control. This subjects the party resorting to this self-help remedy to an additional burden and partially frustrates the effects of the remedy once judicial proceedings have started.

German scholars noticed that since the party who performs in advance is basically giving unsecured credit to the other party, the former faces the risk of not receiving the counterperformance.[70] In reply, the legislator tries to alleviate this risk by granting a special defense according to which a person obliged by a synallagmatic contract to perform his part may refuse performance if, after the conclusion of the contract, a significant deterioration in the financial position of the other party occurs, thus endangering the claim for the counterperformance. In such case, the other party is faced with a double option: either he can offer the counterperformance or he can provide adequate security for it.[71]

Since according to the BGB text parties can derogate from the principle of contemporaneous performance of contractual obligations, the legislator took a critical view with respect to such clauses when contained in general conditions of contract (*Allgemeine Geschäftsbedingungen*). Therefore, the BGB states that the plea of nonperformance cannot be waived in standard form contracts with consumers.[72]

As mentioned earlier, German law provides for a general right of retention, which operates where the duties of the parties are not synallagmatically related to one another. In the cases where the debtor has a matured claim against the creditor arising "from the same legal relationship" on which his own obligation is based, he may, unless a contrary intention appears from the obligation, refuse to render his

---

[69] Markesinis et al. (2006), p. 352.

[70] Markesinis et al. (2006), p. 353.

[71] BGB, Art 321, para 1, reads as follows: "A person who is obliged to perform in advance under a reciprocal contract may refuse to render his performance if, after the contract is entered into, it becomes apparent that his entitlement to consideration is jeopardized by the inability to perform of the other party. The right to refuse performance is not applicable if consideration is rendered or security is given for it." This risk was noticed by English scholars as well: if classified as independent promises, each party would bear the risk with respect to the other's performance. Such consequence led the court to show great reluctance in construing promises as independent. For details and cases: Markesinis et al. (2006), p. 353.

[72] BGB, Art 309, no. 2, (a) reads as follows: "Even to the extent that a deviation from the statutory provisions is permissible, the following are ineffective in standard business terms: [...]2. (Right to refuse performance) a provision by which a) the right to refuse performance to which the other party to the contract with the user is entitled under section 320, is excluded or restricted [...]" Also: Marsh (1994), p. 340.

due obligation until the obligation due to him is performed.[73] Obviously, the effect of this right of retention is comparable with the effect of the *exceptio*,[74] but similarities do not go further.

One last thing is worth emphasizing. Although the remedy consists in withholding performance—a self-help device—**German scholars seem to consider solely the judicial aspect of the defense**, which occurs *ex post facto*, during judicial scrutiny. That is why most of the commentaries (as illustrated above) refer to the parties as "claimant" (the party who did not perform its obligation) and the "defendant" (party who justifiably withholds its own performance). This manner is relevant and telling when it comes to the approach of German law towards self-help: although it is obviously there, it is completely disregarded.

3.4.5 Romania

Due to its French origins, up until 2011, when the Romanian New Civil Code (RNCC) was enacted, Romanian law did not have a dedicated provision to the right to withhold performance (*excepţia de neexecutare a contractului*). Notwithstanding the lack of an explicit provision, cases in which the exception occurred in practice were to be found with reference to sales, exchange or remunerated deposit.[75] Therefore, in the absence of a legal definition the doctrine defined this remedy as a defense at the disposal of one party of a synallagmatic contract to be used in case the other party requires performance of the contractual obligation in the absence of its own performance. Similar to the view taken by French law, it was held that by raising this defense, the invoking party obtains, *without the intervention of the court*, a suspension of performance of its obligations, until the moment when the other party complies with its own. The legal justification of the exception was said to be the interdependence of the mutual obligations of a synallagmatic contract.[76] Additionally, in the same line adopted by French law, the retention right (*dreptul de*

[73] BGB, Art 273, para 1.

[74] For details and applications of the retention right: Markesinis et al. (2006), pp. 354–355.

[75] Statescu and Barsan (2008), p. 86. The authors mention, for example, Art 1322 of the former Civil Code according to which the seller was not obliged to deliver the good unless the buyer paid for it and there was no later term provided for payment, in his favor. Also, according to Art 1364 of the former Civil Code, the buyer facing a mortgage action or a restitution action against the purchased good was authorized to suspend payment of the price until the seller dismissed the actions. With respect to the exchange contract, reference is made to Art 1407 of the former Civil Code, while with respect to the remunerated deposit, the article mentioned is 1619. However, in the latter case, the actual right given is a retention right of the deposited good until the price for the deposit is paid.

[76] Statescu and Barsan (2008), p. 86. Also Vasilescu (2012), p. 515.

retenţie) is considered to be in many situations an application of the right to withhold performance.[77]

Four conditions need to be met cumulatively in order to make use of the exception. The *first* one is that the mutual obligations must have their origin in the same contract, maintaining the French position that the exception cannot be used in order to pressure the other party to comply with its unperformed obligations arising from a different contract[78] and contrary to the German approach. The *second* is that in order to raise the defense, the other party must not have had performed, totally or partially, its own obligations (however, partial nonperformance must be significant). The *third* condition is that the nonperformance must not be the result of the actions of the party raising the exception and stems from the Roman law principle according to which no one can invoke his own wrongdoing as defense (*Nemo auditur propriam turpitudinem allegans*). *Last*, there must not be a mutually agreed term for later performance of one party's obligations, although it is recognized that such an effect may be caused also by the nature of performances or by an expressed legal provision.

Raising the exception was also free from the requirement to put the debtor in default, and it could have been done directly among the parties, without court intervention. However, the party against whom it was raised had the right to address the court, claiming the exception was abusively used.[79] Since the judicial control occurred only *ex post*, such scrutiny does not contradict in anyway the definition of self-help employed by this book.

Despite its evident extrajudicial character, the exception was not until recently referred to as self-help. Romanian law, following its French tradition, took the latter's view towards self-help, maintaining that no one is allowed to do justice on his own. However, after the implementation of the Secured Transactions Law no 99/1999 and of the RNCC, scholars now maintain that self-help (*executarea privată a obligaţiilor contractuale* respectively *justiţia privată*—literally translated as "private enforcement of contractual obligations" and, respectively, "private

[77] Statescu and Barsan (2008), p. 87, and Rizoiu (2011), pp. 573 and 625. In footnote 4 at p. 573, Rizoiu states that the only reminiscences of self-help (the Romanian term used by him is "executare privată," which would literally translate as private enforcement) in Romanian Civil Code until the implementation of the Secured Transactions Law no 99/1999 were the retention right and the possibility of the creditor to fulfill the debtor's obligation on the latter's expense. Additionally, in the field of contractual obligation, there was the defense against an unperformed contract. Rizoiu also takes the view that the retention right was solely a particular form of the right to withhold performance.

[78] However, it is mentioned that courts have admitted the possibility to use the exception in the case of the so-called imperfect synallagmatic contracts, meaning those contracts initially meant to be unilateral during the performance of which an obligation arises for the creditor towards the contractual debtor as result of an extracontractual event (i.e., if the depository undertakes certain expenses for the preservation of the deposited good). See: Statescu and Barsan (2008), p. 87.

[79] Statescu and Barsan (2008), pp. 87–88.

justice") is not something new, introduced by the reform of secured transactions, but it was already allowed in certain situations.[80] Although the process of acceptance of self-help mechanisms was reversed, in the sense that it came through the secured transactions law first, the recognition of the right to withhold performance as a self-help remedy is still a huge cognitive advancement for the Romanian academia and the study of self-help mechanisms.

The right to withhold performance also received recognition from the Romanian legislature, who enshrined it in the RNCC.[81] Additionally, the retention right was legally established: the law now regards it as a good illustration of the right to withhold performance in case of *ad rem*[82] obligations.[83] However, the regulation of these two self-help devices did nothing more than legislatively recognize and strengthen what was deemed as natural effects of synallagmatic relations, without modifying in any way what was already said in the doctrine or the case law about it. By analogy, the process resembled what the drafters of the UCC did in the case of Article 9 with the existing case law on the issue of self-help repossession.

The legal provision differentiates though between important, essential obligations and minor, accessory obligations. The purpose is to emphasize that when one party seeks to use the self-help remedy of withholding performance, it must not do so in a pettifogging, abusive manner. Yet the differentiation was also interpreted to have an emasculating effect on the power of the exception to pressure the debtor, since the wording leads to the conclusion that such pressure can be placed on the nonperforming party only with respect to the main obligations.[84]

Considering that all legal systems analyzed took a similar position, the view adopted by the Romanian legislation is not surprising. However, the shift of perspective with respect to the limiting effect of such a position is rather unique and is worth mentioning. Despite its disregard for the need for reasonableness when

---

[80] See Vasilescu (2012), p. 515, and the references made in footnote 3. The author concludes: "[. . .] private justice, which seems to be illustrated by the *exception non adimpleti*, is nothing but the normal manifestation of the rationale behind and specificity of synallagmatic relations" (in Romanian: "[. . .] justitia privată, pe care pare să o ilustreze *exceptio non adimpleti*, nu este decât manifestarea firească a raţiunii şi specificului raporturilor sinalagmatice." Rizoiu (2011), p. 625: "The secured transactions law introduces in the Romanian legal system an institution whose applications were almost entirely extinct: **private enforcement of contractual obligations**" (in Romanian: "Legea garanţiilor introduce în sistemul român de drept o instituţie ale cărei aplicaţii dispăruseră aproape cu desăvârşire: **executarea (silită) privată a obligaţiilor contractuale**") in opposition to the enforcement procedure of the Code for Civil Procedure, which is a judicial one. However, the same author mentions that certain applications of the right to privately enforce contractual obligations survived in the Civil Code (p. 573).

[81] RNCC, Art 1556.

[82] Ad rem is a Civil law term that translates as "right to a thing." It is a right in specific property arising from another person's duty and valid only against that person, an inchoate or incomplete right to a thing. See Garner (2009), pp. 936–937.

[83] Vasilescu (2012), p. 516.

[84] Vasilescu (2012), pp. 517–518.

resorting to self-help remedies, any such remedy can be subjected *ex post facto* to judicial control and courts will definitely sanction any abusive behavior.

A last note is dedicated to the waiver of the right to withhold performance in standard contracts. According to the RNCC, general dispositions governing contracts, in the case of standard contracts, those provisions that limit the rights of the party to make use of the legal defenses, including the right to withhold performance, are not valid, unless they were expressly accepted, in writing, by the other party.[85] This provision brings Romanian law closer to German law, which also banned the waiver of withholding performance right in standard contracts. However, Romanian law seems to be more permissible since parties may waive their abovementioned right as long as they are fully aware and informed of what they are doing.

3.5 Liquidated Damages and Penalty Clauses

If parties wish to resolve the question of appropriate amount of damages in case of breach, without resorting to litigation,[86] they can agree to a clause for liquidated damages (in common law jurisdictions). The civil law functional equivalent is penalty clauses where a specific amount shall be considered, in anticipation, a just remedy in case of breach.[87] However, the question whether liquidated damages, respectively penalty clauses, represent a self-help remedy might be raised. The book argues that the answer must be positive, for several reasons.

First of all, this remedy's characteristics fit within the boundaries of the definition of self-help employed for the purposes of this work: it tries to remedy or prevent a wrong without resort to court and judicial proceedings. The fact that its validity or application can be later challenged in a court of law does not affect its extrajudicial character since *ex post* judicial control is not inconsistent with any self-help remedy (including self-help repossession). **Second**, a group of American scholars who wrote an extensive study dedicated to self-help[88] refers to liquidated damages as being a self-help remedy. Since the US was chosen as the benchmark for the comparison, it made sense to use their approach for the comparative analysis of this remedy. **Third**, the common law remedy of liquidated damages has an equivalent (similar in purpose but different in technicalities) in civilian jurisdictions, the penalty clause, which fulfills *almost* the same functions and thus provides the adequate basis for a comparative analysis.

[85] RNCC, Art 1203.

[86] Unless the litigation concerns these damages clauses themselves.

[87] Friedman (1981), p. 198.

[88] Brandon et al. (1984), p. 913: "Liquidated damages provisions incorporated in the contracts afford contracting parties a legally enforceable form of prophylactic self-help." For a discussion on whether liquidated damages constitute self-help: Gergen (2009), pp. 1397–1398, footnote 1.

Some additional clarifications must be made. Historically speaking, the liquidated damages clauses have their origin in the penal bonds, which were used under US law to ensure performance. Basically, these bonds were sealed promises to pay a fixed amount of money that could be enforced against the promisor in case of nonperformance.[89] At some point in time, they used to be strictly enforced and, thus, they became a very effective way of discouraging breach. However, they contained a high risk for forfeiture, particularly where the contract was substantially performed. Due to their punitive effect and the need for adequate money damages to compensate the aggrieved party for its actual loss, courts grew unwilling to enforce them.[90] What emerged was an instrument that simplifies the issue of damages to be paid instead of breach and acts less as a coercive factor of performance, although the latter function did not disappear completely, as the following analysis proves.

3.5.1 The US

In the US, liquidated damages clauses, when incorporated, are legally enforceable and constitute an effective self-help remedy, by establishing an amount of money to be paid as damage for any breach without resort to courts.[91] As such, they fulfil three different functions. **First**, the parties avoid any protracted dispute or trial on the issues of damages. By inserting a liquidated damages clause in their agreement, they basically predetermine the amount that is to be paid in case of breach. **Second**, the clause serves as a pressuring factor against the party to perform his obligation, which in the UK is referred to as *in terrorem* effect. The amount will serve as a warning to the promisor that any default will become sanctioned financially. **Third**, liquidated damages may also be designed to diminish the amount of loss borne by the defaulting promisor, though these cases are rare.[92]

However, with respect to the second function, it should be mentioned that liquidated damages clauses serving this purpose face the risk of being invalidated if the agreed amount is too high in relation to the actual damage and the courts deem them to be a masked form of penalty clauses.[93] Unlike liquidated damages clauses, which are considered remedies for a contractual breach (provided that breach occurs), penalties are contractual provisions that are intended to *prevent* a party from breaching the contract and to *punish* that party if their deterring effect proved ineffective.[94]

[89] Ferriell (2009), p. 840.

[90] Ferriell (2009), p. 841.

[91] Ferriell (2009), p. 839.

[92] Friedman (1981), p. 199.

[93] Brizzee (1991), p. 1613. Also: Friedman (1981), p. 200, and Ferriell (2009), p. 840.

[94] Brandon et al. (1984), p. 913.

In order to distinguish between liquidated damages and penalties, US courts have developed a three-pronged test: the *first* step is checking whether the breach caused an uncertain or inestimable amount of damages,[95] the *second* is to ascertain the parties' intention with respect to the damages[96] and the *third* is to check whether the stipulated damages can be deemed a reasonable estimation of the potential loss[97] or they go beyond that. However, the practice focuses more on the third step where, a reasonable estimation would be enforceable, while a disproportionate amount would be a clear indication of a penalty clause.[98] The language used by the parties is not considered to be a determining factor by the US courts[99] in this regard. Another important note concerning the test is that, procedurally speaking, unenforceability of liquidated damages clauses is deemed to be an affirmative defense, which means that it must be specifically pleaded.[100] In the absence of such defense, liquidated damages are enforced without the need of judicial involvement, which underlines their self-help character.

Article 2 of the UCC specifically allows the use of liquidated damages clauses in commercial contracts that have as object sales of goods,[101] although courts are increasingly applying these provisions by analogy to other types of commercial transactions (bailments and leases).[102] A clause providing for liquidated damages is enforceable if two preconditions are met: *first*, that the parties have to establish a

---

[95] Friedman (1981), p. 206. Also: Ferriell (2009), pp. 842–844, and Berendt et al. (2007), pp. 1010–1011. The latter cites *DJ Mfg. Corp. v. U.S.*, 86 F.3d 1130 (Fed. Cir. 1996), with a reference to the position undertaken by the US federal courts with respect to the enforcement of liquidated damages clauses where the amount of damages is difficult to determine at the outset.

[96] Friedman claims that the actual intent of the parties should not be treated as a determining factor in evaluating whether a liquidated damages clause amounts or not to a penalty. Friedman (1981), pp. 204–205. Also: Ferriell (2009), p. 842.

[97] Friedman (1981), p. 209 and Ferriell (2009), pp. 845–848. Also: Farnsworth et al. (2001), p. 552, and Berendt et al. (2007), pp. 996–1001. The former cites *Dave Gustafson & Co. v. State*, 156 N. W.2d 185 (S.D. 1968), while the latter cites several cases, among which: *Truck Rent-A-Center, Inc v. Puritan Farms 2nd, Inc*, 41 N.Y.2d 420, 361 N.E. 2d 1015, 393 N.Y.S. 2d 365 (New York, 1977) and *Layton Mfg. Co. v. Dulien Steel, Inc.*, 277 Or. 343, 560 P.2d 1058 (1977).

[98] Brandon et al. (1984), pp. 913–914, and Ferriell (2009), pp. 845–847.

[99] Friedman (1981), pp. 200–201, and Ferriell (2009), p. 842.

[100] Berendt et al. (2007), p. 1008. The authors refer to *D&D Leasing Co. of South Carolina, Inc. v. David Lipson, Ph. D., P.A.*, 305 S.C. 540, 409 S.E. 2d 794 (S.C. App. 1991), where it was held that because the defendant did not plead unenforceability based on the alleged penalty nature of the contract termination provision, he waived that defense.

[101] UCC, Art 2, Section 718(1) reads: "[...] A term fixing unreasonably large liquidated damages is void as a penalty." For details: Friedman (1981), pp. 208–209.

[102] Brandon et al. (1984), p. 914, footnote 412. Also: Berendt et al. (2007), p. 1007. The authors state that in case of leases, the acceleration clauses, which provided that upon lessee's breach prior to the end of the lease term, the amount of the rent to the end of the lease term becomes immediately due and payable, are construed as liquidated damages clauses and are enforceable as such. They cite *Aurora Business Park Associates, L.P. v. Michael Albert, Inc.*, 548 N.W.2d 153 (Yowa 1996), where in a commercial lease case the court concluded the clause was valid and enforceable and did not amount to a penalty.

just compensation for the anticipated loss that a potential contract breach would cause and, *second*, that the harm caused by the contractual breach cannot be estimated accurately.[103] Otherwise, the UCC is quite clear and specific when stating that any unreasonably large amount of liquidated damage estimates renders the clause void as a penalty.[104]

Despite the similarities with the common law doctrine,[105] the UCC liquidated damages provision differs in the sense that courts may determine reasonableness of the clause under the UCC at either the time of contracting or the time of breach.[106] In other words, the UCC had embraced the approach taken by some courts in cases where no damage occurred although there was breach.[107] The difference is relevant because even if the figure was not reasonable at the time when the parties concluded the contract, courts will uphold it in case it is close to the amount of actual damages when breach occurred.

On a final note, one must mention that despite judicial skepticism, the enforcement of liquidated damages enjoys a significant support from the scholars. And if one considers liquidated damages as self-help remedy, the reasons for support become clearer. In the area of secured transactions, the availability of self-help remedies was meant to increase the level of confidence that the transaction will be performed and, absent such performance, that the creditor will have at his disposal a swift and efficient remedy.

Similar reasons were invoked in the case of liquidated damages: a seller who is willing to make a commitment that he will pay if he is unable to perform may provide sufficient encouragement to a reluctant customer to enter into a deal with him, precisely because of his willingness to put a prize on his failure to perform.[108] These clauses might also benefit new-come undertakings, which must offer some concessions in order to enter and make themselves competitive and attractive on the market. In addition, the availability and enforcement of such self-help remedy

---

[103] UCC, Art 2, Section 718 (1) (a). Also: Ferriell (2009), p. 847.

[104] For examples: Brandon et al. (1984), pp. 914–916. The authors mention *Coast Trading Co. v. Parmac. Inc*, where a provision establishing a 15 % cancellation charge was deemed enforceable by the court under the Washington version of the UCC Art 2-718(1) where the seller was actually able to prove that it had incurred damages in excess of 15 % of the contract price. However, in a different case, *Nu Dimensions Figure Salon v. Beccerra*, a clause that required the breaching party to pay the entire contract price even before the parties have performed any services was held to be unconscionable and unreasonable. On the issue of difficulty to estimate losses, the authors refer to *E.C. Ernest, Inc v. Manhattan Construction Co. of Texas*, where a clause providing for $250 per day of delay was held valid for the fact that neither of the parties disputed the conjectural nature of measuring damages and the loss caused by delay in completion of the building was difficult to measure.

[105] The common law rule in the majority of jurisdictions was that the reasonableness of the liquidated damages clause was to be evaluated solely on the basis of the loss that was anticipated at the time of contract formation. See: Friedman (1981), p. 209.

[106] Friedman (1981), p. 212.

[107] Brandon et al. (1984), p. 915, footnote 424. Also: Friedman (1981)), pp. 212–213.

[108] Ferriell (2009), pp. 847–848.

diminishes the risk of an aggrieved party of ending up uncompensated for different types of harm, and hence should serve to reduce prices.[109] Hence, one may notice that **the logic employed in the US is to provide both secured and unsecured creditors with self-help remedies where such remedies are possible**. Unfortunately, this chapter shows that **the same logic is not applied with consistency in European jurisdictions, where self-help remedies are made available to unsecured creditors in areas of contract law, but they are denied to secured creditors in area of security interests.**

3.5.2 The UK

In UK contract law, similarly to US law, it is also a common practice to include in the contract a specified amount to be paid in case the contract is breached. Such clauses are known as liquidated or agreed damages clauses.[110] They are frequently used in commercial contracts, notwithstanding whether they were individually negotiated or contained in the standard terms of one party. However, they tend to appear more often in relation to late rather than defective performance, especially in fields such as construction and engineering[111] or supply and sale of goods, as well as charter parties agreements (known as demurrage (delay) clauses).[112] As in the US, their purpose is to make recovery of damages easier, mainly by avoiding issues related to proving the actual loss.[113] Additionally, the usage of liquidated damages clauses tries to assure the other party of one's intention to be bound by the contract. However, despite these similarities to US law, liquidated damages clauses are not perceived by UK scholars as self-help remedies.[114]

The similarities with US law are that UK law differentiates between liquidated damages and penalties, and a test has been developed by courts in order to help in making that distinction. In addition, UK law follows a similar public policy concern with respect to upper limits of liquidated damages.

First, UK law makes a distinction between clauses that try to impose a penalty on the defaulting party and clauses that levy liquidated damages from the defaulting party. The distinction is relevant since in the UK, penalty clauses are generally

[109] Ferriell (2009), p. 847.

[110] Peel (2011), pp. 1072–1073.

[111] Peel (2011), pp. 1073–1075. Also: Marsh (1994), p. 316.

[112] Cotton (1999), p. 3. Also: Whincup (1996), p. 289.

[113] Anthony Ogus, Remedies, English Report in Harris and Tallon (1989), p. 246. The author states: "The advantages of this device are clear: avoiding expenses of disputes as to quantification and fixing the 'costs' of breach at the time of making the contract."

[114] Cotton (1999), p. 7. Cotton mentions as self-help remedies retention of title clauses, enforcement of security, withholding payments and setoff, as well as rights against the goods themselves. Liquidated damages are thus treated as regular remedies for contractual breach.

unenforceable[115] as is the case in the US. For a liquidated damages clause to be valid, the amount specified must be a genuine preestimate of the anticipated loss that the performing party is likely to suffer in case of breach. Additionally, a figure that is not in gross excess of the greatest loss that might be incurred is likely to be enforced as well. However, any amount that is provided for *in terrorem* of the defaulting party in order to force the other party to perform (in the US, liquidated damages were deemed a pressuring factor on the debtor) its side of the contract will constitute a penalty clause[116] and will not be enforced. It makes no difference whether the parties used the words penalty or liquidated damages; the courts will always analyze the nature of the amount.[117]

With respect to a claim of a genuine liquidated damages clause, the aggrieved party merely needs to show breach of contract, notwithstanding whether an actual loss was incurred or not.[118] The extent of any loss is also irrelevant. On the other side, the burden of proof that the liquidated damages clause is in fact a penalty lies with the breaching party.[119] However, in case the breaching party is successful in proving the clause to be a penalty, that will not insulate him from liability, since he is still in breach. The only consequence would be that now the plaintiff will have to make use of the judicial process and prove his claim for damages.[120]

The *second* similarity with the US is that courts have developed a test in order to distinguish between penalties and liquidated damages. Hence, a clause will be deemed a penalty where the amount is *extravagant and unconscionable* in comparison to the greatest loss that could have been possibly proved in case of breach.[121] There is also a great likeliness that the clause is a penalty when the obligation breached consisted in paying a sum of money and the stipulated damages are greater than the initial amount to be paid: for example, in the case of hire purchase contracts containing clauses that make larger sums payable for breach at the outset, when the goods are still nearly new.[122] However, liquidated damages are

[115] McKendrick (2010), p. 137.

[116] Peel (2011), p. 1073. Also Marsh (1994), p. 317.

[117] Cotton (1999), p. 3. Also: Whincup (1996), p. 290, and Ogus in Harris and Tallon (1989), p. 246.

[118] Whincup (1996), p. 291. Also: Marsh (1994), p. 317.

[119] Cotton (1999), pp. 3–4.

[120] Marsh (1994), p. 317.

[121] Marsh (1994), p. 317. The author mentions *Dunlop Pneumatic Tyre Co. Ltd v. New Garage & Motor Co. Ltd* [1915] AC 79.

[122] Whincup (1996), pp. 290–291. The author mentions *Bridge v. Campbell Discount*, 1962, where it was held that such a clause was most likely penal. Despite this, one might argue that the greatest depreciation occurs as soon as the goods are used. According to Ogus, courts are concerned with protecting the debtor against extortionate demands by the creditor. Also: Harris and Tallon (1989), p. 247. "A contractual provision of this kind will be enforceable only if it represents a genuine and reasonable preestimate of loss likely to flow from breach." See: McKendrick (2010), p. 137.

not dismissed solely on the ground that a precise preestimation was impossible when the contract was concluded.[123]

Third, with respect to the upper limits of the amounts that can be set as damages through contract, the Unfair Contract Terms Act 1977, which, in certain circumstances, imposes a test of reasonableness in relation to an exclusion clause (which limits or excludes liability), is unlikely to be applied. In the case of a genuine liquidated damages clause, if the amount specified in the clause is higher than the genuine preestimate, it constitutes a penalty and will not be enforced. Therefore, the courts will not benefit a party claiming damages by enforcing a smaller sum.[124] On the other hand, in case of standard term contracts between commercial suppliers and consumer, according to the Unfair Terms in Consumer Contracts Regulations 1999, the latter cannot be bound by any clause that requires him to pay a disproportionately high amount as compensation for his breach.[125]

UK law does not provide whether liquidated damages clauses are intended to be a mutually binding limitation on the amount of damages to be paid. Such an interpretation was upheld in the case of building and engineering contracts,[126] but a carefully drafted contract can expressly state that a party seeking to impose a liquidated damages clause has either the right or the choice[127] to make use of it or not. However, when a liquidated damages clause is invalidated for being a penalty, the amount specified will be used as a limitation on the amount of damages that can be claimed.[128]

With respect to its enforcement,[129] many contracts (especially those in the area of construction where interim payments are usual) will provide for the right to have the damages deducted from subsequent sums due.[130] Contracts also enable the

---

[123] Cotton (1999), p. 4. According to Cotton, the leading case that established the test was *Dunlop Pneumatic Tyre Co Limited v. New Garage & Motor Co Limited [1915] A.C. 79*. The case is also mentioned by Whincup (1996), p. 290, and by Anthony Ogus in Remedies, English Report, in Harris and Tallon (1989), p. 246, footnote 17.

[124] Cotton (1999), p. 4.

[125] Peel (2011), p. 1083.

[126] Cotton (1999), p. 4. Cotton mentions a Court of Appeal case where it was held that where a contract contained an amount of liquidated damages, then the general damages for breach of contract became nonrecoverable in the alternative. See: *Temloc v. Errill Properties, 1987 39 BLR.30*. In addition, Whincup (1996), p. 291, refers to *Cellulose Acetate v. Widnes Foundry*, 1933 (House of Lords), where it was held that a party seeking to enforce a liquidated damages clause cannot then claim more than his genuine preestimate, however great this actual loss is.

[127] The choice in this case refers to the right of the aggrieved party either to sue under the liquidated damages clause or to ignore it and claim general damages. The difference lies with the fact that the latter option includes no limitations on the amount. See: Whincup (1996), p. 291, and his references to a Canadian case: *Raymer v. Stratton Woods*, 1988 (Canada).

[128] The likeliness of this limit to be reached is very low in practice since, by its nature, it was higher than the loss could ever be.

[129] All relevant procedural requirements must be observed—notice periods, time limits—otherwise the defendant will not be required to pay damages.

[130] Marsh (1994), p. 317.

claimant to recover liquidated damages as if they were a debt due by the other party.[131]

Some UK scholars have taken a strong position in criticizing the usage of liquidated damages. Treitel's position is cited in length when claiming that the common law rules for distinguishing between penalties and liquidated damages "manage to get the worst of both worlds."[132] The reasons seem to be, on the one hand, that they are not certain of being enforced, since there is always doubt on whether they will be treated as liquidated damage clauses or penalties and, on the other hand, that they run short of the flexibility present in the civilian systems, where they are enforced by principle, but subject to reduction by courts, since the UK courts do not enjoy the judicial power of reduction. All these debates, however, touch only upon the judicial aspects of liquidated damages, disregarding the fact that the judiciary intervenes only *ex post facto* in their enforcement.

3.5.3 France

According to French law, a contract becomes law (*loi*) for the signatory parties.[133] Therefore, in principle, the parties enjoy the possibility to agree in advance on the amount of damages to be paid in case of breach. Such a clause is known as a *clause pénale*,[134] a term that can be translated as "penalty clause." However, the term is not entirely equivalent with the common law one presented before. Unlike its US and UK counterparts, French law does not distinguish between liquidated damages and penalties,[135] the penalty clause fulfilling both functions at the same time.

There were two characteristics common to both French and English laws. On the one side, once a *clause pénale* was included in the contract, the creditor did not have the right to demand more or less than the agreed amount of the penalty. As it is later shown, now the agreed amount is subject to the court's power to amend. On the other side, the creditor did not have to prove that he has suffered any loss in order to claim the *clause pénale*. But this similarity reveals also a distinction between the two legal systems since French law does not have the requirement that the amount should be a genuine preestimate of the damages in order to be valid.[136]

---

[131] Cotton (1999), p. 5.

[132] Cited by Whincup (1996), pp. 291–292.

[133] FCC, Art 1134, para 1: "Agreements lawfully entered into take the place of the law for those who have made them."

[134] The governing article is FCC, Art 1152, para 1, which reads: "Where an agreement provides that he who fails to perform it will pay a certain sum as damages, the other party may not be awarded a greater or lesser sum."

[135] Nicholas (1992), p. 232. Also Marsh (1994), p. 329.

[136] Marsh (1994), pp. 329–330.

The parties enjoy the possibility to agree on an upper limit (*clause limitative de responsabilité*[137]), instead of going for a fixed amount, which will allow a judge to assess the damages, while, at the same time, subjecting him to the limit. Notwithstanding any of the above, courts are reluctant to uphold clauses that establish derisory limits that have the actual effect of evading liability.[138] At the same time, the legislature has also intervened to exclude or limit exemption clauses, especially in consumer-related cases, where there was a concern with respect to unequal bargaining power.[139]

Coming back to the *clause pénale*, one should first mention that initially the definition provided by the French Civil Code did not include any power in the court to modify the amount. It was therefore agreed that the clause served three purposes[140]: liquidate the damages in advance and remove the need for possibly difficult calculations and consequent delays, limit the debtor's liability (or creditor's entitlement),[141] and exert pressure on the debtor.[142] A *clause pé nale* does not prevent the creditor from claiming specific performance provided he wishes to exercise such option, but the two obligations are not alternative. Thus, the debtor is not entitled to choose to pay the penalty instead of performance.

The third function, that of exerting pressure on the debtor, created difficulties, since the *clause penale* could create in effect a private *astreinte*[143] without, in its

[137] Not to be confused with an exclusion of liability clause (*clause de non-responsabilité* or *d'irresponsibilité*).

[138] Nicholas (1992), p. 233.

[139] For details: Nicholas (1992), pp. 233–234. The author mentions, among others, Art 2 of the decree of 24 March 1978, which provided that in contracts of sale between professionals and nonprofessionals or consumer any clause having as its object or effect to exclude or **to limit** the right of the nonprofessional or consumer to compensation for the breach of any of his obligations is forbidden and therefore void as abusive. However, the author draws attention to the fact that the aforementioned limitations regarded solely sale contracts.

[140] There is also an opinion according to which they fulfill two functions: to preestimate the loss in case of default or to force the other party to fulfill the contract. See: Whincup (1996), p. 298.

[141] With respect to the second purpose, it seems that the *clause pénale* overlaps with a *clause limitative de responsabilité*. Basically, where a *clause limitative* fixes a ceiling, the specified amount in a *clause pénale* will serve as ceiling and floor at the same time. Therefore, it can benefit both parties. However, in cases where it benefits the debtor by acting as a *clause limitative*, it will be subject to certain limitations since the provisions of Art 1152, para 1, will not insulate the debtor from the consequences of his own wrongdoing (*dol*).

[142] Nicholas (1992), p. 234. Also: Marsh (1994), p. 329.

[143] *Astreinte* is a remedy developed by courts in order to ensure enforcement of a specific performance judgment. Basically, the courts attach to a judgment an order that the debtor shall pay to the creditor a specified amount for each day that he remains in default. The main purpose of the device is to place an additional economic burden on the debtor in order to pressure him to perform as soon as possible. For details: Nicholas (1992), pp. 221–224, Denis Tallon, Remedies, French Report, in Harris and Tallon (1989), pp. 268–270, Whincup (1996), pp. 298–299, and Marsh (1994), pp. 331–332.

original form, any power of the court to "liquidate" it.[144] The difficulty was most obvious where the bargaining power of the parties was unequal and, thus, the power to fix the penalties could have amounted to abuse.[145] It is why the French legislature amended the Civil Code in 1985 by empowering the courts to control and alter the amount fixed by the parties.[146] This effect is relevant because it shows that French law recognizes, indirectly, that there is an issue with judicial enforcement itself. Judicial proceedings and court decisions do not guarantee performance. Hence, the regular *astreinte* places additional pressure on the debtor and is payable to the creditor and not to the state.[147] The reason is that where there is an issue with judicial enforcement, it is the aggrieved creditor who needs adequate compensation and not the state. But while *astreinte* remains still within the powers of the judiciary, a penalty clause lies within the powers of the contracting parties. **It is as close to self-help as the French can get in this regard.**

French courts have not developed a similar test to the one developed by US and UK courts, since the question on whether a particular penalty is to be modified lies within the sovereign power of the judge. However, the courts will decide on the matter starting with an assessment of the damage actually incurred, which will serve as the basis for determining whether the agreed amount is excessive or derisory.[148] Furthermore, the Court of Cassation has laid down several limits within which the sovereign power of the judges could be exercised with respect to the modification. Mainly, whenever a judge adjusts the agreed penalty, he has to indicate the reasons why the amount is deemed too large or too small. Additionally, there is a requirement that any stated discrepancy must be "manifest," which means that, similarly to the test developed by common law courts, only considerable differences between the agreed damages and the actual ones shall be taken into account while minor ones shall be disregarded. Lastly, the judge is not entitled to reduce an amount below the level of the damage that has been suffered.[149]

---

[144] Parties can provide for the penalty to increase, similarly to the *astreinte*, in proportion to the delay in performance.

[145] "Unlike English law the power [to revise the penalty] was recognized by the *droit commun* of the right of the court to increase the amount of the penalty where the debtor was guilty of *dol*, and the amount of the penalty was substantially less than the loss suffered by the creditor." See: Marsh (1994), p. 330.

[146] The amendment introduced a second paragraph in FCC, Art 1152, which reads: "Nevertheless, the judge may "even of his own motion" (Act no 85-1097 of 11 Oct. 1985) moderate or increase the agreed penalty, where it is obviously excessive or ridiculously low. Any stipulation to the contrary shall be deemed unwritten."

[147] "The *astreinte*, although it is in reality a fine for having failed to remedy a court order, is nevertheless payable to the creditor and not to the state." For more details and enforcement of the *astreinte:* Marsh (1994), pp. 331–332.

[148] The fact that courts are entitled to modify the penalty's amount both upward and downward means that modification is a device meant to benefit both parties and protect both their interests by either not allowing the creditor to extort from the debtor more than his actual loss or not allowing the debtor to escape liability by paying less than the damage actually caused.

[149] Nicholas (1992), p. 236. Also: Marsh (1994), p. 331.

3.5.4 Germany

Similar to the previous jurisdiction, German law also gives full effect to *penalty clauses*.[150] The breaching party is entitled to have the penalty reduced to a reasonable amount if the courts find it to be disproportionate.[151] Penalty clauses in standard terms involving consumers must meet additional requirements but are still deemed to be valid and enforceable.[152] In such cases, a standard clause will be void if either the damages exceed the amount normally expected in cases where the agreement applies or prevents the other party from proving that the party who inserted the damages did not suffer any or they were substantially less than what was provided for in the contract.[153] This places German law very close to English law, which regards liquidated damages as a genuine preestimate of damages that the creditor would be likely to incur due to breach.

Additional notes on the issue of standard term contracts must be made. It was held that where damages included within such contracts are expressed as a percentage of the contract price, then they are valid under the Gesetz zur Regelung des Rechts der Allgemeinen Geschäftsbedingungen (AGBG)—German Standard Contracts Act—only if a figure was also stated as the maximum amount due under any circumstances.[154] From the principles stemming from the AGBG, if a contract is on the creditor's standard conditions, if a contractor is able to show that the actual loss was smaller than the amount of the liquidated damages, then he will only be liable for the lesser amount. But at the same time, if the creditor is able to prove that the actual loss was bigger than the amount of liquidated damages, then he will be able to claim for the actual loss. This last rule is opposite to the rule applicable in English law.

Compared to all other jurisdictions, it becomes evident that the applicability of the proportionality criterion of German law is likely to produce a similar effect to those established by the courts' tests in the US and the UK or by the legislature in France.[155] But there are some peculiarities. Hence, although the courts are entitled to reduce excessive penalties, they will be precluded from doing so in the case of

---

[150] Penalty clauses are governed by BGB, Arts 339–345. Art 339 reads: "Where the obligor promises the obligee, in the event that he fails to perform his obligation or fails to do so properly, payment of an amount of money as a penalty, the penalty is payable if he is in default. If the performance owed consists in forbearance, the penalty is payable on breach."

[151] The right to ask for reduction is contained in BGB, Art 343, para 1 of BGB, which reads: "If a payable penalty is disproportionately high, it may on the application of the obligor be reduced to a reasonable amount by judicial decision. In judging the appropriateness, every legitimate interest of the obligee, not merely his financial interest, must be taken into account. Once the penalty is paid, reduction is excluded."

[152] Markesinis et al. (2006), p. 444. Also: Whincup (1996), p. 300.

[153] Marsh (1994), p. 233.

[154] Marsh (1994), p. 233, citing a court decision of the Bundesgerichsthof (BGH)—the German Federal Court of Justice—from 1987.

[155] Markesinis et al. (2006), p. 444.

promises undertaken by merchants in the course of their business,[156] the protection focusing on consumers.

German law does not have any provisions to resemble the French feature concerning the promisee's entitlement either to the penalty or to specific performance (with the exception of delay, being deprived of claiming statutory damages): not only that cumulative penalty is permitted but also that the promisee is entitled to claim statutory damages, operating the penalty as the minimum amount of damages.[157] Hence, under German law, the *in terrorem* effect is stronger than in any other jurisdiction, which increases its deterrent effect over breaching parties.

3.5.5 Romania

Following its source of inspiration, namely French law, Romanian law allows the contracting parties to establish, either in their contract or by a separate agreement, the amount of damages owed by the debtor in case of breach, before the actual occurrence of damages as a result of the breach.[158] Therefore, the doctrine went to define the *clauza penală* (literally translated as "penalty clause," although, as in the case of French law, it is not the exact equivalent of the penalty as it appears in the US and UK laws) as the accessory agreement by which the parties determine in advance the equivalent of the loss to be incurred by the creditor in case of delayed, unsatisfactory or non-performance by the debtor.[159] Currently, the penalty clause is governed by the provisions of the RNCC.[160]

Its main effect, according to Romanian scholars, was to offer an evaluation of the losses incurred by the creditor in case of breach by the debtor, without resorting to courts, and, only indirectly, to pressure the debtor to perform. Despite this generally accepted view, a minority of scholars went even as far as to claim that the *clauza penală* is a legal guarantee for performance.[161]

[156] Marsh (1994), p. 232. The author mentions that although big companies or commercial partnerships will be covered, a construction company may not necessarily qualify as merchant under the law.

[157] BGB, Art. 340, para 2, and Art 341, para 2, and Garcia (2012), p. 90. "[T]he penalty constitutes the *minimum* level of the damages which the client can claim if there is nonperformance or delayed performance and is not dependent upon the client being able to prove loss. If the client can establish a claim for damages in excess of the penalty, therefore, he is entitled to recover these *in addition to* the penalty." Marsh (1994), p. 232.

[158] The old regime was established by Arts 1066–1070 of the former Civil Code.

[159] Statescu and Barsan (2008), p. 344.

[160] RNCC, Art 1538, para 1, reads: "The penalty clause is the one by which the parties stipulated that the debtor undertakes to pay a certain amount in case it fails to perform the main obligation." (In Romanian: "Clauza penală este aceea prin care părţile stipulează că debitorul se obligă la o anumită prestaţie în cazul neexecutării obligaţiei principale.")

[161] Statescu and Barsan (2008), p. 344, footnote 2. Also: Vasilescu (2012), p. 540.

In analyzing the legal characters of the clause, several aspects were considered to be relevant. *First*, the clause was in fact an agreement and therefore it was supposed to fully comply with the legal requirements for validity generally applicable to any agreement. At the same time, since it was viewed as an accessory convention, the validity of the main agreement was deemed an essential condition for the actual existence of the penalty clause.[162] Related to the accessory character of the penalty clause, the RNCC introduced special provisions concerning the fate of the penalty where the main obligations are divisible. Therefore, the divisibility of the main obligation will automatically attract the divisibility of the penalty, which shall be paid only by the codebtor who caused the nonperformance and solely for his part. However, if the rationale behind the penalty clause is specifically to prevent a partial payment, the abovementioned rule is not applicable.[163]

Second, its practical utility was emphasized with regard to the possibility of establishing in advance and *without addressing the court* the amount of losses, thereby removing the judicial difficulties of proving it. However, unlike its French counterparts, the Romanian courts focused more on the *limitation effect* of such clauses. It was held that if the actual loss incurred was greater than the amount stated in the penalty clause, the creditor will not be allowed to claim more than what was in the clause itself.[164] *Third*, the purpose of the clause is considered to be solely the evaluation of the loss in case of breach and not to create the possibility for the debtor to free himself of the contractual obligation by paying the clause instead of performing. Therefore, the debtor does not have a right to opt between the two, such option lying with the creditor.[165] *Last*, in order for the penalty to be payable, it must comply with all the conditions for granting damages (nonperformance must be due to the debtor, and he must have been put in default).

An important difference from the other legal systems, especially the French model, was that in principle, given that contracts were considered to be "law" for the signing parties, courts did not have the right to reduce or increase the amount agreed by the parties.[166] Courts were neither empowered to verify the actual loss incurred by the creditor nor to require him to prove the amount of actual losses.[167]

[162] RNCC, Art. 1540, para 1.

[163] See commentaries to RNCC, Art 1543, and additional details in Vasilescu (2012), pp. 541–542.

[164] Statescu and Barsan (2008), p. 345. The authors mention in this regard the Decision no. 818/R from 19.09.2003 of Brasov Court of Appeals.

[165] Two qualifications are needed. On the one hand, the creditor's right to choose between specific performance and the penalty clause appears only after the main obligation has become exigible. On the other hand, if, in case of debtor's breach, the creditor decides to resort to performance by employing a third party on the debtor's expense, the latter shall owe the actual amount of expenses incurred even if it is bigger than the amount specified in the penalty clause. For additional comments and details: Vasilescu (2012), p. 542.

[166] For a detailed analysis of the previous regime: Enache (2012), pp. 1–2.

[167] This view taken by the former Civil Code was heavily criticized by legal scholars for lagging behind reforms taken by other civilian systems such as the Italian, Swiss or French ones. See: Statescu and Barsan (2008), p. 346, footnote 4.

They were only entitled to proportionally reduce the amount of the penalty in case of partial performance. The situation was remedied and clarified by the RNCC, which allows the courts to reduce the amount either when the main obligation was partially performed and the performance benefited the creditor or when the penalty is manifestly excessive[168] in comparison to the loss that could have been foreseen by the parties at the time the contract was concluded, provided that the limit still remains higher than the actual loss.[169] The power of the court to reduce the amount of the penalty, though limited,[170] has a public policy character and cannot be conventionally removed by the parties.[171]

Notwithstanding the differences between legal systems and between civilian jurisdictions,[172] it is obvious that contracting parties benefit from the use of liquidated damages clauses, especially in those cases where the potential damages caused by any of the parties' breach would be difficult to ascertain and asses. They are also helpful because they provide protection to the contracting parties' expectation interests and benefit courts by providing them with an estimate of the damages that would occur in case of breach. However, given the extensive use of standard or adhesion contracts and the fact that bargain inequality is a huge concern nowadays, courts will continue to play an important role in the *ex post* control of liquidated damages clauses.[173] It is why those contracting parties who wish to make

---

[168] The Romanian legislature has not defined what is meant by "excessive," which leaves the task to the courts. This aspect was seen as problematic in practice if one considers the nonunitary case law of the civilian courts. Enache (2012), p. 2. The book contends such risk to be minimum. First, there is a visible tendency of the Romanian courts towards a unitary practice, under the guidance of superior forums such as the Courts of Appeals and the High Court of Cassation and Justice. Second, any legal definition of the term "excessive" would have been more problematic since circumstances and factors to be taken into consideration differ from case to case. Shifting this task to the courts is more beneficial to both parties, since it will allow them to present the peculiarities of their case.

[169] RNCC, Article 1541, paras 1 and 2: "(1) The court may not reduce the penalty unless a) the main obligation was partially performed and this performance has benefited the creditor; b) the penalty is manifestly excessive compared to the loss which could have been foreseen by the parties when the contract was concluded. (2) In the case provided by para 1, letter b) the reduced penalty must remain higher than the main obligation." One author considered these provisions to establish a clear position of the Romanian legislature in the sense that the penalty has mainly a punitive purpose. See: Enache (2012), p. 2.

[170] From the wording of RNCC, Arts 1538 and 1541, it is clear that the norm is still that the debtor owes what was specified in the agreed penalty clause, while the court's intervention is only the exception. Furthermore, the court can be confined to the analysis of the upper limit of the clause, and even here, it must make sure the reduced limit will still be higher than the actual amount of losses incurred. For a detailed analysis: Enache (2012), pp. 2–3.

[171] RNCC, Art 1541, para 3, and the commentaries of Vasilescu in Vasilescu (2012), p. 542.

[172] For a comprehensive analysis of legal provisions and the different outcomes on similar facts in case law concerning enforcement of penalty clauses in common law and civil law systems: Garcia (2012), pp. 83–95.

[173] Brandon et al. (1984), p. 916.

use of liquidated damage clauses as a self-help device should make sure they are carefully drafted and limit the possibility for abuse.

3.6 Extrajudicial Termination[174]

Termination is used in this context to describe the remedy that allows one party to release himself from his obligation to perform, due to the other party's nonperformance or defective performance, without addressing the court and in the absence of a court decision thereof. By excluding the need for judicial proceedings, this remedy falls into the broad definition of self-help to which this work is referring to. Moreover, the importance of the nonjudicial aspect is more visible in civil law jurisdictions that have adopted it and, thus, implicitly recognized the need of aggrieved creditors to be able to quickly and efficaciously exit a contractual relationship[175] without going through lengthy and expensive court proceedings.

3.6.1 The US

In the US, the doctrine of substantial performance was designed to deal with the relatively simple case where the party in breach has finished performing and the innocent party refused to pay the price because the performance was either defective or incomplete. Such disputes also appear often at a much earlier stage of

[174] As in many cases regarding comparative law, a terminology *caveat* is needed. Some of the authors covering the civilian systems use the term "rescission," although in UK law the term is referring to cases where the contract was affected from the very beginning while the US law makes use of rescission for the discharge of contractual obligations by mutual agreement. See: Peel (2011), pp. 850–851. In the US, termination is used for cases where one party ends the contract for any other reason than the other party's breach and cancellation is used for putting an end to the contract for the other party's breach. See: Klass (2012), p. 180. Obviously there is no common understanding on the usage of the terms, even though, often and mistakenly, they are used interchangeably. For the purposes of this chapter, however, "termination" is used as a general term covering situations in which the breach of one party puts an end to the contractual relationship without prior resort to judicial proceedings.

[175] Treitel identifies this as one of the three main interests of the injured party in having the termination remedy at his disposal. The other two are the fact that termination is the only remedy where failure to perform is not, in fact, a breach and that, even where failure to perform is a breach, termination might lead to better results, which are more favorable to the injured party than a monetary claim for damages in court. However, the most important remains the one that allows the aggrieved party to terminate quickly and efficiently. The classic example remains the one of a buyer who has not yet paid for defective goods and who will prefer to "terminate" (refuse the goods and refuse payment) than to perform his side of the obligations and be left to pursue a claim for damages in court. Obviously, by resorting to this self-help remedy, he will be able to avoid both the delays of litigation and the risk that the seller's credit might fail. See: Peel (2011), pp. 851–852.

performance, but the main question remains whether a breach justifies the injured party to exercise its self-help right to either withhold performance or to refuse to perform its own obligation and terminate the contract.[176] Since the self-help remedy of withholding performance was already dealt with, this section is dedicated solely to termination.

The UCC provides strong support for self-help where a party wants to terminate a contract because it believes its expectations will not be fulfilled by the other party, at least in case of sale of goods contracts. The UCC does not explicitly refer to self-help, but it authorizes innocent parties to take many actions without judicial intervention. An analysis of the UCC rules contained in Article 2 leads also to the conclusion that the legislator sought to establish a balance between the various interests involved, of both the innocent party and the breaching one.[177]

The first remedy contained in the UCC[178] refers to the *perfect tender rule*, which enables a buyer to exercise self-help in case the seller breaches. A buyer is authorized to terminate the contract for goods unilaterally when the goods or the tender of delivery are, in any way, nonconform to the contract.[179] It appears then that the UCC is authorizing this response summarily, allowing the buyer to terminate for any minor deviation from the contract's specifications. The justification behind it lies with the fact that at the time when performance is due, the seller either does not deliver or delivers nonperforming goods, thus preventing the fulfillment of the innocent party's interest. Therefore, by providing the innocent party with unilateral termination rights, the perfect tender rule allows the innocent party to satisfy its interests elsewhere.

However, this extreme right is limited,[180] since the UCC also provides the breaching party with a possibility to cure its breach. Cure allows a party to take action independently in order to remedy a breach that, in the absence of a cure, would subject that party to liability. Hence, cure mitigates the perfect tender rule by giving the breaching party an opportunity to protect its own interests and saving the contract by correcting defective performance and removing any danger or abuse and forfeiture from the innocent party's side.[181]

The UCC[182] also provides the innocent party with a posttermination remedy, namely "cover" that enables the buyer who has not received conforming goods to purchase substitute goods without the need to have a third party official confirming

---

[176] Farnsworth et al. (2001), p. 720. The authors clearly refer to termination as being a self-help remedy available to the injured party in case the other party is in breach.

[177] Taylor (1998), p. 868.

[178] UCC, Art 2-601.

[179] For details: Ferriell (2009), pp. 549–551.

[180] UCC, Art 2-508.

[181] Taylor (1998), p. 873. It is not the purpose of this chapter to go into an in-depth analysis of the right to cure and its self-help aspects. For details: Taylor (1998) pp. 874–876. Also: Ferriell (2009), pp. 550 and 563–565.

[182] UCC, Art 2-712.

that it has the right to do so. Of course, this self-help remedy is not arbitrary and must be resorted to in good faith and in a timely manner. Basically, it adds to the buyer's protection by explicitly authorizing self-help at the time of the breach. Its strength and importance lie in the fact that it is a remedy that permits immediate action.

Another interesting fact about cover is that it is a self-help remedy that needed statutory authorization since it was not provided for by the doctrines that dictated when a party is entitled to terminate its own performance under the contract.[183] Now, the innocent party benefits from a low-risk mechanism that allows it to act swiftly and, in case it is later determined that cover was not appropriate, risks only the nonrecovery of extra cost, without suffering any other ill effect.

This self-help remedy removed the uncertainty with respect to what actions an innocent party could take at the time of the other party's breach. It was thus rightfully emphasized that inclusion in the UCC marked a significant departure from the prior law, demonstrating not only the UCC's strong support for self-help[184] but also **the possibility of creating new self-help remedies where they were necessary.**

3.6.2 The UK

Termination under English law (also known as "rescission for failure to perform"[185]) describes the remedy by which one party is released from its obligation to perform because of the other party's defective or non-performance[186] and it is one of the self-help remedies mentioned by Roy Goode in his Commercial Law treatise.[187]

As in the case of any contractual issue, when termination is considered, each party is concerned with its own interests. The innocent party's interests may be grouped under three categories.[188] The *first* is where termination is the only remedy, and the other party's failure to perform is not, in fact, a breach. *Second*, in cases where failure of the other party is breach, termination might not be as favorable in monetary terms than a claim for damages. And *third*, in some cases the innocent party might, by terminating, get a quicker and more efficacious remedy (for example, in the case of defective goods that were not yet paid for).

---

[183] Taylor (1998), p. 869.

[184] Taylor (1998), p. 870.

[185] English law seems to still have debates on the rightful terminology to be used. See for example: Peel (2011), pp. 850–851, and O'Sullivan (2000), pp. 509–513.

[186] McKendrick (2010), p. 137.

[187] McKendrick (2010), p. 123.

[188] Peel (2011), pp. 851–852.

On the other side lay the interests of the breaching party, who may resist termination because it had already incurred expenses in the course of performance. Additionally, it faces a risk when it had already conferred benefits to the innocent party who may be unjustly enriched if allowed to terminate (for example, in case of construction contracts). Therefore, in order to balance these conflicting interests, courts have developed a number of rules and distinctions that will establish *prima facie* whether the right to terminate is available or not. However, even if *prima facie* it would seem that the right is available, there will be further rules that will limit or bar the right to terminate in case of certain supervening factors.[189]

An exhaustive analysis of all the rules and limitations provided by English courts with respect to the right to terminate would exceed the limits of this book. However, several points need to be mentioned. For instance, the question whether the option to terminate has been exercised was regarded as one of fact, but in reality legal requirements must be satisfied, the most important one being that the behavior of the innocent party must unequivocally indicate its intention to exercise its right to terminate. Hence, the option will commonly be exercised by giving notice to this effect to the party in breach.[190]

Similar to US law, in English law there will be no inconsistency between terminating for breach and claiming damages,[191] unless the damages would be penal.[192] With respect to the availability of the right to terminate, it is stated that failure must be substantial,[193] although exceptions are allowed.[194] As in all legal systems, parties are entitled to expressly provide in their contracts that they have a right to terminate in case of a specified failure by the other to perform, the purpose of such clauses being to prevent disputes from arising as to the difficult question whether failure to perform was substantial enough to justify termination and their advantage that they will take effect, even in the absence of such substantial failure.[195] However, courts are reluctant in giving effect to such termination clauses where it is assumed that the contracting parties did not have equal bargaining

[189] Peel (2011), p. 852.

[190] Peel (2011), p. 857.

[191] Peel (2011), p. 862. Also: Whincup (1996), p. 294.

[192] Beale et al. (2005), pp. 600–602. The authors cite *Financings Ltd v. Baldock* [1963] 2 QB 104 and *Thomas Feather & Co (Bradford) Ltd v. Keighley Corpn* (1953) 52 LGR 30. For the difference between liquidated damages and penalties, see *supra*, previous section, Liquidated Damages and Penalty Clauses.

[193] This term is interpreted to mean either that the breach deprived the party of what it had bargained for or that it frustrated his purpose of entering the contract. However, since the abovementioned factors did not prove too helpful in practice, courts have interpreted it in direct correlation to the consequences of breach, for example in case where the award of damages would not adequately compensate the innocent party. For details: Peel (2011), pp. 866–874.

[194] For example, in case of an entire obligation or, due to the English law distinction between conditions, warranties and intermediate terms, in cases of contractual terms, which are referred to as being conditions. For details: Peel (2011), pp. 874–892.

[195] Peel (2011), pp. 892–893.

powers,[196] thus giving prevalence to the trend regarding consumer as a weaker party who needs protection.

With respect to limitations imposed by English law on the right to terminate, it is mentioned that such right can be excluded by the terms of contract, but it can be lost (by affirmation or estoppel).[197] As in the case of rules of determination, a detailed analysis would be too long to have it here. One last note would be to mention here also the criticism brought to the right to terminate, especially where no prejudice occurred (where conditions were inserted in the contracts), since such clauses are seen to provide a party with the means to escape from a bad bargain.[198]

Unlike Roy Goode's Commercial Law, Treitel's Law of Contract, to which most of the references in this section were made, did not mention at any point the term self-help. However, the possibility given to the parties to either unilaterally terminate the contract for lack of performance, by simply giving notice to the party in breach, or define on their own cases and conditions in which termination right can be exercised is definitely a form of self-help. The *ex post* judicial control of whether such remedy was rightfully exercised does not change or alter in any way the nonjudicial character of termination.

3.6.3 France

Despite the Civil Code rule for judicial termination[199] and the well-known French hostility towards self-help, French law does provide for three cases in which a creditor does not need a court order in order to terminate an agreement.

The main one is to provide in the contract for an expressed right of termination, the so-called *pacte commissoire*. Such a clause is normally held valid and allows the parties to establish their own circumstances in which extrajudicial termination will take place. This self-help remedy was criticized for creating room for abuse,

---

[196] Peel (2011), pp. 894–895. With respect to standard form contracts and the right to challenge cancellation clauses under Unfair Terms in Consumer Contracts Regulations 1999, see p. 897. On the distinctions between general law termination and express contract provisions, see pp. 898–902.

[197] Peel (2011), pp. 903–918.

[198] Peel (2011), pp. 919. The author claims that in this case, legislative measures should have been implemented to mitigate the defect in the law under which the right to terminate can be exercised on unmeritorious or technical grounds.

[199] FCC, Art 1184, para 2, 2nd statement, reads: "The party towards whom the undertaking has not been fulfilled has the choice either to compel the other to fulfil the agreement when it is possible, or to request its avoidance with damages." Hence, the general understanding is that in case of breach, the creditor has two options: to address the court either to obtain specific performance (where possible) or to request termination of the contract with damages. The two options are mutually excluding. See: Whincup (1996), p. 298.

especially in those cases where the contractual parties do not enjoy the same bargaining power.[200]

For these reasons, in certain types of contracts such as insurance and tenancies, the legislature intervened either to regulate or to exclude its usage. In addition, courts took more and more a restrictive interpretation[201] and, in the absence of an express and categorical formulation, assume that the parties meant not more than a right for termination, which shall be decided on the basis of the normal, judicial procedure. Hence, careful drafting is required and parties must be explicit in their wish to exclude recourse to court[202] or the legal requirement of a prior notice before termination (*mise en demeure*).[203] In order to exercise its self-help remedy to terminate the contract without any court involvement, the creditor must also act in good faith.[204]

One second instance in which extrajudicial termination can occur is in a contract for sale of commodities or other movables, where a date is specified for the buyer to take delivery and the buyer fails to meet his obligation, in which case the seller is entitled to treat the contract as automatically terminated.[205] However, this remedy has limited effects, for it is restricted to the abovementioned contracts and cannot be extended, not even by analogy, to similar situations, despite its reasonableness and its location in the law.[206]

---

[200] Nicholas (1992), pp. 243–244. Also: Denis Tallon, Remedies, French Report in Harris and Tallon (1989), p. 271: "judicial character is so inherent in the remedy that, although it can be waived by the parties, an automatic terminating condition is regarded with suspicion by the courts and the legislator."

[201] Denis Tallon, Remedies, French Report in Harris and Tallon (1989), p. 273. Also: Marsh (1994), p. 323.

[202] Marsh (1994), pp. 179 and 323.

[203] If in English law it is generally held that in commercial contracts a time clause is regarded as a condition of the contract, the breach of which entitles the purchaser to immediately terminate the contract and seek damages, French law, by contrast, starts from the presumption that a delay in itself by a seller is not sufficient to put the seller in default. Hence, the purchaser must send a formal notice (or an equivalent) requiring performance. It is this issue of such notice (*mise en* demeure) that legally places the seller in default and entitles the purchaser to claim damages of delay from that date. However, parties may exclude this requirement by expressly stating so in their agreement. See: Marsh (1994), pp. 178–179, Nicholas (1992), p. 244, and Denis Tallon, Remedies, French Report in Harris and Tallon (1989), p. 273.

[204] Nicholas (1992), p. 244. The author also provides a list of cases in which the good faith requirement was not met. See footnotes 56–58. Also: Denis Tallon, Remedies, French Report in Harris and Tallon (1989), p. 273.

[205] FCC, Art 1657.

[206] Art 1657 is the last article of Title VI (Of Sales), Chapter V entitled: Of General Obligations of the Buyer. See: Denis Tallon, Remedies, French Report in Harris and Tallon (1989), pp. 271–272. "The case law recognizes the possibility of unilateral rescission for any contract in case of emergency, when continuation of the contract may cause irreparable harm."

The third allowed possibility for extrajudicial termination, was developed by the courts for those circumstances that appear to justify it. Examples referred to dismissal of employees for particularly gross breaches of duty,[207] but the remedy was extended also to other cases where a special relationship of trust or confidence between parties has been breached and there is an urgent need to protect the creditor's interest.[208] Although none of the cases mentioned concerns commercial obligations, the fact that the courts arrived to the conclusion that self-help may be resorted to where urgency demands it is worth mentioning. The question remains why the same need is not observed in the case of creditors with secured interests.

Similarly to the common law cases of extrajudicial termination (and where such termination is the norm),[209] the debtor is entitled to challenge the right of the creditor to act in this way, so ultimately the matter is subject to judicial control. This means that the creditor will be careful not to abuse his self-help remedy, since he will always act on his own risk,[210] but the remedy remains elastic and fast, which led to accusations of undermining the principle that termination must be ordered by the court.

3.6.4 Germany

Germany is tributary to the *pacta sunt servanda* principle in the same way as France and, as shown in the following section, Romania. However, the right to terminate a contract is deemed to be an exception from this principle since it allows the innocent party to withdraw from the contract in case the other party is in breach, without resorting to judicial proceedings. In contrast to French law, German law does not contain a requirement to obtain a court judgment in order to terminate the contract, but in order to protect the rights of the debtor, it followed the French approach in requesting a formal document to put the debtor in default.[211]

The justification of German scholars[212] was that the innocent party's objection to continue the contract is not that the contract itself is flawed but that the debtor's

---

[207] This practice was transformed into law until 2008. See the French Labor Code (Code du travail): L 122-6, 8, both repealed by Ordonnance 2007-329.

[208] Nicholas (1992), p. 245.

[209] Harris and Tallon (1989), p. 270. Denis Tallon, in Remedies, French Report states: "What distinguishes the French system most clearly from the law of most other jurisdictions (notably English law) is indeed its judicial character." Also: p. 290: "[. . .] in English law, a unilateral declaration by the creditor to this effect (rescission for breach) suffices."

[210] Denis Tallon, Remedies, French Report, Harris and Tallon (1989), p. 271.

[211] Marsh (1994), p. 339. The author's view seems to be that the main reason of serving a notice to put the debtor in default is to allow him to cure the breach and perform the contract as it was agreed, which would constitute sufficient protection against extrajudicial termination by the creditor.

[212] Markesinis et al. (2006), pp. 419–420.

performance is not forthcoming and, hence, the creditor must be released form performing his own. Seen from this perspective, the right to terminate seems to be confined to reciprocal contracts or, to use the common law terminology, bilateral contracts.

Therefore, the reason to terminate is the breach of contract and termination is a remedy for that breach. According to German law, termination is (and always was) *effected* by a declaration of will coming from the innocent party.[213] Such declaration is in fact the power of the innocent party to change, by unilateral act, the content of contractual obligations. Once the contract has been terminated, one of the consequences is that any further performance request may be refused.[214] According to the BGB, termination and damages may be combined,[215] and this was considered to be one fact that brings German law closer to its Anglo-American counterparts.[216]

The right to terminate is contained in the BGB,[217] and it entitles the innocent party to terminate the contract, without prior judicial proceedings, if the guilty party failed to perform a reciprocal obligation. Any failure to perform will constitute an objective breach. As already stated, the innocent party is required to provide the debtor with a second opportunity to perform, which consists in a reasonable period of time. Only after this period of time lapses[218] without cure from the debtor's side is the creditor entitled to go further and terminate. Even so, the right to terminate is not entirely absolute, since in case of partial performance or nonconforming performance, the breach must be reasonable and, respectively, serious.[219] But, unlike the French regime, the German one seems not to put so many obstacles in the way of an innocent party seeking release from his own performance.[220]

Termination has two main purposes: to release the innocent party from the obligation to pay the price and, as far as possible, to put matters back into the position in which they were before performance on both sides when the parties entered into their contract.[221]

In the end, the quietness of commentators with respect to the extrajudicial aspect of termination should once again be emphasized. Although it was mentioned that termination occurs by unilateral declaration by the creditor, the fact that courts are

---

213 BGB, Art 349: "Revocation is effected by declaration to the other party."

214 Markesinis et al. (2006), p. 420.

215 BGB, Art 325.

216 Markesinis et al. (2006), pp. 420–421.

217 BGB, Arts 323 and 324.

218 BGB, Art 323, para 2, establishes certain exceptions from the curing period requirement.

219 BGB, Art 323, para 5.

220 Markesinis et al. (2006), p. 422.

221 For a detailed analysis of the two effects of termination, see: Markesinis et al. (2006), pp. 432–435. However, the authors seem to focus more on the second purpose, which is the restitution of what was already performed, which exceeds the interest of this work. Also: Marsh (1994), pp. 338–339.

only involved in this only *ex post facto* is totally disregarded. That unilateral termination, as provided by the BGB, is a self-help remedy completely eludes the attention of German commentators.

3.6.5 Romania

According to the previous Civil Code, in case one of the parties of a synallagmatic contract refused to perform his obligations, the other party had several possibilities: he was entitled to withhold performance, he could ask the court for specific performance or damages and finally he was entitled to ask for the termination of the contract, with damages. Termination was seen as a sanction for breach of a synallagmatic contract, which consisted in the retroactive cancellation of the contract and the restoration of the parties to their situation they were in before the conclusion of the contract,[222] a position closer to the German one described above.

As a norm, termination for breach was only judicial, although the old regime, similarly to the French one, recognized the parties' possibility to resort to conventional termination through express contractual clauses (*pacte comisorii*). Their purpose was to derogate from the norm by reducing or excluding the role of the court in the termination of contracts. Hence, although not specifically referred to as such, they were and continue to be a veritable self-help remedy.

Romanian law recognizes four types of such clauses, each with different effects. Hence, similar to French law, their wording is very important. The *first* type merely restates the legal provision according to which in case of breach by one party the contract is terminated. However, this clause is deemed insufficient to terminate *de jure* the contract and involvement of the court is still necessary. A *second* type establishes that in case of breach, the innocent party is entitled to treat the contract as terminated. The interpretation given to this clause is that the innocent party is required to serve a unilateral termination notice to the breaching party before termination took place. The court is only entitled to ascertain that although the obligation was not performed on time, it was still performed before the termination notice was served. The *third* type states that in case of nonperformance by one party, the contract was deemed terminated at law. Here, the court cannot intervene at all, but still the innocent party is obliged to put the breaching party in default with prior notice, according to the legal requirements of Romanian law. Lastly, the *fourth* type is deemed to be the strongest and the most effective since it states that in case of nonperformance the contract is terminated at law, without putting in

[222] Such consequences made termination (in Romanian original *rezoluţiune*) similar to nullity. However, there were several important differences between the two: while in case of nullity its causes were always contemporary with the conclusion of the contract, in case of termination the cause was always posterior to the conclusion of the contract. Also, in case of nullity the contract was deemed invalid, while termination always regarded a validly concluded contract. See: Statescu and Barsan (2008), p. 88.

default and without any preliminary formalities. This last type removes completely the implication of the courts before the termination.[223]

The only party entitled to appreciate whether termination has occurred or not is the creditor who performed or declared that he is ready to perform his own obligation. However, the existence of termination clauses in the contract does not preclude him from exercising his option of seeking judicial enforcement of the contract instead of having it terminated,[224] which is a common trait of all chosen jurisdictions, underlying that these clauses are remedies at the disposal of the nonbreaching parties.

The current regime governing conventional termination maintained the distinctions described above[225] but added that, in order to produce its effects automatically (meaning, without the involvement of the judiciary), the parties must be specific about which nonperformed obligations will lead to termination, even in the absence of a prior notice.[226] A termination clause cannot be deduced or presumed, but it must be *explicit*, despite the fact that the RNCC imposed only an obligation to expressly determine the nonperformed obligations that would justify termination.

The RNCC introduced an additional remedy that could be looked upon as self-help under contract law: the unilateral termination for breach.[227] Basically, this is a unilateral and irrevocable legal act that provides for the termination of the contract, which occurs at law. From this perspective, the effects of unilateral termination occur similarly as type four of the termination clause: at law, without the court's intervention and without any other formalities.[228] However, the termination declaration takes the form of a notification sent to the debtor, and, in order to be opposable to third parties, it must be filed with the public registries (the Land Registry or the Electronic Archive of Security Interests in Movables).[229] In order to be effective, the declaration must also be sent within the statute of limitations for the action regarding termination.[230]

[223] Statescu and Barsan (2008), pp. 91–92.

[224] Statescu and Barsan (2008), p. 92.

[225] Vasilescu (2012), pp. 521–522. The author provides a detailed presentation of the termination clause with notification. In such a case, the notification must contain clearly the ultimate term in which the debtor should perform its obligation. If the debtor fails to perform even after being provided with such a term, the contract shall be deemed terminated on the basis of a mere unilateral declaration, according to RNCC, Art 1552, para 1, which must be communicated to the debtor.

[226] RNCC, Art 1553, para 1: "A termination clause takes effect if it states explicitly the obligations whose nonperformance will attract the rescission or termination at law of the contract." (In Romanian: "Pactul comisoriu produce efecte dacă prevede, în mod expres, obligaţiile a căror neexecutare atrage rezoluţiunea sau rezilierea de drept a contractului.")

[227] RNCC, Art 1552, para 1.

[228] Vasilescu (2012), p. 522.

[229] RNCC, Art 1552, para 3.

[230] RNCC, Art 1552, para 2.

The RNCC provided for three cases in which termination operates automatically on the basis of a mere unilateral declaration. The *first* case refers to the possibility of terminating the contract when the parties have agreed so. Basically, this is only an application of conventional termination for breach (*pact comisoriu*) discussed above. If the type used is without notification, the declaration of termination shall operate exactly as provided in the clause containing it, automatically and without any other formality. If the type used is with notification, it means the party wishing to declare the contract terminated must first comply with the obligation of putting the debtor in default.[231]

The *other two* cases are comprised into one category, given the fact that both require that the debtor is put in default. One commentator observed that since in these cases the declarations of termination were preceded by the putting in default, the latter procedure renders another notification before termination pointless.[232] Hence, useless formalism and the recourse to courts are avoided. If, however, the debtor will address the court after the valid issuance of the declaration of termination, the court may only ascertain that the termination has already occurred as an effect of a unilateral legal act.

Just to make things more clear, it must be stated here that the unilateral termination established by Romanian law is not to be confused with the homonymous mechanism existent in French law. The latter is only the courts' recognition—given the absence of a legal text—of the possibility to terminate a contract, notwithstanding its duration, by mere declaration of the creditor, on his own risk, in case of gross breach from the debtor. Unlike the French mechanism, the Romanian one is legislated and the conditions required for its usage differ from those established by French courts. Neither has unilateral termination anything in common with the anticipatory breach device used in common law.[233]

3.7 Conclusions: From Passive Self-Help to Active Self-Help

As this chapter illustrated, **all jurisdictions authorize self-help remedies, even if statutes do not nominate them as such and scholars do not necessarily think and speak of them as self-help remedies, especially in the civilian jurisdictions**. These self-help remedies are neither interpreted nor applied evenly. Academic commentaries in civilian jurisdictions tend to focus on legal technicalities, instead of the practicality of these remedies, which is the most important aspect of self-help. The example of German scholars who totally disregard the fact that nonjudicial remedies are a form of self-help is probably the most telling. However,

[231] Vasilescu (2012), p. 522.
[232] Vasilescu (2012), p. 523.
[233] Vasilescu (2012), p. 523.

the fact that French and recent Romanian works talk about the need to allow self-help and private justice[234] in certain cases and legal areas, due to the failure of the judiciary to offer prompt and effective remedies, supports this book's claim that there is a need for recognition and use of extrajudicial enforcement.

Taylor is obviously right when contending that "self-help needs analysis as a cohesive, unified doctrine."[235] The comparison conducted in the previous sections was meant to emphasize the need for such an approach, since despite technical differences the remedies analyzed fulfill, in great lines, the same functions. Taylor argues, for example, that UCC provisions allowing for self-help and applicable only to sales should be extended to all contracts, since they would benefit all parties concerned.[236] She also argues that self-help itself should be strengthened in order to allow contracting parties to protect their interests to their full extent.[237] Following the same line, Gergen argues that current law should focus on contract remedies that favor enforcing simple and predictable terms to protect parties from nonperformance.[238] Self-help remedies definitely fulfill this task, and therefore they should receive more focus than they do currently. This chapter shows clearly that all jurisdictions, directly or indirectly, recognize the need for such remedies. But not all of them recognize self-help remedies.

What is also clear is that *passive* self-help does play an essential part in contract law remedies.[239] Although one may think that the existence of the state with its enforcement mechanism would render self-help pointless, the reality proves otherwise. Even where there are developed laws of contracts, ensured by the state's coercion powers, contracting parties still rely on *passive* self-help techniques. The legal right to enforce a promise will never eliminate in total the insecurity associated with nonsimultaneous performances or asymmetrical exchanges.[240] The rules

---

[234] See Nicholas (1992), p. 213, Harris and Tallon (1989), pp. 244 and 287, Rizoiu (2011), p. 625, and Vasilescu (2012), p. 515.

[235] Taylor (1998), p. 907.

[236] Taylor (1998), p. 907.

[237] Taylor (1998), p. 907.

[238] Gergen (2009), p. 1449.

[239] Rubin (1995), pp. 130–131. "Behind the barrier of litigation costs, in the nonjudicial domain of contract, self-help strategies proliferate and flourish. [...] The point is that self-help makes a difference; it is an important part of contracting behavior, and one whose significance cannot be appreciated through a study of judicial decisions. [...] Self-help provisions are commonly used by contracting parties; they appear in the standard forms that circulate as models, as norms, as private law through the given industry. They have profound effects on the commercial arrangements in our society and on the way in which disputes are resolved by nonjudicial actors."

[240] Kronman (1985), pp. 24–26. "However broadly we define the class of compensable harms, any court-administered damages remedy carries with it a risk of undercompensation. No refinement of doctrine can eliminate this risk."

mentioned above allow parties to settle disputed debts or obligations outside of courts, but without preventing the former from addressing the latter.[241] An *ex post* judicial control is always there, to resort to. Therefore, the reluctance towards recognizing it is not justified. On the contrary, laws regulating it should be promoted to encourage its use and appropriate behavior. Since the use of self-help is evident, it means the state is not the only actor in play.[242] Both businessmen and consumers are in fact exercising their numerous self-help rights, privileges and remedies. However, France and Germany still ban access of secured creditors to self-help remedies when it comes to enforcement of security interests. This position is nonconsistent with the rationale and logic behind the remedies analyzed in this chapter, which are available to unsecured creditors, and it should be changed. This chapter proves to great extent that there is no incompatibility between extrajudicial remedies and legal principles applicable in civil law jurisdictions.

One last thing must be taken into account when considering the implementation of self-help remedies: **the careful examination of its desirability as a social policy, since some of the procedures used might seem dangerous and unfair and might not be equally attractive and beneficial to all segments of society,**[243] especially to weaker parties. As the analysis revealed, various legal systems recognized the need and implemented limits and exclusions in their laws with respect to the availability of self-help remedies, especially in the area of standard or adhesion contracts and where consumers are the main concern. The reason is that **contractual safeguards and the *ex post* judicial control are not always enough to insulate consumers from abuse.**

The need for additional regulation in the sense of providing enhanced legal safeguards and procedural rules with respect to employment of self-help remedies is better revealed in the case of self-help repossession—an *active* form of self-help—which constitutes the topic of the next chapter.

References

Beale HG, Bishop WD, Furmston MP (2005) Contract. Cases and materials. Oxford University Press, New York

---

[241] Gergen (2009), p. 1445. Also see: Lichtman (2004), pp. 22–23. Lichtman notices that most legal rules do not require self-help as a precondition to formal legal process and argues that the reason might be the fact that the private incentive to resort to self-help is in all cases already strong. He states that where self-help is truly the more efficient alternative, the creditors will opt for it. However, he adds, there will be exceptional instances where contracting parties will lack the adequate incentives to engage in efficient self-help and in those cases laws might cast self-help as a prerequisite to legal relief.

[242] Lichtman (2004), p. 12. "[. . .] the existence of a plausible self-help remedy poses a challenge to the government's claim that direct intervention is required. But [. . .] absence of a plausible self-help mechanism is taken to be an argument in favor of direct government regulation."

[243] Black and Baumgartner (1987), p. 41.

Berendt GE, Cochran RA, Long DE, Nye RJ, Scheid JH (2007) Contract law and practice. Lexis Nexis, United States
Black D, Baumgartner MP (1987) On self-help in modern society. Dialect Anthropol 12:33
Brandon DI, Cooper ML, Greshin JH, Harris AL, Head JM Jr, Jacques KR, Wiggins L (1984) Special Project. Self-help: extrajudicial rights, privileges and remedies in contemporary American society. Vanderbilt Law Rev 37:845
Brizzee D (1991) Liquidated damages and the penalty rule: a reassessment. Brigham Young Univ Law Rev 1991
Cotton S (1999) Remedies for breach of contract. In: Practical law PLC magazine. Thomson Reuters (Professional) UK Limited, London
Dolly C (2000) The electronic self-help provisions of UCITA: a virtual repo man? John Marshall Law Rev 33:663
Drake HH (1905) Consideration v. Causa in Roman-American Law. Michigan Law Rev 4
Enache E-M (2012) Reductibilitatea clauzei penale (The reduction of the penalty clause), www.juridice.ro. Available at http://www.juridice.ro/198931/reductibilitatea-clauzei-penale.html
Farnsworth EA, Young WF, Sanger C (2001) Contracts. Foundation Press, New York
Ferriell J (2009) Contracts. Lexis Nexis, United States
Friedman JM (1981) Contract remedies in a nutshell. West Publishing Co., St. Paul
G. G. W. (1859) Right of stoppage in transitu. Am Law Regist (1852–1891) 7:577
Garcia IM (2012) Enforcement of penalty clauses in civil and common law: a puzzle to be solved by the contracting parties. Eur J Leg Stud 5:98
Garner BA (2009) Black's law dictionary. WEST, US
Gergen MP (2009) A theory of self-help remedies in contract. Boston Univ Law Rev 89:1397
Harris D, Tallon T (1989) Contract law today. Anglo-French comparisons. Clarendon Press, Oxford
Hillman RA (1990) Contract modification and "self-help specific performance": a reaction to Professor Narasimhan. Cornell Law Fac Publ 62:62
Klass G (2012) Contract law in the United States. Wolters Kluwer Law & Business, The Netherlands
Kronman AT (1985) Contract law and the state of nature. J Law Econ Organ 1:5
Lichtman D (2004) How the law responds to self-help. The Chicago Working Paper Series 1
Lorenzen EG (1919) Causa and consideration in the law of contracts. Yale Law J XXVIII:621
Markesinis SB, Unberath H, Johnston A (2006) The German law of contract. A comparative treatise. Hart Publishing, Oxford and Portland, Oregon
Marsh PDV (1994) Comparative contract law: England, France, Germany. Gower Publishing, Hampshire
McKendrick E (2010) Goode on commercial law. Penguin Books, London
Narasimhan S (1987) Modification: the self-help specific performance remedy. Yale Law J 97:61
Nicholas B (1992) The French law of contract. Oxford University Press, New York
O'Sullivan J (2000) Rescission as a self-help remedy: a critical analysis. Cambridge Law J 59:509
Peel E (2011) The law of contract. Sweet & Maxwell, London
Rizoiu R (2011) Garantiile reale imobiliare. O abordare functionala – Analiza economica a dreptului garantiilor reale – Introducere in regimul juridic al ipotecilor mobiliare. Universul Juridic, Bucharest
Rubin EL (1995) Symposium: the nonjudicial life of contract: beyond the shadow of the law. Northwest Univ Law Rev 90:107
Statescu C, Barsan C (2008) Drept civil. Teoria generala a obligatiilor (Civil law. General theory of obligations). Editura Hamangiu, Bucuresti (Bucharest)
Tajti T (2013a) Post-1990 secured transaction law reforms in Central and Eastern Europe. Szegedi Közjegyzői Közlöny II:1
Tajti T (2013b) Systemic and topical mapping of the relationship of the draft common frame of reference and arbitration. Kazimieras Simonavicius University, Vilnius
Taylor CR (1998) Self-help in contract law: an exploration and proposal. Wake Forest Law Rev 33

Vasilescu P (2012) Drept civil. Obligatii – in reglementarea Noului Cod Civil (Civil law. Obligations – in the light of the New Civil Code). Hamangiu, Bucuresti

Whincup MH (1996) Contract law and practice. The English system and continental comparisons. Kluwer Law International, The Hague

Yergin D (2012) The prize. Simon & Schuster UK Ltd, London

Chapter 4
Active Self-Help: Self-Help Repossession, Administrative Receivership, Private Disposition of Collateral and Strict Foreclosure

If the previous chapter dealt with *passive self-help* remedies[1] and showed that they are not only compatible with all legal systems analyzed, but also heavily relied upon in contract law, this chapter focuses on *active self-help* remedies and will prove that they are also compatible with civilian systems. When analyzing *passive help-help*, the book considered the ways in which creditors try to ensure, by means of contract, that they will be paid. But despite contractual covenants and the pressure they pose, these means do not guarantee payment. Events, both dependable and nondependable on the debtors' will, could affect their possibility of making payments in accordance with the contract.

As pointed out by Grant Gilmore, one of the fathers of UCC Article 9 and its leading commentator, in the US, once default occurs, the initiative lies with the creditor, because in case of default he is the aggrieved party. The creditor has the right to sue the debtor for judgment, take out execution and have a levy on the debtor's assets on the basis of such judgment, followed by a judicial sale.[2] This is the general way of action, available to all types of creditors, secured or unsecured, in all jurisdictions covered. **But in the US, the UK and Romania, those who have taken the precaution of securing the transaction**—secured creditors or secured parties—**enjoy the additional possibility of resorting to private enforcement by taking the collateral into their possession**[3] (if they do not have it in their hands already), **sell it and apply the proceeds to the debt and then sue for any deficiency** (if necessary). **Getting the possession may be acquired (where the law so allows) either by private means, without a legal process or support of public organs, or by bringing an action in replevin** (or similar action).[4] Since the

---

[1] Rizoiu (2011), p. 581.

[2] Gilmore (1999), p. 1189.

[3] In this regard, American terminology uses "repossession," while the UK one uses "recaption"; hence, for the purposes of this work, the two terms are used interchangeably.

[4] Gilmore (1999), p. 1190.

C.G. Stănescu, *Self-Help, Private Debt Collection and the Concomitant Risks*,
DOI 10.1007/978-3-319-21503-7_4

US has been used as the benchmark for the purposes of this work, all comparative analyses in this chapter refer back to the provisions of American law.

Once in possession, creditors must decide what to do with the collateral—depending on the security agreement and the provisions of the law—keep it for themselves in full or partial discharge of the debt or dispose of it (typically by private or public sale) and file for deficiency (if the sale did not cover the debt and ancillary expenses). At this point, creditors' rights collide with the rights of the debtors[5] to have certain formalities complied with (prior notice, time, place or manner of sale, proper distribution of proceeds and return of any surplus). All this time, the debtors play a waiting game[6] with the hope that the creditors will make some mistake, which would trigger the legal protections and bring some relief to the debtors' situation.

Repossession of intangible goods[7] is also possible where the secured creditor takes possession of the debtor's accounts, but that constitutes the object of the following chapter, so it will not be addressed here. Those involved in the recovery of debts, including those specialized in repossessions (who must comply with the "without breach of peace" standard), might also have to comply in certain situations with the Fair Debt Collection Practices regulations, but this obligation is addressed in the next chapter as well.

Despite the fact that what has been described above on default commonly occurs everywhere, the rights and obligations of both creditors and debtors vary from one jurisdiction to another, depending on the policies that govern the legal safeguards and the attitude towards access to credit in general. Hence, a comparative analysis of such rights and obligations is needed in order to understand what lessons could be learned in terms of efficiency. The comparison is useful for the civil law jurisdictions not having upgraded their laws established by old civil codes or codes of civil procedure, which need reforms in order to adapt to the requirements of modern credit markets.

Since the topic of the book is nonjudicial means of recovery, this chapter will not discuss the option to bring suit for a debt judgment, neither judicial enforcement nor repossession by court action, despite that such alternatives are available in all jurisdictions covered. The focus of this chapter is solely on extrajudicial remedies available to secured creditors—self-help repossession and administrative receivership—as they are the only category of creditors who enjoy the right to use self-help means in repossessing the collateral or administering the business and the assets of the debtor. The chapter analyzes the legal requirements for self-help repossession

[5] Nowka (2009), p. 241.

[6] Gilmore (1999), p. 1190.

[7] Without being settled, there is even a discussion concerning the availability of self-help repossession with respect to licensed software or other copyright-protected digital content. However, most authors claim that self-help repossession should not be allowed (or should be allowed restrictively) in case of software since the losses caused are higher than the value of the disputed software. For details: Roditti (1995), pp. 452–459; Cohen (1998), pp. 1103–1119; Gitter (1993), pp. 416–420.

and administrative receivership and the issue of constitutionality of private repossession and briefly touches upon the aftermath of repossession (private sales and strict foreclosure[8]), thus proving that there is no incompatibility in resorting to such remedies in civilian systems, as long as the adequate legal safeguards and consumer protection regulations are in place.[9]

4.1 Self-Help Repossession

Repossession, as defined by the 2004 edition of Black's Law Dictionary, consists in "any act or instance of retaking property,"[10] and throughout history it allowed individuals to regain possession of their property without resorting to a formal judicial process. **In time, repossession became the most powerful self-remedy available to secured creditors in the US, in the UK and, recently, in Romania**, whose secured transaction law is based on the US model. Therefore, this section is dedicated solely to repossession through self-help and its legal requirements. Since France and Germany do not allow for repossession without judicial control, they will only be mentioned where similar institutions were identified for the purposes of the comparison. A similar solution was used in the case of strict foreclosure, which is not recognized in the UK.

4.1.1 Creditor's Options upon Debtor's Default. Election of Remedies Doctrine

Upon debtor's default, the creditor's right to repossess is triggered.[11] Therefore, the creditor is now facing a choice with respect to the measures and paths to follow in order to recover his debt. In the US, under UCC Article 9, he has the option of

[8] UCC, Section 9-620. From the wording of the Section and the Official Comment, it is clear that strict foreclosure is a procedure by which the secured party acquires the debtor's interest in the collateral without the need for a sale or other disposition upon default. In such cases, repossession will only be necessary where the secured creditor is not in possession of the collateral, but it is also a precondition of strict foreclosure, for the creditor must be in possession before acceptance. According to Comment 7 to Section 9.620, if the collateral is consumer goods, strict foreclosure occurs only when the creditor is in possession. The American Law Institute National Conference of Commissioners on Uniform State Laws (2009), p. 107.

[9] Tajti (2013), p. 13. Also: Tajti (2012), p. 117.

[10] McRobert (2012), p. 569.

[11] 17, (Inalta Curte de Casatie si Justitie, Completul de 9 Judecatori) In Decision 3/2003, the court held: "The realization of a security interest is done by taking into possession the collateral." The court also acknowledged the right of the secured party to choose private enforcement over judicial one.

attempting a workout under the threat of repossession and, if unsuccessful, he may place additional pressure on the debtor by actually repossessing the goods that he may either keep in realization of the debt (strict foreclosure) or sell. But he also has the option to ignore repossession and bring suit, obtain a judgment and seek execution through judicial process.[12] Any attempts of the debtor or other lien creditors or third party purchasers to oppose possession of collateral to the secured creditor might be liable for conversion, under tort law.[13]

Similar options are available in the UK, where in order to seize the goods, the creditor may attempt recaption of collateral or simply bring action in tort, once the debtor's possession of the goods becomes adverse to the creditor's rights.[14] The same position was taken by the Romanian law after the modernization of its STL and maintained by the RNCC,[15] both of them inspired by UCC Article 9.

4.1.1.1 Election of Remedies Doctrine in the US

In order to understand one of the revolutionary reforms brought by the UCC, it must be mentioned that under pre-UCC law, in the US, the creditor was subjected to the *election of remedies* doctrine, which meant that once a path was chosen, the other one was automatically waived and thus no longer unavailable.[16] The extraordinary innovation of the UCC was therefore to state[17] that the creditor's rights and options were now cumulative (as well as his duties[18]) and could be exercised simultaneously (but not both at the same time, which would amount to harassment)[19] or combined (repossession by judicial process and sale by Article 9 rules).[20] The other breakthrough provision was to allow the creditor to sell the collateral in a private sale, but this will be addressed in the next section.

---

[12] In some cases, where the value of the collateral has decreased and it is obvious that court action will be sought for deficiency, the creditor might prefer addressing directly the court, which will save him not only money and time but also the risk of an unlawful repossession or a suit for commercially unreasonable disposition of collateral. Evidently, the creditor will choose how to act depending on the actual circumstances and information he holds in each case. See: White and Summers (2010), p. 1331.

[13] For a detailed analysis of conversion claims faced by lien creditors or third party purchasers of collateral: Hayes (2006), pp. 734–739.

[14] Macleod (2007), p. 807. For a detailed description of the doctrine and its application in US law: *Cumulative Remedies Under Article 9 of the Uniform Commercial Code: An Answer to Fuentes v. Shevin at* http://scholarship.law.wm.edu/wmlr/vol14/iss1/8, pp. 217–222.

[15] Rizoiu (2009), p. 4/36.

[16] White and Summers (2010), p. 1332.

[17] UCC, Section 9-601 (c).

[18] Rusch and Sepinuck (2010), p. 141.

[19] Official Comment 5 to UCC, Section 9-601, The American Law Institute National Conference of Commissioners on Uniform State Laws (2009), p. 1045. Also: White and Summers (2010), p. 1332.

[20] Rusch and Sepinuck (2010), p. 140.

4.1.1.2 Election of Remedies Doctrine in the UK, France and Germany

The election of remedies doctrine is still existent in the UK.[21] This places the creditor in an inferior position compared to his US counterpart, by limiting his options and forcing him to choose between private and judicial enforcement.

Given the fact that France[22] and Germany[23] do not recognize self-help repossession, there cannot be any discussion on the election between self-help repossession and judicial repossession in these jurisdictions. The sole notable exception will be the possibility of strict foreclosure in France or the repossession of aircraft in Germany, with the debtor's consent, which will be discussed *infra*, Sect. 4.4.

4.1.1.3 Election of Remedies Doctrine in Romania

Romanian law, as opposed to UK or German law, took over the American position towards the election of remedies doctrine.[24] It enabled creditors to resort to any enforcement solution they deemed fit, without facing the risk of opting for one path and thus be precluded from turning to the other in case the first one did not provide the expected results.

To conclude, when dealing with Article 9 remedies given to secured creditors,[25] one should take a look first at what the UCC tried to achieve. The policies behind the revised provisions of UCC Article 9 allow upon debtor's default, on the one hand, to obtain possession of collateral with *minimum* resort to judicial proceedings and, on the other hand, encourage higher yields upon disposition of collateral by allowing *private* sales as well as public sales.[26]

With respect to the policies behind the STL, the Romanian doctrine went even further and stated that **once default has occurred, the party in an unprivileged situation and requiring protection is the creditor as he already complied with his obligation and now needs the debtor to comply with his.**[27] The creditor will be limited though in his wish to buy the collateral through a private sale.[28] Obviously, the absence of similar policies and options for the creditors in Germany and France, as well as the maintenance of the *election of remedies* doctrine in the

[21] Ramsay (2012), p. 484.

[22] Dahan and Simpson (2008), p. 270.

[23] Franklin and Harms (2010), p. 131; and Tajti (2002), p. 274.

[24] Rizoiu (2009), p. 7/36.

[25] Repossession is available *only* to secured parties who formed a security interest according to the legal provisions of the UCC. See McRobert (2012), p. 570.

[26] Kieninger (2004), p. 79.

[27] Rizoiu (2009), p. 7/36.

[28] Art. 73, Title 6, of Law 99/1999 concerning measures for accelerating the economic reform provides that the creditor cannot adjudicate the collateral in a private sale that he organized without allowing first participation of third parties, unless otherwise agreed with the debtor.

UK, places the creditors in these jurisdictions in a weaker position than their counterparts in the US or even Romania, by confining them to the lengthy and costly judicial proceedings.

4.1.2 Taking Possession of Collateral

According to UCC Article 9 and RNCC, self-help repossession consists in taking possession or rendering the collateral unusable or disposing of it on the debtor's premises without a judicial process.[29]

4.1.2.1 Common Aspects

In exercising this right, the US creditor must make sure that the entire process takes place without *breach of peace*,[30] while the Romanian counterpart needs, *besides the without breach of peace* standard, to also ensure that such possibility is *expressly allowed*[31] by the security agreement. Otherwise, the creditor faces liability for his failure to observe the abovementioned rules.[32] As was underlined, self-help repossession is "desirable from the secured party's point of view because it provides a quick and economical means of obtaining the collateral."[33]

The position of UK commentators is not very different. While characterizing the self-help repossession remedy, Roy Goode underlined that in exercising his right the creditor "must take the greatest care not to commit any of the numerous offences that lie in store for him" and concluded that "where the exercise of the right to self-help involves the use of violence against the person or property of another, it ceases to operate."[34]

A concurring view was expressed by the Romanian law and doctrine.[35] The rights of the creditor are not unlimited and the fact that the law has basically delegated some of the coercive powers of the state to him should make him very careful not to act outside the statutory boundaries. Under the first reformed RSTL, repossession was allowed *only* for nonpossessory secured creditors and for leasing companies, deemed to have retained ownership under suspensive condition. The creditor was entitled to retake the collateral from any person, including junior

[29] UCC Section 9-609 and RNCC, Art 2435 corroborated with Art 2439.

[30] UCC, Section 9-609. For details: White and Summers (2007), p. 218.

[31] RNCC, Art 2440 and the comment in Colectiv (2012), p. 873.

[32] White and Summers (2007), p. 219. For Romania, RNCC, Art. 2475, Para 1.

[33] Duncan et al. (2012), (Rel. 29), pp. 5–17.

[34] Goode (1999), Issue 26/IE/3053.

[35] Rizoiu (2009), p. 12/36.

creditors who repossessed as well.[36] Repossession was to be conducted personally, through a representative or through a third party professional, a collection agency. No prior notice or authorization was required under the old regime, no fees similar to those required by judicial enforcement needed to be paid.[37] The creditor was allowed to retake the collateral by private means without breach of public order, without physical violence or any other means of intimidating the debtor and without any act that might constrain the debtor in the moment of the repossession.[38]

4.1.2.2 The Sacrosanct Formula: Protection of Debtors Under Former Romanian Secured Transactions Law

With respect to *express consent*, the former RSTL contained a peculiarity: the consent was *not only express* but had to be given *in a specifically described form*—a statutory phrase written in capital letters, of a certain font size.[39] Furthermore, given probably the novelty of the institution, the law made the formula mandatory even for nonconsumer contracts, providing equal status to both consumers and traders, who were deemed equally uninformed[40] and unprotected, unlike the US where such protective measures are provided solely for consumers.[41]

The sacrosanct formula was dropped though by the implementation of the RNCC, and it was considered that dropping it is a proof of maturity of the law, an implied statement of the Romanian legislator that the accommodation period with this self-help remedy has ended, and legal subjects are sufficiently familiarized with it.[42]

4.1.2.3 Taking Over the Collateral Under the Romanian New Civil Code

In characterizing the implementation of an Article-9-based STL in Romania, Radu Rizoiu underlined that the Romanian law found "a middle way" between the right

---

[36] Rizoiu (2009), p. 15/36.

[37] RSTL, Art. 63 (1). By taxes or tariffs, the law understood mandatory taxes or tariffs similar to those imposed by judicial foreclosure. Fees paid to third parties involved in the repossession were not covered by this provision.

[38] Rizoiu (2008), p. 6/8.

[39] RSTL, Art 63 (4).

[40] The doctrine criticized harshly the mandatory formula arguing, among others, that it is a step back, since commercial agreements under the former Commercial Code were supposed to be less formalistic; it is a rigid measure because it does not allow the parties to formulate their own. The parties were allowed though to define the procedure as long as it complied with the statutory requirements. See: Rizoiu (2009), pp. 31–32/36.

[41] Rizoiu (2009), p. 30/36.

[42] Rizoiu (2011), p. 623.

of the creditors to get private enforcement (more efficient) and ensuring a good protection of debtor's rights. Therefore, the law ensures that what the creditor can do is take a *pre-emptive* possession of the collateral while no property rights are affected.[43]

The new regime introduced by the RNCC makes no more reference to prior authorizations, taxes and fees but requires the creditor to serve notice, through a judicial enforcement officer, to the debtor thereof.[44] The creditor is still not allowed to "breach the public order"—which is the Romanian equivalent of the US no "breach of peace" standard or recourse to any direct or indirect means of constraint, even if such means do not amount to a criminal offense. Any contractual clause that would limit these obligations would be invalid. The Romanian legislator has dropped the former attempt of the STRL to classify (but not clarify) what may constitute a breach and resorted to a type of open definition, more similar to its UCC model.[45]

These modifications seem to emphasize that according to the legislators, **Romanian debtors and creditors have reached a level of maturity that allows them to deal in full knowledge with means of private enforcement**, i.e. self-help repossession. However, **the lack of case law and scarce literature as well as legislative developments should not be construed in the sense that no problems exist in practice.** On the contrary, they seem to suggest more that creditors still rely on judicial enforcement, less risky and more familiar to Romanian practitioners, and reality might be less bright than it looks on paper.

4.1.3 The Issue of Constitutionality and Human Rights Violations

In both the US and Romania, self-help repossession was subjected to a constitutionality control. However, the reasons were not entirely similar. In the US, the concern was twofold: on the one hand, an apparent violation of the 14th Amendment, given the fact that debtors were deprived of their property without due process (absence of prior notice and hearing), and on the other hand the issue of significant state involvement, which would amount to a violation of due process, based on the fact that self-help repossession was explicitly authorized by state statutes.

In Romania, the main issue regarded the compatibility of self-help with the legal system in place. Since self-help repossession is an exception from the civil law principle that no one is allowed to do justice on their own and the realization of justice is an attribute of the state's organs, **private enforcement meant that certain attributes of the state were "transferred" to secured creditors, which**

---

[43] Rizoiu (2009), p. 15/36.

[44] RNCC, Art. 2440.

[45] Rizoiu (2009), p. 21/36.

required a legislative consecration.[46] However, Romania did not encounter a constitutional challenge strictly on the issue of self-help repossession as it was the case in the US, but on a particular provision of the previous Code of Civil Procedure related to the possibility of enforcing a title without resort to judicial process.

4.1.3.1 Constitutional Control in the US

Coming back to the issue of constitutionality of self-help repossession in the US, taking over someone's property without judicial involvement raised the question whether self-help repossession is in accordance with the Constitution's requirement for due process. Under the 14th Amendment, a state is not allowed to deprive a person of property without due process, which requires at a minimum to notify the person on the proposed taking and to give that person an opportunity to be heard, unless certain stringent circumstances justify such action to be performed *ex parte*. Such possibilities create obvious risks for the debtor. A mistaken or malicious party could cause serious disruptions to a debtor's business by wrongfully or abusively taking possession—a situation that could be prevented if the debtor would receive a prior notice and be given an opportunity to be heard before the actual repossession.[47] Thus, since the due process requirements apply even in the absence of direct action from the state,[48] debtors raised the issue of constitutionality in courts, with various outcomes.

4.1.3.1.1 Only Deprivations of Property Conducted by the State Could Violate Due Process

An example of partial success is the decision in *Fuentes v. Shevin*,[49] in which the court held that replevin statutes of Florida and Pennsylvania were unconstitutional because they allowed a prejudgment seizure of a debtor's property without prior notice and hearing.[50] The decision makes sense because although the property was

---

[46] Rizoiu (2011), p. 582.

[47] Horvathova et al. (2011), p. 89.

[48] Duncan et al. (2012), (Rel. 29) 5-17.

[49] *Fuentes v. Shevin*, 407 US 67, 92 S. Ct. 1983, 32 L.Ed.2d 556 (1972), cited in Duncan et al. (2012), (Rel. 29) 5-17. See also the analysis in Symposium on Commercial Law (1973), pp. 443–445, and the point-by-point analysis in Brodsky (1974), pp. 296–297. The case became relevant due to the fact that an action in replevin to repossess collateral under a conditional sales agreement is very closely related to the self-help remedy permitted by the UCC. For a discussion concerning cases that followed *Fuentes v. Shevin* and a summary of the requirements of due process: TeSelle and Love (1977), pp. 256–260.

[50] For a detailed analysis, with history and legal implications: McDonnell (1973). Also: Symposium on Commercial Law (1973), pp 441–443. For a call of reform of self-help repossession law, based on the outcome of *Fuentes*: McDonald (1972), p. 540, and the following. The author argues

seized for the benefit of creditors and not the state, the writ of replevin was issued by the judiciary and the actual repossession was accomplished by representatives of the state. Therefore, there was sufficient state action involved to successfully invoke the safeguards of the 14th Amendment.

Fuentes was used by majority of lower courts to invalidate state statutes that allowed provisional seizure without notice or hearing, which affected state's procedures concerning the writ of sequestration. As a result, the US Supreme Court overruled the standard of procedural due process applied in Fuentes and, in *Mitchell v. W.T. Grant Co*,[51] it returned to the rule that where only property rights are involved, postponement of judicial review does not necessarily violate the right to due process and recognized the creditor's strong interest in protecting the property from any action the debtor might take against that interest.[52]

A similar outcome to Fuentes, but this time concerning self-help repossession itself, was reached in *Adams v. Egley*,[53] where it was held that self-help provisions of Section 9-503 of the California Commercial Code were unconstitutional, unless the presence of extraordinary circumstances could justify the deprivation of the debtor of his property.[54] The real outcome of these challenges at US states' level was the observation of the fact that the 14th Amendment only ensured protection against deprivations of property conducted by the state, which *per a contrario* meant that **a private repossession conducted by the secured creditor was not violating the due process requirements.**[55]

that the most important outcome of *Fuentes* is that debtors in default should be provided with a notice and an opportunity to be heard "at a meaningful time," where meaningful time is understood as "before the property is repossessed" (p. 560).

[51] *Mitchell v. W.T. Grant Co.*, 94 S. Ct. 1895 (1974).

[52] For a detailed analysis of Mitchel and the way it departed from Fuentes, Guidry (1974), pp. 225–229.

[53] 338 F. Supp. 614 (S.D. Cal. 1972).

[54] Symposium on Commercial Law (1973), pp 446–448. However, the case focused more on the efficacy of waivers found in usual consumer agreements, the majority of the judges criticizing previous decisions that upheld waivers of due process in security agreements. It was reversed in *Adam v. Southern California First National Bank*, but the decision cited *D.H. Overmyer Co. v. Frick*, 405 U.S. 174 (1972), to confirm the proposition that in certain instances, summary repossession, without notice and an opportunity for a hearing, may be unconscionable and void as a matter of public policy. See: *"Self-Help" Repossession and Due Process* (1974), p. 674. The decision was discussed and harshly criticized for creating adverse economic implications for all borrowers and affecting lower income groups even more severely. See: McAnally (1973), pp. 710–712 and 723–725.

[55] King and Cook (1996), p. 56. The authors, citing *Arcoten v. Peters*, 829 F.2d 671 (8th Cir. 1987), show: "The court noted that had Arcoren's lender been private, it clearly would have been entitled to repossess without notice or hearing."

4.1.3.1.2 Statutory Authorization of Self-Help Repossession Does Not Amount to State Action

Debtors, however, tried to convince the courts that the secured creditor's remedy ought to be treated as state action.[56] Hence, they have argued that state action was present since self-help repossession was statutorily authorized,[57] which converted it into a governmental function. The great majority of the courts held that Section 9-609 is constitutional[58] unless the state's involvement was "significant"[59] and

[56] Following *Fuentes*, six decisions have declared self-help repossession under 9-503 to be state action. Three of them were overturned by courts of appeals. However, three survived: *Michel v. Rex-Noreco, Inc., Boland v. Essex County Bank & Trust Co., Watson v. Branch County Bank.* For details see Del Duca (1974), pp. 216–217.

[57] H. (1973), p. 585. On same case, see discussion at Brodsky (1974), pp. 299–300. Brodsky also mentions the eighth Circuit Court of Appeal's Decision in *Bichel Optical Laboratories, Inc v. Marquette National Bank*, which held that the prejudgment self-help remedies authorized in Minnesota's Commercial Code did not significantly involve the state in the self-help process (pp. 300–301).

[58] Laswell (1974), pp. 98–100. The four circuit courts that have considered the issue have found that the states were merely regulating the contractual right to repossess and as such were lending only their passive support, but they were not *requiring* the use of the self-help remedy. Hence, they concluded that no significant state action was involved and the cases were dismissed for failing to make a federal cause of action. However, district courts did not reach the same consensus on whether a state's enactment of the UCC constitutes significant state action or not. Those that found that there was no significant state action relied on the fact that secured creditors are acting independently, under their contracts, and not under color of state law. Therefore, it was not the arm of the state that acted directly against an individual's property and depriving him of it without notice and hearing but rather an individual. Those that have found that the enactment of the self-help repossession provisions by the states encouraged and involved the states in private repossessions thought it constituted sufficient action to raise a federal question. However, the latter position was dropped after the decision rendered in *Mitchell v. W.T. Grant Co.* (42 U.S.L.W. 4671 (U.s. May 14, 1974). On the position of federal Court of Appeals as well as a discussion on the district courts' decisions finding sufficient state action in Article 9 and an analysis of *Mitchel*: Buckley Jr (1976), pp. 167–169. Also: H. (1973), p. 587, mainly footnote 9, for an extensive list of cases where state and federal courts have disagreed with the contention according to which explicit authorization by state statutes of self-help repossession constitutes sufficient state involvement to be a violation of 14th Amendment. The author also discusses in detail *Adam v. First National Bank* (9th Cir., Oct 4, 1973), where the Court of Appeals held that "where private individuals employ self-help based on a contractual agreement and without explicit aid, from the state there is no significant state involvement by reason of state allowing such action." Similarly, in *King v. South Jersey Nat'l Bank*, the court held that self-help repossession was a contracting matter rather than state action and therefore immune from constitutional challenge, despite a dissenting opinion. See: T. (1975), pp. 177–178. Relatively recent, the Louisiana Supreme Court reached the same outcome in *Price v. U-Haul Co.*, 745 So 2d 593, 594 (La 1999), where it held that self-help repossession did not violate the Federal Constitution. See: Hamilton (2000), p. 2241.

[59] See the decision in *Boland v. Essex County Bank and Trust Co.*, where the court stated that the statute created an election of remedies that was unavailable under the common law and, hence, the expansion of the common law remedy involved the state to such a significant degree that it became state action, at Buckley (1976), p. 168. For contrary outcomes, see *Adam v. First National Bank*, at H. (1973), p. 589; and Del Duca (1974), pp. 217–219. Also see *James v. Pinnix* (495 F.2d 206 (5th

amounted to "affirmative conduct."[60] The attempt of shifting from federal constitutional law to state constitutional law on grounds of due process violations was not more successful.[61] It was also claimed that, in case the US Supreme Court would ever rule on the constitutionality of self-help repossession, there is no reason to believe that it would reverse the decisions of the Circuit Courts.[62] Hence, the constitutionality of self-help repossession in the US seems to be settled.

What seemed to make a difference were the self-help repossession attempts with the assistance of law enforcement personnel.[63] Courts reached opposite conclusions

---

Cir. 1974), cited and discussed at McRae (1974), p. 1421, where the fifth Circuit Court of Appeals held that the state of Mississippi did not significantly involve itself in self-help repossession actions taken by the creditor. Similar outcome was reached in *Northside Motors, Inc v. Brinkley*, 282 So 2d 617 (Fla. 1973), discussed at Smith (1973), pp. 231–232, and in *Price v. U-Haul Co*, 745 So 2d 593, 594 (La 1999), where the Louisiana Supreme Court noted that "the state did not encourage or benefit from private action authorized by the Act and that the Act did not compel U-Haul's action" and "private enforcement of possessory liens was justified by avoiding expenses that would otherwise be incurred in judicial recovery of debt." Hence, by applying the "state encouragement theory" and "public function concept," the court determined that the state's enactment of the Act was not itself state action. See: Hamilton (2000), p. 2243. A discussion on the rejection of three theories of state action—partnership, encouragement and traditional state—and relevant cases are to be found also in "Self-Help" repossession and due process (1974), pp. 668–675.

[60] *King v. South Jersey Nat'l Bank,* at T. (1975), p. 178.

[61] In *King v. South Jersey Nat'l Bank,* the court found that Section 9-503 was not invalid under the Constitution of New Jersey. The court relied on the notion that only those absolute rights that were part of common law when the constitution was enacted are protected by the courts. Therefore, even if the property right of the debtor was fundamental, by contract the secured party was granted a property interest in the collateral, and these interests of both debtor and creditor needed to be balanced. See: T. (1975), p. 178. Also: TeSelle and Love (1977), pp. 291–293, citing and discussing several state courts' decisions in which constitutionality of self-help repossession was upheld: *Benschoter v. First National Bank of Lawrence* (218 Kan. 144, 542 P.2d 1042 (1975), *Borg-Warner Acceptance Corp. v. Scott*, 86 Wash. 2d 276, 543 P.2d 638 (1975), *HiU v. Michigan Nat'l Bank,* 58 Mich. App. 430, 228 N.W.2d 407 (1975), and *Helfinstine v. Martin*, 48 OxLA. B.A.J. 668 (Mar. 19, 1977). For a detailed list of federal and state court cases dealing with the issue of constitutionality: Duncan et al. (2012) (Rel. 29) 5-17, footnote 12. For a case with a different outcome, see same source, footnote 13.

[62] Brodsky (1974), pp. 301–302. The author substantiates his position by relying and restating the arguments of James J. White with respect to the benefits of self-help repossession. For a different opinion: Buckley Jr (1976), p. 170. The author contends that Section 9-503 does not meet the substantive due process tests of the Supreme Court, despite the fact that most Courts of Appeals have upheld the Code provision. Since more than 30 years have passed and the Supreme Court has not ruled against self-help repossession, this opinion can only be mentioned in the footnote.

[63] Debtors tried to expand the concept of state action to include private conduct under circumstances of significant state involvement. The four theories on which the debtors relied were as follows: (1) that the involvement of the police in repossession activities constituted concerted action between state and private parties, (2) that private parties were performing a public function in repossession property because seizure of property was traditionally done by state officials, (3) that the extensive regulation of the activities surrounding consumer financing and motor vehicle resale and certification constituted significant state involvement and (4) that the enactment of Section 9-503 amounted to significant action because it authorized and encouraged creditors to

on the matter. While the New Mexico Supreme Court held that "as a matter of law, repossession conducted on an Air Force base with the assistance of an armed security police sergeant was unconstitutional even though the sergeant accompanied the repossessor in accordance with the policy of the Air Force base to protect the repossessor,"[64] the New Jersey Superior court reached the opposite conclusion in a case that involved a constable who assisted a self-help repossession, holding that "although the constable was a state actor, the secured creditor's right [. . .] is not state granted. Thus, the involvement of the constable, without more, did not violate the debtor's due process rights."[65]

The threshold is not only the actual involvement of the state actor but the way his presence is perceived at the moment of the actual repossession. But as some authors have pointed out, the focus on whether self-help involves sufficient action to invoke due process protection "really obscures the underlying question of whether, as a matter of public policy, repossession ought to be in the exclusive domain of the state."[66] Therefore, the presence of a police officer at the time of repossession has better chances to be considered breach of peace[67] than actual state involvement, as it is shown *infra*, Sect. 4.1.4.3.

---

make use of self-help repossession. As already stated, the overwhelming majority of courts did not find these arguments persuasive. T. (1975), pp. 182–183. For a case in which the District Court argued that "when a statute or even a common law custom allows an individual to unilaterally transcend the fundamental and inalienable level of equality incident to all dealings between people in this country, that statute is clothing the individual with a power which can only truly be consistent with the state. It is this power given an individual by the state, that constitutes 'state action,'" see the discussion on *Gibbs v. Titelman,* 369 F. Supp. 38 (E.D. Pa. 1973) at Del Duca (1974), pp. 219–223. It should be noted though that the District Court's decision was overruled by the Court of Appeals. See also *Oller v. Bank of America*, 342 F. Supp. At 21, where the court stated that "the requirement of 'state action' can rarely be satisfied when the action is taken by one not a state official," cited and discussed by McAnally (1973), pp. 712–713.

[64] *Waisner v. Jones*, 107 N.M. 260, 755 P.2d 598 (1988), cited in Duncan et al. (2012) (Rel. 29) 5-18 and footnote 14. On the issue of constitutional provisions and their convergence with self-help repossession: Laswell (1974), pp. 108–109.

[65] *Santa Barbara, Inc. v. Heart of Cedar Lane*, Inc., 226 N.J. Super. 509, 545 A. 2d 180, *cert. denied and appeal dismissed sub nom. Priovolos v. Heart of Cedar Lane*, Inc. 109 S. Ct. 485 (1988) cited in Duncan et al. (2012) (Rel. 29) 5-18. For an extensive list of similar decisions, see same source, footnote 16. The position of Justice Pashman, dissenting in *King v. South Jersey Nat'l Bank*, was that the cooperation between the police and creditors constitutes state action in those cases where creditors keep the police apprised of their repossession activities to avoid being arrested as car thieves. T. (1975), p. 179. The author provides a list of cases where the police accompanied the repossessor and helped him, directly or indirectly, to repossess the car, at same page, footnote 29.

[66] Duncan et al. (2012) (Rel. 33), 5-19.

[67] UCC, Section 9-609, Official Comment 3 states: "This section does not authorize a secured party who repossesses without judicial process to utilize the assistance of a law-enforcement officer. [A] repossessing party's use of a law enforcement officer without benefit of judicial process constitute[s] a failure to comply with former Section 9-503." The American Law Institute National Conference of Commissioners on Uniform State Laws (2009), p. 1054.

4.1.3.2 Constitutional Control in the UK and the Issue of Human Rights Violation

In the UK, the issue of constitutionality was not raised, but it was contended that even peaceful reentry may infringe human rights. This, together with the foregoing legal difficulties arising from repossessions, has led to the flourish of repossession agents, although their use might give rise to vicarious criminal liability as well.[68] However, no case of the European Court of Human Rights has yet touched upon the matter of due process with respect to the area of secured transactions.[69]

4.1.3.3 Constitutional Control in Romania

With respect to the compatibility of self-help repossession with Romanian constitutional law, the doctrine took the position that it is "fully compatible."[70] However, at the time when this opinion was expressed, there was yet no decision to touch on the matter of due process in private enforcement. But a few months later, the Constitutional Court has rendered a decision on a provision of the previous Code of Civil Procedure, which raised the issue of what would have been the actual outcome of a constitutional plea against private enforcement in Romania:[71]

> [T]he foreclosure should not be viewed unilaterally, only from the perspective of the creditor and its rights, but also from the perspective of the debtor, who must be protected and have those guarantees that characterize the right to a fair trial, by removing any possibilities of abuse and possible abusing approaches. Giving access to court - by ensuring the possibility of challenging the acts of an execution which was contrary to law - is not always a sufficient remedy provided to the person against whom the execution procedure was started in an unlawful manner. It is necessary to have a procedural guarantee for the debtor to prevent any abuse from the creditor and the judicial control of the commencement of enforcement proceedings also constituted an adequate and effective guarantee of the right to a fair trial for all parties involved in this procedure.[72]

To summarize, the Constitutional Court decided that discarding courts' approval in execution procedure is in fact a violation of due process, exactly the opposite of what their peers from the US said.

The issue remained open until the RNCC was adopted and implemented in 2011. Although maintaining the US model, the new regime established the obligation of the creditor who wishes to dispose of the repossessed collateral to first ask for the approval of the court, thus bringing the new legal provisions in line with the decision of the Constitutional Court. The mandatory notification, prior to the

[68] Macleod (2007), p. 809.

[69] Rizoiu (2011), p. 583.

[70] Rizoiu (2009), p. 13/36.

[71] For a detailed discussion, see: Horvathova et al. (2011), pp. 103–104.

[72] Decision no 458/2009 of the Constitutional Court of Romania, published in the Official Gazette no 256/17.04.2009.

exercise of self-help repossession, plays a similar role in defending the rights of the defaulting debtor. In this way, one can conclude that the private enforcement procedure established by the RNCC adequately protects the procedural rights of the debtor and is, thus, fully compatible with the Romanian constitutional law without impeaching on the strategic rights of secured creditors.

4.1.4 The No "Breach of the Peace" Standard

As mentioned before, revised Section 9-609 of the UCC authorized self-help repossession or rendering the collateral unusable[73] without the involvement of courts, provided it could be done without "breach of peace." However, neither the previous nor the current version of the UCC defined the concept of *breach of peace*, but they left it to be developed by courts, during their *ex post facto* control. For these reasons, despite that the number of decisions dealing with it in the US is "legion," they are not entirely consistent,[74] causing even today considerable uncertainty.

A classic understanding of breach of peace defines it as "a violation of public order, a disturbance of the public tranquility, by an act or conduct inciting to violence or tending to provoke or excite others to break the peace [. . .] including any violation of any law enacted to preserve peace and good order."[75]

In the US, given the lack of a statutory definition for breach of peace, courts have opted, in a large majority, for a case-by-case approach, taking into account the specific factual circumstances.[76] Only a minor group of courts have adopted tests to determine whether breach of peace occurred in the course of repossession.[77] Therefore, to ease the understanding of what constitutes breach of peace, cases must be categorized on the basis of the factors that determine or might determine

[73] The former Section 9-503 on self-help repossession did not provide for this possibility. White and Summers (2010), p. 1335.

[74] Rusch and Sepinuck (2010), p. 143. McRobert (2012), p. 578; Martin (2013), *at* http://papers.ssrn.com/sol3/papers.cfm?abstract_id=2331708, p. 3; and Braucher (1997), pp. 566–591.

[75] Lloyd and Kuney (2008), p. 196.

[76] McRobert (2012), p. 580. The author criticizes this approach because, by analyzing each case individually and creating new factors and rules, courts fail to give adequate guidance for future determination of breach of peace.

[77] White and Summers (2010), p. 1336. In summarizing the pre-Code cases, they mention that courts inquire mainly into "(1) whether there was an entry by the creditor upon the debtor's premises and (2) whether the debtor or someone acting on his behalf consented (or objected) to the entry and repossession." However, recent cases (*Clarin v. Minn Repossessors*, 198 F 3d 661, 664 (8th Cir. 1999); *Giles v. First va. Credit Serv.*, 560 S.E. 2d 557, 565 (N.C. Ct. App. 2002); *Davenport v. Chrysler Credit Corp.*, 818 S.W. 2d 23, 29 (Tenn. Ct. Appl. 1991), brought up more factors to be considered: "1) where the repossession took place; 2) the debtor's express or constructive consent; the reaction of third parties; 4) the type of premises entered; and the creditor's use of deception." For details: McRobert (2012), p. 579.

breach: use or threat of violence, trespass, use of law enforcement officers, verbal confrontation and disturbance to third parties. As the following discussion will point out, if some factors are clear-cut and courts have reached a consensus, i.e. use of physical violence, others are quite hard to determine and courts' decisions are still inconsistent. Such situation can defeat the very purpose of the UCC Article 9.[78]

Things are not much different in the UK or Romania. The lack of a statutory definition raised serious issues with respect to the application of the breach of peace standard by Romanian courts since, unlike their common law counterparts, civilian courts can only interpret law, not make it,[79] and are not usually bound by precedents.[80] Hence, Romanian courts enjoy less freedom in developing the law regarding the breach of peace standard, which is why Romanian academia sought for alternative solutions in statutory definitions of breach of public order, offered by criminal law.

4.1.4.1 Use or Threat of Violence

The use of violence against the debtor or debtor's property would most likely be perceived as an automatic breach of peace. However, where there is only a threat of violence, courts are not on the same page anymore since not every kind of threat would suffice.

4.1.4.1.1 Use or Threat of Violence in the US

US courts are consistent on the issue of use of violence, and no case has held that an act of violence did not amount to breach of peace in the course of self-help repossession. However, the situation is different with respect to what kind of threat of violence would constitute breach of peace.

In *Salisbury Livestock Co. v. Colo. Cent. Union*,[81] it was held, for example, that in order for the threat to constitute breach of peace, violence must be "reasonably likely" and not just a "remote possibility," but without defining any of the two mentioned terms.[82] Since the uncertainty is high, creditors either resort to professional repossessors, despite the fact that they would still be liable for any breach of peace caused by the latter, or try to recapture the goods by avoiding confrontation with debtors.

---

[78] McRobert (2012), p. 587.

[79] Rizoiu (2009), p. 21/36.

[80] The sole exceptions are the Guidance Decisions for the unitary application of the law of the High Court of Cassation and Justice, Art 517, Para 4 of New Code of Civil Procedure.

[81] *Salisbury Livestock Co. v. Colo. Cent. Union,* 793 P. 2d 470, 474 n. 3 (1990).

[82] McRobert (2012), p. 582.

4.1.4.1.2 Use or Threat of Violence in the UK

With respect to use of force, the English courts have taken the position that in case the debtor fails to pay and return the goods to the creditor upon his request, the owner is entitled to use *reasonable* force to recapture them. Only unreasonable force would amount to a breach of peace and would attract even criminal liability for assault.[83]

Since uncertainty lies over what constitutes "reasonable force," creditors or repossessors try to avoid confrontation by conducting repossession in the early hours (especially when the goods repossessed are motor vehicles) or resorting to experienced and specialized agencies. However, as it is the case in the US, resorting to professional repossessors does not insulate the secured creditor from liability towards the debtor for wrongful repossession,[84] so the major advantage in hiring a third party repossessor lies with their expertise, which allows secured parties to assume that the likelihood of breaching the peace is smaller.

4.1.4.1.3 Use or Threat of Violence in Romania

Similar to the US and the UK, Romanian law, both in its former secured transactions regime and the current one, bans any use of force and violence during repossession efforts, be it physical or verbal, against the debtor. Additionally, any illegitimate threat to use force, inflicting a real fear to the debtor for his own, his relatives' or good's safety, could invalidate repossession no matter whether it was direct or indirect and took place contemporarily or before the actual repossession. The doctrine made a valid point that the banned use of violence must be *an action* (such as the act of grabbing or pulling the goods from the debtor's arms). The passive form, involved in defending the collateral *after* a successful (and legal) repossession, would not attract any form of liability, be it civil or criminal.[85]

However, Romanian law does not specifically provide for the situations where the secured creditor hires a third party repossessor. One may only speculate, on the basis of general civil law principles, that if the third party acts as an agent of the secured creditor, then the latter will be held liable for any damages caused by the agent on his behalf. Unfortunately, **Romanian law does not provide for any licensing system for professional repossessors, which makes it really hard to distinguish crooks from genuine professionals.** This legislative gap is therefore

[83] Macleod (2007), p. 809.

[84] UCC, Section 9-609, Official Comment 3, "[C]ourts should hold the secured party responsible for the actions of others taken on the secured party's behalf, including independent contractors engaged by the secured party to take possession of collateral." The American Law Institute National Conference of Commissioners on Uniform State Laws (2009), p. 1054.

[85] Rizoiu (2009), p. 26/36.

detrimental to both secured creditors and debtors, for general principles of private law do not provide an adequate protection to either of the two categories involved.

4.1.4.2 Trespass

Cases involving trespassing are widely litigated and cover numerous unique facts that led to divergent solutions. An important question related to trespass is whether consent given by the debtor, either prior or at the time of repossession, may insulate the creditor or the repossessor from liability. Additionally, it is important to determine who gave the consent and if such consent is opposable to the debtor.

4.1.4.2.1 The Issue of Consent

Generally, in the US, the creditor is not allowed to enter the debtor's home or garage in the absence of the debtor's consent, freely given,[86] *at the time* of the entry (or *near to it*),[87] since any *a priori* consent to the breach of peace standard or its alteration would be voided on the ground that the rule is one of public policy.[88] Clearly, where the repossessor is unable to collect the collateral without serious trespass,[89] the lender must resort to judicial action or wait until the debtor brings the collateral to a more public place.[90]

The issue of consent requires more attention due to the peculiarities of the other chosen jurisdictions. For example, under UK law, any of the statutory limitations of repossession can be overwritten by obtaining consent *at the time* of the repossession, coming either from the debtor or from the person in occupation or control of

[86] White and Summers (2010), p. 1336; Martin (2013), p. 7; McRobert (2012), p. 582. White and Summers mention *Girard v. Anderson,* 257 N.W. 400, 402–403 (Iowa 1934), as the most articulate and forceful statement of the rule that entry into the debtor's residence in the absence of the debtor is a breach of peace, even if the debtor admitted that the door was unlocked at the time of the creditor's entry. Martin mentions *Pantoja-Cahue v. Ford Motor Credit Co.* 872 N.E. 2d 1039 (III App. Ct. 2007), where the court held that where a repossession takes place by actually breaking into the debtor's premises or by breaching or cutting chains, gates, barricades, doors or any kind of barriers designed to exclude trespassers, the likelihood for breach of peace is high. Lastly, McRobert mentions *Girard* as well and adds a list of similar cases in footnote 123: *Evers-Jordan Furniture Co v. Hartzog,* 187 So 491, 493 (Ala. 1939); *Girard v. Anderson*; *Hileman v. Harter Bank & Trust Co.*, 186 N.E 2d 853, 855 (Ohio 1962).

[87] White and Summers (2010), p. 1337. The authors mention that with respect to debtor's consent, even an oral one would suffice.

[88] White and Summers (2007), p. 221. Also: Martin (2013), p. 5.

[89] There is no legal distinction between serious and light trespass. Hence, whether trespass has occurred and it is deemed "serious" enough to constitute breach of peace is fact specific and is determined on a case-by-case basis.

[90] Martin (2013), p. 7.

the premises.[91] Despite the fact that Germany does not generally allow self-help repossession, this remedy might be permissible in the case of aircraft lease, provided that the lessee cooperates.[92] Most likely, the lessee's cooperation is in fact his consent to the repossession, at the time when it takes place. Absence of the lessee's consent, however, immediately requires the creditor to resort to judicial proceedings; otherwise, he faces criminal liability.[93]

Under Romanian law, consent *at the time* of repossession is not required, since it is presumed to be given *ex ante* as a mandatory legal requirement for the legality of the repossession.[94] However, obtaining consent at the time of the repossession can only be beneficial to the creditor and spare him of any issues that might arise later.[95] Of course, in order to be valid, consent has to come from either the spouse or a relative of the debtor, who can express a valid consent. Therefore, consent given by underaged persons or those lacking legal capacity would be void, while in the case of a legal person, consent must come either from a legal representative or from a person exercising a certain degree of control over the collateral (such as a night security officer).[96]

Similarly to what was mentioned in the case of use or threat of violence, hiring a third party repossessor will not insulate the secured creditor from liability for breach of peace, neither in the US nor in the UK[97] or Romania.[98] It is safe to assume that even in the absence of liability under repossession statutes, liability may be incurred under general tort law.

However, returning to the issue of trespass, some qualifications of the abovementioned situation need to be made by taking into account additional factors such as proximity to the debtor's household and the debtor's efforts to protect the repossessed property and possible creditor deceit in procuring consent.

---

[91] Guest et al. (2009), p. 2091.

[92] Tajti (2013), p. 134.

[93] Tajti (2013), p. 134.

[94] Rizoiu (2009), p. 32/36. See: RNCC, Art. 2440, requiring for expressed consent to self-help repossession in the contract between the secured creditor and the debtor.

[95] Rizoiu (2011), p. 617.

[96] Rizoiu (2009), p. 33/36.

[97] Official Comment 3 to UCC Rev Section 9-609 (1999), cited in Duncan et al. (2012) (Rel. 35) 5-23. Also: Rusch and Sepinuck (2010), p. 151. In the UK, the Administration of Justice Act 1970 extends any offense committed during debt collection to "any person 'who concerts with others in taking such action...' notwithstanding that his own course of conduct does not by itself amount to harassment." See Macleod (2007), p. 809; and Martin (2013), p. 6.

[98] Under Romanian law, the creditor would be liable in tort for *culpa in eligendo*. See Rizoiu (2009), p. 15/36.

4.1.4.2.2 Trespass in the US

In the US, if entry into the debtor's house may be automatically construed as breach of peace, moving away from the residence to the yard, driveway or street, the debtor's argument weakens.[99] Cases are even more inconsistent where the creditor did not trespass into the debtor's home but disregarded express measures taken by the debtor to protect his property, such as breaking a lock or a chain, in order to enter.

In most cases,[100] it was held that such actions constitute breach of peace. However, on several occasions[101] it was held that, where the entry occurred by using a key obtained without authorization or by cutting locks or where the creditor ignored the "no trespassing" sign of the debtor,[102] there was no breach of peace.

---

[99] White and Summers (2010), p. 1336. The authors mention that they have found no case in which the repossession of an automobile from a driveway or a public street (absent any other circumstances, such as debtor objection) constituted breach of peace in itself, and, in footnote 4, they provide a list of examples in which courts upheld such a repossession: repossession of car from driveway at 5 AM (*Ragde v. Peoples Bank*, 53 Wash App. 173, 767 P.2d, 949, 7 UCC 2d 1314 (1989)); repossession of vehicles not visible from public place when repossessed from a secluded years, on an isolated ranch (*Salisbury Livestock Co. v. Colorado Central Credit Union,* 793 P. 2d 470, 12, UCC2d 894 (Wyo. 1990)). Salisbury is also discussed in Picker et al. (2002), pp. 310–317. The previous authors' position is confirmed and strengthened by McRobert, who claims that no reported decision has held that mere trespassing onto debtor's property, without entering the home, constitutes breach of peace. He also offers an extensive list of such cases at footnote 128: no breach of peace where secured creditor made an unauthorized entry onto driveway of debtor's residence to remove vehicle (*Butler v. Ford Motor Credit Co.*, 829 F.2d 568, 570 (5th Cir. 1987)); simply going upon the private driveway of the debtor and taking possession of secured collateral is not breach of peace (*Hester v. Bandy,* 627 So. 2d 833, 840 (Miss. 1993)). See: McRobert (2012), p. 583. Several other cases (*Chrysler Credit Corp v. Koontz*, 661 N.E. 2d 1171 (III App. Ct. 1996) and *Oakloan Bank v. Baldwin*, 709 S.W. 2d 91 (Ark. 1986)) where no breach of peace occurred, although the lender had entered the debtor's premises, but encountered no barriers, are found at Martin (2013), p. 7, footnote 38.

[100] McRobert (2012), p. 583, footnote 130. The author mentions that cutting chains connected to a lock is breach of peace (*Martin v. Dorn Equip. Co.* 821 P.2d 1025, 1026–1028 (Mont. 1991)) and so is cutting the gate's chain without permission (*Williamson v. Fowler Toyota, Inc.*, 956 P.2d 858, 859, 862 (Okla. 1998)) or entering a garage and cutting chains that attached car to post in garage to repossess the car (*Davenport v. Chrysler Credit Corp,* 818 S.W. 2d23, 26, 29–30 (Tenn. Ct. App. 1991)). See also *Pantoja-Cahue v. Ford Motor Credit Co.* 872 N.E. 2d 1039 (III App. Ct. 2007) cited and discussed by Martin (2013), p. 7.

[101] McRobert (2012), p. 583, footnote 131. All mentioned cases are from New York: *Global casting Indus., Inc. v. Daley-Hodkin Corp.*, 432 N.Y.S. 2d 453, 456 (N.Y. Sup. Ct. 1980); *Cherno v. Bank of Babylon*, 282 N.Y.S. 2d 114, 120 (N.Y. Sup. Ct. 1967), *aff'd*, 288 N.Y.S. 2d 862 (N.Y. App. Div. 1968).

[102] See: *Chrysler Fin. Co. v. Flynn,* 88 S.W. 3d 142, 147–152 (Mo. Ct. App. 2002).

4.1.4.2.3 Trespass in the UK

The question was raised in the UK as well, and since the common law was uncertain, agreements usually provided the creditor with a license to enter the debtor's land and seize the good, though nowadays such a provision is prohibited by law.[103] However, the creditor can obtain the debtor's expressed permission to enter premises, at the time of the entry. The license, unless unfair, insulated the creditor from liability for trespassing, if only reasonable force was used, which is a major advantage for the UK creditors compared to their US counterparts, who are not allowed to use force in the course of repossession. Since the term reasonable force is not defined by law but determined on a case-by-case basis, a certain degree of caution is still advisable.

Entry to recapture on the basis of the same license can, however, amount to a criminal offense.[104] As for what "premises" are, it is presumed that the term connotes the land to which the public does not have access as of right and extends to car ports and private driveways, whether or not occupied by the debtor,[105] and caravan sites and it is contended that the term does not require the existence of a building structure.[106] In this regard, it is obvious that the protections offered to the debtor under UK law are more extensive than their US counterparts, where repossession of goods from a driveway might have a chance to stand if no breach of peace occurred.

4.1.4.2.4 Trespass in Romania

Given the increased protection and broader meaning of the requirement not to breach "public order," it appears that the Romanian law raises the possibility that a repossession conducted in a public space (such as public parking space or the side of a public street) might constitute a breach if it causes public outrage or scandal,[107] which would hardly be the case in the US or the UK. Of course, these breaching acts should take place *at the time* of the repossession and should occur in public in order to impeach the retaking; otherwise, although they might amount to criminal liability, they would bear no effect on repossession.

---

[103] Although common, such provisions were avoided by the Hire Purchase Act 1938 in some hire purchase agreements. This protection was extended by the CCA to include conditional sales and simple hirings. Section 92(1) of the CCA provides that "except under an order of the court, the creditor shall not be entitled to enter any premises to take possession of goods subject to a regulated hire purchase agreement, regulated conditional sale agreement or regulated consumer hire agreement." See: Macleod (2007), p. 821.

[104] Violent entry without consent or a court order may be an offense under s6 (as amended) of the Criminal Law Act 1977. See Macleod (2007), p. 809.

[105] Macleod (2007), p. 821.

[106] For a detailed discussion supported by relevant court cases, see: Guest et al. (2009), p. 2091.

[107] Rizoiu (2009), p. 22/36. Any breach of public order that occurs after the repossession, even if it involves a repossessed good, would not bear any effects on the repossession itself.

4.1.4.3 Use of Law Enforcement Officers

At first glance, impersonating an officer would most definitely be considered breach of peace in the US,[108] since it contradicts the extrajudicial aspect of a self-help remedy. Having a real police officer present would not help either,[109] despite a few dissenting opinions.[110] Official Comment 3 to UCC Section 9-609 specifically indicated that the use of law enforcement during self-help repossession equals to breach of peace. However, given the nonbinding effect of the Commentary, courts have varied in their interpretation of the statutory provision.[111]

Variations were generated mainly by the two ways in which creditors relied on law enforcement to the effect of self-help repossession: the officer *helped* with the repossession itself—which clearly constituted breach of peace[112]—or the officer was merely present to provide *passive protection* for the creditor and *deter* potential violence—in which cases courts reached inconsistent and contradictory conclusions.[113]

Impersonating a law enforcement officer would also be sanctionable in the US under the FDCPA,[114] while in the UK it would fall under the provisions of the Administration of Justice Act 1970[115] and in Romania would constitute a criminal

[108] White and Summers (2010), p. 1337.

[109] Walker v. Walthall, 588 P.2d 863 (Ariz. Ct. App. 1978), cited by Lloyd and Kuney (2008), p. 206. The court held: "the introduction of law enforcement officers in self-help repossession, regardless of the degree of participation or non-participation, in the actual events would constitute state action, thereby invalidating repossession without a proper notice or hearing."

[110] White and Summers (2007), p. 220. Putting the case law under a question mark the authors express their doubts, which seem correct, at least from a logical point of view: "[W]hy is it wrong for a person who is entitled to possession to take along a "peace officer" to insure that it gets possession "peacefully"?" For an elaborate recent study and criticism of the consequences of involvement of law officers in repossession: Loterstein (2013), pp. 1365–1372.

[111] *Pride Hyundai, Inc. v. Chrysler Fin. Co.*, 369 F 3d 603, 613 (1st Cir. 2004) and *Smith v. First Union Nat'l Bank of Tenn.*, 958 S.W. 2d 113, 116 (Tenn. Ct. App. 1997), where it was held that secured parties are not allowed to use the assistance of law enforcement personnel to accomplish self-help repossession, cited by McRobert (2012), p. 577, footnote 75.

[112] *Harris v. City of Rosenburg*, 664 F. 2d 1121, 1127 (9th Cir. 1981); *Jackson v. Richards*, 433 A.2d 888, 895–896, n. 11 (Pa. Super. Ct. 1981); *Stone Mach. Co. v. Kessler*, 1 Wash. App. 750, 757, 463 P. 2d 651, 655 (1970). In the latter case, it was held that even an officer's verbal assistance amounts to constructive force, intimidation and oppression, which constitutes breach of peace. McRobert (2012), pp. 580–581; and Picker et al. (2002), pp. 322–326.

[113] *Walker v. Walthall*, 588 P.2d 863 (Ariz. 1978), where the court decided that the mere presence of a uniformed deputy sheriff at the site of repossession constituted a breach of peace. Similar view was adopted in *United States v. Coleman*, 628 F.2d 961 (6th Cir. 1980), but the court refused to extend it to mere surveillance by the officers. Basically, in the mentioned case, the police officer remained around the corner from the location of the repossession and was out of sight of the debtor.

[114] See *infra*, Chap. 6, Sect. 6.2.3.3.1.

[115] Falsely representing himself to be authorized in some official capacity to claim or enforce payment or uttering a document falsely represented by him to have some official character or

act.[116] With respect to the use of law enforcement, in Romania the regime implemented by the former RSTL was very clear and resumed the majority position of the US courts deciding on the matter: in the retake process of the collateral, the creditor may not be assisted by a public or police officer.[117] Self-help repossession was thus statutorily incompatible with the use of public enforcement. Such provision obviously reduced the amount of debate over the matter.[118] Unfortunately, the provision was not maintained by the provisions of the RNCC, so the topic is now relevant for Romanian practitioners as well.

4.1.4.4 Verbal Confrontation

According to White and Summers,[119] the debtor's opposition, however slight and even if merely oral, would normally make any entry or seizure a breach of peace. The logic behind his argument is that the law should not make a debtor physically confront a repossessor in order to be able to claim a breach of peace. Obviously, if the law would require physical confrontation, then it would be encouraging antisocial behavior and violence against the repossessor. Despite such arguments, US courts have not reached a consistent position with respect to the legal effect of debtor's verbal objection to self-help repossession, some of them holding that any verbal opposition, however minor, would amount to breach of peace,[120] while others have required a higher level of protest.[121] In the case of the latter, the main idea was that the nature of the objection suggested that there was no likelihood to

purporting to have some official character is unlawful harassment and is criminally liable. Macleod (2007), pp. 809–810.

[116] Art. 241 of the New Romanian Criminal Code, sanctioning the illegal use of official uniforms or insignia. The liability will be incurred by the person actually impersonating a law enforcement officer and not by the creditor, unless it is the creditor himself who made use of official uniforms or insignia.

[117] RSTL, Art 63 (3).

[118] Given the silence of the law, the doctrine asked what would be the outcome if the police officer is the creditor or what if he does not reveal he is a police officer or what if he is simply present, without getting involved or "actively assisting" the creditor. Rizoiu (2009), p. 27/36.

[119] White and Summers (2010), p. 1337.

[120] *Marcus v. McCollum*, 394 F.3d 13, 820 (10th Cir. 2004), where the court determined that any debtor's request for secured creditor to stop constitutes breach of peace, and *Hollibush v. Ford Motor Credit Co.*, 508 N.W. 2d 449, 451–453 (Wis. Ct. App. 1993), where the court held that the debtor's protest to repossessing agent "You are not going to take the Bronco" was enough to constitute breach of peace.

[121] *Dixon v. Ford Motor credit Co.*, 391 N.E. 2d 493, 497 (Ill Ct. App. 1979), where the court required "an unequivocal oral protest," or *First & Farmers Bank, Inc. v. Henderson*, 763 S.W.2d 137, 140 (Ky. Ct. App. 1988), where the court required "repossession in the face of debtor's objection."

lead to a physical confrontation,[122] which, as pointed out earlier, would constitute an automatic breach of peace. Cases or academic debates concerning verbal confrontation as breach of peace were not identified in the UK or Romania, thus it would be hard to speculate on the outcome in these jurisdictions.

4.1.4.5 Disturbance of Third Parties

The practice of American courts[123] with respect to disturbances caused to third parties has been consistent in the sense that such disturbance does not constitute breach of peace, despite recent criticism calling for a change.[124] The reason behind these positions seems to be the principle according to which breach of peace can

---

[122] McRobert (2012), p. 584. The author refers to *Chrysler Credit Corp v. Koontz*, 661 N.E.2d 1171, 1173–1174 (Ill. Ct. App. 1996), where the court found no breach of peace where the debtor yelled "Don't take it" to the secured creditor attempting to repossess his car. To find so, the court defined breach of peace as "a conduct which incites or is likely to incite to immediate public turbulence." Given the fact that the repossessor made no physical or verbal response to the debtor's request and the debtor did not act in a violent either, the court reasoned there was not breach of peace. A similar reasoning was used in *Williams v. Ford Motor Credit Co.*, 674 F.2d 717, 720 (8th Cir. 1982), where the court found no breach of peace where repossessor completed the repossession after the debtor interrupted and was allowed to recover personal items from the car. The court held that there was no evidence to reveal that the repossessors have performed any act that was oppressive, threatening or tended to cause physical violence. However, the dissenting opinion makes a good argument to the contrary and should be mentioned here.

[123] In *Chapa v. Tracier & Associates*, 267 S.W. 3d 386 (Tex. Ct. App. 2008), the court refused to find breach of peace where harm to third parties has occurred during a self-help repossession. In the mentioned case, the secured creditor's repossession agent repossessed a car from a public street, during the absence of the driver. However, the repossessor failed to observe the fact that in the backseat of the car were the debtor's two young children. When he finally realized that fact, the repossessor returned the children and the vehicle to the mother. Surprisingly, the court found no breach of peace, for the reason that at the time of the repossession no objection was expressed. Any harm done, after the repossession has taken place, was not considered. Therefore, the harm done to the children, to the mother and her brother, who was present and was later diagnosed with post-traumatic stress disorder due to this event, was totally disregarded. Similarly, in *Jordan v. Citizens & Southern National Bank of South Carolina*, 298 S>E. 2d 213, 214 (S.C 1982), where, after the debtor's truck has been repossessed and the debtor engaged in a pursuit of the creditor, in another vehicle, for up to 30 min, resulting in repossessor's reckless driving and endangerment of public safety, the court found no breach of peace. McRobert (2012), pp. 585–586. See also the discussion on *Smith v. AFS acceptance, LLC*, 77 U.C.C. Rep. Serv. 2d 794 (N.D. III. June 1, 2012), and *Thompson v. Gateway Fin. Servs.*, 2012 U.S. Dist. LEXIS 169377 (N.D. III. Nov. 29, 2012) at Martin (2013), pp. 4–5. In the former case, where the vehicle was repossessed although the debtor and her daughter were inside, with the doors opened, and both of them, together with the neighbors, were shouting at the repossessors, the court held that only the debtor's claims were allowed, but not those of the daughter's, for the simple reason that the daughter was not a debtor for the purposes of the statutory requirements of Section 9-609. In the latter case, the court held that the debtor's child and car passenger did not have standing to bring claims under Section 9-609 after the vehicle repossessor frightened them and caused the diabetic passenger to urinate on himself.

[124] McRobert (2012), p. 593. Also see: Martin (2013), pp. 4 and 7.

only stem from the interactions between debtors and creditors at the time of the repossession, such as violence, verbal confrontation or trespass. According to this principle, any harm or threatened harm to third parties immediately following the repossession does not amount to breach of peace.[125] However, this position should be changed, since it does not consider the effect that the disturbance caused to a third party can have on the debtor, like in the case of *Chapa v. Tracier and Associates*,[126] where the repossessor repossessed the car while the two young children of the debtor were inside, thus creating enormous distress to the debtor and the debtor's family.

In Romania, the result is different due to the usage of the term "public order," which was interpreted by the leading scholar in the field as having a broader meaning than the US "breach of peace" standard.[127] This led to a peculiar result: the protection awarded by the Romanian law, seems to give more emphasis to protecting the social *status quo*. This means that the creditor's rights are to prevail *only* over the defaulting debtor but not over the society's or community's interests. Hence, it is possible to have a breach of peace *even if* the debtor was not involved.[128]

4.1.5 Restrictions on Self-Help Repossession

In the US, the UCC did not impose any restrictions on who can resort to self-help repossession, as long as they comply with the without "breach of peace" standard. Despite the fact that US law, similar to UK law, recognizes the equity interest acquired by the debtor in the collateral (the 60 % rule), it did not impose any ban on repossession of such consumer goods, but merely on the possibility of the creditor to strict foreclose on them.[129] On the contrary, repossession was made generally available to all secured creditors, thus expanding its application.[130]

According to UK law, in case of a sale on credit the property passes on delivery (and the creditor will be treated as an unsecured creditor), while in case of a hiring agreement, the supplier retains the entire property interest (which will make him also a secured creditor).[131] In between these two options are the conditional sales and the hire purchase agreements, under which the value of the supplier's interest

[125] The assumption seems to be that the creditor's obligations regarding breach of peace under Section 9-609 cease when the repossession is completed. See Martin (2013), p. 5.

[126] For details and other similar cases, *supra* footnote 123.

[127] The doctrine underlined that "public order" is a fluctuating concept regarding the essential social interests of the state and local communities. See: Rizoiu (2009), p. 24/36.

[128] Rizoiu (2009), p. 22/36.

[129] UCC, Section 9-620, e).

[130] McRobert (2012), p. 577.

[131] Macleod (2007), pp. 806–807.

diminishes pro tanto with every payment made.[132] This was because general law conceptualized the hirer as having no property right or equity in the good, which meant that the goods could be immediately repossessed on the slightest breach, and this resulted in the abusive practice of "snatch back."[133] Therefore, unlike the US law, UK law has considered it necessary to impose certain restrictions on self-help repossession in consumer-regulated agreements, due to the peculiarities of its quasi-security interests' regime.

4.1.5.1 Restrictions of Self-Help Repossession in the UK

Given the situation described above, in the UK statutory provisions were implemented to respond to unfair practices such as "snatch back" and protect the equity that a consumer may have built up against arbitrary seizure.[134]

4.1.5.1.1 The "One Third" Rule and Regulated Agreements

The 1938 Hire Purchase Act (HPA) implemented the *one-third rule*, which forbids the recaption of consumer goods after one-third of the hire price was paid. These goods became commonly known as "protected goods."[135] The HPA revision of 1964 added the default notice and the procedure concerning death (the latter being also extended to conditional sales). The CCA 1974 adopted all the abovementioned rules and extended their application to all regulated consumer credit agreements, namely agreements between two parties, one of whom is an individual[136] and the other of whom is any person that provides credit to the former. Under the same category of regulated agreements fall consumer hire agreements, which are concluded between two bodies, one of whom is an individual and the other of whom is a person, by which goods are loaned to the hirer for use without an option to purchase. Finally, the 2006 revision of the CCA added the default notice sheets, the

---

[132] This is not valid in case of mortgages.

[133] The practice of snatch back was described as follows: "[w]hile most firms wanted payment in full rather than repossession, there was a significant proportion – including some who engaged in considerable advertising – that specialized in repossessing good after most payments were made... many cases were reported of debtors who had almost completed contracts having their goods snatched within hours of missing a single payment. (Scott 2002, 195, 215)." See: Ramsay (2012), p. 481.

[134] Ramsay (2012), p. 482.

[135] Macleod (2007), p. 821. Where the hirer had paid more than one-third of the hire purchase price, HPA 1938 termed them "protected goods": in respect of these, the exercise of any common law right of recaption was totally prohibited and, if the owner alternatively sought to recover the goods through court action, introduced a number of substantive and procedural protections.

[136] Under the definition of "individual," the CCA covers also partnerships and any other unincorporated bodies.

provisions with respect to default interest and the possibility of the debtor that once served with a default notice to apply in court for a Time Order.[137]

4.1.5.1.2 The Notion of "Protected Goods"

Currently the CCA, concerning strictly regulated hire purchase or conditional sales agreements, maintains the concept of "protected goods,"[138] which was derived from the HPA, and if one-third of the total price of the goods has been paid or tendered,[139] the creditor is not entitled to recover possession of the goods, except on order of the court and only if the debtor is *in breach.*[140] In order to establish the applicability of Section 90's provisions, the total price was defined[141] to mean the total sum payable by the debtor under the agreement, including any sum payable on the exercise of an option to purchase but excluding any sum payable as a penalty or as compensation of damages for breach.[142] The total price does *not* include default interest due in respect of late payment of installments or expenses incurred by the creditor in communicating with the debtor, which are recoverable from the debtor under the terms of the agreement.[143]

4.1.5.1.3 Safe Harbors in Repossessing Protected Goods

The law established several safe harbors with respect to repossession of protected goods in cases where the debtor has transferred the good, and the creditor is

---

[137] Furmston and Chuah (2010), p. 529. "The central point of a time order is that whilst it is in force and being complied with, the creditor's right to terminate the agreement, demand early payment of any sum, recover possession of any goods or land, enforce any security, etc. – in effect the creditor's rights – are put on hold and if the breach is remedied by meeting the payments under the time order the breach is deemed never to have taken place."

[138] The notion extends to "add on" agreements. According to Section 90 (3) of CCA, once the debtor has paid 1/3 or more of the total price of the goods under an earlier agreement and a later agreement is made between the same debtor and creditor relating to any such goods, then all goods under the later agreement (including the old goods) are automatically protected goods. This result *only* follows where the debtor has *not* paid 1/3 or more under the later agreement. If he had, then Section 90 (1) would apply anyway. Thus, the creditor is not entitled to recover possession of the goods subject to a later agreement except on an order of court, *even if* less than a third (or indeed nothing) has been paid under the later agreement. Same result is obtained under subsection 4 where the earlier agreement is modified under Section 82(2) as well as when a completely new agreement was entered into. For details: Guest et al. (2009), p. 2089.

[139] Furmston and Chuah (2010), p. 528. Payment by a surety is also taken into consideration in establishing whether one-third of the price was paid. See Goode (1999), Issue 36/II B/264.

[140] Goode (1999), Issue 36/II B/263. Also: Furmston and Chuah (2010), p. 528.

[141] CCA, Section 189 (1).

[142] Guest et al. (2009), p. 2088.

[143] Guest et al. (2009), pp. 2088–2089.

attempting repossession from the transferee, where the debtor has consented to the repossession or where the debtor has voluntarily terminated the agreement.

As mentioned, the restriction concerning protected goods will not apply when *a transfer of possession* occurred and the creditor attempts repossession of the goods from a person other than the debtor. Problems appear when the debtor has only given possession to a third party over the protected good.[144] In *Kassam v. Chartered Trust Plc.*,[145] the debtor had given possession over his car to a dealer, intending to have it sold. The court decided that if the sale has not taken place yet, the dealer was merely a bailee for the debtor, and hence, repossession from the dealer was in fact still "from the debtor."[146]

The situation would change though if the dealer had bought the car or sold it to a third party, because in such cases the dealer would be in possession as purchaser or bailee of a third party and therefore the repossession would not breach the provisions concerning protected goods. Courts have also taken the position that abandoned goods may be repossessed without a court order,[147] as long as the abandonment can be established with certainty.[148]

Another safe harbor is obtaining *debtor's consent to repossession.*[149] Under the CCA, only consenting *in advance* to the repossession of protected goods is invalid. As was pointed out, *de facto* consent is frequently given by the debtor in the hope that resale by the creditor will discharge the balance due.[150] According to courts, the consent must be "unqualified and informed,"[151] genuine and voluntary, albeit reluctant.[152]

Last safe harbor is provided by *voluntary termination* of agreement by the debtor.[153] Burden of proof of termination is on the creditor alleging it.[154] Any repossession of protected goods outside these safe harbors will attract severe penalties under the CCA.[155]

---

[144] Goode (1999), issue 36/II/B 265.

[145] *Kassam v. Chartered Trust Plc.*, [1998] R.T.T. 220.

[146] Guest et al. (2009), p. 2089.

[147] *Bentink Ltd v. Cromwell Engineering Co* [1071] 1 Q.B. 324 CA.

[148] *FC Finance Ltd v. Francis* [1970] 114 SJ 568. Goods merely left by the debtor with a garage for repair do not constitute abandoned goods.

[149] For a comprehensive analysis of consent: Goode (1999), Issue 36/II/B 266.

[150] Macleod (2007), p. 824.

[151] *Chartered Trust Plc v. Pitcher* [1988] RTR 72 CA.

[152] *Mercantile Credit Co Ltd v. Cross* [1965] 2 QB 205, [1965] 1 All ER 577, [1999] GCCR 251).

[153] "Termination" means primarily termination under a contractual power. It probably also includes the case where the debtor purports to terminate without complying with the contractual conditions attached to his power, for he is equally manifesting his intention to be rid of the agreement. It does not, however, include the case where the debtor repudiates and the creditor accepts the breach as terminating the agreement. Goode (1999), Issue 36/II/B 264–265.

[154] Guest et al. (2009), pp. 2089–2090. Also: Macleod (2007), pp. 824—825. For a detailed discussion: Goode (1999), Issue 36/II/B 264–265.

[155] Penalties are provided by Section 91 of the CCA.

4.1.5.1.4 Restrictions on Repossession of Nonprotected Goods

Another limitation on repossession is further provided by the CCA in the case of goods subjected to a regulated hire purchase or a conditional sale agreement (even if they do not qualify as "protected goods") or a regulated consumer hire agreement. According to the CCA,[156] the creditor is prohibited from entering premises in order to take possession of goods, unless he has a court order.

This prohibition seems to extend to entry on premises of third parties as well as premises of debtor,[157] and failure to comply may bring, besides statutory penalties,[158] criminal charges for theft, blackmail, burglary, use of violence for the purposes of securing entry, criminal damage, harassment of debtors and demanding payment for unsolicited goods.[159]

4.1.6 Restrictions of Self-Help Repossession in Romania

Initially, the RSTL did not impose any restrictions on self-help repossession, besides the nonbreach of public order or the ban on use or threat of using force and the like, but with the implementation of the RNCC, the legislator conditioned the use of private enforcement of serving a prior notice through a judicial enforcement officer to the debtor. It is unclear what the nature of this notice is and what it should contain. Most likely it should point out that the debtor is now in default and the creditor deems himself entitled to resort to self-help repossession of the collateral.

Another limitation is related to the right of the creditor to take possession of the collateral from another party than the debtor. The third party can only oppose delivery of the good if the creditor does not prove his right. According to the law, the proof can be made by presenting the security agreement, concluded with the observance of all legal formalities and a certificate attesting the priority rank issued by the Electronic Archive under the conditions of the law.[160] Given the lack of case law at the current moment, it is hard to estimate how this limitation works in practice and how well qualified a third party in possession is to assert the documents submitted by an alleged secured creditor. The likelihood is that such cases end up with a request for judicial repossession under the RNCC.[161]

---

[156] CCA, Section 92 (1).

[157] Guest et al. (2009), p. 2091.

[158] Goode (1999), Issue 36/II/B 269.

[159] For a detailed discussion of all criminal liabilities faced by a creditor trying to retake goods that are the subject of a regulated hire purchase or conditional sale agreement, see: Goode (1999), Issue 26/IE/3054–3060.

[160] Colectiv (2012), p. 873. Comment to Art. 2441.

[161] RNCC, Art 2442, provides for the right of the creditor to request the support of the bailiff (executor judecătoresc) for repossessing the collateral.

4.2 Rights of the Secured Party: Disposition of Collateral

Once the secured creditor comes into possession of the collateral, he enjoys two options: to dispose of the collateral or to accept the collateral as discharge of the debtor's obligation, also known as strict foreclosure. **Although these options do not constitute self-help as such, they are in fact a direct consequence of repossession and the actual purpose of it.** Hence, any analysis of self-help repossession and its importance in debt recovery would not be complete without addressing the issue of disposition of collateral or strict foreclosure. However, one must mention with respect to the disposition of collateral that, similar to repossession, it can be conducted either privately, by the creditor, or by employing the state's apparatus. Since the book deals strictly with the nonjudicial aspects of enforcement, here only the private disposition of collateral is covered.

4.2.1 Disposition of Collateral in the US

In the US, the UCC authorizes the creditor in possession to sell, lease or otherwise dispose of any or all of the collateral after default. UK and Romanian laws provide, in addition to the rights above, the right of the creditor to administer, directly or indirectly, the collateral, under the supervision of the court.[162] All these possibilities materialize either by a public transaction (a public auction[163]) or by a private sale (which would include every other method that is not a public auction).[164] Looking at this authorization from the traditional civilian perspective, Kieninger considered it to be the *key remedy* added by the UCC in supplement to the available

---

[162] For UK: Ali (2002), p. 249. For Romania, RNCC, Art. 2468–2473. Details are provided *infra*, Sect. 4.2.3.

[163] Since neither the public sale nor the private sale is statutorily defined, the doctrine tried to establish what is understood by both of them. Based on pre-Code case law, Gilmore concluded, for example, that the essence of a public sale is not that the relevant public is not only invited to attend but is also informed, by whatever means of publicity are deemed appropriate, when and where the sale is to take place. Otherwise, in the absence of proper publicity, it would not be a public sale, no matter the place or time when it was conducted. On the matter whether a public sale must be an auction sale, Gilmore answered positively, for reasons that have more to do with the protection of the purchaser, though he noted that if the legislator would have intended to require an auction it would have said so specifically. Gilmore (1999), pp. 1242–1243. After the revised version of Article 9, the comments seem to agree on the auction requirement by describing the public sale as "one at which the price is determined after the public has had a meaningful opportunity for competitive bidding." UCC Rev. Section 9-610, Official Comment 7 (1999), cited in Duncan et al. (2012), (Rel. 29) 5-30.3, footnote 30. Most courts follow the comment's guideline and thus require that a public disposition be open to the public and not just a limited segment of the public. Therefore, dealers' only auctions might not satisfy the requirements and will be classified as private dispositions. See Nowka (2009), p. 251.

[164] Rusch and Sepinuck (2010), p. 156.

judicial remedies since "[A] far better price is likely to be realized when the collateral is sold, in a public or private sale, by the secured party on a businesslike basis than would be obtained at a sale by a court officer, and likely also more rapidly and at a lower cost."[165]

4.2.2 Disposition of Collateral in the UK

Creditors are entitled to dispose of the collateral and seek deficiency in the UK as well, but the issue is complicated by the concept of hire purchase, since technically the transaction is not a credit sale or a security agreement and consumers are able to return the goods at any time during the agreement. Therefore, creditors insert now "minimum payment clauses"—a charge for depreciation in hire purchase and conditional sale as a method of obtaining a deficiency payment.[166]

It should be emphasized though that a "minimum payment" clause that entitles the finance company to recover more than what would be recovered under the CCA[167] would be considered a penalty by the courts and dismissed as such. However, the provisions related to protected goods and Section 100[168] apply to regulated hire purchase and conditional sales agreements and do *not* apply to a loan that is secured against the personal property of a debtor.[169]

4.2.3 Disposition of Collateral in Romania

In Romania, the sale of the collateral may take place *only after* a court has approved the foreclosure. The request is trialed in open court, with the subpoena of all parties,

[165] Official Comment 2 to UCC, Section 9-610: "[. . .] This section encourages private dispositions on the assumption that they will result in higher realization on collateral for the benefit of all concerned.[. . .]," The American Law Institute National Conference of Commissioners on Uniform State Laws (2009), pp. 1055–1056. Also Kieninger (2004), p. 79. For a similar opinion: Nowka (2009), p. 249: "The court does not hold, approve, or oversees a Section 9-610 disposition. The secured party may dispose of the collateral in a public or private disposition, in a single unit or separate parcels, when and where It chooses, and on terms it chooses. This freedom theoretically helps produce higher disposition price, but the freedom is not unlimited."

[166] Ramsay (2012), p. 482.

[167] See *infra* Section 100 of CCA.

[168] Section 100 introduced a 50 % rule intended to provide a form of justice between hirer and owner: "100-(1) Where a regulated hire purchase or regulated conditional sale agreement is terminated under section 99 the debtor shall be liable, unless the agreement provides for a smaller payment, or does not provide for any payment, to pay to the creditor the amount (if any) by which one-half of the total price exceeds the aggregate of the sums paid and the sums due in respect of the total price immediately before termination."

[169] Ramsay (2012), p. 483.

and the creditor must attach all documents attesting the existence *and perfection*[170] of his security interest.[171] Besides this mandatory prior approval from the court, the creditor enjoys pretty much the same rights as his US counterpart: he may sell the goods "as they are," or after taking commercially reasonable measure to increase their value, he may sell them at a public auction or directly, notwithstanding the method, manner, time, place[172] or conditions as long as the "commercially reasonable standard" is complied with.[173] If the proceeds resulting from the sale do not suffice in covering the debt and reasonable expenses, the debtor shall remain personally liable for the difference, but the creditor will now have the status of an unsecured creditor.[174]

4.2.4 Debtor Protection Measures

In order to ensure debtors' protection, the UCC established a few duties that the secured party must comply with: *a prior notice* to the debtor of the proposed disposition and the obligation *to dispose of the collateral in a "commercially reasonable" manner* (analyzed in the following section). As it will be shown, similar standards exist in Romanian law but not in UK law. The absence of such protections comes as a surprise, if one considers the effort put by the UK legislation into debtor's protection upon default and during repossession. It would seem that in the legislator's view, once the default was not cured and the good was repossessed, the debtor has exhausted all his possibilities to remedy the situation and must now face the consequences, no matter how (financially) harsh they will be.

4.3 The Commercially Reasonable Standard

In analyzing the provisions of the UCC with respect to the sale of collateral by the secured party, Gilmore underlined two significant additions: the express statement of the "commercially reasonable" standard, which the secured party must meet when conducting such a sale, and an equally important statement of the availability

---

[170] If the security interest was not perfected according to the law, the creditor shall not be entitled to sell the collateral. See: Colectiv (2012), p. 875.

[171] RNCC, Art 2445 (1).

[172] The good can be sold by the creditor even if it is still in the possession of the debtor, since the law expressly empowers the creditor to take possession of the goods (Art. 2447). But the right of the buyer to take into possession the good, after the sale, covers only the situation where the good is still in the possession of the debtor. If the good is in the possession of a third party, the sale must occur *after* the good was taken into possession by the creditor. See: Colectiv (2012), p. 876.

[173] RNCC, Art 2445 (2)–(5).

[174] RNCC, Art. 2456, and its commentary in Colectiv (2012), p. 879.

of judicial control over what the secured creditor planned to do or already did in respect of the sale.[175] The secured creditor's duties (to act in a commercially reasonable manner and to account for surplus) and the correlative rights of the debtor related to the disposal of collateral could not be waived or varied by parties' agreement, though parties were allowed to determine the standards by which these right and duties were to be measured, as long as the established standards were not manifestly unreasonable.[176] Otherwise, with the full observance of the commercially reasonable standard, a sale or any other disposition of the collateral can take any form: as a unit or in parcels, at any time and place and on any terms.

4.3.1 The Commercially Reasonable Standard in the US

As far as commercial reasonableness was concerned, the key provision of the UCC, which was adopted by the RNCC as well, is that every aspect of the disposition, including the method, manner, time, place and terms, must be commercially reasonable. This mandatory rule is not subjected to disclaimer or limitation. Since the standard was not defined by the UCC, the job was left to the courts.

4.3.1.1 Judicial Determination of Commercially Reasonable Standard: Factors and Circumstances

In fulfilling this task, US courts are accustomed to formulate the duty in terms of a fiduciary obligation (to use his best efforts to see that the highest possible price is received for the collateral)[177] and look to a number of factors (relationship of price obtained to market price, conformity to commercially reasonable standards, presence or absence of a recognized market for the collateral and secured party's utilization of that market, overall reasonableness of means and method of disposition under the circumstances),[178] taking into account all of the facts and circumstances of each case.[179] The case law also made clear the fact that a secured party has a duty to publicize the proposed sale, but the type and extent of publicity depend

---

[175] Gilmore (1999), p. 1228.

[176] Gilmore (1999), p. 1229.

[177] Gilmore (1999), pp. 1232–1233.

[178] Duncan et al. (2012), (Rel. 32) 5-42, footnote 88.

[179] In *R & J of Tennessee, Inc. v. Blankenship-Melton Real Estate, Inc.*, 55 UCC Rep Serv. 2d 278, (Tenn. App. 2004), the court held that the sale was not commercially reasonable under Revised Article 9 because the secured party failed to provide adequate notice to a secondary obligor, did not advertise the sale, did not hire an experienced auctioneer, held the collateral for over 7 months before conducting the sale and permitted others to use the collateral during the extended time period. For a list of court decisions on the applicability of the commercially reasonable standard, see: Duncan et al. (2012), (Rel. 32) 5-43, footnote 90[1].

on the type of collateral. Delaying the sale or disposing of the collateral in a haze are other factors with an impact on the assessment done by the courts.[180]

The Revised Article 9 added several provisions that impact the secured creditors' conduct in the disposition of collateral: the predisposition notice with respect to the detailed information that must be given to debtors and other obligors in advance of the disposition (see previous section). Moreover, the official comments emphasize the need to prepare the collateral for sale, in order to maximize the proceeds that would result from it[181] and the fact that all warranties related to the title, possession and quiet enjoyment will pass together with the collateral. Revised Article 9 also addressed the controversial issue of the "low" price, together with the sanctions for failure to comply with the legal requirements of the sale,[182] a matter developed in the following section.

4.3.1.2 Relevance of the Obtained Price

The price has been a disputed topic and factor in the assessment of commercial reasonableness. A higher price, which could have been obtained under a different method and at a different time than those elected by the creditor, was not deemed to lead to the conclusion that the sale was made in an unreasonable manner. But this does not mean the secured party should disregard the actual value of the collateral at the time of the sale either.

Gilmore commented that the law definitely does not require the secured creditor to be a "seer or a prophet" but "to [also] act with due diligence, to use his best efforts, to have a reasonable regard for the debtor's interests."[183] In addition, he noticed that there are no mechanisms to automatically produce a high price in default sales and that in order to get a fair price, the UCC relied on the mechanism of public sale, notification and publicity and as long as all these have been properly operated, failure to obtain a good price cannot be imputed to the creditor.[184] He also underlined that the debtor shares some of the burden as well once he receives proper notification of the sale, being in a position that enables him to protect his interests in

[180] Duncan et al. (2012), (Rel. 35) 5-48, footnotes 108 and 113.

[181] Before the Revision, Prof. Gilmore stated that among the secured party's powers in conducting the sale of collateral lies the authorization to prepare or even process the goods in order to maximize the proceeds. Gilmore (1999), p. 1238. The courts, although not entirely unanimous, have taken the same position and held that it would be unreasonable for the secured creditor not to take any action to prepare the collateral such as minor repairs or cleaning it up before the sale. See: Duncan et al. (2012), (Rel. 35) 5-46.

[182] Duncan et al. (2012), (Rel. 32) 5-44.

[183] Gilmore (1999), p. 1237.

[184] This view is also supported by the case law, which held that mere inadequacy in the price obtained will not make the disposition commercially unreasonable as long as there was no fraud or wrongdoing from the creditor's side. For a detailed list of cases: Duncan et al. (2012), (Rel. 33) 5-50.2, footnote 123.

the collateral even if he does not manage to redeem it: "If he does nothing, his later allegation that the property was worth a great deal more [...] should be received with a degree of skepticism."[185]

Revised Article 9 sought to find a compromise, and while maintaining that the price obtained is not of itself sufficient to conclude that the collection, sale or acceptance was commercially unreasonable, the secured party has to establish compliance with the standard. This actually represented a major change as it shifted the burden of proof from the debtor to the creditor, in affirmatively proving the sale was commercially reasonable.[186] Unfortunately, as it will be shown later, the Romanian law did not adopt the shifted burden of proof, which leaves the debtor in a very weak position to defend against unfair sales.

4.3.1.3 Safe Harbors Concerning Commercially Reasonable Sales

There are a few safe harbors provided for by the law. The sale will be deemed to have met the commercially reasonable standard if the secured creditor sells the collateral in the *usual manner* in any recognized market therefor or at the *current market price* in a recognized market at the time of the sale or if the sale was in conformity with reasonable commercial practices among dealers of the type of property sold. Two aspects require qualification. *First*, the courts have interpreted the "recognized market" in a very narrow language,[187] in line with Comment 9 to the Revised Section 9-610, which described it as a market "in which the items sold are fungible and prices are not subject to individual negotiation, such as the New York Exchange Market."[188] *Second*, as emphasized by Gilmore, a used car auction at or through which dealers sell repossessed cars to other dealers does not provide safe harbor since in such market there is no possibility to say with objectivity and certainty what the price was. However, he further underlined, the secured party might still be protected from any attacks if the sale was in conformity with reasonable commercial practices among dealers in the type of property sold.[189]

---

[185] Gilmore (1999), p. 1245.

[186] Commenting on the previous provisions of the UCC, Prof. Gilmore observed that "Allegations of fraud or of failure to exercise a required degree of diligence are easily made" and, hence, he concluded that the burden of bringing convincing proof "should be on the party who makes these allegations." Gilmore (1999), p. 1235.

[187] *Reno Financial Ltd. v. Valleroy*, 229 S.W. 3d 622 (Mo. App. 2007).

[188] Duncan et al. (2012), (Rel. 33) 5-50, footnote 116[1].

[189] Gilmore (1999), p. 1236.

4.3.2 Commercially Reasonable Standard in the UK

In the UK, there are no similar standards to govern the sale of the collateral, but the creditor of a conditional sale who is also seeking damages in addition to the price obtained in the resale is under a duty of care to get the best price obtainable.[190] Otherwise, he bears no duty towards the debtor.

In the case of a hire purchase, as mentioned before, the debtor is in a more difficult position as he will not even be entitled to plead that the creditor made a double recovery in the legal sense or that installments paid are in fact a part payment of the price,[191] since the creditor is under no duty to account for the surplus.

4.3.3 Commercially Reasonable Standard in Romania

The Romanian law seems to have quantified some of the experience of the American courts. Therefore, by the provisions of the RNCC,[192] a sale is deemed to have complied with commercial reasonableness when it took place in the way in which similar goods are sold regularly in an organized market, if the sale price was established by an organized market and valid at the time of the sale, if the commercial tactics employed were those established and followed by those regularly dealing in the same type of goods or in accordance with the standards established by the parties in the security agreement when there is no organized market for the collateral or no established commercial tactics.

The rule states that whenever the price can be determined on an organized market, that is the price to follow. In reality, especially in the case of used products, this rule would become an exception, leaving the creditor the power to use whatever methods he wishes. Additionally, the Romanian legislator clearly expressed the fact that if a better price could have been obtained by using another selling method or choosing a different time to sell, that shall not automatically deem the sale as commercially unreasonable.[193] Hence, the sale enjoys an *absolute presumption of commercial reasonableness*,[194] and it is therefore the debtor's burden to prove it otherwise, which is a totally different view than the one taken by the UCC.

Unfortunately, this creditor-friendly approach taken by the RNCC places the debtor in a very weak position, compared to its US counterparts. An explanation might be that, as mentioned earlier, the RNCC does not distinguish between

---

[190] Macleod (2007), p. 808. The author mentions an unreported case in which the court ruled in this way: *Contra Forward Trust Ltd. v. Best* (1983).

[191] Macleod (2007), p. 808.

[192] RNCC, Art 2446.

[193] Art 2446 of RNCC, Para 2.

[194] Colectiv (2012), p. 875.

consumers and businesses in this regard, although this is obviously a big legislative gap that exposes the debtor to the risk of abuse.

4.4 Strict Foreclosure

Strict foreclosure is acceptance of secured creditor of the collateral in full or partial satisfaction of the debt. Legally speaking, this means that the secured creditor will become the owner of the collateral without judicial process or resorting to private or public sales.

4.4.1 Strict Foreclosure in the US

In the US, in the case of consumer goods, only full strict foreclosure is allowed, i.e. acceptance by the creditor of the collateral in full satisfaction of the debt. This is aimed at protecting consumer debtors. The logic behind prohibition of partial strict foreclosure in consumer goods is, on the one hand, the need to protect weaker parties from being tricked into relinquishing the collateral and still be in debt, especially when professional creditors will rarely grant credit for a collateral that would not cover the debt and interest entirely, and, on the other hand, to make sure that the consumers do not fall victims to the adhesion contracts providing for partial strict foreclosure.

As Gilmore emphasized, historically strict foreclosure used to be the normal remedy, and, in his opinion, it was the best and the simplest way of liquidating any secured transaction upon default[195] since the power to sell the collateral, together with permission to sue for deficiency, might prove tougher on the debtor. The benefits were evident for both parties: if the value of the collateral suffices to cover not only the debt but also the expenses for foreclosure, the secured party avoids all issues related to commercially reasonable standard disposition.[196] On the other side, if the value of the collateral is smaller, the debtor faces the risk of being sued for deficiency, and hence he might wish to avoid additional charges and expenses by simply allowing the creditor to keep the collateral, without a sale.

Of course, if the value of the collateral is significantly bigger than the amount owed, the debtor maintains an equity interest in the collateral, which should be maintained for the debtor or his other creditors. Hence, Article 9 has limited the secured party's right to exercise the option of strict foreclosure, and under the

---

[195] Gilmore (1999), p. 1220.

[196] However, in *Reeves v. Foutz and Tanner, Inc.*, 617 P.2d 149 (New Mexico Supreme Court, 1980), cited by Picker et al. (2002), pp. 344–346, the court held that where the creditor retained the collateral, but sold it in the normal course of his business, he must account for the surplus.

Revised rules the debtor must first consent to the secured party's acceptance of the collateral. The consent can be evidenced in two ways, either by affirmatively agreeing to the acceptance of the secured creditor by an authenticated record *after* default or by not replying or objecting within 20 days after a proposal to accept the collateral in full satisfaction from the secured creditor was sent.[197]

Since other parties might hold an interest in the collateral, the UCC established three classes of parties that should also be notified[198] of the proposal in order to provide them with the possibility to object. One objection, from any of these classes, suffices in forcing the creditor to resort to a sale of collateral under Article 9 rules.[199] The notification is pretty much similar in all aspects to the one that the creditor must give prior to the disposition of collateral with one difference: the notification with respect to strict foreclosure must reach its addressee, while the one with respect to the disposition need only to be sent under the letter of the law, the addressee bearing the risk of miscarriage in the mail.[200]

4.4.2 *Strict Foreclosure in France*

France's appearance may be construed as a surprise. Strict foreclosure is the *only exception* from its judicial enforcement tradition,[201] though strictly banned in the case of consumer credit debts.[202] The recent reform of the French STL removed the prohibition of foreclosure clauses, thus enabling creditors to keep the collateral in satisfaction of the debt, though the good's value would have to be determined by an expert appointed by the parties,[203] an overprotective condition if one considers the fact that strict foreclosure can only occur between professionals but logical if one considers situations such as those of mega-corporation type of creditors versus a family SME.

---

[197] Official Comment 2 to UCC, Section 9-620, The American Law Institute National Conference of Commissioners on Uniform State Laws (2009), p. 1074. "This section [. . .] reflect the belief that strict foreclosure should be encouraged and often will produce better results than a disposition for all the concerned." Also: Duncan et al. (2012), (Rel. 33) 5-56.3.

[198] For a detailed discussion on the contents of the notice and the categories entitled to receive such notice, see Gilmore (1999), pp. 1223–1227.

[199] See: Gilmore (1999), p. 1226. Gilmore made a good observation that a "commercially reasonable" proposal should not be defeated by a "commercially unreasonable" objection, but he also pointed out that such an issue, although interesting from a theoretical point of view, has slim chances of being argued in practice since the secured party is better of disposing of the collateral via sale than spending time and money in court trying to determine if the objection was done in good faith and based on sufficient reasons.

[200] Gilmore (1999), p. 1240.

[201] Dahan and Simpson (2008), p. 270.

[202] Dahan and Simpson (2008), p. 266.

[203] Dahan and Simpson (2008), p. 266.

The introduction of strict foreclosure, however, allows for a swift, and most likely cheaper, way of settling the debt and the dispute between a creditor and his debtor. One may wonder why the reform did not push for the right to self-help repossession, given the fact that, as revealed by the previous chapter, France does allow for passive self-help remedies and wishes to implement a modern and an efficient secured transactions system. The allowance of strict foreclosure is yet another step towards a private enforcement regime.

4.4.3 Strict Foreclosure in Germany

In Germany, as well, strict foreclosure is possible in practice, although not expressly allowed by the BGB.[204] The possibility of keeping the collateral in realization of the debt may be deduced implicitly from the provisions covering pledged goods.[205] Basically, German law permits strict foreclosure as long as the agreement was entered into *after default* has occurred. However, unlike US or French law, Germany lacks detailed rules on how strict foreclosure functions, leaving it entirely up to the parties' agreement.

Additionally, German law does not draw a distinction between agreements on strict foreclosure involving consumer transactions, between written or oral agreements or between full or partial strict foreclosure. Although the fact that strict foreclosure is valid only if the parties agreed on it after default may be construed also as a measure of protection for consumers, German law lacks the certainty of the other jurisdictions in this regard and should consider these legal gaps by reforming its legislation concerning security rights in movable property.

4.4.4 Strict Foreclosure in Romania

In the case of Romanian law, the situation is closer to its American model. The creditor is entitled to make a proposal for strict foreclosure, if the law does not provide otherwise, by giving notice to the debtor and all interested parties, if the

[204] The DCFR might offer an idea about how strict foreclosure is perceived in Germany given the number of German scholars involved in the drafting. In particular, Arts. IX-7:105 and IX-7:216 and the corresponding comments are relevant. An agreement for strict foreclosure that is predefault will not be deemed effective. Strict foreclosure may be total or partial; however, in case there is a surplus, its value must be returned to the debtor, while in case of deficiency, the debtor will still be liable for it. von Bar and Clive (2010), pp. 5621–5623 and 5659–5661.

[205] BGB, Art. 1229, prohibits agreements reached before default that transfer ownership over the pledged collateral to the pledgee, in case the debtor defaults. The prohibition strictly refers to agreements reached *before* default but mentioned nothing with respect to such agreements concluded *after* default. *Per a contrario* this may be interpreted that the latter are allowed.

debtor consents and there is no opposition.[206] The consent must be *written and after default*, the latter provision bringing the RNCC closer to the German BGB. Similarly to the notice of sale, the proposal must be filed with the Archive for publicity and information purposes. This time there is no provision with respect to the term in which the notice shall be served, but for reasons of equality of treatment with other notices required by the STL, one may presume it to be the minimum 15 days. Any opposition must also be communicated to the creditor within 15 days from notification. Obviously, since the term for opposition runs from the notice, it is implied that the notice has to be received, which clears the doubts raised with respect to the notice of sale, where such qualification was not made.

Under Romanian law, strict foreclosure can *only* be *full* and, besides the normal effects of a sale, it will also extinguish the creditor's right to sue for any deficiency.[207] Unfortunately, **Romanian law did not establish any ban on strict foreclosure in case of consumer goods, as the US and the French laws did, nor did it establish any specific rules, such as the evaluation of the collateral by an independent expert, as is the case in France.** Since partial strict foreclosure is banned by Romanian law, having the good evaluated by an independent expert did not make much sense. However, this does not mean that the creditor might not profit from strict foreclosure by retaining the surplus (the difference between the actual value of the collateral and what is owed). Probably the legislator considered that allowing strict foreclosure agreements *only* after default, on the one hand, and the notification of all interested parties, on the other, represent an adequate and sufficient protection. However, **the current regime fails to acknowledge any kind of equity gained by the debtor in the collateral,** which exposes him to a greater loss than similar debtors from the US or the UK.

4.4.5 Consumer Goods with Substantial Equity

As pointed out in the previous sections of this chapter, the legislators have tried to implement rules to protect the debtors from any kind of abuse coming from the creditors. The prior notice or commercially reasonable standard is part of such protection mechanisms. The book turns now to those rules with sole application in the case of consumers, which represent a more specialized and narrower set of rules designed to cover those situations in which consumers managed to acquire a substantial equity in the collateral before the defaulting event. The reason behind this designated body of rules is the fact that usually "the consumer security agreement is a contract of adhesion" and therefore "the consumer needs protection."[208] Same position was expressed in the UK, and although the facilitation of

[206] RNCC, Art. 2460, Para 1.

[207] See Colectiv (2012), p. 881, comment to Art. 2463.

[208] Gilmore (1999), p. 1221.

self-help is a characteristic of commercial law, in consumer law the unequal bargaining position of the consumer had to led to significant *controls on repossession* by creditors.[209] Romania does not have such rules since it makes no distinction between the regimes applicable to professionals and consumers.

4.4.5.1 The Issue of Substantial Equity in Consumer Goods in the US: The Sixty Percent Rule

Article 9[210] has expressly prohibited strict foreclosure in two situations: when the security interest is a purchase money security interest in consumer goods *and* the debtor has paid 60 %[211] of the *cash price*[212] for the collateral or when the collateral is consumer goods, the security interest is a *non*-purchase money security interest *and* the debtor has paid 60 % of the *loan*. Since strict foreclosure is banned in these cases, it follows that the creditor must dispose of the collateral *via* private or public disposition. But the drafters have added even here *an additional* measure: the collateral must be disposed of within 90 days from the moment it came into the possession of the creditor, in any of the two situations mentioned; otherwise, the creditor will face recovery from the debtor either in tort for conversion or under Section 6.[213] The law also established an exception from this rule, which allows the creditor to dispose of the collateral over the 90-day term if, *after default*, the debtor provides the creditor with a *written* waiver of this protection. As for partial strict foreclosure in case of consumer goods, it should be mentioned that it is forbidden.

4.4.5.2 The Issue of Substantial Equity in Consumer Goods in the UK, France and Germany

The UK did not limit the protection of a debtor's substantial equity to strict foreclosure, since the law does not allow for strict foreclosure, but to repossession itself.[214] As pointed out earlier, France excluded consumers from the application of strict foreclosure clauses, while in Germany, the lack of provisions leaves the issue in complete darkness and opened only to speculation.

---

[209] Ramsay (2012), p. 481.

[210] UCC, Section 9-620 (e).

[211] The underlining idea is simple: if the debtor has paid as much as 60 %, then he has built up an equity that should be protected by requiring a compulsory disposition that will produce a surplus to be returned to him. Gilmore (1999), p. 1222.

[212] For a detailed discussion and explanation on the difference between the cash price and the loan: Duncan et al. (2012), (Rel. 15) 5-57–5-58.

[213] Duncan et al. (2012), (Rel. 15) 5-57.

[214] See *supra* Sect. 4.1.5.1.

4.4.5.3 The Issue of Substantial Equity in Consumer Goods in Romania

Surprisingly, besides the general provision that precludes creditors opting for strict foreclosure to seek deficiency afterwards, the Romanian law did not follow the UCC model in granting debtors with substantial equity in their acquired goods any additional protection. This is a major loophole in the Romanian law since common law jurisdictions recognize the importance of protecting such equity. The probable explanation lies with the fact that the Romanian law does no longer make a difference between commercial and consumer debtors.

4.4.6 Other Consequences of Strict Foreclosure

The previous section covered the case where consumer goods were involved and the debtor had a substantial equity in the collateral. This section focuses on the situations in which such equity did not reach the legal threshold and the creditor still made the proposal to retain the collateral in satisfaction of the debt.

The UCC provides that if the secured party wishes to make such proposal, he should follow certain steps: (1) if the debtor has not signed an *after* default waiver to his rights under the section, then the secured creditor must send the debtor a written notice of such proposal, unless the collateral is consumer goods and no further notice is required; (2) in all other cases, the secured creditor must send notice to all other secured parties from whom he had received written notices of a claim of an interest in the collateral.[215] If from any of the above there is an objection to the proposal within 21 days after the notice was sent, then the secured party must dispose of the collateral. If no objection is received, then the secured party may keep the collateral in satisfaction of the debt. Until the Revised Article 9, once the secured party had chosen to keep the collateral it gave up any right to a deficiency judgment, but now this rule was amended[216] and the secured party may keep it only in partial satisfaction, allowing him to seek deficiency afterwards.

One last situation deserves mention. In the case the secured party neither disposes of the collateral nor makes a proposal to retain it in satisfaction of the debt, the question is: what are the rights of the debtor? Must he wait and remain in uncertainty, or is there any kind of remedy he can resort to? Some authors[217] answered that although the UCC is silent on establishing a time limit for the secured party to act, at some point a court could conclude that the secured party must be deemed to have accepted the collateral in satisfaction of the debt, with the corollary conclusion that he loses the right to sue for deficiency.

---

[215] UCC, Section 9-620 (f).

[216] Duncan et al. (2012), (Rel. 23), 5-60, footnote 16.

[217] For a discussion of the problem and a few cases addressing it: Duncan et al. (2012), (Rel. 15) 5-62–5.5.63, footnotes 25, 26 and 30.

This issue of *constructive* strict foreclosure has been resolved by the Revised Article 9, which provided that a purported or apparent acceptance of collateral in full or partial satisfaction of the obligation is ineffective unless the secured party consents to the acceptance in an authenticated record or sends the debtor a written statement containing the terms on which the secured party is willing to do so. The position taken by the Code cannot be interpreted otherwise than a major setback with respect to debtor protection, since the debtor must now wait for the secured creditor's decision and action and try to defend himself only under the "commercially reasonable" standard.

4.5 Sanctions Against the Secured Party for Wrongful Repossession and Failure to Observe Debtor's Rights

The duty of the secured creditor to respect and observe the debtor's rights would be totally useless without means and sanctions to which the creditor may be subjected to for noncompliance. Therefore, the chosen jurisdictions have resorted to different sanctions of either criminal or civil nature. However, their efficiency varies.

4.5.1 Criminal and Tort Liability

If breach of peace should occur during self-help repossession, it would amount to tort (compensatory and punitive damages),[218] criminal liabilities,[219] or statutory liability under the UCC[220] or, in consumer cases, would deprive the creditor of the

[218] White and Summers (2010), pp. 1335–1336 and 1356–1357. On the same issue of tort liability: Rusch and Sepinuck (2010), pp. 12, 151 and 187; and Martin (2013), pp. 1 and 9. On the issue of punitive damages, at page 9, footnote 47, Martin provides an extensive list of cases where punitive damages were declined. Without restating them all again here, it is worth mentioning that in order for the court to grant punitive damages, one must prove that the repossessor's behavior was outrageous, indicating spite or malice, fraudulent evil or willful improper motives, conscious and deliberate or reckless disregard for debtor's interests, oppression or wanton.

[219] White and Summers (2010), p. 1336. An example of criminal act that happens often in the course of repossession is to repossess a car with people inside (kidnapping). See: Rusch and Sepinuck (2010), p. 151.

[220] UCC, Section 9-625, provides for statutory remedies in case of secured party's failure to comply with Article 9: judicial orders concerning noncompliance, damages for loss caused by failure to comply, statutory damages in consumer goods transactions in the amount of not less than the credit service plus 10 % of the principal amount of the obligation or the time price differential plus 10 % of the cash price, damages for the loss of any surplus. In addition, the same Section established at letters e) and f) a list of cases in which noncompliance with the specified provision would amount to statutory damages in the value of 500 dollars for each case. For details, White and Summers (2010), pp. 1355–1356.

right to sue for deficiency.[221] Moreover, such behavior might constitute a violation of statutes[222] governing fair debt collection practices. Finally, secured party's behavior might violate state tort law (trespassing when entering the debtor's house without permission, battery when pushing the debtor or a member of his family, conversion when taking other property of the debtor[223] as well as the collateral). Secured creditor's demeanor or conduct might intentionally inflict mental distress.

Similarly to US law, under UK law, an overzealous creditor attempting to repossess goods via self-help might fall foul of a number of offenses designed to protect the debtor. Especially, recapture of goods from the debtor without being entitled by a court order or by securing debtor's consent at the time of the repossession might face criminal consequences. The offenses that might be committed are theft, blackmail, burglary, using violence for the purposes of securing entry, criminal damage, harassment of debtors or demanding payment for unsolicited goods. Without having such a standard as "without breach of peace," under UK law, a wrongful recaption of the goods would deprive the creditor of his other remedies under the agreement and would constitute both a tort and a repudiation of the agreement.[224] In addition, besides statutory restrictions, recaption raised a series of legal problems such as entitlement to use force, whether the creditor is allowed to enter the debtor's premises, whether wrongful recaption would be sanctioned under debt collection legislation or whether it amounts to violation of human rights.

Since France and Germany do not allow self-help repossession, anyone engaging in repossessing goods would be committing a criminal act, most likely theft, if violence or breaking into someone's property occurred. In addition, they would most likely be held liable for any damages caused as well under general civil law.

Similarly, in Romania, any criminal offense is subjected to the provisions of the Criminal Code (and ancillary laws) or contravention rules. What does not amount to a criminal offense might be subjected to tort law (civil liability) under the general rules of the RNCC. However, the situation in Romania is hardly similar to those in the US or the UK. First of all, not all wrongful conducts give rise to liability in tort. For example, there is no tort of conversion in Romania. The only provisions dealing

[221] Rusch and Sepinuck (2010), pp. 187–191. Also: White and Summers (2010), pp. 1354–1355, and *In Re Downing*, U.S. Bankruptcy Court, W.D. Missouri (2002), 286 B.R. 900, where the court held that the notice concerning the sale of collateral given by the secured creditor to the debtor was insufficient and hence the secured creditor lost its right to a deficiency judgment under Missouri law.

[222] Martin (2013), p. 1.

[223] In tort and criminal law, conversion is defined as the wrongful possession or disposition of another's property as if it were one's own; an act or series of acts of willful interference, without lawful justification, with an item of property in a manner inconsistent with another's right, whereby that other person is deprived of the use and possession of the property. See: Garner (2009), p. 381.

[224] Macleod (2007), p. 808.

with the disposition of another's goods[225] are to be found in the section dedicated to the sale contract. What is worse is that the new established regime, although "commercial friendly,"[226] places the person whose goods were disposed by another without right in a very weak position, since, according to the courts, the aggrieved party can only annul the contract if both the seller and the buyer knew the good did not belong to the seller and, hence, there was a unlawful cause[227] or both contracting parties acted in ill faith.[228] Hence, leaving the matter to be solved by tort rules is not a good solution because tort law does not grasp it.

Otherwise, the only remedy available is the action of restitution (*acţiune în revendicare*), which is both complex and expensive, due to the fact that the judicial fees are calculated based on the value of the good to be restituted. However, nothing affects the Romanian debtor more than the absence of parallel, sector-specific prudential and consumer protection regulations,[229] similar to the US FDCPA.[230] Despite the fact that Romania has adopted and recognized self-help repossession, the Romanian system suffers in terms of efficiency when it comes to preventing and remedying creditor abuse.

4.5.2 Secured Party's Statutory Liability

As seen in the previous sections, in the US, the secured party enjoys total discretion in disposing the collateral, as long as it acts in good faith and complies with the commercially reasonable standard. The possibility of challenging an unreasonable sale in court was not considered enough pressure on the creditor to ensure his compliance, and hence, the UCC has provided for additional remedies available to both the debtor and to other secured parties.

---

[225] RNCC, Art. 1683.

[226] Reftu (2012), the author fails to recognize the risks of having personal property sold by a third party, once the owner has lost possession, claiming that such sale needs to be validated by the real owner. In fact, goods sold on black market or fairs do not require such validation and a good faith purchaser would acquire valid title, while the real owner would be left with an action for damages against the seller.

[227] Decision no 14/2009 of Suceava Court of Appeals.

[228] Decision no 543/2012 of Gorj County Court.

[229] Tajti (2013), p. 13. The author emphasizes that lack of proper regulation has actually encouraged out-of-court enforcement, but placing it somewhere on the boundaries of legality and on the expense of consumers.

[230] For a detailed analysis and a comparison of FDCPA and Romanian law, see *infra*, Chap. 6, Sect. 6.1.

4.5.2.1 Statutory Remedies in the US

A first important remedy is the opportunity offered to all interested parties to seek an injunctive relief to prevent an unreasonable disposition of collateral, provided that the person who tries to obtain it satisfies all state law requirements to obtain it.[231] Seeking an injunction might prove useful in the case the secured party did not yet dispose of the collateral. But in the case he already did and caused a loss to the debtor (or any person entitled to notification or whose security interest has been made known to the secured creditor) by not complying with the provisions of Part 6 of Article 9, then the latter has the possibility to seek damages.

Some other aspects are worth mentioning. *First,* since the law only refers to secured parties who notified their interest to the secured creditor, it means that those who failed to do so cannot seek recovery, even in the case of improper disposition. *Second,* in the absence of an action for deficiency from the secured creditor's side, it is the debtor's burden to prove that the secured party failed to comply with the provisions of Part 6, Article 9. With respect to damages, since the UCC's text refers to damages for "any loss," courts have interpreted this phrase to exclude consequential damages but allowed punitive damages,[232] in those cases where secured creditors acted with reckless disregard of the rights of the debtor or other secured parties.[233]

Another important aspect concerns loss and consumer goods. Since the law only refers to loss, it might be possible for a person to establish that the secured party acted commercially unreasonable but to fail proving the loss resulting from such behavior. Therefore, the UCC[234] has specifically provided for payment of a minimum amount to the debtor *if* the collateral is consumer goods, *regardless of whether the debtor or other person suffered any loss.* In such case, the debtor may recover an amount not less than the credit service charge plus 10 % of the principal amount of the debt or the time price differential plus 10 % of the cash price. In effect, this provision imposes a statutory penalty on the erring secured party, given the fact that the debtor does not have to prove any actual damages to recover the statutory amount. The clear purpose of this provision is its deterring effect on secured parties so that they refrain from engaging in wrongful activity.[235]

The Revised Article 9[236] permits recovery of damages for any loss caused by secured creditor's noncompliance with any of Article 9's provisions. The Revised version also added lien holders to the categories of those entitled to seek damages. Moreover, the language used allows recovery for emotional distress damages, which represent two major novelties. However, where a debtor's deficiency is

[231] Duncan et al. (2012), (Rel. 32) 5-75.

[232] White and Summers (2007), pp. 242–243.

[233] For a list of cases, see Duncan et al. (2012), (Rel. 35), 5-77, footnotes 16 and 17.

[234] UCC, Section 9-507 (1).

[235] Duncan et al. (2012), (Rel. 35), 5-77.

[236] UCC, Section 9-625 (b).

eliminated,[237] Revised Article 9 also prohibited recovery of any additional damages, the Official Comment claiming that in this way any double recovery for noncompliance would be prevented.[238]

Revised Article 9 contains several specific damage provisions for consumer goods transactions. There is again a minimum, statutory damages rule for debtors and secondary obligor in consumer goods transactions, which will apply in any case in which the creditor has failed to comply with the provisions of Revised Article 9. Additionally, the Revised version imposed a $500 penalty on persons who fail to comply with specific statutory provisions.[239]

Last but not least, the noncompliant secured party faces the risk of losing the right to sue for deficiency.[240] While Gilmore pointed out that there is no direction in Article 9 to help answer the question whether the secured creditor loses the right to a deficiency judgment against the debtor in the cases where he failed to observe the duties imposed on him by the UCC, the courts dealing with the issue have reached heterogeneous conclusions.[241] Unfortunately, the drafters of Revised Article 9 did not answer either, leaving the issue still to be determined by state courts, and therefore differing rules continue to apply.

4.5.2.2 Statutory Remedies in the UK

As already pointed out,[242] under UK consumer credit law dedicated to restrictions of repossession, it was established that in case of a regulated hire purchase or conditional sale agreement, if the debtor fails to remedy the default notified to him in a default notice, then the creditor is entitled to repossess goods *only after* obtaining a court order or the consent of the debtor at the moment of the repossession. But if the creditor disregards these obligations and goes on repossessing protected goods without the debtor's consent or in the absence of a court order, the agreement is terminated, and the debtor will be released from *all* liability under it.

Moreover, he will be entitled to recover all payments he has previously made to the creditor under the agreement.[243] This is a particularly severe sanction, as once the statutory duty has been breached, it cannot be remedied by the creditor returning the goods to the debtor.[244]

---

[237] UCC, Section 9-626.

[238] Duncan et al. (2012), (Rel. 35), 5-78, footnote 23. Official Comment 3 to Section 9-625, The American Law Institute National Conference of Commissioners on Uniform State Laws (2009), p. 1081.

[239] See *infra*, footnote 11 in Chap. 7.

[240] White and Summers (2007), pp. 239–241.

[241] For a detailed discussion and list of court decisions and their position: Duncan et al. (2012), (Rel. 35), 5-80–5-84, footnotes 31–38.

[242] See *supra*, Sect. 4.1.5.1.

[243] Furmston and Chuah (2010), p. 528.

[244] Harding (1995), p. 114.

4.5.2.3 Statutory Liability in Romania

In Romania, the RNCC has kept the sanctions introduced by the previous RSTL and thus maintained the statutory penalties, which had, beyond doubt, a strong deterrence effect on creditors. What the legislator did was to **add a civil penalty on top of the obligation to repair any damages or cover any losses caused by creditor's noncompliance with the legal provisions concerning either the retake or the sale of the collateral.**[245] Hence, for any breach of rules governing repossession or foreclosure, the creditor is to pay a penalty of one-third of the value of repossessed, respectively, sold goods.[246]

This penalty is not conditioned on the actual existence of any losses or damages; hence, it can be asked in court by a challenge to enforcement. It is worth mentioning that under the old STL, the penalty was even harsher as it amounted to one-third of the secured obligation,[247] which attracted criticism from the doctrine.[248] Either way, awarding damages in the absence of an actual loss represented (and still does) a novelty in the Romanian legislation (as a civil law jurisdiction) and its introduction can only be explained by the need to set an example for creditors and prevent any eventual abuses from their side. If the possibility of *ex post* challenge was illusory and the actual benefits of the aggrieved debtor would have been minor, the creditors would have abused both the taking into possession and the private sale.

4.6 Administrative Receivership (The Right to Administer Debtor's Assets)[249]

As shown in the previous sections, in case of debtor's default, in several of the chosen jurisdictions (the US, the UK and Romania), the creditor can resort to a self-help remedy—self-help repossession—in order to gain control and possession over the collateral or render it unusable by removing an essential component, in those cases where the collateral cannot be removed easily from the debtor's premises. However, self-help repossession is not the only self-help remedy available to

---

[245] Noncompliance for disobeying the rules established for distribution of proceeds that resulted from the sale of collateral only gives rise to an action for damages, based on general civil law.

[246] RNCC, Art. 2475, Para 2.

[247] RSTL, Art 87 and 88.

[248] Rizoiu (2009), p. 19/36.

[249] One must mention here that "receivership" in the sense used in Anglo-American law does not exist as a legal institution in Romania. The RNCC uses the term "administration." However, the right of the creditor to administer the collateral for the purposes of recovering the secured debt is a proper equivalent of administrative receivership as it existed in UK law. Hence, for the purposes of this work, administrative receivership and the right to administer the collateral will be used interchangeably when referring to Romanian law.

aggrieved creditors. In the UK[250] and Romania, the creditors enjoy the option of administrative receivership, a self-help tool that enables them to appoint[251] a receiver[252] and manage over the debtor's property. In the US, the book's benchmark, although receivership is known, it does not fall in the category of self-help remedies for the receiver is appointed by and acts as an agent of the court, while France and Germany do not know this legal institution.[253]

Despite several common features, administrative receivership in the UK and Romania has also many differences of regime, as the following analysis will point out. First, one must answer whether administrative receivership is a self-help remedy indeed, in full accordance with the definition employed for the purposes of this work. Since under the legal regimes established in the UK and Romania, administrative receivership is a legal, but not mandatory, out-of-court remedy, meant to help the secured creditor recover his debt without the involvement of state officials,[254] the answer can only be positive and the differences between the UK and Romanian systems do not affect in any way its character.

In the following sections, the book will comparatively analyze the legal regime applicable to this self-help remedy by focusing on four main issues: the *conditions required* to use administrative receivership as a self-help remedy, *who can act as a receiver* (administrator), his *legal status* (and liabilities) and his *legal powers*. There will also be a discussion on future prospect of implementing this remedy in Romania, when the UK has recently decided to drastically limit its application.

---

[250] Ali (2002), p. 249. The author mentions four self-help remedies available to secured parties: taking possession of secured property, selling the secured property, appointing a receiver in respect of the secured property and foreclosing the security interest. These remedies are considered self-help remedies because "they do not depend upon the grant of a judicial order or the intervention of a regulatory authority." Also: Getzler and Payne (2006), p. 136.

[251] The appointment was subjected in the UK to certain limitations: the secured creditor needed to have such right granted through the security agreement and the remedy was available only for a floating charge. In Romania, only the first condition was required. Ali (2002), pp. 259–260.

[252] According to the definition, a receiver is "a disinterested person appointed by a court, or by a corporation or other person, for the protection or collection of property that is the subject of diverse claims (for example, because it belongs to a bankrupt or is otherwise being litigated)." See: Garner (2009), p. 1383.

[253] "Other jurisdictions [. . .] do not permit a creditor to run a debtor's business, either because *this is simply a form of enforcement remedy which does not exist in that jurisdiction* (as is the case with many continental legal systems) or because the jurisdiction in question has developed a bankruptcy procedure which actually *prohibits secured creditors running a debtor's business effectively for their own account* (as is the case with Chapter 11 proceedings in the United States of America)." Vinter (1998), p. 150.

[254] See *infra*, footnote 261.

4.6.1 Character and Conditions of the Administrative Receivership and the Right to Administer the Debtor's Goods

Given that UK's personal property security law is spread in several normative acts, the legal regime of administrative receivership is to be found in the Insolvency Act. According to the previous Insolvency Act (1986), an administrative receiver could have been appointed by a secured party who held a debenture granting security interests that entitled the appointment of a receiver and manager over the whole, or substantially the whole, of a company's property, provided that one of the securities was a floating charge.[255] As noted by Armour and Frisby, this doubled the effect of the floating charge, which was able to cover the entirety of the debtor's assets by itself, the reason being that the priority granted by the floating charge had gradually been eroded by various types of claims that ranked ahead of it.[256] Under the old regime, the secured creditor was also able to block the effective operations of other insolvency procedures[257] and was allowed to confer appointment without any precondition of a demand for repayment to the debtor company.[258] Administrative receivership ended when either the floating chargee's debt was discharged or when there were no more assets to be used or sold to discharge the debt.[259]

Administrative receivership was, in fact, a privatized insolvency regime,[260] and a firm was able to *opt in* to this regime by granting an appropriate package of charges to a secured creditor. The direct result was that the secured creditor and his appointee gained after-default control and decision-making powers over the debtor company,[261] which at least in theory could have generated efficiencies. The rights of control granted to the secured creditor meant that junior creditors were stayed from enforcing their claims against the company's assets during receivership and prevented any "race to collect." This allowed the receiver to deploy the assets in a manner best suited to promote the dominant secured creditor's interests.[262] Seen

---

[255] Section 29 (2) of Insolvency Act 1986. According to one author, "the essential characteristic of a "floating" charge is that the company which grants it remains free to carry on its business and use its assets in the normal course of its business, until the lender intervenes, by appointing a receiver or in certain other ways, to enforce his security." Collins (1978), p. 691. Also: McCormack (2009), p. 126.

[256] Armour and Frisby (2001), p. 75.

[257] Section 9 (2) (a) of the Insolvency Act 1986.

[258] Armour and Frisby (2001), p. 76.

[259] Sheehan (2011), p. 403. Also Hunter (2005), p. 513.

[260] Armour and Frisby (2001), pp. 87–88. However, a receiver could have been displaced by the court and only by the court, provided other debenture holders or the appointor has requested so. For details, effects of removal, resignation or vacancy: Hunter (2005), pp. 570–575.

[261] Collins (1978), pp. 692–693.

[262] Sheehan (2011), pp. 400–401. "The administrative receiver has control over the assets for the purpose of paying off one particular creditor (the floating charge), and his or her management powers are ancillary to that aim."

from this perspective, administrative receivership was a remedy that facilitated the efficient disposal of assets by the secured creditor, following his decision to enforce.

Administrative receivership in Romania is a brand new private enforcement method and self-help remedy introduced by the RNCC,[263] following its model, the Civil Code of Quebec.[264] It did not exist in the previous RSTL, based entirely on UCC Article 9, which does not acknowledge such an institution. It is worth mentioning here that, unlike the UK law analyzed above, the Romanian legislators specifically considered the right to administer the collateral a private enforcement method, available to the choice of the creditor upon debtor's default. However, similarly to UK law this enforcement method is limited to security interests (mortgages) taken over the assets of an enterprise,[265] although it requires both the notification of any interested person[266] and the filing with the Electronic Archive of an enforcement notice.[267] Similar also to UK law, the bankruptcy of the debtor company does not lead to the termination of the administration right[268] and the administration right ceases when the creditor has covered his debt,[269] including interest and expenses incurred during enforcement; when he has chosen another method of enforcement; or, in other cases, when it is provided by law.[270]

---

[263] RNCC, Art. 2435, letter b) states: "Upon default, the creditor is entitled, at his choice to [...] take over the collateral for the purpose of administer it under the provisions of Art 2468-2473." In Romanian: "Î}\^{I}{n caz de neexecutare, creditorul are dreptul, la alegerea sa, să preia bunul în scop de administrare în condiţiile Art 2468-2473."

[264] Taking over the collateral for the purpose of administering it is considered a special case of administering the goods of another, an institution that was adopted from the Civil Code of Quebec. See for details: Boti (2011) and Boti and Boti (2010), http://www.juridice.ro/130791/institutia-administrarii-bunurilor-altuia-in-noul-cod-civil-roman.html.

[265] RNCC, Art 2468, and the provisions of Art 3 (3). The former defines the condition required for the creditor to exercise his right of administration of the collateral, while the latter defines what the exploitation of the enterprise is.

[266] The categories of interested persons to be notified are specified in RNCC, Art 2450, and are the same categories upon which a creditor must serve notice in case of enforcement by sale of collateral.

[267] According to the wording of Art 2468, the three conditions must be met cumulatively.

[268] RNC, Art 2472, last thesis. At the moment when the RNCC was adopted, commentators appreciated that this article created a veritable exception from the provisions of Art 36 of Insolvency Act no 85/2006. See: Colectiv (2012), p. 883. Given the fact that the Insolvency Act no 85/2006 was replaced by a new Insolvency Act no 85/2014, it is highly debatable if such an exception still survives.

[269] The right to take over the collateral in order to administer it is a temporary right. RNCC, Art 2468, para 2.

[270] These cases are the general cases established by the RNCC with respect to termination of administration of another's goods—which constitutes general law with respect to administration right—and they are listed in Art. 846: termination of the creditor's or beneficiary's rights over the administered goods, the expiry of the term, the achievement of the purpose, the denunciation of the creditor or of the beneficiary of the appointment, the replacement of the administrator by the

4.6.2 *Who Can Act as Receiver*

A question raised in the UK, before the modifications brought by the Enterprise Act 2002, which severely limited the creditors' possibility to appoint a receiver and the receiver's powers, was who could have been appointed as a receiver and what the first duties and effects were. Since in Romania the right to administer debtor's goods is brand new, a comparative analysis with the UK can only benefit Romanian scholars and practitioners.

4.6.2.1 Administrative Receivers in the UK

In the vast majority of cases, the receiver was an insolvency practitioner,[271] although no provision precludes the secured party to act as a receiver himself. However, a body corporate cannot act as receiver of the company's property.[272] The administrative receiver first had to verify that his appointment was in accordance with the provision of the security instrument,[273] for otherwise he would have been liable for trespassing.[274] In order to protect the rights of third parties, notification of the appointment had to be given to interested parties[275] and to the Registrar of Companies, and after the appointment all invoices, orders for goods or business letters issued by or on behalf of the debtor company had to contain the statement that a receiver or manager has been appointed.[276] The appointment of the administrative receiver out of court also had the effect of "crystallization" of the floating charge into a fixed one.[277]

---

creditor, beneficiary or the court, at the request of any interested person, by death, incapacity or insolvency of the administrator or of the beneficiary.

[271] Hunter (2005), p. 470

[272] Hunter (2005), p. 471.

[273] The security agreement must contain the possibility of the secured party to appoint a receiver, the circumstances in which a receiver can be appointed and the range of powers conferred upon the receiver, which may extend the statutory powers that were provided by the Insolvency Act 1986. Ali (2002), p. 260.

[274] Hunter (2005), pp. 478–479.

[275] Hunter (2005), p. 508.

[276] Section 39 (1) of the Insolvency Act 1986.

[277] Hunter (2005), p. 473. On the effects of crystallization over the powers of the company and its directors, see Hunter (2005), p. 474. Also: Collins (1978), pp. 691–692.

4.6.2.2 Administrators of Debtor's Goods in Romania

With respect to who can act as administrator, Romanian law[278] states that there is no impediment for the creditor to exercise the function himself, similar to UK law, but the creditor can also appoint another person of his own choice, or it can be someone appointed by the court. The latter case does not present any interest since the involvement of the court would undermine the self-help character of this enforcement method. Going back to who can administer the collateral on behalf of the secured creditor, one must notice that there is no requirement, similar to UK law, that he is an insolvency practitioner. The explanation is that the administration right is a general civil law institution, established by the RNCC and not a special one, established and strongly embedded in the insolvency proceedings, like in the UK. Another difference from the UK regime is that, given the lack of specification in the wording of the RNCC, it seems a legal person can administer the collateral for the benefit of the creditor. However, based on the analysis of the Civil Code of Quebec and practice of Canadian courts, it was postulated that such possibility should be allowed only exceptionally.[279]

4.6.3 Status of Receiver

The appointed administrative receiver's status[280] in the UK was somehow complicated. Therefore, UK scholars had to find suitable explanations for the extensive powers he enjoyed over the debtor's assets. As the following comparative analysis will point out, the status of the Romanian administrator is not less complex and the legal provisions governing its status are insufficient to justify or support his powers.

4.6.3.1 Status of the Administrative Receiver in the UK

By statute,[281] he was deemed to be a company's agent[282] (until or unless the company went into liquidation). Concomitantly, he should have been subjected to a fiduciary duty of loyalty and a duty of care towards the company, in accordance with the principles of agency law. These fiduciary duties did not apply to the

[278] RNCC, Art 2469.

[279] Boti (2011), para 13.1.

[280] For details: Collins (1978), pp. 707–710. The author mentions a "dual" status of the receiver and discusses the complications that arise where foreign jurisdictions are involved, especially those where the institution is unknown, such as France and Germany, or has a different regime, such as Canada or the US.

[281] Section 44 (1) of the Insolvency Act 1986.

[282] However, given the peculiarities of the receiver's agency, the principal does not have the right to dismiss the agent. Section 45 (1) of the Insolvency Act 1986.

administrative receiver, since his main duty was to exercise his powers *bona fide* in the interest of the secured creditor who appointed him[283] rather than those of his nominal "principal."[284] However, if he decided to carry on the business, he was obliged to do it with due diligence.[285]

The logic behind is simple:

> Provided the business was to be sold as a going concern, it had to continue trading. Hence, it meant that new contracts were to be negotiated and concluded after the appointment of the administrative receiver. Were the receiver to enter into contracts as a principal, he would have been personally and exclusively liable to them. Were he to act as agent for his appointor, the latter would have been liable.[286]

Therefore, the agency status ensured that the company continues as principal and that the secured creditor remains stranger to the contract.[287] Were the secured creditor not distanced from potential liability[288] in this fashion, there would have been a strong disincentive to continue trading, thus restricting the outcomes that could have realistically been achieved.

---

[283] For these reasons, McCormack notes that although "the receiver is designated by statute as an agent of the company [...] this is a very curious and unusual form of agency." McCormack (2009), p. 126.

[284] McCormack (2008), p. 49. Also: Armour and Frisby (2001), p. 77. Keeping in mind that they are referring to the previous legal regime, the authors mention that a receiver owed to the "principal" (the debtor company) no duty of obedience nor any general duty to provide information as to the conduct of its affairs. They also mention that the common belief according to which the receiver's duty of care was limited to the requirement to take reasonable steps to obtain a proper price on the exercise of his power to sale was overturned by the decision rendered in *Medforth v. Blake & Ors* [2000] Ch 86 (CA), where the court ruled that if the receiver decided to continue trading, then he owes an equitable duty of skill and care to the debtor company. However, this duty was not supposed to conflict with the main duty of acting in the interest of the secured creditor. For details on *Medforth v. Blake & Ors* and on the duty of good faith and duty of care to obtain the best price for assets sold, see: Sheehan (2011), p. 401. Also: Collins (1978), p. 692. "The primary duty of the receiver is to the debenture holders and not to the company. He is receiver and manager of the property of the company for the debenture holders, not manager of the company."

[285] Sheehan (2011), p. 401.

[286] Armour and Frisby (2001), p. 88.

[287] This contention requires some qualification. A receiver would not be personally liable on the contracts he enters into in the name of the principal. However, Section 44 (1) of Insolvency Act 1986 established an exception from this rule in relation to both commercial and employment contracts. The receiver was allowed to escape this personal liability by contracting it out. Hence, the company was to be liable as principal only in these cases where receivers managed to contract out their personal liability. See: McCormack (2008), p. 51.

[288] Sheehan (2011), p. 401. However, the creditor owes a duty to exercise his appointment right in good faith by not appointing an incompetent person. See: Hunter (2005), pp. 469, 491 and 522. Additionally, the creditor could have been held liable in case he sought to direct or influence the judgment of the receiver. Hunter (2005), p. 496.

4.6.3.2 Status of the Administrator of Debtor's Goods in Romania

In Romanian law,[289] either the creditor or the person empowered by him with the administering of the collateral bears the status of an "administrator of another's goods" with "complete administration" powers.[290] Hence, the person empowered with complete administration must conserve and exploit profitably the assets, enrich the patrimony as long as these operations are in the benefit of the beneficiary.[291] For this purpose, the administrator is able to sell or encumber the assets or change their destination and also to perform any kind of investment he deems fit.[292] However, unlike in the UK where the receiver was able to terminate any prior-appointment obligation, he is not allowed to touch upon any rights obtained prior appointment by any tenants.[293]

4.6.4 Powers of the Receiver

Administrative receivers in the UK and administrators of the debtor's goods in Romania enjoy a wide range of powers in order to fulfill their ultimate purpose, recovering the creditor's debt. However, as the following comparison shows, their powers are not entirely similar, due to both differences in status and legislative gaps in Romanian law.

4.6.4.1 Powers of the Administrative Receiver in the UK

With respect to the powers conferred to the administrative receiver, UK law provided him with a wide range of statutory[294] powers to manage the company's business, to commit it to new contracts and to take control of and sell its assets.[295] Additionally, he may have caused the company to terminate its preappointment

---

[289] RNCC, Art 2470.

[290] The legal regime applicable to complete administration is provided by RNCC, Arts 800 and 801, corroborated with the general legal regime applicable to any administration of another's goods, as established by RNCC, Arts 792–857 and Arts 79 and 80, points 15, 16 from the Law for the Application of the Civil Code.

[291] RNCC, Art 800.

[292] RNCC, Art 801.

[293] RNCC, Art 2471.

[294] The administrative receiver had a standard list of powers in Section 42 (1) and Schedule 1 of the Insolvency Act 1986, if the absence of any explicit powers in the security instrument. See Sheehan (2011), p. 402.

[295] Section 42 (1) of the Insolvency Act 1986 and Armour and Frisby (2001), p. 77. However, the powers were not completely discretionary. The receiver was supposed to take note and pay the preferential debts ranking in priority to the floating charge. See: Sheehan (2011), pp. 401–402.

contract in order to further the interests of the secured creditor.[296] The termination leaves the contracting party with a remedy in damages for breach of contract against the company, as long as the contracting party did not acquire a proprietary right superior to that of the secured creditor, prior to crystallization of the former's floating charge. However, if this was not the case, the contracting party was left unsecured against an insolvent enterprise, which may have proved worthless.

Obviously, the powers of the administrative receiver in pursuing the interests of the secured creditor were extremely strong,[297] which brought it to the attention of the legislators, who in 2002[298] decided to amend the Insolvency Act and limit the availability[299] of this self-help remedy. Therefore, where a floating charge was executed after the 15th of September 2003, the charge is unable to appoint an administrative receiver but may, if the charge would have been able to appoint such a receiver before 2003, appoint an administrator.[300] Since basically the Enterprise Act 2002 removed the floating chargee's possibility to displace management or assert control over the debtor's assets and replaced it with an ability to appoint an administrator who has to consider by law the interest of all creditors,[301] one can

---

Also: Hunter (2005), p. 480. For a detailed list and analysis of powers and privileges conferred to the administrative receiver, see: Hunter (2005), pp. 508–511.

[296] The reason lies in the fact that the rule established in *Said v. Butt* ([1920] 2 KB 497) according to which an agent cannot be liable in tort for inducing a breach of his principal's contract has been held to apply to receivers as well according to several cases: *Lathia v. Dronsfield Bros* [1987] QB 357; *Re Sobam BV (In Receivership)* [1996] 1 BCLC 446.

[297] "The 'New Labour' government saw receivership as too heavily creditor oriented. There the concern was that the economic recession of the early 1990s had been prolonged by banks protecting their returns through appointing receivers and consequently, many companies had been driven unnecessarily into insolvency." McCormack (2009), p. 126. Also: Sheehan (2011), p. 402: "It was thought that administrative receivers and their appointors held too much power and were able to look after their own interests in the detriment of other corporate stakeholders."

[298] The Insolvency Act 1986 was modified by the Enterprise Act 2002. "Receivership was not seen as sufficiently responsive to the concerns of other stakeholders." McCormack (2009), p. 126.

[299] Section 176 A of the Insolvency Act 1986, inserted by Section 252 of the Enterprise Act 2002, provides, for example, that the liquidator of an insolvent company should use a prescribed portion of the assets subject to the floating charge to satisfy unsecured debts. Moreover, floating and fixed charges cannot participate in the distribution of these assets should there be a shortfall in money owed to them, unless all the unsecured creditors have been paid in full. However, it is contended that despite the harshness of this measure, the prescribed part makes little difference in practice to unsecured creditors. Sheehan (2011), pp. 402–403. Whether that is true or not, this work cannot verify. However, insulating part of the debtor's assets from a secured creditor's reach has an obvious, negative impact on the secured creditor's recovery and undermines the purpose of the security interest, which is even more important. Additionally, Section 72 of the Insolvency Act 1986 now makes it impossible for a floating charge to appoint an administrative receiver except where the charge was created before the date or where the charge was created after the date with the observation of several circumstances. See for details Sheehan (2011), p. 403; and Hunter (2005), pp. 437–439 and 503–504. It is why authors have claimed that floating charge should even be dropped off altogether. For details: Sheehan (2011), pp. 411–413.

[300] Hunter (2005), pp. 462, 503; and Sheehan (2011), p. 400.

[301] Sheehan (2011), p. 413. Also: Hunter (2005), p. 550.

easily claim that the reform of the Insolvency Act meant in fact the death of administrative receivership[302] and of a very effective (at least in theory) self-help remedy.

4.6.4.2 Powers of the Administrator of Debtor's Goods in Romania

In Romania, the situation is far more complicated. According to the general regime applicable to the administration of another's goods, the administrator bears the obligation to act only within the powers conferred to him[303] and must act with due diligence, honesty and loyalty,[304] in order to realize the interests of the beneficiary. Similarly to UK law, he is empowered to take over the goods to be administered wherever they are, even from another secured creditor, provided the sale of the collateral has not been started.[305] Moreover, as long as he acts within the powers conferred and undertakes obligations in the name of the beneficiary, he will not be personally held liable towards third parties.[306] However, opposite to UK law, the beneficiary is liable towards third parties for any damages caused by the administrator during the exercise of his powers, but the liability is limited to the profits made.[307]

The numerous differences in the applicable regime lie with the fact that Romanian law did not clarify the status of the creditor acting as administrator or of the administrator himself. As shown in the case of the UK, in order to answer the practical issues, the receiver was assimilated to an agent of the company with exceptional limited duties towards the principal (the debtor company), acting mainly to the benefit of the secured creditor. This allowed him to conduct the business effectively but insulated both him and the secured creditor from liability. The Romanian legislator did not address these concerns,[308] which will definitely cause difficulties in practice and render this enforcement method useless.

---

[302] The Enterprise Act 2002 prohibited the appointment of an administrative receiver altogether with the exception of charges created before the 15th of September 2003 and of charges created after that date, in cases which fell under statutory exempted categories (Section 250 of Enterprise Act 2002). The exemptions are meant to protect large capital market financings, step-in rights in public–private partnership projects, utility projects, urban regeneration projects, financial market charges, registered social landlords and protected railway companies. McKendrick (2010), pp. 926–927. Also: McCormack (2008), pp. 53–56.

[303] RNCC, Art 802.

[304] RNCC, Art 803.

[305] RNCC Art 2441, para 2.

[306] RNCC, Art 813. However, he is liable if he acts outside the powers conferred and the third parties were unware that the administrator is acting outside granted powers (RNCC, Art 814).

[307] RNCC, Art 816.

[308] When addressing the general legal regime applicable to the administrator of another's goods, the RNCC refers only to duties towards the beneficiary (the party whose goods are administered). However, if one extrapolates these provisions to the special case established by Art 2435, para 2, the beneficiary of the administration is not the party whose goods are administered but the

One explanation might be the novelty of this remedy and the fact that the legislators were satisfied with the mere translation of the Quebec's Civil Code and did not pay attention to the way it can be applied to the Romanian legal system.[309] Whatever the explanations are, this self-help remedy remains both complex and uncertain on paper with unpredictable results in practice.[310] One may also raise the question of opportunity considering the fact that the UK, where administrative receivership had a long-standing tradition, decided to drop it. Whether it will prove an efficient and useful tool remains to be seen.

4.7 Conclusions: Death of the Repo Industry or a More Efficient System?

This chapter analyzed the mechanisms behind private enforcement and tried to point out both similarities and peculiarities between the chosen jurisdictions that recognize it as a useful legal tool in the realization of secured interests. In the US, the focus is on the balance between the aggrieved creditor's rights to recover his debts and the debtor's rights not to be subjected to any abuse in the process. The UCC tried and managed to find that balance by implementing and developing standards such as the prohibition of breach of peace during self-help repossession and commercial reasonableness of any private sale of the collateral. Additional rules were designed to protect consumers, especially those who built up a considerable equity in the collateral and insulate them from any arbitrary decisions the creditor might take during foreclosure procedures, such as the 60 % rule.

In the UK, the focus on the consumer is even stronger. Given the influence of the EU perspective on consumer protection, UK law tries to keep the consumer debtor informed so that he can make the best decision in the circumstances. Before going on the path of foreclosure, UK law also provides the consumer debtor with several opportunities of complying or dealing with his obligations. In certain cases, the legislator deemed that it would be better to preclude creditors from using self-help means against consumers in regulated agreements, thus imposing restrictions of

---

secured creditor, since the purpose of the administration right is the repayment of the debt. Similarly, when the general regime refers to the liability of the beneficiary, it refers to the party whose goods are administered as well, but under the special regime, the beneficiary secured party cannot and should not be held liable for the obligations undertaken by the administrator since that would undermine the whole purpose of the administration. Unfortunately, Romanian law left all these issues to be answered by the practice and since the Romanian courts can only interpret law (and not create it as common law courts can) the results are hard to predict.

[309] Boti and Boti (2010), Para 11.

[310] See Boti (2011), *at* http://www.juridice.ro/152502/influenta-codului-civil-din-quebec-asupra-noului-cod-civil-din-romania.html, Para 13.1. The author claims that with respect to the administration of another's goods, only the practice will decide the utility and pertinence of this activity.

repossession. However, once default was not cured and repossession has occurred, the debtor is left entirely defenseless, at creditor's will.

Last but not least, the Romanian law, in its quest for modernization and in order to provide an incentive for investors, has chosen a *hybrid* system that combines the private enforcement means of the UCC with limited judicial control. Unlike its American model, the Romanian law made—and still makes—no differentiation between professional and consumer debtors, both of them enjoying the same legal safeguards, although that means in practice less protection for consumers, for general consumer protection law cannot step in.

Unfortunately, private enforcement also generated other effects than those prescribed by the legal norms. Despite efforts put in by legislators, courts and legal doctrine, interpretation- and application-related issues still arise. Moreover, besides the legal analysis there are also other factors to be taken into consideration, such as the need, the development and the future of the repo industry[311] or the need to constrain it in a tighter legal jacket.

Recent calls for reformation underline the inconsistency of court decisions regarding breach of peace and consider that it undermines predictability and promotes needless litigation.[312] The proposed solution is to implement a uniform, open-end definition to be used by the courts at a nationwide level. The definition is to contain, first, a standard description of circumstances that would amount to breach of peace *per se* and, second, in case there was no *per se* breach, a case-by-case assessment of the level of trespass required in the process and the level of harm caused to third parties (which was totally disregarded until now).[313] Only time will tell if such proposals are adopted[314] or have the expected results.

In the UK, MacLeod[315] has expressed concerns with the effects of enhanced consumer protection and restrictions on repossession over access to credit. He contended that such measures reduce the advantage of repossession and the total charge for credit will increase, which will be reflected especially on the debtors ("good payers will pay for the bad"). Additionally, creditors will be encouraged to seek ways to separate the loan from the supply of goods because although they will be deprived of security over the goods, they will escape the provisions limiting the liability of debtors who exercise their right to statutory termination in case of regulated agreements or consumer hirings. Last but not least, another effect of extra-statutory restrictions is that it will trigger an increased number of domestic consumers to resort to illegal lenders and mob repossession methods since their credit rating will not enable them to secure financial accommodation with the

[311] Over two million repossessions occurred in the US in 2009, according to an American NGO monitoring consumer protection. See Van Alst and Jurgens (2010), p. 1.

[312] McRobert (2012), p. 586.

[313] McRobert (2012), p. 593.

[314] Such proposals to define breach of peace were made during the revision of Article 9, but they were dismissed by the legislators. See: Loterstein (2013), p. 1363.

[315] Macleod (2007), pp. 834–836.

creditors anymore. The concern seems to be related to the business as well, but in this case it is the credit business that takes the blow. Therefore, alternatives via various forms of chattel mortgage[316] are being examined in a quest for reformation.

As for Romania, the RNCC seems to have found the middle way between private enforcement and judicial control. Similarly to the previous RSTL, the RNCC did not establish any special rules for consumer protection. Absence of relevant court cases raises the question of whether debtors (either professional or consumers) are equally protected or exposed. The provisions with respect to judicial control suggest the former, but reality might support the latter. Interestingly enough, the doctrine analyzing private enforcement could not come up with an actual case in which any of the aspects of private enforcement as they were regulated by the previous RSTL were put into discussion.

The current RNCC regime is too new to have generated a practice. It is hard to believe that private enforcements do not occur, but it is even harder to assume what the reason for lack of court cases may be: reluctance and total compliance of creditors with self-help repossession rules? Total collaboration from the debtors' side? Preference of judicial enforcement methods? Obviously difficulties generated by the differences between the competences of common law and civil law courts are in place: open statutory definitions left up to the courts to determine cannot generate the same effects in a country where courts lack the power to make law and are limited to interpret it.

Undeniably, the initial EBRD model implemented[317] generated a significant decrease in credit costs since it facilitated the collateralization of personal property[318] and had a beneficial impact on the development of the credit business,[319] which was the main purpose from the very beginning. Additionally, the repossession business knew a rapid expansion as well, generating important revenues.[320] In its path to modernity, nineteenth-century Romania adopted from the West the newest legal instruments and methods, in an attempt to jump over a historical development gap and catch up with its neighbors and models. This policy was heavily criticized by the Romanian academics as being "a form without substance."[321] The main idea behind this phrase was that the Romanian society and realities were not suitable for implementing such modern means, and hence appropriate means, designed for such realities, were in fact needed to ensure development. After 15 years since the reformation of its STL, one cannot tell for sure if this is still the case.

[316] Macleod (2007), p. 836.

[317] Dahan and Simpson (2008), p. 90.

[318] Rizoiu (2009), p. 3/36.

[319] Dahan and Simpson (2008), p. 234.

[320] Horvathova et al. (2011), p. 105, specifically footnote 61.

[321] Maiorescu (1868).

References

Ali P (2002) The law of secured finance. An international survey of security interests over personal property. Oxford University Press, USA

Armour J, Frisby S (2001) Rethinking receivership. Oxford J Legal Stud 21:73

Boti I (2011) Influenta Codului Civil din Quebec asupra Noului Cod Civil din Romania. www.juridice.ro

Boti I, Boti V (2010) Institutia administrarii bunului altuia in Noul Cod Civil Roman. www.juridice.ro

Braucher J (1997) The Repo Code: a study of adjustment to uncertainty in commercial law. Wash Univ Law Rev 75:549

Brodsky JA (1974) Constitutionality of self-help repossession under the Uniform Commercial Code: the Eighth and Ninth Circuits Speak. South Dakota Law Rev 19:295

Buckley LW Jr (1976) The future of self-help repossession under the Uniform Commercial Code. Commer Law J 81:165

Cohen JE (1998) Copyright and the jurisprudence of self-help. Berkeley Technol Law J 13:1089

Colectiv (2012) Noul Cod civil. Comentarii, doctrina, jurisprudenta. Ed. Hamangiu, Bucuresti

Collins L (1978) Floating charges, receivers and managers and the conflict of laws. Int Comp Law Q 27:691

Dahan F, Simpson J (2008) Secured transactions reform and access to credit. Edward Elgar, Cheltenham/Northampton

Del Duca LF (1974) Pre-notice, pre-hearing, pre-judgment seizure of assets – self-help repossession under UCC Section 9-503, its antecedents and future. Dickinson Law Rev 79:211

Duncan RF, Lyons WH, Wilson CL (2012) The law and practice of secured transactions: working with Article 9. Law Journal Press, New York

Franklin D, Harms SA (2010) International commercial secured transactions. Carswell, Toronto

Furmston M, Chuah J (2010) Commercial and consumer law. Pearson Education Limited, Essex

Garner BA (2009) Black's law dictionary. WEST, US

Getzler J, Payne J (2006) Company charges. Spectrum and beyond. Oxford University Press, Oxford

Gilmore G (1999) Security interests in personal property. The Lawbook Exchange, LTD, Union, New Jersey

Gitter H (1993) Self-help remedies for software vendors. Santa Clara Comput High Technol Law J 9:413

Goode R (eds) (1999) Goode: consumer credit law and practice. LexisNexis Butterworths, UK

Guest AG, Lloyd MG, Lomnicka E, Dobson P (2009) Encyclopedia of consumer credit law. Thomson Reuters (Legal) Limited, London

Guidry G (1974) Mitchell v. W.T. Grant Co.: procedural due process reexamined. LA Law Rev 35:221

H. WR (1973) Prejudgment self-help repossession of secured property held not to violate due process – Adams v. Southern California First National Bank, No. 72-1484 (9th Cir., Oct. 4, 1973). Univ Richmond Law Rev 8:585

Hamilton AW (2000) Price v. U-Haul Co: the Louisiana Supreme Court authorizes self-help repossession. Tulane Law Rev 74:2237

Harding GW (1995) Consumer credit and consumer hire law: a practical guide. Sweet & Maxwell, London

Hayes TG (2006) Secured creditors holding lien creditors hostage: have a little faith in revised Article 9. Indiana Law J 81:733

Horvathova A, Fabian K, Stanescu C-G (2011) Is self-help repossession possible in central Europe? The case of Hungary, Romania and Slovakia. J Euroasian Law 4

Hunter Q.C. M (2005) Kerr and Hunter on receivers and administrators. Sweet & Maxwell, London

Kieninger E-M (2004) Security rights in movable property in European private law. Cambridge University Press, Cambridge
King LP, Cook ML (1996) Creditors' rights, debtors' protection, and bankruptcy. Mathew Bender, New York
Laswell DL (1974) Commercial transactions: the future of self-help repossession. John Marshall J Pract Proced 8:98–100
Lloyd RM, Kuney GW (2008) Secured transactions: UCC Article 9 & Bankruptcy. University of Tennessee College of Law, Knoxville
Loterstein A (2013) Law-enforcement officers and self-help repossession: a state-action approach. Mich Law Rev 111
Macleod JK (2007) Consumer sales law. Routledge-Cavendish, Abingdon
Maiorescu T (1868) In contra directiei de astazi in cultura romana. Convorbiri Literare
Martin JS (2013) The repo man did what? A secured creditor's Article 9 right to repossess collateral and when lenders have liability for repossessions gone awry. Commercial Damages Reporter 1. www.ssrn.com
McAnally JW (1973) State action considerations and economic implications of holding self-help repossessions unconstitutional. Law Soc Order 707
McCormack G (2008) Corporate rescue law – an Anglo-American perspective. Edward Elgar, Cheltenham
McCormack G (2009) Apples and oranges? Corporate rescue and functional convergence in the US and UK. Int Insolv Rev 18
McDonald KK (1972) Self-help repossession: Fuentes and judicial process. Temple Law Q 46:540
McDonnell JB (1973) Sniadach, The Replevin Cases and self-help repossession – due process tokenism? Boston Coll Law Rev 14
McKendrick E (2010) Goode on commercial law. Penguin Books, London
McRae MD (1974) Commercial law-self-help repossession – Section 9-503 of the UCC Held Constitutional. Mercer Law Rev 26:1421
McRobert R (2012) Defining 'Breach of the Peace' in self-help repossessions. Wash Law Rev 87
Nowka RH (2009) Mastering secured transactions: UCC Article 9. Carolina Academic Press, Durham
Picker RC, Baird DG, Jackson TH (2002) Security interests in personal property. Foundation Press, New York
Ramsay I (2012) Consumer law and policy. Hart Publishing, Oxford/Portland
Reftu R (2012) Conventia de vanzare a bunului altuia – o sursa de nesiguranta? www.lexcafe.ro. http://lexcafe.ro/articole/valabilitatea-conventiei-de-vanzare-a-bunului-altuia-o-sursa-de-nesiguranta/
Rizoiu R (2008) Garantie reala mobiliara. Executare prin mijloace pasnice. Intelesul notiunii "in mod pasnic". Revista romana de drept privat
Rizoiu R (2009) Mecanismele executarii private in cazul luarii pasnice in posesie a bunului afectat unei garantii reale mobiliare. Revista romana de drept privat
Rizoiu R (2011) Garantiile reale imobiliare. O abordare functionala – Analiza economica a dreptului garantiilor reale – Introducere in regimul juridic al ipotecilor mobiliare. Universul Juridic, Bucharest
Roditti EC (1995) Is self-help a lawful contractual remedy? Rutgers Comput Technol Law J 21:431
Rusch LJ, Sepinuck SL (2010) Problems and materials on secured transactions. Thomson & West, St. Paul
"Self-Help" repossession and due process (1974) St. John's Law Rev 48:661
Sheehan D (2011) The principles of personal property law. Hart Publishing, Oregon
Smith D (1973) Security interests: self-help still an available method of repossession. Univ Miami Law Rev XXVIII:231
Symposium on Commercial Law (1973) Self-help repossession of consumer goods: a constitutional look at Section 9-503 of the Uniform Commercial Code. Valparaiso Univ Law Rev 7:439

T. SM (1975) Self-help repossession pursuant to private contract held constitutional. King v. South Jersey Nat'l Bank, 66 N. j. 161, 330 A.2d 1 (1974). Rutgers Camden Law J 7:176

Tajti T (2002) Comparative secured transactions law. Akadémiai Kiadó, Budapest

Tajti T (2012) When and why is the rubberstamp of the European Union insufficient? Caveats to systems on the road towards the European Union. Zbornik. Pravnog Fakulteta U Zagrebu

Tajti T (2013) Post-1990 secured transaction law reforms in central and eastern Europe. Szegedi Közjegyzői Közlöny II:1

TeSelle J, Love JJ (1977) Attachment, garnishment, replevin and self-help repossession in Oklahoma. Oklahoma Law Rev 30

The American Law Institute National Conference of Commissioners on Uniform State Laws (2009) Uniform Commercial Code 2009–2010 Edition. Official Text and Comments. Thomson Reuters United States

Van Alst JW, Jurgens R (2010) Repo madness. How automobile repossessions endanger owners, agents and the public. National Consumer Law Center, Boston

Vinter G (1998) Project finance. Sweet & Maxwell, London

von Bar C, Clive E (2010) Principles, definition and model rules of European Private Law. Draft Common Frame of Reference (DCFR). Oxford University Press, Oxford

White JJ, Summers RS (2007) Principles of secured transactions. Thomson & West, St. Paul

White JJ, Summers RS (2010) Uniform commercial code. In Practitioner treatise series. Thomson Reuters, USA

Chapter 5
Factoring, Bad Debt and Collection Agencies

As stated in the previous chapters, creditors are skeptical about the efficacy of the judicial process when it comes to collection of debts, given the lengthy procedures, high expenses incurred, inherent risks and uncertainties.[1] In such circumstances, the creditors will not resort to litigation until all self-help remedies (where available) and nonjudicial collection efforts have been exhausted without result. Having analyzed self-help repossession and administrative receivership in Chap. 4, the book now turns to factoring and nonjudicial debt collection by debt collection agencies. As it will be shown, factoring is a sale or purchase of account receivables[2] for the purpose of collection, although account receivables may also be used as collateral.

However, using receivables as collateral is not going to be specifically covered by this chapter for two main reasons. **First**, the book is not concerned with collateralization of accounts receivables as such but with nonjudicial debt collection. **Second**, although in case of default the collateral needs to be recovered, it will be recovered either by selling the receivables (factoring) or by resorting to debt collection (be it private[3] or judicial) in the ways that will be analyzed later in this

[1] King and Cook (1996), p. 7.

[2] The terminology used in the UK for "account receivables" or "receivables" is "book debts." Book debts, in their turn, belong to the species of property called choses in action, which have been defined as property rights that can be enforced only by action and not by taking possession. See: Biscoe (1975), p. 95. For a detailed discussion concerning whether "receivables" is the exact equivalent of "book debts": Johnston (2008), pp. 147–148; and Beale et al. (2012), p. 273. Since the benchmark of this work is the US, the terminology employed for the purposes of this chapter will be the American one.

[3] UCC, Section 9-109 (d) (5) UCC, actually states that Article 9 will not cover assignments of accounts made for the purpose of collection only. Hence, abusive debt collection will be sanctioned under the FDCPA and not by provisions of the UCC. However, according to Official Comment 5 to Section 9-109, Article 9 will cover both transactions—sale of receivables (factoring) and assignment of receivables (invoice discounting)—but mainly with respect to perfection and priority rules. Laws (2009), p. 875.

C.G. Stănescu, *Self-Help, Private Debt Collection and the Concomitant Risks*,
DOI 10.1007/978-3-319-21503-7_5

chapter. There are no substantial differences in the collection process that would justify a separate analysis[4] of factoring (sale of receivables) and invoice discounting (assignment of receivables). The issue of abusive debt collection practices and remedies against them will be dealt with in the remaining two chapters.

5.1 Factoring

Generally, factoring is defined as a continuing legal relationship between a financial institution (the factor) and a business concern (the obligor[5]) selling goods or providing services to trade customers (the customers/debtors/account debtors) whereby the factor purchases the obligor's account receivables without or with recourse to the obligor and in relation thereto controls the credit extended to the customers (including the debt collection) and administers the sales ledger.[6]

5.1.1 Historical Background and Development

Factoring has a history dating back more than 400 years.[7] It is one of the oldest commercial activities and, at the same time—given its current use—one of the newest financing methods.[8] In its modern form, it had emerged about 100 years ago in the US[9] and spread in the 1960s in the UK, continental Europe and Asia. This activity was strongly related to the textile industry, but it evolved beyond that into a

---

[4] In the UK, invoice discounting is in fact considered a form of factoring and is reported together with factoring for statistics purposes. Bickers (2011), p. 147.

[5] UK terminology refers to the obligor as "client." Same term is used in the decisions of the Court of Justice of the EU (ECJ). However, since the benchmark of this book is the US, the terminology adopted is the American one.

[6] Biscoe (1975), p. 3. This definition is consistent with the more restrictive definition of factoring accepted in the US: "a continuing arrangement between a factoring concern and a seller of goods or services on open accounts, pursuant to which the factor performs the following services with respect to the accounts receivable arising from sales of such goods and services: purchases all accounts receivable for immediate cash, maintains the ledgers and performs other book-keeping duties, collects the accounts receivable, assumes the losses which may arise from the customer's financial inability to pay." Ruddy et al. (2006), pp. 1–2.

[7] There are authors who identify the origin of factoring in Ancient Rome. Silverman (1948), p. 593. Others went as far as to establish an origin back to ancient Babylon, 5,000 years ago. Ruddy et al. (2006), p. 5.

[8] Hiller (1939), p. 305.

[9] Gilmore (1999), pp. 250–251; Ruddy et al. (2006), p. 5; Biscoe (1975), pp. 30, 37; and Hilson (2010), pp. 2–4.

wide area such as shoes, petroleum, furs, lumber, rubber, metal and paper products.[10]

Just to emphasize the rapid growth and the magnitude of this business, in the US, in 1939, the revenues generated by factoring were already around one billion dollars per year.[11] Another study, this time focused on the situation in the UK, showed the factoring market to be one with a constant growth, in 1990s recording a total turnover of about 48 billion British pounds.[12] Since factoring deals basically with the collection of receivables, such staggering figures show exactly how important this financing method and the debt collection service are.

Nowadays, the term factoring is generally referred to as a "specialized service of credit checking and of financing the producer and distributor of merchandize."[13] Factors fulfill certain functions such as purchasing accounts receivable, guaranteeing the seller against customer credit failures, billing, ledgering and **collecting** the receivables, as well as financing clients' operations.[14] As this work is dedicated to debt collection, the focus of the analysis of factoring will refer primarily on the aspects related to the purchase and collection of accounts receivables. In the US, these services became important and proved very successful in the early 1940s where small and middle-sized Enterprises (SME's) were looking for short-term loans, which the banks were not interested or willing to provide. Thus, factors took over the collection of amounts, which the banks could not or would not do.[15] They also undertook for extra premium, in some cases, the loss of account when nonpayment occurred (nonrecourse factoring, known in Europe as *del credere*). At the same time, the borrowers were relieved from bookkeeping and accounting expenses.[16]

When it comes to factoring, one deals with **a triadic relationship**, in which all three parties are supposed to be professionals, active players in the field of commerce, although, as it is shown later in this chapter, that is not necessarily the case anymore. The factor is "a specialized type of either privately or bank-owned finance company, that purchases accounts receivable from a client firm and then receives payments directly from clients' customers."[17] In time, factoring developed into two types: *recourse* factoring—which entitles the factoring company to claim payment directly from the obligor in the event that an obligor's customer defaults on

---

[10] Hiller (1939), p. 310.

[11] Hiller (1939), p. 310. The spectacular growth of factoring in that period may be explained by two causes: "the need for credit advice and credit warranty to manufacturers who do not have the organization to handle their own credit problems efficiently and the need for working capital which arises at one time or another in the conduct of most business." See: Silverman (1948), p. 595. For the purposes of this work, the focus will be on the first function.

[12] Soufani (2002), p. 21.

[13] Silverman (1948), p. 593.

[14] Silverman (1948), p. 594.

[15] Fleming and Hopkins (2011). Also: Blackburn (2010).

[16] Silverman (1948), p. 596.

[17] Soufani (2002), p. 23.

payment—and *non-recourse* factoring—where the risk of nonpayment is entirely undertaken by the factor. Given the fact that usually the factors' profits stem out of the difference between the price they pay to the client and the face value of the purchased debt, in the case of nonrecourse factoring, the previously mentioned difference will be bigger.

5.1.2 Factoring Consumer Debt

Given the definition of factoring and the details above, it would appear that debts incurred by individuals in their private capacity (such as debts incurred for personal, family or domestic use—consumer debts) are excluded from factoring.[18] There were two arguments. On the one hand, usually the invoice values of consumer debts were less than the minimum, which would allow the factor to perform his functions at a reasonable cost to the obligor. On the other hand, obtaining adequate current credit information on which to base credit decisions and assume credit risks was much more difficult with respect to the consumer than a trader, considering that the factor was under no contractual relationship with the consumer.[19]

Notwithstanding the above, factoring does not fall outside the topic of this work for several reasons. **First**, due to the fact that under nonrecourse factoring the obligor sells his debts (at a discount) and manages to obtain cash while avoiding the risk of customer's inability to pay, from his point of view, the debt was collected without recourse to judicial proceedings, which constitutes the topic of this book. **Second,** despite the exclusion of consumer debt from the definition of factoring, it must be mentioned that the circumstances that gave rise to their exclusion have changed. Today, selling consumer debts in bulk (i.e., selling uncollected parking tickets or electricity bills) is a standard practice. Advancement in technology and computers has much simplified and reduced the costs of ledger administration, while consumer credit information became more available already.[20] Hence, it is now possible to factor consumer debts, which can expose consumers to abusive debt collection practices. **Last**, either because of lack of understanding[21] or because of existing legal gaps, factoring has been used as cover for debt collection services (either by outsourcing the collection or by selling debt portfolios), causing a phenomenon that this book describes as "pseudo-factoring." The following section

---

[18] Ruddy et al. (2006), p. 2.

[19] Biscoe (1975), p. 29.

[20] Biscoe (1975), p. 29.

[21] "Another subsidiary of the second defendants are (X) Ltd, who carry on the business nowadays confusingly called factoring," *Hamilton finance Co., Ltd v. Coverley, Westray, Walbaum and Tosetti, Ltd, and Portland Finance Co. Ltd.*, [1969] I Lloyds Rep. 53, at p. 58, cited by Biscoe (1975), p. 3.

focuses mainly on this particular issue that is the key reason for covering factoring in this work.

5.1.3 Factoring and Debt Collection: The Issue of Pseudo-Factoring

Given that factoring applied only to commercial contracts meant that consumers' debt did not constitute the object of factoring, although, as stated earlier in this chapter, that situation changed already.[22] This aspect bears additional consequences. In the US, for example, as long as the factoring relationship does not cover consumer debt, factoring companies will not fall under the provisions of the Fair Debt Collection Practices Act (FDCPA) and will not qualify as debt collectors under the definition provided by the very same law. Their actions, rights and obligations will be ruled by contract and the provisions of the UCC. Moreover, in case of assignment of receivables, which is done solely for the purposes of debt collection, not even the provisions of the UCC will be applicable.[23]

Despite the differences between the legal systems, factoring is a growing business and a useful financing tool. However, for the purposes of this work, what is important is that in all jurisdictions the factor will fulfill, among others, the task of collecting debts. Put in other words, "debt factoring means selling your invoices on to a third party. [...] In essence a factoring company is a source of finance, a debt collector and an accounts ledger management service rolled into one."[24]

[22] *West v. Costen*, United States District Court, Western District of Virginia, 558 F. Supp. 564 (1983), cited by King and Cook (1996), pp. 8–24. The mentioned case was brought for alleged violations of the FDCPA, and among the defendants was Multi-service Factors, Inc (MSF), a corporation that mostly attempted to collect dishonored checks from both merchants and retailers (p. 9). Although the scheme in place and the services offered would not fall entirely under the classic definition of factoring, the corporation was held to be a debt collector under the FDCPA, due to the activities of its own collection agents (pp. 11–12). However, absent collections from consumers, it is doubtful that the same conclusion would be reached. For the moment, it is worth emphasizing that a factoring company might collect consumer debt, and so it will fall within the requirements of FDCPA with respect to its collection practices. In the UK, block discounting is a form of assignment that resembles nonnotification, recourse factoring (meaning that the client assumes the risk of nonpayment by the debtor) under a facultative agreement, the main difference being that the installments are due from consumers. Beale et al. (2012), pp. 294–295.

[23] UCC, Section 9-109 (d) (5).

[24] Strachan (2011), *at* http://www.thefreelibrary.com/Improve+cashflow+and+cut+overheads%3b+Ian+Strachan+gives+a+beginner's...-a0261914288.

5.1.3.1 True Factoring v. Quasi Factoring in Europe

In Europe, factors are generally governed by the provisions of general law applicable to contracts or special laws dedicated to such operations. However, similar to the situation in the US, things would become problematic as soon as factors would attempt to collect consumer debt,[25] especially in those countries where no adequate sector-specific protection against abusive debt collection practices is in place. Probably, the best solution for the future would be to enact a special statute with respect to factoring agreements, which should properly define the scope and object of the contract, together with the rights and obligations of the parties, including the debt collection function.

The issue of true factoring, quasi factoring and their relationship to debt collection was raised in front of the Court of Justice of the EU (ECJ), in matters related to taxation of services and VAT. Since the book does not deal with taxation, these matters are not going to be addressed here. However, the rationale applied by the ECJ is relevant in understanding the view of the European judiciary towards the strong connection between debt collection and factoring.

The key case is *Finanzamt Groß-Gerau and MKG-Kraftfahrzeuge-Factory GmbH* on the interpretation of certain provision of the Sixth Council Directive (77/388/EEC) on the harmonization of the laws of the Member States relating to turnover taxes—Common system of value-added tax: uniform basis of assessment.[26] In answering the preliminary questions raised by the German court, the ECJ distinguished between 'true factoring,' seen as "purchase of debts with full assumption of risk of loss"[27] (usually referred to as nonrecourse factoring), and "quasi-factoring," where the factor does not assume the risk for loss but in fact grants credit to the other party[28] and engages in the business activity of the obligor (operations that fall either under recourse factoring or invoice discounting).

---

[25] For example, in the UK, it was stated that the provisions of CCA 1974 would have been applicable to the factor's agreement with his client and to his relations with debtors. Three points had to be borne in mind: that the credit, which did not exceed 25,000 pounds, was provided to an individual (which included partnerships); that the term creditor included an assignee; and that the act did not regulate a consumer credit agreement for fixed sum credit under which the number of payments to be made by the debtor did not exceed four and those payments were to be made within 12 months of the date of the agreement. Or these three points were applicable to virtually all debts, which were the subject of an agreement for the factoring of trade debts. Therefore, in case the factor provides his services for partnerships or sole traders and his recourse is framed as a repurchase, it would have been possible (although deemed unlikely) to have the agreement considered a "personal credit agreement," which would have fallen within the scope of CCA 1974. Despite theoretical debates, a factor would have to be licensed as a debt collector under UK law, even if collection services are only ancillary. See: Ruddy et al. (2006), p. 248.

[26] *Finanzamt Groß-Gerau and MKG-Kraftfahrzeuge-Factory GmbH* (C-305/01) [2003] (Sixth Chamber).

[27] Ruddy et al. (2006), Para 26.

[28] Ruddy et al. (2006), Para 30.

However, despite the noted differences in legal regime, the ECJ took the view that true factoring, quasi-factoring and debt collection cannot be separated from each other. The Court stated that "where [. . .] the factor engages in true factoring by purchasing debts owed to his client without enjoying a right of recourse against the client if debtors default, he indisputably supplies a service [. . .] consisting essentially in relieving [. . .] of debt recovery operations."[29] In other words, **true factoring (nonrecourse factoring) is in fact pure debt collection**, an aspect that was further underlined and developed by the ECJ:

> [T]he term debt collection must be interpreted as encompassing *all forms of factoring*. In accordance with its objective character, the essential aim of factoring is *the recovery and collection of debt owed to a third party*. Therefore, *factoring must be regarded as constituting merely a variant of a more general concept of debt collection, whatever the manner in which it is carried out*[30] (emphasis added).

The interpretation of the ECJ is clear-cut and self-explanatory; hence, it does not require additional comments. Even if the arguments above were mentioned in the reasoning and for determining whether factoring and debt collection should be subjected to taxation according to EU law, the position of the court is valuable for understanding the linkage between factoring and debt collection in Europe.

In a case decided in 2010,[31] also on the issue of taxing factoring operations, the ECJ again analyzed the nature of the services provided by factoring companies. Relying on its reasoning in *Finanzamt Groß-Gerau and MKG-Kraftfahrzeuge-Factory GmbH* (C-305/01) [2003] (Sixth Chamber), it found that "it [the nature of debt collection and factoring] was to be construed broadly"[32] and held that the services provided by the appellant were within those broad terms: "by undertaking the recovery of debts for the account of those entitled to them, [it] frees its clients of tasks which, without its interventions, those clients, as creditors, would have to perform themselves."[33]

According to the court, it does not matter that the collection relates to debts that were not in default and does not involve coercive measures to obtain payment:[34] "it is irrelevant that such service supplied at the time when the debts concerned become due. "[. . .] *factoring, all forms of which are included in the terms 'debt collection and factoring' is not limited to debts in respect of which the debtor has already defaulted. It can also have as its object debts which have not yet become due and will be paid on the due date*."[35] Once again, the decision of the ECJ represents a

[29] Ruddy et al. (2006), Para 49.

[30] Ruddy et al. (2006), Para 77.

[31] *Revenue and Customs Commissioners v. AXA UK Plc* (C-175/09) [2010] STC 2825 (ECJ (3rd Chamber)) cited by Allen (2010).

[32] *Revenue and Customs Commissioners v. AXA UK Plc* (C-175/09) [2010] STC 2825 (ECJ (3rd Chamber)), Para 30.

[33] Allen (2010), Para 33.

[34] Allen (2010), Para 35.

[35] Allen (2010), Para 34.

substantial widening in scope of debt collection and factoring and underlines and maintains the strong connection that exists in Europe between the two.

An interesting case is also the one of Romania, where debt collectors use factoring as a coverage for their activities, since under the provisions of the previous Civil Code the assignment of receivables was not valid until the debtor had accepted it by an authenticated document or was officially notified, via a court officer, about the assignment.[36] The decision and its consequences, as well as the issue of pseudo-factoring and debt collection, are discussed in the following section.

5.1.3.2 Pseudo-Factoring v. Debt Collection in Romania

In a 2009 case decided by the First Instance Court of Ploiesti,[37] the judge dismissed a claim brought by a company called Top Factoring Ltd[38] against a private person (consumer) on the ground that the former lacked standing.[39] To reach this conclusion, the court first analyzed the provisions of Law no. 469/2002 concerning several measures for strengthening contractual discipline, which defined factoring as contract concluded between a merchant (as defined by the Romanian Company Law[40] of that time) and the factor (which was supposed to be a bank or specialized financial institution).[41] In other words, according to the law, factoring was a contract between businesses, where the factor could only be a financial organization.

The court then proceeded to check whether the claimant fulfilled the legal conditions and concluded that the factor was neither a bank nor a specialized financial institution. On the contrary, it was merely a limited liability company (as its name stated), registered under the general rules of the Romanian Company Law. Thus, said the court, the claimant was precluded by law to buy a debt portfolio because such a sale was legal only when performed by a bank or specialized financial institution, within the limits of the authorization issued by the National

---

[36] Art 1393 of the previous Romanian Civil Code.

[37] Civil Decision no 2509/05.03.2009, unpublished, available in Romanian online at: http://portal.just.ro/281/Lists/Jurisprudenta/DispForm.aspx?ID=32, last visited on 23.01.2015.

[38] In Romanian: SC TOP FACTORING SRL.

[39] In the case, the "factoring company" brought a civil claim action against a private person asking for payment of several mobile phone invoices that were due. The claims belonged to a phone company and were assigned to the claimant. The court, exercising its procedural rights, raised the plea of lack of standing and after allowing the parties to state their positions on it, admitted it and dismissed the case.

[40] Law no. 31/1990, republished in the Official Gazette of Romania no 1066/2004, Part I.

[41] Art 6 (2) b) of Law 469/2002, concerning certain measures for strengthening the contractual discipline, published in the Official Gazette of Romania, Part 1, No. 529/19.07.2002, currently repealed by Law 246/2009.

Bank of Romania.[42] Given the fact that the claimant was not a real factor and so it did not possess the authorization of the National Bank, the agreement concluded with the client was not legal and thus the claimant lacked standing.

It is safe to presume that such a case in which nonfinancial business organizations were hiding debt collection efforts behind factoring operations was not isolated. For example, SC Top Factoring SRL is one of the top collecting companies of Romania, still operating in the same manner as the one described by the court. Despite the fact that they are not registered according to the law governing factoring operations, they still present themselves as a factoring company[43] when what they do is outright debt buying and debt collecting, as it is indicated on their webpage.[44] The question that arises is—if debt collectors take advantage of the legislative gaps and extend normal factoring services to private consumers, can one look at pseudo-factoring also as a form of debt collection? An additional question would be whether in hiding behind the mask of factoring operations—be it true, quasi- or pseudo—debt collectors would be able to escape liability for abusive practices, where legislation against such abuses is in place.[45]

---

[42] In Romanian: "[. . .] SC T Factoring SRL nu este o societate bancară sau o instituţie financiară specializată, ci o societate cu răspundere limitată (astfel cum rezultă din chiar denumirea ei!). Prin urmare, din aceasta perspectivă şi în temeiul art 11 alin 1 lit b) din Legea 58/1998 privind activitatea bancară, operaţiunea de cumpărare a unui portofoliu de creanţe nu este legală, deoarece ea nu poate fi desfaşurată decât de o societate bancară sau o instituţie financiară specializată, aceasta din urmă în limita autorizaţiei acordate de Banca Naţională a României." Civil Decision no 2509/05.03.2009, unpublished, available in Romanian online at: http://portal.just.ro/281/Lists/Jurisprudenta/DispForm.aspx?ID=32, last visited on 23.01.2015.

[43] The website was initially consulted in 2012. Currently, however, references to factoring are only implied by the company's name and by the services offered.

[44] http://www.topfactoring.ro/Services, last visited 23.01.2015. There were slight differences between the Romanian and the English versions, especially with respect to the last service offered: debt purchase, which on the Romanian version states: "achiziţie de portofolii de creanţe neîncasate," which would be more accurately translated as purchase of unpaid (due, defaulted) debt portfolios. After 2012, when it was initially consulted, the website was redesigned. The English version states as service offered: cash flow management consisting in the purchase of accounts receivable portfolios. The translation still does not match entirely since the English version left "unpaid" out. A similar case might be the one of RomFactor SRL, which defines itself as a "one-stop cross-border trade finance boutique." See: http://www.romfactor.ro/about-us/#WhoWeAre, last visited on 23.01.2015. However, although according to the law (Government Ordinance no 28/2006 published in the official Gazette, Part I, No. 89/31.01.2006) any nonbank financial institution providing factoring services should be organized as a joint stock company (Art 5 (1) and 7 (1)), registered with the National Bank of Romania (Art 34), there is no mention of this company in the Registries. Basically, according to the data coming from the bank, there is only one nonbank financial institution engaged in factoring at 07.08.2014. See: http://www.bnro.ro/files/d/RegistreBNR/ifn/RegistrulGeneral/registrul_general_ifn_active_e.htm, last visited on 23.01.2015.

[45] As shown earlier, in *West v. Costen*, in the US masking debt collection under factoring services would not insulate debt collectors from liability under the FDCPA. In countries such as Romania, where no legislation concerning abusive debt collection exists, such question would not arise. Most likely, in Romania, the factoring agreement was used to overcome the limitations imposed by

An unpublished Romanian conference paper[46] indirectly addressed this ongoing concern by advancing the hypothesis that the difference between factoring and mere debt collection stems from the allocation of risks. If in factoring the risk is borne by the factor (with the exception of recourse factoring) in case of mere debt collection, the collection agencies only promise to cash in the invoices without assuming the risk of nonpayment.[47] The authors emphasize that in such situations, which they refer to as "pseudo-factoring," the client remains the owner of the account receivable and only pays the collection agency the commission for "stimulating" the account debtor.[48]

Their view is consistent with the position of the ECJ; however, it fails to address the issue of concomitant risks. Romania does not have a law against abusive debt collection practices or a licensing system of debt collectors. Hence, the minimum protection offered came from the legal definition of factoring as a specialized operation between business entities, one of them being a financial institution under the supervision of the National Bank. Allowing nonfinancial business organizations to engage in debt collection under the cover of factoring operations against consumers while escaping supervision of the regulatory body adds **two additional risks**. On the one hand, **collecting consumer debt** in the absence of any kind of sector-specific consumer protection regulation **by unlicensed and unsupervised business entities puts consumers in great danger to incur unsanctioned abuse**. On the other hand, **tolerating unsupervised nonfinancial business entities to conduct specialized services in a wider area than that of supervised financial entities exposes the latter to unfair competition**.

These reasons are the very reasons that led to the enactment of the Fair Debt Collection Practices Act in the US, as sector-specific regulation and consumer protection against unfair debt collection practices. Romania must realize and grasp the practical risks of tolerating pseudo-factoring and its consequences and, following the US and the UK experiences, address these issues and the need for sector-specific consumer protection. Chapters 5 and 6 of the book focus specifically on the building blocks of an efficient fair debt collection practices act.

---

the previous Civil Code to assignment of debts. However, after the implementation of the RNCC the issue of debt assignments is not a concern for debt collectors anymore.

[46] Ionut Daniel Gogorita and Ovidiu Florian—CONTRACTUL DE FACTORING, p. 8. The paper is not available online anymore.

[47] Although not without merits, this theory is not complete, since many debt collectors engage now in acquisition of large portfolios of unpaid or bad debt, at huge discounts, for they undertake the entire risk of nonpayment. However, in case of successful collection, any amount beyond what was paid at purchase will remain with the debt collector as profit.

[48] Gogorita and Florian, p. 8, not available on-line anymore. In Romanian: "Sunt numeroase firme de recuperări ce promit doar încasarea facturilor şi nu preiau riscul de neîncasare. In asemenea situaţii rămâneţi proprietarul creanţei ca în cazul pseudo contractelor de factoring, societăţii de recuperare urmând să-i achitaţi comisionul perceput pentru serviciul de "stimulare" a clientului rău platnic."

The following section is dedicated to obstacles to factoring in each chosen jurisdiction, namely nonassignability clauses and the requirement to notify the assignment together with their effects on actual collection.

5.1.4 Obstacles to Factoring

Since the debtor is not part in the contract between the creditor and the factor and hence he does not have knowledge of the sale or assignment of his debt to a third party, he may still make valid payment to the creditor. Therefore, he should be informed of the assignment as soon as possible. Another obstacle might be the existence of a nonassignability clause, which could be opposed by the debtor to the factor. As the following discussion will reveal, given the peculiarities of each jurisdictions, the effects of these obstacles vary.

5.1.4.1 Notification of Assignment

Notification of assignment bears important consequences both for the debtor, because until he receives one, he may make valid payment to the original creditor, and for the factor, for once he delivered the notification he may ask the debtor to pay him directly.[49] The following sections analyze the issue of notice in the chosen jurisdictions.

5.1.4.1.1 The US

Loans secured by the assignment of accounts receivable, together with sales of accounts, chattel paper and payment intangibles or promissory notes, have received extensive coverage under the UCC.[50] The justification for subjecting all the above to the same legal treatment was that such an approach has proved successful in "avoiding the difficult problems of distinguishing between transactions in which obligations were secured by receivables and those where the receivables were actually sold,"[51] due to the fact that in commercial financial transactions the

---

[49] A response to the issue of notification of assignment is the nonrecourse factoring (a.k.a. confidential factoring) where the communication between the factor and the debtor is reduced to a minimum, by using the creditor's corporate image and letterhead. However, even in such cases, the factor retains the right to notify the debtor in the event of a covenant breach or serious default. http://www.comcapfactoring.com/blog/what-is-non-notification-factoring/, last visited 23.01.2015.

[50] UCC, Section 9-109 (a) (3). Also: Posel (1982), p. 294.

[51] Official Comment 4, Laws (2009), p. 875.

distinction was often blurred.[52] Therefore, even if factoring is a sale of accounts receivables and no credit is involved, the rules of Article 9 expand to sales of account receivables as well.[53] The main effect is that factoring was "put upon a detailed statutory base, highly protected against unbargained–for risks."[54]

According to UCC, in order to be valid against third parties, the assignment of accounts receivables must be perfected like any other Article 9 security interest,[55] but the method always follows the nature of the collateral and the connected industry.[56] For attachment, there is a requirement for a written agreement between the client and the factor, for value to be given by the factor and, finally, for filing a financial statement with the appropriate authorities. The exceptions from the latter requirement do not apply in the case of factoring.[57] After attachment has taken place and the assignment has been perfected, the factor can notify the account debtor to make payment to him, in case there is such an agreement between the client and the factor or upon the default of the client.[58]

---

[52] Gilmore (1999), pp. 250–286. Gilmore describes that in the pre-UCC period the law relating to accounts receivables financing—in which he includes the assignment of monies due and to become due as well as factoring (pp. 250–251)—had been almost entirely common law. Hence, any nonnotification financing agreement risked being set aside in bankruptcy as a voidable preference (p. 253). However, the rule adopted in *Benedict v. Ratner*, 268 U.S. 353, 45 S. Ct. 566, 69 L. Ed. 991 (1925), according to which a reservation of dominion by the assignor was inconsistent with the effective disposition of title and creation of a lien, did not affect factoring operations, for factoring always required notification to the account debtor and direct payment to the factor (p. 259). Even if the decision would have been applicable, there would have been no major effects on factoring operations since the factor was already accustomed to "police" the affairs of his clients, in the way the *Benedict* rule now required lenders to do (p. 261). The story gets more complicated with the introduction of the accounts receivable statutes, first in the form of validation statutes—according to which assignments were to receive statutory protection without either notification or filing—which basically established an automatic perfection of assignments (p. 274), on the false premise that still survives in the UK and Germany that once the assignment is made public bankruptcy is just around the corner (p. 275) and later with the return to the traditional favoring of publicity against secret liens (p. 275). The latter position prevailed and was maintained by the UCC.

[53] Posel (1982), p. 294.

[54] Posel (1982), p. 294.

[55] Girsberger (1992), p. 472.

[56] UCC, Section 9-309 (2), concerning assignments that do not transfer a significant part of the assignor's outstanding accounts. According to Comment 4, the purpose of Para 2 of Section 9-309 is to save from *ex post facto* invalidation casual or isolated assignments, which no one would think of filing. However, any person who regularly takes assignments of any debtor's accounts or payment intangibles should file.

[57] These conclusions stem out from the provisions of UCC, Arts. 9-204 (1) and 9-302 (1). Girsberger (1992), p. 472.

[58] UCC, Section 9-406 (1). According to Comment 2, the revision of the UCC made clear that once the account debtor receives the notification, the account debtor cannot discharge its obligation by paying the assignor. It also makes explicit that payment to the assignor before notification or payment to the assignee after notification discharges the obligation. However, the effectiveness of the notification is not in any way affected by the identity of the person who gives it. With respect to the requirement of authentication, the comment states that this requirement is satisfied by sending

Since the US is a filing-based system,[59] unlike the UK, France or Germany, which are notification-based systems, notification of the account debtor will matter only in determining whether he has validly discharged his duty[60] but it will not affect the assignment itself, which makes the factoring operation easier and more efficient. It becomes obvious that by submitting factoring to the general rules applicable to secured transactions as established by UCC Article 9, the filing requirement affects many issues in the field[61] and constitutes, together with the invalidity of nonassignability clauses,[62] the greatest difference between the US system and the majority of the European jurisdictions chosen,[63] and the most important lesson to be learned.

5.1.4.1.2 The UK

In UK law, a factoring agreement affects an assignment of the present and future book debts owing to the creditor that are comprised in the agreement. The assignment[64] must be in writing under the hand of the debtor,[65] must be an absolute one,[66]

---

notification on the notifying person's letterhead or on a form on which the notifying person's name appears. (Section 9-102 defines authentication.) See: Laws (2009), p. 994. Obviously, the meaning of the term is different from the European understanding where it commonly means a document that has been certified by a public notary or an attorney.

[59] As Gilmore put it, in the history of the American security law there has been "one constant factor: whenever a common law device has been covered by a statute, some form of public recordation or filing has been required as a condition of perfection of the security interest." He further notes that despite opinions claiming that filing statutes concerning accounts receivable might destroy business credits, the reality proved otherwise: "receivables financing kept on growing, no matter what kind of statute was adopted." Hence, even in the pre-UCC era, accounts receivable statutes have included both transfers, which were sales or outright assignments and transfers for security. The reason was the need to protect not only straight accounts receivables but also arrangements of the factoring type (which had either a notification or a nonnotification form). Gilmore (1999), pp. 274–276.

[60] Girsberger (1992), pp. 474–475.

[61] Girsberger (1992), p. 484.

[62] See *infra* Sect. 5.1.4.2.

[63] The sole exception among the chosen jurisdictions is constituted by Romania, which implemented a filing system similar to the US one in 1999 by means of Law no. 99/1999. The law was repealed in 2011 by the RNCC, but the system was maintained. Currently, the filing system is provided by RNCC, Art. 2413–2419.

[64] The assignment referred to here is the statutory or the legal assignment, whose formalities are set out in Section 136 of Law of Property Act 1925.

[65] Johnston (2008), p. 148.

[66] Provided that there is no nonassignment clause in the contract between the client and the debtor, the factor obtains, by assignment of debts to him, the absolute right to be paid by the debtor, even without the latter's consent. However, he will not obtain more rights than the client had and, thus, he may collect only according to the contractual terms between the client and the debtor. Ruddy et al. (2006), p. 71. Also: Biscoe (1975), pp. 99–100.

and not a security by way of charge over the book debts,[67] even if the client accepts personal liability to the factor for payment of the debts if its customers do not pay them.[68] An express written notice of it should be given to the debtor.[69] In case all the legal requirements are complied with and notice has been received by the debtor, the assignment will have the effect of transferring to the factor[70] the legal right to the debt, all available methods of recovering the debt and the possibility to validly discharge the debt without concurrence of the debtor. According to Beale,[71] this form of notification factoring grew in the UK out of the debt-collecting industry, which confirms once more the strong relationship and the overlap between the two.

Unlike the US (a filing-based system), the UK is a notification-based system, and thus an assignment must be completed by notice to the debtor,[72] for there is at present no way of registering a security interest as there is in the US under the UCC. Distinguishing factoring by outright purchase of debts from lending on security of debts[73] is important under the UK law, for normal factoring agreements in the UK

[67] English scholars recognize as their American peers that lending against a fixed charge on the book debts of the client might have the same practical effect as factoring by the purchase of the debts and payment on account for them by the factor on invoice date. It is emphasized that lending on security overcomes the difficulties put by the prohibition of assignment in contracts between sellers and buyers of goods and services, as well as conflicts with other charges. However, on the other side, a purchase of debts provides the factor with the benefit of direct recovery from debtor, the client does not need to register a charge and payment of charges by the client is without deduction of tax. This last approach has prevailed in the UK. One must bear in mind the difference between a mortgage and a charge, for while a mortgage comprises the transfer of ownership of the mortgaged property to the security holder subject to the mortgagor's right of redemption, a charge does not include any transfer of ownership but merely gives the security holder the right to have his debt paid out of the proceeds of the charged goods. See: Ruddy et al. (2006), pp. 4–5 and 322. Biscoe adds to the above that purchases and mortgages are both forms of assignment, whereas the charge is not. However, a purchase is an absolute transfer of property for consideration, whereas mortgages and charges are secured loans. Biscoe (1975), pp. 89–91; and Johnston (2008), p. 148.

[68] Drury and Xuereb (1991), p. 225.

[69] Ruddy et al. (2006), p. 139. There is no special requirement concerning the notice other than that it should be in writing. Since the statutory requirement provides for "notice" and not "a notice," the understanding is that there is no need for a separate document. However, the notice should state clearly that there has been an assignment, what has been assigned and to whom, but there is no need to include the date of the assignment. The three requirements concern only the statutory assignments; hence, any assignment that does not fulfill all of them may be valid in equity, provided the intention of the parties is clear and value has been given. According to another source, the notice is also "the primary collection device, endorsed on invoices directing customers to pay the factor." See: Biscoe (1975), pp. 3 and 100–103.

[70] Ruddy et al. (2006), p. 139; and Beale et al. (2012), p. 274.

[71] Beale et al. (2012), p. 290.

[72] Johnston (2008), p. 149; and Beale et al. (2012), p. 282.

[73] Biscoe also distinguishes between factoring and invoice discounting, the latter being a purely financial facility without the nonfinancial elements of factoring. The author points out that the distinction is blurred and confusion is maintained by the fact that in practice many refer to invoice discounting as "confidential factoring," which is in fact a form of nonrecourse factoring. Even if

are based on sale and purchase of the debts and vesting the debts in the factor. The result is that the factor becomes the owner of the debts. If it would be determined that the operation is in fact a secured loan, then the transaction would be registrable[74] and, in such event, the factor who has not registered would be unable to recover in competition with a liquidator, an administrator or any other creditor of the company with an interest in the charged property.[75]

Obviously, the factor must avoid the complicated issue of priority of rights and interests in receivables, for the UK lacks a comprehensive statutory regulation relating to priorities such as is found in the US's UCC. Hence, notice to the debtor has an important bearing[76] on the conflicts between the factor and other claims. Basically, in case a client assigns its book debts to more than one assignee, then the competing claimants will normally rank for priority according to the order[77] in which they gave notice to the account debtor.[78] The logic behind it is threefold:

---

invoice discounting agreements resemble factoring agreements in that the financier purchases the debts and the client makes much the same warranties concerning their validity and enforceability, the differences are numerous: the purchase is always with recourse to the client, notice of assignment is not given to the customers, the client collects the debts as the financier's agent and usually has a discretion as to the frequency of assignments and, also, the financier provides no nonfinancial services to the client. Biscoe (1975), pp. 24–25. On the distinction between outright sale of receivables at a discount or a loan secured on receivables, see also: Beale et al. (2012), pp. 286–289.

[74] Charges and mortgages have to be registered with the Registrar of Companies in order to be valid against any liquidator of the company. However, purchases of debts are not subjected to the registration requirement. Public registration of assignments was seen as deterring some businesses from factoring. Although not everyone shared this opinion, lack of registration requirement was presented as one of the major advantages of assignments by way of purchase of client's debts. Biscoe notices though that in commercial reality, the sale of debts to a factor is similar in effect to giving security whatever the law may say, which is why it is treated the same under the American UCC and why the Crowther Committee and the Diamond Report recommended the same treatment in the UK. Biscoe (1975), pp. 89–91; and Beale et al. (2012), pp. 288, 446 and 772–776.

[75] Ruddy et al. (2006), p. 147; and Beale et al. (2012), p. 290.

[76] Ruddy et al. (2006), p. 161.

[77] English law also establishes an exception from the abovementioned rule, in the case of adjusting priority claims that arise from a contract of sale when the supplier of goods has retained the ownership of the goods and also over the proceeds generated by these goods, until they are entirely paid for. The conflict might appear in case the company has also entered into a factoring contract with respect to its customers' debt arising on the resale. The exception consists in the fact that the law will enable the unpaid supplier to recover the resale price of the goods from the person who bought them from the company or, from the company itself, if the price has been paid to it. The legal justification stems from the fact that the resale company has been acting merely as an agent of the unpaid supplier. For details: Drury and Xuereb (1991), pp. 225–226.

[78] The general rule of priorities between competing assignees of the same debt is known as the Rule in *Dearle v. Hall* (1828) 3 Russ 1. The rule states that the first assignee who is acting in good faith, without knowledge of an earlier assignment to a competing assignee, to obtain a receipt by the debtor of notice of his assignment is entitled to collect and give a good discharge for the debt. However, if the debtor receives more notices on the same day, it will be the earlier assignment that will have priority. Same solution will be applied in case no notice at all has been given by any of the assignees, provided the equities are equal. Ruddy et al. (2006), pp. 161–163; and Biscoe

first, since receivables are intangibles and one cannot take possession of an intangible, notice is considered to be the closest equivalent to it; *second*, the notice to the debtor has a deterrent effect to any attempt of fraud by multiple assignments of the same debt; *third*, failure by an assignee to give prompt notice to the debtor is deemed negligence and is thus sanctioned with loss of priority.[79] The account debtor can raise against the factor all the defenses he had against the obligor, but only if the terms of the account debtor's contract do not preclude him from doing so.[80] Such defenses cannot be raised after notification was given, and thus there is another strong incentive[81] for the factor to notify the account debtor as soon as possible after the conclusion of the factoring contract.

Obviously, all these issues would be easily avoided in case a UCC model filing system would be in place, but that is not the case for the moment. Hence, if under US law the notice serves only the purpose of validating the payment of the assigned debt by registering it, under UK law one must inform the account debtor of the assignment. Hence, **in the UK, the notification** has a more important and complex role, for it **may affect the validity of the factoring operation itself** and adds additional burdens to the debt collection efforts.

5.1.4.1.3 France

Factoring appeared in France in the 1960s as a three-party, short-term contract, under which the factor purchased the receivables from the client and then collected the debts owed to the client from the debtor.[82] For this purpose, the factor was subrogated to the rights of the seller.[83]

(1975), pp. 122–125. For a detailed analysis and criticism of the rule, see: Beale et al. (2012), pp. 477–479.

[79] Ruddy et al. (2006), p. 163. An interesting discussion on the rationales of the rule is available in Biscoe (1975), pp. 125–127.

[80] Drury and Xuereb (1991), p. 225; and Beale et al. (2012), p. 275.

[81] As emphasized, besides assisting the factor in his claim for priority against competing interests in the assigned debts, the receipt of notice by debtor has several other important effects: it fixes the rights of the parties in relation to the debtor's countervailing rights, it prevents the discharge of the debtor by subsequent payment to the client, it avoids changes in terms in the contract between the client and the customer and it also enables the factor to take proceedings to recover the debt in his own name. For details: Ruddy et al. (2006), pp. 163–167; and Biscoe (1975), pp. 111–118.

[82] Mesnooh (1994), p. 254.

[83] Rodière (1976), p. 580. For such an operation to remain, at least by analogy, within the confinements of the Civil Code, French jurists offered four possible theories: novation by change of creditor, delegation, assignment of receivables or conventional subrogation with the consent of the client (subrogating creditor) and of the factor (subrogated creditor). Currently, delegation is used to take security over insurance policies and rental payments. The *délégant* asks for the *délé gué*, who accepts it, to pay certain sums to the *délégatire*, though the *délégant* is still not discharged. The right and obligations of the debtor and third party involved will be defined by contract and customs, not by law. There are no legal requirements concerning the validity of the

As seen in the introductory part of this chapter, by contract the factor undertakes to pay to his cocontractor the sum that the account debtor owes him against submission of documents that prove the accounts receivables and the delivery documents. After payment, the factor is subrogated to the cocontractor, which will allow him to go after the debtor by using the previous rights that the cocontractor had against the debtor. Basically, the payment done by the factor is an advance on his part and it transfers the risk of the possible insolvency of the debtor.

In 1981, the Loi Dailly was enacted with the purpose of making the transfer of receivables between the financial institution and the commercial borrower simpler[84] than through subrogation. The law, which basically introduced a method of assignment of receivables by way of security,[85] allowed multiple assignments, including those that were not yet into existence, by means of submitting a list (bordereau) to the financial institution (the factor).[86] Hence, the law made possible both assignment in bulk and of future receivables,[87] which basically meant a big step towards the "Americanization" of French commercial law.

Interestingly, where the US and the UK were focusing on how to distinguish between debts securing a loan and debts that were merely sold, for they had different legal regimes, the French took the position that debts securing a loan will provide an easier and much more effective method of financing than the outright purchase. However, this position is due solely to the obvious shortcomings

---

delegation, but in practice it is advisable to have a written contract in which to clearly state the rights and obligations of the parties. The document is usually a tripartite security agreement in which the security provider asks that one of his own debtors pays the secured creditor. See: Hilson (2010), pp. 19–46. On the assignment, it was noted: "Assignment of accounts receivables and subrogation are closely related and many issues in the law of subrogation have been resolved by analogy to the law of assignment. [. . .] Under French law, unlike under German law [. . .] a transfer of accounts receivable, in order to be valid, must be founded on a valid agreement, such as purchase or a credit agreement ("cause"). [. . .] Unlike in German and Swiss law or under the UCC, any assignment in order to be valid must be notified to the account debtor by a so called "signification" a notification which must be delivered by a court clerk, Art. 1690 (1) Code Civil. Alternatively, an assignment may be formally accepted by the account debtor through a public declaration ("acceptation" Art. 1690 (2) Code Civile)." See Girsberger (1992), pp. 477–478. However, out of the four theories, the one favored was the last one, conventional subrogation, for it offered several advantages: it did not require the participation of the debtor or a notice to be given to the debtor or an authenticated acceptance from the debtor. These requirements are contained in FCC, Art 1690, concerning assignments. The debtor's acceptance by authentic act is necessary in order for the assignment to have effect as against both third parties and the debtor of the accounts receivable. See Rodière (1976), p. 580.

[84] For details concerning the advantages and disadvantages of a Loi Dailly assignment as well as the procedure: Johnston (2008), pp. 180, 182.

[85] Hilson (2010), pp. 19–44; and Johnston (2008), pp. 179–180.

[86] Drury and Xuereb (1991), p. 231; and Mesnooh (1994), p. 254.

[87] The only condition was that future receivables or future contracts were sufficiently identified. Otherwise, it covered a wide range of receivables, including goods sold or subsidies by public bodies. Hilson (2010), pp. 19–45.

of the Civil Code's framework of assignments:[88] the requirement of a notice served by enforcement officers and an authenticated acceptance by the debtor.

The novelty introduced by Loi Dailly was the removal of the requirement to give notice to the debtors in order to perfect the security against third parties. However, notice had to be served to ensure that payments were made directly to the factor.[89] The assignment was valid and enforceable against third parties upon the execution of the client of an assignment document (*acte de cession de créances professionelle*) and took priority as from the date of the document. How such a document could be opposable to third parties in the absence of a filing system like the one in the US remains unclear.

Coming back to the method of subrogation, French law is clear on the fact that in order to prevent the account debtor to pay the client, the former must be notified.[90] Basically, from the moment the agreement between the factor and the client was concluded, the receivables transferred to the factor are part of his assets. As he just stepped into the shoes of the client, it is debatable if he will have any preference in case the account debtor goes bankrupt. Posel expressed the view that a French factor's position is similar to that of a successor, rather than of a secured creditor. Thus, "it would seem entirely free to collect the account in spite of the client's intervening bankruptcy, without hindrance from prohibitions of individual action outside the bankruptcy proceeding."[91]

Similarly to US and Germany, if the account debtor pays in good faith to the client, before being notified about the subrogation, he will be validly discharged.[92] Also, the account debtor enjoys all the defenses he could have raised against the original creditor, as well as all the defenses he has against the factor personally. One peculiarity of the French system remains the fact that the account debtor can refuse to pay the face value of the debt if the factor paid less than that in consideration of the subrogation.[93] This stems from the fact that subrogation puts the factor in the position of the client only to the extent that the factor has discharged the client's duties.[94] This being the case, the debt collection services offered by factors under the rules of subrogation are severely affected. As seen in the US and the UK, the factor purchases invoices at a discount and reserves a factoring fee. However, once the invoices have been paid by the debtor in full, the factor will release the

---

[88] FCC, Art 1690. See also: Tajti (2002a, b), p. 101.

[89] Provided notice was not served and payment was made to the client, the latter was deemed to hold the funds as the agent of the factor. As long as the payments made by the debtor were in good faith, in the abovementioned circumstances, they were valid and the debtor was discharged. See: Hilson (2010), pp. 19–45.

[90] Posel (1982), p. 298.

[91] Posel (1982), p. 300.

[92] Girsberger (1992), p. 480; and Johnston (2008), p. 191.

[93] "Because the subrogation theory gives rise only to a right of reimbursement, the factor cannot require payment which exceeds its own payment to the creditor." Posel (1982), p. 296; and Johnston (2008), p. 191.

[94] Girsberger (1992), p. 480.

difference to the creditor, retaining only his fee. In France, however, by resorting to factoring by way of subrogation, the creditor assumes from the very beginning the loss of the discount.

5.1.4.1.4 Germany

The factoring contract, similar to most civil law countries, is not governed by a dedicated statute[95] in Germany. It is considered a "global assignment,"[96] and it is covered generally by the rules of assignment established by the Civil Code (BGB).[97] German law divides the transaction between the factor and the client in two: the agreement by which the client agrees to assign receivables and the transfer of receivables itself.[98] Once with the transfer of the debt, the factor will also take over the risk for the debtor's insolvency (*delcredere* risk).[99] German law was perceived as more flexible[100] than its French counterpart at least with respect to mechanisms for assigning and charging debts and commercial rights in order to meet commercial needs, due to the successful efforts of practitioners of using effectively existing and future debts as security (without the need to notify the account debtor) and convincing courts to recognize such devices (*kautelarische Sicherheiten*).[101]

With respect to the form required by the rules of BGB, the assignment must be in a written form, but authentication is not required.[102] Moreover, the assignment will be valid *without* the notification or the consent of the account debtor,[103] given the

[95] The factoring contract is considered an atypical contract, since the obligations of the parties cannot be linked to any of the types of contracts to be found in the BGB. Even the fact that factoring is used under its English name is considered a proof of the strong influence of Anglo-American law and business practices. The rules for this type of contract are to a great extent shaped by case law, but, tributary to the civilian system tradition, they seek to draw on their resemblance to known types of contracts in order to apply the provisions of BGB, at least by analogy. Markesinis et al. (2006), p. 163.

[96] Hilson (2010), pp. 19–60. In practice, an assignment concerns all receivables from business transactions with customers (Globalzession). Since under German law there is no equivalent of the US floating lien or the UK floating charge, global assignments and blanket assignments (Mantelzession) are used to assign a yet undefined number of present and future receivables. In the former case, the company assigns all present and future receivables from the outset, while in the latter they are assigned after they come into existence. Another difference between the two is that in the former case, the assignment is automatic. For details, see Johnston (2008), pp. 196–199; and Serick (1990), pp. 90–92.

[97] BGB, Art 398, and Johnston (2008), pp. 193–195.

[98] Girsberger (1992), p. 475. Also: Grundmann (2013), p. 131.

[99] Grundmann (2013), p. 121.

[100] Drury and Xuereb (1991), p. 233.

[101] Tajti (2002a, b), p. 283.

[102] BGB, Art. 398, and Hilson (2010), pp. 19–59.

[103] Hilson (2010), pp. 19–59. Also Serick (1990), pp. 56, 102.

fact that there is no such legal requirement. The effect is that once the transfer has been made, the accounts assigned belong to the factor, but if the creditor goes bankrupt and the account comes into existence after its assignment, then such an assignment will not be recognized with respect to the bankruptcy estate,[104] a major shortcoming of the absence of a filing system like the one in the US. However, the Federal Court of Justice has questioned this approach[105] and held that the assignment of claims arising during the restricted period is not necessarily subject to contestation. Obviously, the Federal Court's decision took into consideration the economic importance of factoring (seen as global assignment) and realized that if contestation under insolvency proceedings would be generally possible, factoring operations would become ineffective and would limit access to credit and finance, thus having a negative impact on the economy.[106]

German law considers a fundamental principle that the position of third parties not involved in a contractual relationship cannot be affected by the contracting parties.[107] For this reason and given that notification or consent of the assigned debtor is not mandatory, it aimed to protect the debtor by statutory provisions.[108] Thus, the account debtor is entitled to use against the factor all defenses that he had available in the moment of the assignment.[109] If the account debtor has paid the client without knowing of the assignment, he will also be considered discharged and the factor will have no claim against him.[110]

If the creditor has assigned the same receivable to more than one person, German law will consider the first assignee as being entitled to the account.[111] Thus, it will be the factor's responsibility to check before the contract is concluded if the receivables are not already assigned to third parties.[112] Such a task cannot be

[104] Girsberger (1992), p. 476; and Hilson (2010), pp. 19–60.

[105] Decision of the *Bundesgerichtshof* from 29.11.2007, published in *Zeitschrift für Wirtschaftsrecht (ZIP)* (2008) 183-9, cited in Johnston (2008), pp. 198–199.

[106] Johnston (2008), p. 199.

[107] Markesinis et al. (2006), p. 181.

[108] One must mention here that in Germany the assignor is authorized to collect and/or receive any and all of the receivables and to exercise all other rights assigned to the security holder during the ordinary course of business, unless the assignee has revoked such authorization for default or for other reasons defined in the assignment agreement. Upon such an event, the assignee is entitled to inform the obligors of the transferred claims of the assignment. In that case, this information is deemed notice and the obligor must discharge his obligation by paying directly to the assignee. Hence, the protection offered to the debtor by the BGB refers only to payments done before such notification, even if the default or any other triggering event has already occurred.

[109] BGB, Art 404.

[110] BGB, Art 407. Also: Girsberger (1992), p. 476.

[111] Serick (1990), p. 98.

[112] Girsberger (1992), p. 477.

easy in the absence of a filing system like the one in the US,[113] and hence a German creditor faces more risks than his American counterpart.

5.1.4.1.5 Romania

The first mention of factoring in Romanian law was in Government's Emergency Ordinance no 10/1997,[114] which contained no definition but mistakenly qualified it as a "payment instrument."[115] The error was corrected by Art 6, Para. 2, letter b) of Law no 469/2002,[116] which defined factoring as a contract between a party, called obligor (in Romanian *aderent*), providing goods or services, and a banking company or a specialized financial institution, called factor, on the basis of which the latter provides funding, monitors the claims and safeguards the credit risk and the former assigns to factor, by way of sale, claims arising from the sale of goods or services to third parties.

Despite the fact that factoring received a statutory definition, given that there were no other provisions to govern it and the law was later repealed, the Romanian scholars considered the factoring contract to be an unnamed, consensual, mutually binding, commutative, *intuitu personae*,[117] with successive execution, adhesion, fundamentally commercial contract.[118] Similarly to what the French or German scholars and courts were doing, one can notice that the Romanians were also trying to fit this atypical contract within the confinements of the Civil Code, at least by analogy. Identifying its traits was obviously seen as a first and necessary step.

Another similarity to Germany is the view that the factoring contract consists actually of two distinct agreements. The first is a frame agreement, usually concluded for a determined period of time, which contains the factor's promise to buy

---

[113] "The one defect of German law is that it provides no machinery for publicizing the arrangements a company makes in order to secure money which it raises by charging or transferring its assets other than land, ships, aircraft and industrial property rights. This results in greater opportunities for conflicting priority claims to arise between the various banks and institutions which finance a company." See Drury and Xuereb (1991), p. 233; and Johnston (2008), p. 203.

[114] OUG no. 10/1997 for diminishing the financial blockage and the economic losses (in Romanian original: OUG nr 10/1997 cu privire la diminuarea blocajului financiar şi a pierderilor din economie), published in the Official Gazette no. 72/22.04.1997, repealed by Art 13 of Law no. 469/2002.

[115] For a more detailed description of the legislative evolution of factoring in Romania: Vartolomei (2006), pp. 90–94.

[116] Law no. 469/2002 with respect to some measures concerning the strengthening of contractual discipline (in Romanian original: Legea nr. 469/2002 privind unele măsuri pentru întărirea disciplinei contractuale), published in the Official Gazette no. 529/19.07.2002, repealed by Law no. 246/2009, published in the Official Gazette nr 450/30.06.2009.

[117] The *intuitu personae* character of the factoring contract is not fully supported by Romanian scholars, but as all of them mention it, the book refers to it as well.

[118] Carpenaru et al. (2009), p. 472, Patlageanu and Lefter (2004), p. 108, Mircea (2000), p. 121, Vartolomei (2006), p. 94.

and the client's promise to sell the account receivable, which correspond to certain conditions and criteria established by the two parties. The second is the pure factoring agreement, by which one or more actual account receivables are transferred. A frame contract is justified by the fact that the parties agree to transfer also account receivables that are not yet into existence, and both might wish to avoid a bulk transfer. On the other side, through the pure factoring agreement the actual subrogation together with the actual payment take place.[119] By stepping into the shoes of the client, the factor will obtain also all the guarantees and pledges of the debt.[120]

As in the case of the UK, Romanian law does not require a specific written form or a separate document for the validity of the factoring contract.[121] A written document has only an *ad probationem* value given the fact that the legal institutions used to fundament the factoring operation—the assignment (in Romanian, *cesiunea de creanţă*) and subrogation (in Romanian, *subrogaţia prin plată consimţită de creditor*)[122]—do not require a written form for their validity either.[123] The position did not change after the enactment of the New Civil Code (RNCC) in 2011, but after analyzing the two legal institutions mentioned above, the comments support the opinion that assignment is now better suited than subrogation for conceptualizing factoring. The reason is that by assignment the assignee (in this case the factor) would be entitled to the entire face value of the debt, no matter what was the price he paid for it, while by subrogation—similar to the situation in France—he would be entitled only to the price he paid,[124] which has a negative impact on factoring operations. This is a **major break from the French tradition**, but totally understandable given the US-like approach taken by Romanian secured transactions law.

As peculiarities, Romanian scholars mention first that factoring is reserved exclusively to commercial activities and commercial debt. These aspects have important consequences relevant to the topic, especially when addressing the issue of pseudo-factoring,[125] where, under the coverage of factoring, debt collectors are in fact pursuing the collection of consumer debt as well.

What is certain is that the creditor and the account debtor have to be merchants[126] as defined by the law, and it is of no importance whether they are legal

[119] For details: Mircea (2000), pp. 124–126; and Patlageanu and Lefter (2004), pp. 111–112.

[120] RNCC, Art 1568.

[121] RNCC, Art 1579.

[122] There is also an opinion that there is a third legal institution on which factoring is based: the mandate. Patlageanu and Lefter (2004), p. 106; and Mircea (2000), p. 125.

[123] Carpenaru et al. (2009), p. 474; and Patlageanu and Lefter (2004), p. 108.

[124] Turcu (2011), comment to Art. 1598—Subrogaţia parţială (partial subrogation), p. 681.

[125] See *supra* Sect. 5.1.3.

[126] By the enactment of the RNCC, the division between civil and commercial codes was extinguished. Thus, the merchant's definition offered by the former Commercial Code does not exist as such anymore but was included in the RNCC together with a new category, that of the professional, the latter not being defined by the code.

or natural persons.[127] The factor, on the other side, must be either a specialized financial institution or a bank and also a nonbanking financial institution or a credit institution that has as a business scope factoring operations.[128] The latter have to be registered with the National Bank and lay under its supervision.[129] Only a legal person can be a factor.[130]

With respect to opposability and multiple assignments, it must be emphasized that the public notice must be performed by way of filing with the Electronic Archive of Secured Transactions (EAST),[131] introduced in Romanian law by Law no. 99/1999. Although Law no. 99/1999 was repealed in 2011 by the NCC, the provisions concerning filing with the EAST were maintained.[132] This makes Romania a filing-based system, closer to the US, since notification is now given to the whole world. Although the filing will solve the priority issue and the opposability concerns,[133] some scholars[134] argued that such a filing does not suffice and a written notification of the account debtor is also necessary.

Surprisingly, the RNCC took the same position[135] and the assignment will not be opposable to the debtor until notice is served. One can only speculate why a public notice was not deemed sufficient for opposability of the assignment to the debtor. Whether the Romanian legislator did not fully understand the mechanism behind the UCC Article 9 or it was only overcautious with a newly and foreign institution, the fact remains that under Romanian law public notice and notification of the debtor must be combined.[136] This places an unnecessary additional burden on factors attempting to collect commercial debts, but it makes sense if one considers that additional time is needed for business men to learn to conduct research based on a skeletal notice in a register.

---

[127] Carpenaru et al. (2009), p. 474.

[128] For details: Carpenaru et al. (2009), p. 474. There was also the opinion that such operations can be undertaken only by commercial banks given the fact that Romanian Company Law does not provide for the existence of commercial companies that have as sole activity factoring operations. Vartolomei (2006), p. 96.

[129] According to Government Ordinance no 28/2006 published in the official Gazette, Part I, No. 89/31.01.2006, any nonbank financial institution providing factoring services should be organized as a joint stock company (Arts 5 (1) and 7 (1)), registered with and under the supervision the National Bank of Romania (Art 34).

[130] Vartolomei (2006), p. 96; and Carpenaru et al. (2009), p. 475.

[131] In Romanian original: Arhiva Electronica de Garantii Reale Imobiliare.

[132] RNCC, Art 2413–2419.

[133] Turcu (2011), p. 681, comment to Art. 1598—Subrogaţia parţială (partial subrogation).

[134] Carpenaru et al. (2009), p. 480.

[135] RNCC, Arts 1579 and 1583.

[136] To sum up, filing with the EAST makes the assignment opposable to third parties and establishes the priority between multiple assignees. On the other hand, the notification of the debtor will matter only for making the assignment opposable to him. However, with or without notice to the debtor, the assignment will have full effect between the assignor and the assignee (RNCC, Art 1575). In practice, notice will most likely be served by the factor upon assignment for this will be the only way in which the factor will be paid directly by the debtor.

5.1.4.2 Nonassignability Clauses

Debtors have tried to prevent creditors from assigning their debts to a third party by inserting in their contracts nonassignability clauses. The validity of such clauses is treated differently among the chosen jurisdictions. However, as the following sections will reveal, all chosen jurisdictions agree that money claims may be validly assigned.

5.1.4.2.1 The US

The UCC strictly forbids the nonassignment contractual clauses,[137] which, as it will be shown, constitutes a major difference between the US system and the German one, which acknowledges such clauses. However, things are neither as clear-cut nor as simple as they would seem at first glance.

In reality, certain restrictions on alienation—especially those concerning medical insurance, software licenses or leased goods—are considered justified and will be recognized by courts.[138] It is the rights to payment that should not be barred or restricted through a nonassignability clause, and in this regard most chosen jurisdictions seem to agree nowadays.

5.1.4.2.2 The UK

With respect to nonassignability clauses precluding an assignee from acquiring direct rights against the debtor from the creditor with respect to the receivables arising from the contract, UK law upholds them, but the courts will first try to determine what the clause was actually looking to prohibit. However, despite any interpretation given to the clause, it will not be construed so as to affect amounts already paid or to exclude the assignment of monetary payments, which is a solution comparable to the one adopted in all chosen jurisdictions.[139] The justification offered in the UK is that the debtor has no legitimate interest as to the identity of his creditor when he has to pay a pure debt, and it is an explanation suitable for all other jurisdictions.

---

[137] UCC, Section 9-406 (d). According to Comment 5, the current version of UCC has expanded the rule of free assignability to chattel paper and promissory notes and explicitly overrode both restrictions and prohibitions of assignment. The comment also addresses the meaning of the term "ineffective" which is to be construed in the sense that the clause is of no effect whatsoever, and hence, the presence of such a clause will not prevent the assignment from taking effect between the parties and the prohibited assignment will not constitute a default under the agreement between the account debtor and the assignor. See Laws (2009), pp. 995–996. For details also: White and Summers (2010), pp. 438–441.

[138] White and Summers (2010), pp. 440–441.

[139] Beale et al. (2012), p. 277.

5.1.4.2.3 France

Nonassignability clauses are permitted under French law, usually in the form that requires consent of the debtor prior to the assignment of the said receivables. If at the date it purchased the receivables the factor ignored the presence of such clause, he could be liable for any damages caused to the debtor having knowingly contributed to the violation of the contractual provisions agreed between the client and the debtor, for in many cases, assignment absent the consent of the debtor amounts to breach of contract.[140]

Liability for damages, together with a right of setoff, might cause the factor to lose the receivable altogether. One must also add that according to French law, several specific claims—salaries or pensions—cannot be assigned. Additionally, a duty of confidentiality or of professional secrecy might also impede the assignment of receivables.[141] However, it would be difficult to assert what kind of damages the account debtor had incurred due to the fact that it has to pay the same debt (or the discounted one) to a different person. Hence, this protective measure appears as unjustified and obsolete, at least with respect to monetary debts.

5.1.4.2.4 Germany

Despite some degree of flexibility, contrary to the system established by the UCC, German law recognizes the validity of nonassignability clauses between the account debtor and the client,[142] which poses a serious obstacle for factoring operations. Since many debtors had such nonassignability clauses in their general terms and conditions—especially the economically powerful companies, such as those from the automobile industry, chemical industry or supermarkets—their debts were basically excluded from factoring.[143] It is why the German legislator has introduced provisions[144] in the sense that a restriction to assignability of money claims can be overridden, in order to make receivables suitable as security for financing disregarding any prior agreement between the parties, a solution similar in its reasons and effects with the one adopted in the UK.

However, nonassignability clauses were not the only obstacles for factoring operations in Germany. Issues arise from retention of title clauses,[145] where seller and buyer agree to transfer the property of the delivered goods only after full

---

[140] Johnston (2008), pp. 183–184.

[141] Johnston (2008), p. 184.

[142] BGB, Art 399. Also: Girsberger (1992), p. 475; and Hilson (2010), pp. 19–59.

[143] Grundmann (2013), p. 130. The explanation offered by the author is that by including nonassignability clauses, debtors try to avoid the erroneous double payment of the same debt, by paying the factor after they have paid the original debtor already.

[144] Art 354 of the German Commercial code (Handelsgesetzbuch). Also: Johnston (2008), p. 195.

[145] BGB, Art. 455.

payment. These clauses are often included in the general terms and conditions of the sellers. Moreover, factoring operations are also confronting a "stigmata" since debtors who have been notified by the factors of the assignment assume that the client is in fact facing bankruptcy. The reason behind this belief is that most of the times German banks reveal the assignment when the credited client does not have much time left.[146] Obviously, this issue is false and misleading, if one considers the fact that in case of factoring, notification of assignment is the rule, in order for the factor to be paid directly by the debtor. Hence, notification of the debtor does not imply that the client is insolvent in any way.

5.1.4.2.5 Romania

With respect to nonassignability clauses, the solution adopted by the RNCC resembles the ones adopted in France and Germany. Generally, they will be upheld, but there are certain legal exceptions.[147] In case the contract between the creditor and the debtor contains a nonassignment clause, the assignment can still be valid if the debtor consents to it, the assignee did not know and could not know about the existence of the nonassignability clause at the time of the assignment or the assignment regards a money claim, the last statutory exception being consistent with the positions adopted in the other jurisdictions (even if in the UK and Germany such exception was developed by courts). However, similarly to other civilian jurisdictions, the law provides for nonassignable claims and bans any assignments that would make the claim substantially onerous.[148]

The analysis of factoring in Romania reveals a rather eclectic system, with multiple sources of inspiration. The novelty of the operation combined with several failed attempts to legislate it have led to **a combination of solutions and overprotective measures** (such as the double notice requirement: to both the debtor and other third parties). It seems the Romanian legislators feared to fully take the American approach concerning the ban of nonassignment clauses but also feared the effects of such clauses on the credit industry (which lead to the prohibition of such clauses in the case of monetary payments, which proved to be a sound solution in Germany). All things considered, factoring managed to become a big business in Romania too,[149] taking advantage of the confusion between the activities of factoring institutions and those of collection agencies.

---

[146] Grundmann (2013), pp. 129–130.

[147] RNCC, Art 1570, Para 1. According to the legal provision, nonassignment clauses will be upheld unless the debtor has consented to the assignment, the clause was not expressly stated in the contract and the assignee (the factor) did not and could not know of its existence at the time of the assignment or the assignment regards a monetary payment.

[148] RNCC, Art 1569.

[149] See: https://www.brd.ro/stiri/brd-este-liderul-pietei-de-factoring-din-romania-cu-o-cota-de-piata-de-34-si-cifra-de-afaceri. According to data provided by the leading factoring operations provider, only in 2013, the factoring market amounted to 2.7 billion euros and had an increase of

This section dedicated to Factoring has also showed that due to the link between factoring, debt acquisition and debt collection, it sometimes becomes hard to identify which one is which, especially where the factoring operations were only recently introduced, as in the case of Romania. It is necessary to be able to correctly distinguish between them for both creditors' and debtors' sake. In the case of creditors, they need to be able to understand their rights and their risks and must be allowed to compete fairly, while in case of debtors, they need to make sure they have made a valid payment, under a legal assignment and to the right creditor. In addition, debtors should be insulated from abusive debt collection practices, through sector-specific consumer protection regulation. Due to the blur covering factoring, pseudo-factoring and debt collection, these issues have been tolerated in most of the civilian jurisdictions. Since the implications of these blur are severe, the book now turns its attention to debt collectors and collection agencies.

5.2 Collection Agencies

Addressing the topic of collection agencies is not easy, as debt collectors were not really a federal concern in the US until 40 years ago, while in continental Europe they are not a concern almost at all even today, despite recent calls for a change of approach with respect to debt collection and consumer-debtor protection.[150] In the US, their activity, which goes back to the nineteenth century, was subjected to regulation only from 1977, when the Fair Debt Collection Practices Act (FDCPA) was enacted,[151] and even then, only with respect to their abusive practices against consumers.[152] Regarding commercial debt, they are covered by the UCC Article 9, but the UCC does not provide for any kind of defenses[153] against those engaging in unfair collecting practices, for example.

In Europe—including most of the chosen jurisdictions—their activity is either scarcely covered by sector-specific regulation (France and Germany) or even not

6 % in the first trimester of 2014. The situation was not much different in 2012, which seems to prove that the market has stabilized. See: http://www.romania-insider.com/romanias-factoring-market-worth-nearly-eur-3-billion-in-2012/77482/ both last visited 23.01.2015.

[150] An article from 2012 states that in the past 25 years significant progress has been achieved in Europe since the old regime favoring creditors has been replaced by a more debtor-friendly system. However, the change is still deemed unsatisfactory. According to the author: "the credit crunch made it clear once again that the comprehensive consumer protection system is certainly not an obsolete notion. [. . .] The character of debt help must become more businesslike, whereas debt collection should gain a more social character." Huls (2012), p. 498.

[151] Warren and Westbrook (2009), p. 14.

[152] For what is understood as consumer under FDCPA, see *infra* Chap. 6, Sect. 6.1.3.

[153] One may argue that the "no breach of peace standard" could be considered a defense of the debtor against abusive repossessions. However, given the fact that the standard is one of the conditions specifically stated by the law, the book's opinion is that the "no breach of peace standard" is a validity condition of self-help repossession and not a defense against it.

covered at all (Romania), the only notable exception being the UK, whose Consumer Credit Handbook (CONC) has an entire chapter dedicated to regulation of nonjudicial debt collection (including repossession).[154] They function under the provisions of factoring—with respect to commercial debts—those of the general rules applicable to contracts and those of the Civil Codes (Romania), or under specific statutes (UK, France and Germany). Where regulation is available in the civil law countries, it mainly concerns licensing and establishes several norms with respect to the content of the notice to be sent to debtors,[155] thus establishing a minimum of prudential rules for the latter.

In order to analyze collection agencies, given the absence of information regarding their activity in Europe, the starting point is the definition given by the FDCPA to debt collectors and the focus will be mostly on collection agencies that concentrate their efforts on consumer debtors. For the purpose of this chapter, the book will briefly present the development and evolution of the collection industry from the enactment of the FDCPA in 1977 until today, will identify who the debt collectors are and what their main legitimate activities are and will define and analyze bad debt. The issue of bad debt is analyzed here because, as it will be shown, it lies at the border of legitimate and unfair debt collection practices, in the sense that while legally one may attempt to collect it, the methods in which bad debt is revived might be regarded as abusive. Unfair and forbidden collection practices, defenses against abuses and calls for reformations will be left for and dealt with in the final chapters of the book.

5.2.1 An Ever-Growing Business

The debt collection industry is not new. By 1977, when the US decided that it is time to enact laws to regulate the activity of debt collectors—at least with respect to consumers—it was already a huge industry generating substantial revenues.[156] Recently, the industry has grown even bigger due to the expansion of consumer

[154] Whether existent general consumer protection laws available at EU and Member States levels are sufficient in dealing with debt collection is a matter for debate and is specifically addressed in the following chapter. However, for now one should notice that the examples of the US and the UK make a compelling argument for the need of sector-specific regulation to deal exclusively with debt collection, while the fact that France and Germany have introduced additional legislation in the field, even if not as extensively as the US or the UK, indicates a recognition of the same need.

[155] See Chap. 6, Sects. 6.1.5 and 6.1.6.

[156] "The legislative history of FDCPA notes that in 1976, companies turned over five billion dollars in debt to the approximately five thousands agencies across the country." Hector (2011), p. 5.

credit[157] and the financial crisis.[158] Since in times of crisis the need for money increases, debt collectors flourish.[159] Not surprisingly, so does the number of complaints against them, but that will constitute the topic of the following chapter.

To fully understand the importance and the development of the industry, one must mention here that although home mortgages were considered the principal cause of the financial crisis that still haunts the world today, unsecured consumer credit also played an important role in the crisis being exacerbated.[160] Expansion of the market and an increased number of players[161] on the market were not the only effects. The industry had to change and adapt in order to keep up with the increasing amount of delinquent consumer debt, some of them implicating numerous innovations[162] for avoiding the law and consumers' safeguards. Some of them are finally noticeable even in Europe: "Debt collectors use tweets, sms, and e-mail, etc. The well-known and unknown opportunities and risks (privacy) will be hot items in the coming years."[163] New opportunities were also created to cover all segments of the collection industry, such as debt buying.[164] The first question to be answered is who are those involved in this huge and innovative business.

---

[157] See Hector (2011), p. 5. "The explosive growth, which followed an enormous increase in credit card debt [...]. As the amount of unsecured credit card debt has risen, so have the default rates on credit card payments." Also: Huls (2012), p. 502.

[158] De Boer (2013), pp. 1–2. According to data offered by the BCFP, about 30 million Americans, nearly 10 % of the population, was subjected to debt collection in 2013, for amounts averaging 1,500 dollars per person.

[159] "The debt collection industry is one of the few booming industries left in America. [...] [E] xperts estimated that debt collection firms' revenues will "increase from 10 billion dollars in 2006 to 11.6 billion in 2011." Fox (2012), p. 357. "As the US economy continues to struggle, one sector flourishes: the debt collection industry. With literally trillions in outstanding debt nationwide, businesses have stepped up their efforts to recover debts owed to them." Gogel (2011), p. 358. Additional data can be found in Holland (2011).

[160] Spector (2011), p. 260. Also: Fox (2012), p. 358.

[161] "According to the Bureau of Labor Statistics, jobs in debt collection are expected to increase by 19 % for the period from 2008 through 2018, faster than any other occupation." Fox (2012), p. 357. Also: Spector (2011), p. 262: "An industry trade association [...] estimates that the debt-buying industry employs 150.000 people nationwide and, by 2005, was responsible for collecting nearly 40 billion dollars in outstanding debt."

[162] "[C]ollectors are going to have to get creative in order to keep the liquidations up." See Jurgens and Hobbs (2010), p. 17.

[163] Huls (2012), p. 503.

[164] Spector (2011), p. 262. BFCP and FTC have identified debt buying as one of the major developments that did not exist when the FDCPA was enacted and hence requires the amendment of the FDCPA. Also: De Boer (2013), pp. 2–3.

5.2.2 Who Are the Debt Collectors?

A creditor faced with his debtor's default has several possibilities: collect the debt himself, hire a specialized debt collection agency or law firm, sell or assign his debt to a third party (i.e., either a debt buyer or, respectively, a factor).[165] All of them will have the possibility of using either judicial or extrajudicial means, as they might deem fit.[166] Although according to the FDCPA the original creditors are not considered debt collectors, many of the state FDCPAs (mini-FDCPAs) do include original creditors in the definition of debt collectors,[167] a solution that makes sense from the point of view of the aim that such fair debt collection practice acts are trying to achieve: why would the same practice be considered less abusive if employed by an original creditor than if employed by a third party debt collector?

For the purposes of this work, the benchmark definition of the debt collector is the one provided by the federal FDCPA, for it encompasses all aspects of private debt collection, including enforcement of security rights (although as it will be shown, repossessors rarely fall under the provisions of the FDCPA).[168] One must also notice that the legislator does not distinguish between direct and indirect collection or between the methods employed, nor does it touch upon the provenience of the debt that is to be collected, since the debt's origin is not relevant. What is relevant though, to qualify as a debt collector, is the aspect of regularity of collection operations, although, as it will be later revealed, in the absence of a statutory standard, regularity is ascertained by courts on a case-by-case basis:

> The term "debt collector" means any person who uses any instrumentality of interstate commerce or the mails in any business the principal purpose of which is the collection of any debts, or who regularly collects or attempts to collect, directly or indirectly, debts owed or due or asserted to be owed or due another. [...] [T]he term includes any creditor who, in the process of collecting his own debts, uses any name other than his own which would indicate that a third person is collecting or attempting to collect such debts. [...] [S]uch term also includes any person who uses any instrumentality of interstate commerce or the mails in any business the principal purpose of which is the enforcement of security interests.[169]

In defining who is a debt collector, the FDCPA establishes also who is not to be considered a debt collector, even if his activity involves collection of debts. These legal exceptions[170] set basically clear limits for the application of the Act. Thus, a

---

165 "The debt collection industry can be broken into two parts. One encompasses the debt that creditors sell to debt recovery agencies for a discount.[...] The other part is made up of in-house or third-party collectors whom creditors employ to recover debts on their behalf." Gogel (2011), p. 359.

166 King and Cook (1996), p. 7.

167 King and Cook (1996), p. 28. For details, *infra*, Chap. 6, Sect. 6.2.1.1.

168 *Infra*, Chap. 6, Sect. 6.2.1.1.

169 FDCPA, Section 803, Para 6.

170 FDCPA, Section 803.

creditor will never be considered a debt collector[171]—unless during the collection he will present himself under a different name in order to indicate that a third person is attempting to collect on behalf of the original creditor—and neither will his agents, employees, affiliates or subsidiaries. Public employees collecting state debt or taxes are not to be considered debt collectors either, nor will those agents serving debtors with documents concerning the debt. NGOs performing collection services or private persons[172] are also excluded. The last provision excludes those who are collecting debts that are not defaulted yet and those who are collecting secured commercial debts.

Thus, according the FDCPA, a debt collector is usually a third party agency that has as a principal and regular scope of business collection of debts, or its agents/ employees, as well as attorneys who engage primarily and regularly in debt collection, being of no importance whether the actual collection takes place outside or inside the US.[173] Once debt collectors have been defined, the analysis turns now to the markets where they are active on and on how they grew to today's magnitude.

5.2.3 *Primary and Secondary Markets: New Players on the Scene*

Normally, in the US, the process of collecting a delinquent debt begins in-house, and it is conducted by the creditor's agents or employees.[174] This is the primary market, which is only relevant from the perspective of state legislation.[175] If they prove unsuccessful, after 180 days, the debt is charged off, though the collection efforts continue on the secondary market.[176] This type of outsourcing debt collection efforts has been around for years, and, as shown above, it came to grow into a multibillion dollar business.[177]

---

[171] The term "never" refers here only to the federal legislation, which is a *de minimis* rule. However, as stated already, original creditors are considered debt collectors by most of the states' FDCPAs, the so-called, mini-FDCPAs, which are state level legislation. Whether the original creditors should be considered debt collector is addressed in more detail in the next chapter.

[172] See the legal conditions established by FDCPA, Section 803, Paragraph 6, letter F.

[173] For detailed examples and explanations of who qualifies and who doesn't qualify as a debt collector under FDCPA, see: The Federal Trade Commission—Staff Commentary on the Fair Debt Collection Practices Act, Commentary to Section 803 (6), available online at: https://www.fdic.gov/regulations/laws/rules/6500-1325.html, last visited on 23.01.2015.

[174] Fox (2012), p. 357.

[175] Only according to state law (mini-FDCPAs) are the original creditors considered debt collectors.

[176] Fox (2012), p. 357.

[177] For details: Goldberg (2006), pp. 725–729. "Debt collectors previously pursued only a few accounts to collect the highest amount available from each debtor, thereby incurring high costs with small returns. The companies learned, however, that they could buy large portfolios of debt

The secondary market is represented by firms that collect for a contingency fee, which can go up to 30 % of the debt's face amount,[178] and if their efforts are also unsuccessful, the debt is then resold in its entirety to other debt-buying entities.[179] The process of selling debt can contain more transmissions from one unsuccessful collecting firm to another before a judicial action is brought in a state court. The debt is qualified as a delinquent one, and so it sells at a bargain price,[180] usually at a few cents per dollar.

Such bargains have drawn the attention of investors and speculators.[181] Thus, they now acquire portfolios made up of receivables,[182] which represent claims against debtors and which can prove very valuable if they can generate bigger revenues than the price paid for their acquisition, together with the cost of the actual collection. To have an idea about the amount of profit that can be gained out of such transactions, it should be interesting to mention that Asset Acceptance Capital Corporation, one of the largest debt buyers, announced that in the first 3 months of 2009 it spent 22.1 million dollars to purchase charged-off debt with a face value of 747.8 million and reported for the same period of time collection of more than 94 million dollars.[183]

These new actors learned fast the secrets of the business and became specialists in prolonging the life of debt[184] or "resurrecting it," despite the fact that efforts have been made to encourage them to employ due diligence in order to avoid purchasing bankruptcy discharged debts or time-barred debts.[185] These issues are addressed in more detail in the section dedicated to bad debt.

Such a profiting business did not limit itself to the US, and investors have spread their activity overseas[186] as well. At the same time, European creditors—especially banks—have realized the advantages of disposing and clearing their books of nonperforming loans (NPL). A recent German study showed that "beginning in 2003, German banks began to dispose of NPL portfolios. Since then, the sale and

---

for relatively small fixed costs and then fully exploit their technology and personnel to reach thousands of debtors each day and accept lower recovery amounts. This process reduced costs while producing higher returns. Accordingly, economies of scale provided debt-buying companies with increased profits and the opportunity for extended growth" (p. 726). Additional data can be found in Spector (2011), pp. 257–299.

[178] Fox (2012), p. 357.

[179] See Fox (2012), p. 357.

[180] Prices vary in different geographical areas due to requirements of FDCPA and to different state laws. For details: Fox (2012), p. 357.

[181] Jurgens and Hobbs (2010), p. 18.

[182] Spector (2011), p. 262.

[183] Spector (2011), p. 262.

[184] Jurgens and Hobbs (2010), p. 18.

[185] Spector (2011), p. 262.

[186] Huls (2012), p. 503. The author notices and explains the profitability of the new market noticing the wide range of consultants, intermediaries, relief providers, debt collection agencies, bailiffs and also NGOs acting in the field.

acquisition of NPL portfolios has become almost an industry in itself and many financial investors, especially Anglo-Saxon and US – American are active in this field in Germany."[187] The study also revealed that German banks are more inclined to get rid of NPL or delinquent debts faster than their American counterparts: "German banks consider [...] those loans as non-performing which have been written-off or have not been paid back by the lender within 90 days after final maturity,"[188] and also include in such categories "loans which the creditor is entitled to terminate due to a default of the lender or because of a decline of the security rights"[189] and also "loan portfolios which consist exclusively of performing loans which are sold for reasons of credit policy by the seller."[190]

Similar studies with respect to the UK, France or Romania were not found, although it is hard to believe that such activities and "investments" do not take place in these jurisdictions as well. The German study pointed out that some of the great debt buyers on the German market are actually Anglo-Saxon companies, while nowadays, the collection agencies active in Eastern Europe are in fact of German or Scandinavian origin.[191] A simple look on the websites of the Romanian collection agencies[192] reveals that they are also engaging in debt-portfolio acquisitions, just that the latter has not drawn the attention of scholars or researchers. The legislative void, lack of concern for consumer-debtors, absence of a sector-specific consumer protection similar to the FDCPA or simply ignorance of such practices by academia and practitioners[193] could explain the absence of data or empirical studies. It is one of this book's aims to fill in the void and raise awareness with respect to the concomitant risks related to nonjudicial debt collection and abusive debt collection practices. However, now that it is established who they are and where they act, it is time to turn towards their main activity, the debt collection.

---

[187] Schwarze and Storjohann (2006), p. 77.

[188] Schwarze and Storjohann (2006), p. 77.

[189] Schwarze and Storjohann (2006), p. 77.

[190] Schwarze and Storjohann (2006), p. 77.

[191] Tajti (2013a, b), p. 127, particularly footnotes 310 and 311.

[192] Some examples: the Romanian version of the official website of SC Top Factoring SRL states under "Services": "acquisition of defaulted debt portfolios," available at http://www.topfactoring.ro/Servicii, last visited 23.01.2015. The English version of the official website of EOS KSI Romania states under "Services": "EOS KSI Romania purchases receivables portfolios of various compositions. We offer debt purchase for our client's defaulting debts, unsecured, or secured by movable goods or real estate," available at: http://ro.eos-solutions.com/en/services/receivable-management/debt-purchase/, last visited on 23.01.2015. The English version of the official website of Urban si Asociatii also states that "receivables purchase" is part of their offered services, available at: http://www.urbansiasociatii.ro/en/services.php, last visited on 23.01.2015. The Romanian website of GCA specifies that they offer purchase of receivables (available online at http://gca.ro/ro/achizitii.php, last visited on 23.01.2015) as part of their services, but the provided link will actually send customers to the website of a private person involved in the purchasing business (available online at: http://lucianbagia.ro/ro/achizitii.php, last visited on 23.01.2015), which has major implications that will be analyzed in the following chapter.

[193] Tajti (2013a, b), pp. 129–130.

5.2.4 Collecting the Debt

In the US, debt collection is regulated by the enactment of federal statutes like the FDCPA[194] or similar state laws,[195] which were designed to prevent any abuses against consumers that might arise during the process.[196] The FDCPA enumerates a number of practices that are strictly forbidden as deceptive and fraudulent, which *per a contrario* meant that any other practices—unless causing similar effects as those specifically stated in the Act—were to be considered legal and valid.[197] The apparition of such new practices not covered by the act, along with the forbidden practices, will be analyzed in the following chapter, so they will not be addressed here. However, this section offers a description of legitimate collection practices and their potential for abuse.

The collection process knows generally two stages: the *informal* collection (also called extra (non) judicial/soft collection) and the collection *litigation* (also called judicial/hard collection). The stages and the tactics employed are the same everywhere, so an analysis of each jurisdiction might not bring many novelties in terms of practices and services offered but will help emphasize the need for regulations in all of them. Unfortunately, there is a lack of similar empirical studies to those conducted in the recent years in the US. One explanation may be the fact that the phenomenon did not yet catch the attention of the scholars and researchers, while the other may stem out of the fact that the US seems to become very much aware that its regulations with respect to debt collection cannot keep up with the technological innovations and the new tactics employed by the debt-collecting business[198] and try to justify with data the need to update and reform their legal framework. As in Europe, such a framework is not really a concern (with the exception of the UK); reports and the calls for reform are generally absent.

---

[194] Similar federal statues are Equal Credit Opportunity Act (prohibits discrimination in connection with a credit transaction), Fair Credit Reporting Act (limits collector's ability to report accounts in collections that predate the report by more than 7 years. Spector (2011), p. 263.

[195] "Forty two states supplement the FDCPA with legislation governing debt collection." For discussion, see Spector (2011), p. 263.

[196] "While the FDCPA protects consumers from unlawful practices of third party debt collectors, it does not protect consumers from the original creditor or debt buying agency except in extremely narrow circumstances." Gogel (2011), p. 358.

[197] "The modern debt collection industry has found new ways around consumer protection laws that allow it to continue squeezing money out of debtor's pockets. Unfair but legal collection methods include: outsourcing early collection services overseas to bypass US laws, using sophisticated databases to target individuals who are statistically likely to pay debts, taking advantage of the liberal procedure requirements in small claim courts to obtain judgments against unsophisticated debtors, and collecting debts well after the expiry of the statute of limitations." For details: Goldberg (2006), pp. 713, 724–752.

[198] "[F]DCPA simply made collectors implement a new business model tailored to the new law. In order to carry out the new model, debt collection industry has resorted to many abusive strategies that have allowed companies to disregard the spirit of FDCPA, while still complying with the letter of the law." Goldberg (2006), p. 729.

5.2.4.1 Informal Collection

Informal collection usually contains attempts to convince the consumer debtor, by means of private communication (telephone[199] or mail), or "otherwise encouraging payment" to pay his debt.[200] In the US, these attempts have to fulfill the requirements of the FDCPA with respect to validation of debt,[201] while in most European jurisdiction such attempts are basically left to the debt collectors' will, out of the chosen jurisdictions the UK being the notable exception. Problems appear also as effects of globalization. According to a report, "collectors have expanded globally, enlisting low-wage employees in distant countries in the campaign to extract payments from American consumers."[202]

The situation is not much different in European countries, where restrictions and safeguards as those imposed by the FDCPA do not exist or focus mostly on the administrative aspect of the debt collection business,[203] such as licensing. In France, one collection agency refers to a three-stage process (according to which prior to the informal/amiable stage, there is a "precontentious stage"),[204] but most agencies stick to the classic two-stage process. The informal stage will include summons to pay, phone calls from call centers, direct meetings with the debtor.[205] Some also advertise "tough, persistent and highly aggressive"[206] techniques and "using the legal system as a weapon."[207] This could be easily understood as using

---

[199] "The basic tool of the debt collector is the telephone. Each day tens of thousands of collectors file into cubicles [. . .] and use automated dialers to call alleged debtors and try to persuade them to send money." Jurgens and Hobbs (2010), p. 6.

[200] Spector (2011), p. 263.

[201] **Section 809(a)** requires a collector, within 5 days of the first communication, to provide the consumer a written notice (if not provided in that communication) containing (1) the amount of the debt and (2) the name of the creditor, along with a statement that he will (3) assume the debt's validity unless the consumer disputes it within 30 days, (4) send a verification or copy of the judgment if the consumer timely disputes the debt and (5) identify the original creditor upon written request. For details https://www.fdic.gov/regulations/laws/rules/6500-1325.html, last visited on 23.01.2015.

[202] Jurgens and Hobbs (2010), p. 6. On the same topic: Goldberg (2006), p. 731. Among the advantages of outsourcing overseas, the author mentions "improved returns on capital, lowered risk, greater flexibility, and better responsiveness to customer needs at a lower cost," but there are also a large number of problems such as "sending extensive databases of debtor information to other countries compromising debtor's privacy rights" and "loss of control over third party operators." For details, see *infra* Chap. 7, Sect. 7.2.1.1.

[203] Huls (2012), pp. 504–505.

[204] http://en.france-contentieux.com/debt-collection-process.html, last visited 23.01.2015.

[205] http://en.france-contentieux.com/debt-collection-process.html, and http://www.collection-agency-france.com/, both last visited on 23.01.2015.

[206] http://www.abad-debt.com/france-collection-agency.htm, last visited on 19.06.2012 (page not available anymore).

[207] http://www.abad-debt.com/services.htm, last visited on 19.06.2012 (page not available anymore).

the legal gaps as a weapon against debtors, for sector-specific regulation in France is extremely scarce as the following chapter will reveal.

In Germany, collection agencies engage in amiable collection efforts, called "out of court or prejudicial court proceedings," which include investigation of "the actual address and financial standing of the debtor," "sending a dunning letter with a deadline for payment (within 8–10 days)," "correspondence with the debtor in written and by telephone," "negotiations concerning an installment agreement (if recommendable)."[208] The procedure might further involve checking for "information at different sources like trade register, internet databases, commercial agencies and resident's address registration office."[209] This is the most preferred method of collection in Germany as court proceedings are quite expensive.[210]

In the UK, letters are also the first step,[211] before face-to-face encounter,[212] some agencies expressing their doubts about the success of writing letters.[213] The explanation given by collectors is that debtors have become immune to the pressure of such informal techniques and ignore letters or phone calls, make empty promises or send invalid checks. Thus, the probability to encounter a debt collector on the doorstep is very high[214] in the UK, which reminds somehow of the tactics employed by the Mafia.

The situation is similar in Romania. A simple review of collection agencies' websites will unveil the tactics employed by them in the informal stage. In its online presentation, one of the leading collection agencies mentions as legal stages "Amiable collection through call-center services as well as field collection, at the debtor's location"; "Judicial collection stage through a national network of lawyers as well as forced execution phase with the support of a national cover of officers of court."[215] The Romanian version of another agency's website elaborates on the same stages: amiable (by phone or mail) and then judicial collection.[216] Some are

---

[208] http://www.debtcollectioningermany.com/FAQ.html, last visited on 23.01.2015.

[209] http://www.debtcollectioningermany.com/FAQ.html, last visited on 23.01.2015.

[210] Explanations for "Mahnbescheid" and "Widerspruch": http://www.europeancollectors.org/debt-collection-in-germany, last visited on 23.01.2015.

[211] "Letters before action: This service allows you to easily send out overdue account reminder letters to your customers." The website even provides for an automatic method of submitting the data for such bulk letters. http://www.creditcollections.co.uk/bulkletters.htm, last visited on 23.01.2015.

[212] "We personally talk to your debtor on a continuing programmed basis, creatively and psychologically obtaining debtor commitment and payment to you." http://www.arhelp.com/howdoesitwork.asp?GUID=apoc9sin8e, last visited 23.01.2015.

[213] The motto of one UK collection agency is as follows: "It is the **Personal Contact** of your debtor that gets the result you want.[...] Letters don't collect, we do!" http://www.arhelp.com/howdoesitwork.asp?GUID=apoc9sin8e, last visited 23.01.2015.

[214] http://www.directcollectionsltd.co.uk/, last visited on 23.01.2015.

[215] http://www.topfactoring.ro/Company, visited on 19.06.2012. The current content of the page suffered modifications with respect to services offered.

[216] http://www.toprecuperari.ro/index-2.html, last visited 23.01.2015. The Romanian text reads: "Activitatea de recuperare creanţe se desfaşoară în 2 etape: - colectarea pe cale amiabilă -

taking quite a descriptive approach in advertising their services, by developing on each stage: "During this stage, our company which, based on the customers and investments in Romania is the leading specialized company, successfully renders collection services by phone, notices and summons, visits on the field at the debtor domicile/registered office/working place, the investigation of the debtor assets [...]." The same collection agency gets involved in parallel proceedings, if the judicial collection effort was successful and a writ of execution was issued:

> We take parallel actions regarding: [a] negotiations with the debtors for an amiable payment of the debt that implies new court transactions; [b] the initiation of forced execution proceedings by means of the official receiver, which implies: [1] the identification of personal property and real estate held by the debtor with banks, insurance companies, leasing companies, local taxes and charges departments, land books, IT registrar offices; [2] pursuing the forced execution approval by the court regarding the claim filed by the official receiver; [3] defending our customer interests in potential challenging proceedings related to the forced execution or title, filed by the debtors; [4] monitoring the seizure and capitalization stage of the seized assets.[217]

If the communication is successful, the debtor and the debt collector may agree on a repayment schedule or on a lump sum payment that might erase the debt.[218] In case the debt is not settled, normally hard collection follows. In the case of debt buyers, they have the additional option of reselling the debt and letting the buyers deal with collection at a later date.[219]

Given that this work is dedicated to nonjudicial debt collection, hard collection was supposed to be left out. However, since most debt collectors in the US resort more and more to judicial proceedings in order to revive bad debt or to obtain rapidly (and most of the time abusively) a writ of execution, thus circumventing the protection provided by the FDCPA, several considerations must be made. Therefore, the book will not make an exhaustive analysis of judicial collection but will focus on its potential for abusive nonjudicial debt collection.

5.2.4.2 Judicial Collection

If informal methods were not successful, debt collectors have the option of resorting to litigation or arbitration. "Hard collection" used to be avoided by debt

telefoane, notificări, concilieri directe, etc., conform unei proceduri interne adaptate de la caz la caz. - recuperarea pe cale judecătorească - reprezintă declanşarea procedurilor judiciare în vederea recuperării creanţei."

[217] http://www.urbansiasociatii.ro/en/the_dispute_stage.html, last visited on 23.01.2015.

[218] Where such a possibility exists, the debt collectors can resort to repossession. For details, see *supra* Chap. 4, Sect. 4.1.

[219] Spector (2011), p. 263.

collectors in the US,[220] but empirical studies show that there is an increasing turn to it,[221] and it has even become the preferred method of debt collection.[222] The reason for such a change is easy to identify. Although the FDCPA established rules of conduct for all stages of collection, "it imposed no obligations on collector's conduct in litigation other than requiring that suits be filed in the venue in which the consumer signed the contract or in which the consumer resides at the commencement of the litigation."[223] In other words, debt collectors have identified the gap between the protections offered by the FDCPA in private/informal collections and those offered in judicial/formal collection, and they are now massively exploiting them.[224] Given that litigation of debts is generally governed entirely by state law procedures and only few of them provide additional safeguards to the requirements of fair notice and opportunity to be heard, there is no wonder that this venue is nowadays the preferred one. Just one short look at the success rate of debt collection suits and the picture is complete.[225]

The situation is different in Europe, especially in countries where contingency fees are not (yet) allowed[226] such as the UK,[227] France, Germany and Romania.

---

[220] "After a careful empirical study [...] many creditors are unlikely to use courts for collection because they see litigation as loaded with unnecessary costs." Other risks, especially when it comes to consumer debt, is that of losing the case entirely or getting a decision stating that the creditor does not hold a valid debt. For details: Warren and Westbrook (2009), p. 5.

[221] Spector (2011), p. 263, Jurgens and Hobbs (2010), pp. 12–16, The Legal Aid Society, *Debt Deception. How Debt Buyers Abuse the Legal System to Prey on Lower-Income New Yorkers at* http://www.nedap.org/pressroom/documents/DEBT_DECEPTION_FINAL_WEB.pdf, pp. 6, 8–9.

[222] "Recently litigation has moved from a method of last resort to a preferred method of collecting debts." Fox (2012), p. 358.

[223] Spector (2011), p. 263.

[224] "Unfortunately the FDCPA was written at a time when most collection activity was non-judicial. It has not kept up with the changes in the practice of debt collection and is largely silent when it comes to litigation abuse." Fox (2012), p. 359.

[225] "The rate of default judgments in consumer debt collection cases is reported to have reached 95 % and may be double the default judgments rate in debt cases generally." Spector (2011), p. 263. "Collectors have taken over small claims courts and other low level courts in state after state. In Massachusetts, "the people's court has become the collectors' court."[...] The vast majority of court cases resulted in judgments in favor of the creditors." Jurgens and Hobbs (2010), p. 13. "According to industry reports, close to 80 % of the debtors fail to respond to collection lawsuits and most result in default judgments." Fox (2012), p. 358. Similar data can be found at Holland (2011), p. 267.

[226] Emons (2007). According to this paper, the UK introduced conditional fees (success fees), while France and Germany are considering introducing them (pages 89–90). For the moment, the contingency fee is strictly forbidden in Europe by the ethical code of the European association of lawyers. On the contingency fee in France: http://www.triplet.com/70-10_litigation/70-30_structure.asp, last visited on 23.01.2015.

[227] On the proposal of having actual contingency costs introduced in the UK, see European Justice Forum's paper UK: Government Implementation of Jackson Reforms on the Costs and Funding of Litigation. Introduction of Contingency Fees and increased Mediation, p. 2, available online at http://europeanjusticeforum.org/storage/UK%20Government%20Implementation%20of%20Jackson%20Reforms%20on%20the%20Costs%20and%20Funding%20of%20Litigation.pdf, last visited on 23.01.2015.

Debt collectors advise their clients that the costs (both in time and money) of the proceedings are not at all small.[228] This must be a major setback for debt collectors in Europe as many clients will not be willing or able to pay the judicial and attorney fees asked by the state and, respectively, by the collection agency. Further details on debt collection litigation are offered in Chap. 6 where the abuses occurring in this stage are addressed. It is worth noting here though that the ban of contingency fees or look-alikes may function as a good consumer protection method, although it would be hard to claim that this is the main reason behind the ban.

If the court proceeding proves unsuccessful, most likely if the collection was attempted by a debt buyer, the debt is often resold, provided there is a market for it.[229] If the "hard collection" mechanism is successful, a judgment is issued, which will empower the creditor to garnish the wage of the debtor or to seize his car, bank account or any other property.[230] The judgment has also a very important effect, that of prolonging the life of the consumer's obligation to pay the alleged debt, sometimes for decades,[231] this being the second important reason for which, after the massive expansion of the debt-buying industry, the judicial debt collection has become so heavily used. It is also why the analysis turns now to the topic of bad debt and the way the collection industry is trying and many times succeeds to resuscitate it.

5.3 Bad Debt[232]

Bad debt is not only a defaulted debt but a debt that for some reason cannot be collected anymore. Normally, a debt becomes uncollectable after the statute of limitations produced its effects with respect to it or after the debt has been discharged in bankruptcy. The above-named mechanisms are legal ways of "killing" a debt, but that does not preclude a debt collector from contacting a debtor

---

[228] http://www.debtcollectioningermany.com/FAQ.html, last visited on 23.01.2015.

[229] "A dismissal without prejudice can create as many problem for defendant as it solves. The debt will likely be sold back into the debt market and eventually come back to haunt the defendant. [...] A dismissal without prejudice leaves the collection agency with a valuable asset it can sell." Fox (2012), p. 368. Also: Spector (2011), p. 260.

[230] Jurgens and Hobbs (2010), p. 3.

[231] "These judgments can be used – depending on each state's laws – to garnish wages or seize assets from a debtor. A judgment can also extend the life of a claim decades beyond limits imposed by state statutes." Jurgens and Hobbs (2010), p. 12. "A summary judgment granted in error on, for example, a debt that is beyond the statute of limitation, has the effect of laundering the defect from that debt. The debt is now a judgment that can be collected for the next twenty years." Fox (2012), p. 368.

[232] Bad Debt is defined as "A debt that is uncollectible and that may be deductible for tax purposes"—Garner (2007), p. 432.

about it,[233] and neither does it preclude a debtor from voluntarily paying it.[234] There are also ways to bring back to life a time-barred or a discharged debt,[235] despite the efforts made in the US by the FDCPA to preclude such practices.[236] Resurrecting bad debt became very important with the entrance on the collection market of debt buyers because, as pointed out in the previous section, it sells very cheap and can generate enormous amounts of money.[237]

In general, the statute of limitations of contract or tort law claims is determined by state law in the US or national laws in continental Europe.[238] Normally, the calculation starts with failure of consumer to make a payment. States also determine when the countdown stops depending on two things: the type of debt and the law that applies either in the state where the debtor lives or the state specified in the credit contract.[239] The situation is similar in Europe: in the UK, the term is 6 years according to the Limitations Act from 1980;[240] in Germany, the general term is 3 years, but it can be subject to interruption,[241] while in France it is 5 years after the

[233] http://www.ftc.gov/bcp/edu/pubs/consumer/alerts/alt144.shtm, last visited on 23.01.2015.

[234] In the US, the Federal Trade Commission actually informs consumers that paying an old debt is entirely up to them. See http://www.ftc.gov/bcp/edu/pubs/consumer/alerts/alt144.shtm, last visited on 23.01.2015.

[235] The decision to sue for a discharged debt may serve other purposes as well: "some creditors may believe, perhaps erroneously, that they need a judgment for a tax or regulatory purposes," to "impose costs on the consumer by damaging the consumer's credit rating," "to maintain a reputation as a tough debt-collector and discourage other debtors from defaulting." But the main purpose remains the one of convincing "the current defendant to pay." Hynes (2008), pp. 19–20.

[236] The safeguards offered by the FDCPA, when it comes to time-barred debt, are limited and refer strictly to litigation. "FDCPA bars debt collectors from threatening litigation, or actually using litigation, after the statute of limitations for suing to recover the debt has passed. But FDCPA does permit debt collectors to pursue time-barred debts that are still otherwise valid using out of court collection methods. Thus, when contacted about old debts, debtors are left without recourse unless the collection agents threaten litigation or actually file suit." See Goldberg (2006), p. 750. In a recent case addressing the issue of trying to collect time-barred debt, the court "explained that [. . .] [the] obligation was not extinguished by the expiration of the statute of limitations [. . .]. Although he [the debtor n.n.] had a complete legal defense against paying the debt, he still owed it. The statute of limitation merely rendered the debt unenforceable, but it did not invalidate it." Author unknown (2011), pp. 18–19.

[237] "Secondary markets have grown, where creditors sell "bad" debts for pennies on the dollar to bargain hunters who know how to squeeze more money out of debtors." Jurgens and Hobbs (2010), p. 5. Also: Goldsmith and Martin (2010), p. 372.

[238] "Each state imposes a statute of limitations, typically ranging from three to six years, after which a debtor is no longer legally obligated to pay the debt and can have a judgment dismissed in court." See Goldberg (2006), p. 750.

[239] For example, the statute of limitations for credit card debt in a few states may be as long as 10 years, but most states impose a period of 3–6 years. See: http://www.ftc.gov/bcp/edu/pubs/consumer/alerts/alt144.shtm, last visited on 23.01.2015.

[240] The full text of the Limitations Act from 1980 is available online at http://www.legislation.gov.uk/ukpga/1980/58, last visited on 23.01.2015.

[241] "According to German civil law, claims are generally statute-barred after 3 years." http://www.debtcollectioningermany.com/FAQ.html, last visited on 23.01.2015.

recent reform in 2008,[242] but the term starts to flow from the moment the plaintiff—in this case the creditor—knew or should have known the facts giving rise to the claim. In Romania, the general term is 3 years, according to the RNCC,[243] if the law does not provide for a different term.

When it comes to developing techniques that can resurrect debts, one may notice that, if in the US the old FDCPA provides at least some minimal safeguards to consumers, in the chosen European jurisdictions (with the exception of the UK) there is none, leaving the consumers totally exposed. Even so, collection agencies have found ways to circumvent the legal provision in the US and trick consumers into paying old or discharged debts.

For example, one firm sends to the targeted debtors letter every 60 days with different settlement offers—including prizes such as flat TVs or other gifts for those who make payments.[244] Others use credit card offers—so-called "zombie cards," which are designed to function as a "debt collection device, not new credit":[245] debtors are offered "the possibility to charge debts to the new zombie cards because the transaction has the potential to erase statutes of limitations on the old debt and restart the clock for a new cycle of delinquency and default for the debtor."[246] A least a successful technique proved to be the one of offering debtors settlements for half of the face value under the threat of being reported for the old debt with the credit reporting agencies.[247]

Some debt collectors go even further and try to collect "dead-debt," meaning the debts of the deceased that cannot be the subject of collection unless the surviving family members signed a coloan agreement. Attempting to collect from surviving relatives is probably one of the oldest abusive practice identified as such by the law, if one considers the fact that it has been present and banned since the reign of the Roman Emperor Justinian,[248] and its survival can only be explained by its efficiency. Collection agencies took advantage of the fact that surviving family members did not know that they do not have a legal obligation to pay[249] and tried, many

[242] See the new prescription period at http://www.debevoise.com/files/Publication/d41d2d1d-0b7a-4806-ae59-79c55d1ea0a0/Presentation/PublicationAttachment/30e6df7b-791d-4192-b024-88960400ca72/RecentModification.pdf, last visited on 19.06.2012 (page unavailable anymore). The original French text of Loi no 2008/561 from 17 June 2008 "portant réforme de la prescription en matière civile" is available online at: http://www.legifrance.gouv.fr/affichTexte.do?cidTexte=JORFTEXT000019013696&dateTexte=, last visited on 23.01.2015.

[243] RNCC, Art. 2517.

[244] Jurgens and Hobbs (2010), p. 19.

[245] Jurgens and Hobbs (2010), p. 20.

[246] Jurgens and Hobbs (2010), p. 20.

[247] "Under the FDCPA, an obsolete debt cannot be reported to a credit reporting agency. Accordingly, the court found that under the "least sophisticated debtor" standard the letters were misleading and impliedly threatened to take action that could not legally be taken." See Author unknown (2011), p. 1.

[248] See *supra* Chap. 2, Sect. 2.2.1.

[249] Silver-Greenberg (2011).

times successfully, to collect debts on moral grounds.[250] To make things even worse, debt collectors targeting money owed by deceased people take pride in their ability to get the client's money back without causing any bad publicity: for example, while one promises help "to protect our clients' brands and maximize their recoveries,"[251] another offers "a proven approach that yields high returns at a low risk to the client's reputation."[252] Some finally went as far as to send "condolences cards that double as collection letters."[253] In a case decided in 2011, a court found that attempts to collect dead debt from a nonowing survivor relative amount to harassment and thus constitutes a violation of the FDCPA.[254]

The success of such techniques is strongly connected to the debtor's options and actions. Once confronted with an old debt, the debtor has three options, each of them bearing their own consequences: to pay, to partially pay or to continue not paying.[255] The consequence of payment is that even if the debtor finds out that the debt was time barred, he cannot reclaim it. Also, another consequence might be that he will face collection efforts for all penalties, damages or interests that attached to the initial debt.[256] The consequence of partial payment is the reanimation of the debt. Basically, a new term will start flowing from the moment of the partial payment and the consumer will even face the possibility of being sued for the remaining amounts.[257] In case of nonpayment, the collectors can still try to convince the debtor to pay and also it might prove harder for the debtor to ask for credit or insurance as nonpayment usually affects the credit rating.[258]

In the US, the ability of collection agencies to adapt to the existing legal framework and invent more and more instruments to trick consumers into resurrecting old debts did not go unnoticed and the Federal Trade Commission tried to respond as strong as possible,[259] but further action and regulation are needed, as shown in the next chapters.

---

[250] Silver-Greenberg (2011) at http://online.wsj.com/news/articles/SB20001424052970204224604577030043890121710.

[251] Silver-Greenberg (2011) at http://online.wsj.com/news/articles/SB20001424052970204224604577030043890121710.

[252] Silver-Greenberg (2011) at http://online.wsj.com/news/articles/SB20001424052970204224604577030043890121710.

[253] Silver-Greenberg (2011) at http://online.wsj.com/news/articles/SB20001424052970204224604577030043890121710.

[254] Silver-Greenberg (2011) at http://online.wsj.com/news/articles/SB20001424052970204224604577030043890121710.

[255] http://www.ftc.gov/bcp/edu/pubs/consumer/alerts/alt144.shtm, last visited 23.01.2015.

[256] http://www.ftc.gov/bcp/edu/pubs/consumer/alerts/alt144.shtm, last visited 23.01.2015.

[257] http://www.ftc.gov/bcp/edu/pubs/consumer/alerts/alt144.shtm, last visited 23.01.2015.

[258] http://www.ftc.gov/bcp/edu/pubs/consumer/alerts/alt144.shtm, last visited 23.01.2015.

[259] Latest settlement concerning reanimation of bad debt has reached 2.5 million dollars. For details: http://moneyland.time.com/2012/02/02/2-5-million-ftc-settlement-targets-collection-of-expired-debt/, last visited on 23.01.2015.

But debts can also be cured in or by courts, as mentioned in the previous section. In the US, the high number of cases—usually finalized with default judgments—has blocked the activity of courts[260] and has decreased the ability of judges to properly analyze them,[261] with some authors going as far as to accuse judges of willingly helping creditors to keep the debt alive.[262] Advantages are also drawn from the fact that many of the targeted debtors do not really understand the legal process they are submitted to, while the attorneys are intimately familiarized with the courts and hope that debtors will either fail to contest or will be unable to put up a proper defense.[263]

The European counterparts of collection agencies are operating in the same way, some making resurrection of old debt their principal object of activity, some advertising their successful tactics in acquiring the same result. In the UK, a collection agency advertises on its website the fact that it would take debt of "any age and size";[264] in Germany, another collection agency announces that it specializes in "collecting outstanding debts (bad debts) in Germany -and all European countries,"[265] while in France one debt collector lets its clients know that besides the traditional collection services its "recent interventions" with some clients have enabled it to "acquire a particular know-how" in fields like handling of claims written-off as bad debts,[266] and another praises its own "tremendous solution to the problems of bad debts, charge offs, and delinquent receivables."[267] All these might be just bragging, but in the absence of proper regulations with respect to fair collection practices, one can never know. In Romania, similar advertisements were not identified, but the fact that the debt-buying business is well developed leads to the belief that tactics as those employed in the other jurisdictions analyzed take place as well.

The issue of bad debt is far from being settled. Although in the US the FTC and a large number of NGOs are struggling and fighting for reform and implementing tougher regulations against those engaged in resurrection of debts, in Europe things are rather silent. However, attempts to collect time-barred debts or discharged debts need to be addressed by the European jurisdiction as well and as soon as possible, despite any possible resistance from the current procreditor status quo,[268] for

---

[260] For details: Jurgens and Hobbs (2010), pp. 12–16. Another analysis on exploiting small claim courts is available at: Goldberg (2006), pp. 741–749.

[261] A practice seems to be the one of giving applications for default judgments to clerks instead of judges, who often lack legal training and are unable to assess whether the application meets the minimum required standards. Society (2010), p. 14.

[262] Fox (2012), pp. 368–369.

[263] Goldberg (2006), pp. 744–745.

[264] http://www.arhelp.com/faq.asp?GUID=apoc9sin8e#q2, last visited on 23.01.2015.

[265] http://www.debtcollectioningermany.com/, last visited on 23.01.2015.

[266] http://en.france-contentieux.com/debt-collection.html, last visited on 23.01.2015.

[267] http://www.abad-debt.com/services.htm, last visited on 19.06.2012 (page currently unavailable).

[268] Huls (2012), p. 508.

debtors are far from being insulated from abusive debt collection practices. The following chapters will show that the American model and experience provide a good and valuable source of inspiration.

References

Allen S (2010) ECJ says payment handling service is taxable supply of debt collection, Nov/Dec. Busy Practitioner

Author unknown (2011) Recent developments. Debt collection. Debt collector may attempt to collect time-barred debt (Guertas v. Galaxy Asset Mgmt., 641 F. 3d 28 (3rd Cir. 2011)). J Consum Commer Law. http://www.jtexconsumerlaw.com/V15N1/V15N1_DebtCol.pdf

Beale H, Bridge M, Gullifer L, Lomnicka E (2012) The law of security and title-based financing. Oxford University Press, Oxford

Bickers M (2011) World factoring yearbook 2011. BCR Publishing, Kent

Biscoe PM (1975) Law and practice of credit factoring. Butterworths, London

Blackburn V (2010) The Cinderella of finance steps out of the shadows. The Daily Telegraph, London

Carpenaru SD, Stanciulescu L, Nemes V (2009) Contracte civile si comerciale. Ed. Hamangiu, Bucuresti

De Boer S (2013) Fair debt collection practices act. Overview, analyses, and administration. Novinka, New York

Drury RR, Xuereb PG (1991) European company laws. A comparative approach. Dartmouth Pub Co

Emons W (2007) Conditional versus contingent fees. Oxford Econ Pap. http://oep.oxfordjournals.org/content/59/1/89.full.pdf+html

Fleming S, Hopkins K (2011) Fears for their overdrafts drive small firms away from banks. The Times, London

Fox JL (2012) Do we have a debt collection crisis? Some cautionary tales of debt collection in Indiana. Loyola Consum Law Rev. http://ssrn.com/abstract=2023829

Garner BA (2007) Black's law dictionary. Thomson/West, St. Paul

Gilmore G (1999) Security interests in personal property. The Lawbook Exchange, LTD, Union

Girsberger DI (1992) Defenses of the account debtor in international factoring. Am J Comp Law 40:467

Gogel JA (2011) Remedies for abusive debt collection: an Illinois lawyer's guide. Illinois Bar J 99:358

Goldberg L (2006) Dealing in debt: the high-stakes world of debt collection after FDCPA. South Calif Law Rev 79:711

Goldsmith TE, Martin N (2010) Testing materiality under the unfair practices acts: what information matters when collecting time-barred debts? Winter Consumer Finance Law Quarterly Report 372

Grundmann W (2013) Leasing und Factoring. Formen, Rechtsgrundlagen, Verträge. Springer Gabler, Germany

Hector C (2011) Debt collection in the information age: new technologies and the fair debt collection practices act. Calif Law Rev 99:1601

Hiller WH (1939) Four centuries of factoring. Q J Econ 53:305

Hilson JF (2010) Asset-based lending. A practical guide to secured financing. Practising Law Institute, New York

Holland PA (2011) The one hundred billion dollar problem in small claim court: Robo signing and lack of proof in debt buyer cases. J Bus Technol Law. http://papers.ssrn.com/sol3/papers.cfm?abstract_id=1875727

Huls N (2012) A next step in debt enforcement: the merger of debt help and debt collection. J Consum Policy 35:497
Hynes RM (2008) Broke but not bankrupt: consumer debt collection in state courts. Florida Law Rev. http://www.floridalawreview.com/wp-content/uploads/2010/01/Hynes_A2.pdf
Johnston W (2008) Security over receivables. Oxford University Press, Oxford
Jurgens R, Hobbs RJ (2010) The debt machine: how the collection industry hounds consumers and overwhelms courts. National Consumer Law Center Report. http://www.nclc.org/images/pdf/pr-reports/debt-machine.pdf
King LP, Cook ML (1996) Creditors' rights, debtors' protection, and bankruptcy. Mathew Bender, New York
Laws (2009) T. A. L. I. N. C. o. C. o. U. S. Uniform Commercial Code 2009–2010 edition. Official text and comments. Thomson Reuters, United States
Markesinis SB, Unberath H, Johnston A (2006) The German law of contract. A comparative treatise. Hart Publishing, Oxford and Portland, Oregon
Mesnooh CJ (1994) Law and business in France. A guide to French commercial and corporate law. Martinus Nijhoff Publishers, Netherlands
Mircea V (2000) Contractul de factoring. Revista de drept comercial
Patlageanu A, Lefter A (2004) Contractul de factoring. Revista de Drept Comercial
Posel S (1982) Factoring accounts receivable in France: some legal aspects and American comparisons. Tulane Law Rev 57
Rodière R (1976) The code civil and modern procedures of payment. Tulane Law Rev 50:577
Ruddy N, Mills S, Davidson N (2006) Salinger on factoring. Sweet & Maxwell, London
Schwarze T, Storjohann J (2006) The sale and acquisition of non-performing loans under German law. J Int Bank Law Regul 21
Serick R (1990) Securities in movables in German law: an outline. Kluwer Law and Taxation Publishers, Deventer
Silver-Greenberg J (2011) For the families of some debtors, death offers no respite. Wall Street Journal. http://online.wsj.com/news/articles/SB20001424052970204224604577030043890121710
Silverman HR (1948) Factoring: its legal aspects and economic justification. Law Contemp Probl 13:593
Society TLA (2010) Debt deception. How debt buyers abuse the legal system to prey on lower-income New Yorkers
Soufani K (2002) The decision to finance account receivables: the factoring option. Manag Decis Econ 23:21
Spector M (2011) Debts, defaults and details: exploring the impact of debt collection litigation on consumers and courts. Virginia Law Bus Rev. http://ssrn.com/abstract=1975121
Strachan I (2011) Improve cashflow and cut overheads; Ian Strachan gives a beginner's guide to the world of factoring and invoice discounting and what it means to businesses. Birmingham Post & Mail Ltd, Birmingham Post
Tajti T (2002a) Comparative secured transactions law. Akadémiai Kiadó, Budapest
Tajti T (2002b) Viehweg's topics, Article 9 UCC, the "Kautelarische Sicherheiten" and the Hungarian secured transactions law reform. Vindobona J Int Commer Law Arbitr
Tajti T (2013a) Post-1990 secured transaction law reforms in Central and Eastern Europe. Szegedi Közjegyzői Közlöny
Tajti T (2013b) Systemic and topical mapping of the relationship of the draft common frame of reference and arbitration. Kazimieras Simonavicius University, Vilnius
Turcu I (2011) Noul Cod Civil republicat. Cartea a V-a. Despre obligatii (Art 1164–1649) – Comentarii si explicatii. C.H. Beck, Bucuresti
Vartolomei B (2006) Admisibilitatea incheierii contractelor de factoring in contextul legislatiei romane actuale. Dreptul
Warren E, Westbrook JL (2009) The law of debtors and creditors: text, cases, and problems. Wolters Kluwer Law & Business, New York
White JJ, Summers RS (2010) Uniform commercial code. In: Practitioner treatise series. Thomson Reuters, U.S.A.

Chapter 6
Abusive Debt Collection Practices and the Building Blocks of an Efficient Debt Collection Regime

As shown in the previous chapter, the debt-collecting industry in America has been under continuous expansion and development, strongly fueled by the higher degree of unemployment and the increasing number of bankruptcies generated by economic crises. The proportions reached and the large numbers involved have brought from the very beginning a myriad of devious and abusive collection practices,[1] in particular harassment (at home or at the work place), impersonation of lawyers or law officers by collectors, use of false documents or physical threats.[2]

Given that creditors would like to get paid and would, normally, resort to almost any means in order to achieve their goal, the **traditional remedies did not prove efficient in providing debtors with enough protection against the abusive practices** such as those mentioned above.[3] In the US, the problem of intrastate debt collection abuses,[4] has added to the already existing—absent or inadequate - state law,[5] and has led to calls for federal intervention in dealing with the problem.[6] The Fair Debt Collection Practices Act (FDCPA) has provided thus a general

[1] Potach (1978).

[2] Potach (1978), p. 895.

[3] The Congressional findings and the declaration of purpose of the FDCPA state in 15 USC 1692 (Section 802) (a) and (b) that "There is abundant evidence of the use of abusive, deceptive, and unfair debt collection practices [. . .]. Existing laws and procedures for redressing these injuries are inadequate to protect consumers."

[4] "Abusive collection practices are carried on to a substantial extent in interstate commerce and through means and instrumentalities of such commerce. Even where abusive debt collection practices are purely intrastate in character, they nevertheless affect intrastate commerce." FDCPA, 15 USC 1692 (Section 802) (d).

[5] Griffith (2012), p. 179: "It was a serious turn of events because until then many states had no effective laws to control the conduct of collectors."

[6] One should not ignore the fact that the Congress passed the FDCPA in an attempt to balance two competing interests: consumers' right to be treated with care and respect and not be subjected to abusive collection practices and creditors' and debt collectors' interest in recovering the money they were owed. See Akina (2012), p. 145 at 149.

C.G. Stănescu, *Self-Help, Private Debt Collection and the Concomitant Risks*,
DOI 10.1007/978-3-319-21503-7_6

background and a solid starting point, despite the emergence of ever newer types of abuses and the repeated calls for reform,[7] which will be addressed in the next chapter. In Europe, however, though similar issues have risen, the response is not yet as strong and adequate as in the US (with the UK being a notable exception). The explanation might be that the dimension of abuses related to debt collection in Europe is significantly lower than in the US, but in the absence of concrete statistics one may only speculate.

This chapter deals with the abusive practices regulated by the FDCPA, the legal remedies it provides and the current European framework in the field, while the next chapter discusses the reasons why the FDCPA has been criticized in recent years and the areas proposed for reform. The critical assessment is based on a matrix of analysis consisting of several proposed building blocks, which help in evaluating the efficiency of any law regulating abusive debt collection.

6.1 Current Legal Framework Concerning Abusive Debt Collection

The severity and forms of abusive debt collection are hardly identical in the jurisdictions in the purview of this work, which explains the differences in concern and regulation of abusive debt collection practices. Moreover, while the US literature is anything but scarce, and the US case law is very well developed at both federal and state levels, the situation is almost the opposite in European jurisdictions. Obviously, where both regulation and concern are lacking—such as the case of Romania—the absence of relevant case law and discourse is not really surprising, but in countries such as the UK, France or Germany, where such regulation is in place (although with different levels of development), such absence might be a sign that the legal framework is either insufficient or inefficient. Put differently, one should ask whether the absence of case law and literature is a sign that the system (either in total or in certain parts) is, in fact, malfunctioning and why.

Due to the fact that statutes are changing or might change in the near future, analysis limited to the law in force might lead to a distorted picture. Therefore, the following sections do not focus purely on the current the wording of the statutes, but they also propose a matrix of analysis consisting of six building blocks and then critically asses the current legal provisions, in search of the best suited solutions against abusive debt collection practices.

It might be useful to first summarize the current frameworks in place (provided they exist), at both EU and national levels, or proposed projects (for Romania), together with the policies behind them, for they will reveal, from the very beginning, the jurisdiction's approach to the issue of abusive debt collection. For

[7] "The recent increase in reported debt collection complaints is proof enough that the FDCPA is still a necessary shield for consumers." Akina (2012), p. 150.

example, the EU protects consumers in general, without addressing in detail the specific issue of debt collection. In the US, the legal framework consists mainly in statutory law, be it at federal or at state level. In the UK, the legal framework consists mainly of agency regulations, such as the former Office for Fair Trading (OFT), whose attributes were taken over by the new Financial Conduct Authority (FCA). In those countries lacking specific legislation, the starting issue is, obviously, the absence of sector-specific legislation itself.

6.1.1 General Consumer Protection v. Sector-Specific Legislation: Why the EU Consumer Protection Regime Against Unfair Commercial Practices Is Insufficient

The EU does not have sector-specific legislation dedicated strictly to nonjudicial debt collection. Consumer protection enjoys a general coverage under Directive 2011/83/EU; however, according to the EU Guidance to Directive 2005/29/EC (UCPD), debt collection falls under the scope of this directive, since it qualifies as an "after-sale service": "debt collection should be regarded as after-sales commercial practices regulated by the Directive. Indeed, when a consumer owes a trader certain amount of money (as a consumer debt), the collection of this debt (in house or by a third party) is directly connected with the sale or supply of products."[8]

If debt collection falls within the scope of UCPD, it means that it qualifies as an unfair commercial practice and is prohibited if it is either contrary to professional diligence or if it is misleading (Art. 6 and 7) or aggressive (Art. 8 and 9), in particular.[9] By "professional diligence," the UCPD understands the "standard of special skill and care which a trader may reasonably be expected to exercise towards consumers, commensurate with honest market practice and/or the general principle of good faith in the trader's field of activity."[10] Hence, the trader's field of activity is regarded as the standard for honest market practices, which "could lead to the argument that, in sectors where bad practice is rife, the standard demanded is

[8] https://webgate.ec.europa.eu/UCPD/public/index.cfm?event=public.guidance.browse&elemID=1, last visited 09.12.2014. Recital 13 of Directive 2005/29/EC states that "In order to support consumer confidence the general prohibition should apply to unfair commercial practices [...] following the conclusion of a contract and during its execution." According to Art 3.1, the Directive applies "to unfair business – to – consumer practices, as laid down in Article 5, before, during and after a commercial transaction in relation to a product." Given the wording of Art 3, business-to-business transactions do not fall within the scope of the Directive. See also: Ramsay (2012), p. 163. However, no scholarly work dedicated to the issue of unfair debt collection under the UCPD or developing the issue of debt collection under the UCPD was identified during the research conducted for this work.

[9] Art 5.1, Art 5.4 and Art 5.5 of Directive 2005/29/EC. On difficulties raised by the UCPD's definition of "professional diligence," see: Micklitz et al. (2009), p. 85.

[10] Art 2, letter h) of Directive 2005/29/EC.

correspondingly low."[11] If one extrapolates the requirement of professional diligence to debt collectors—whether in-house or third parties—then **debt collectors are expected to receive training and be specialized in the field** (attorneys or accountants), **maintaining a fair approach towards consumers and exercising their services in good faith**[12] (unless bad practice is in fact the actual standard in the debt collection business). Since none of these standards are defined by the UCPD, however, they are left up to national laws and national courts to establish on a case-by-case basis, which might affect the declared purpose of maximum harmonization sought by the UCPD.[13] Member states have different takes on traders' fields of activity and expected standards of good practice, i.e. Romania does not even license its debt collectors, while all other chosen European jurisdictions do.

As shown above, the UCPD distinguishes between two types of behaviors that will qualify as unfair practices: on the one hand, *misleading* practices (actions[14] and omissions[15]) and, on the other hand, *aggressive* practices (including harassment,

[11] Poncibo and Incardona (2005), p. 317 at 319.

[12] On the standard of "good faith," see *Freiburger Kommunalbauten GmbH Baugesellschaft & Co. KG v. Ludger Hofstetter and Ulrike Hofstetter*, C-237/02 [2004] of the ECJ, Para 19, available online at: http://curia.europa.eu/juris/showPdf.jsf?text=&docid=49062&pageIndex=0&doclang=EN&mode=lst&dir=&occ=first&part=1&cid=255716, last visited 10.12.2014.

[13] On the debate concerning maximum harmonization sought by the UCPD: Micklitz et al. (2009), pp. 78–81.

[14] "A misleading action occurs when a practice misleads through the information it contains, or, through the deceptive presentation of that information, and causes or is likely to cause the average consumer to take a different transactional decision than he or she would have taken otherwise. The definition of a misleading action used in the Directive has taken into account the current state of knowledge of how consumers take decisions in the market space. For example, new insights from behavioral economics show that not only the content of the information provided, but also the way the information is presented can have a serious impact on how consumers respond to it. The Directive has therefore explicit provisions to cover situations of practices which are capable of deceiving consumers 'in any way, including overall presentation', even if the information provided is factually correct." https://webgate.ec.europa.eu/UCPD/public/index.cfm?event=public.guidance.browse&elemID=74#article_62, last visited 09.12.2014. General misleading information is covered by Article 6 of Directive 2005/29/EC.

[15] A misleading omission occurs when a practice misleads through omitting material information that the average consumer needs, in a particular context, in order to make an informed transactional decision. Misleading omissions are covered by Art 7 of Directive 2005/29/EC and need to be read in correlation to Art 2, letter (k), which defines transactional decisions as "decisions taken by consumers concerning whether, how and on what terms to [. . .] make payment in whole or in part [. . .]." Given the broad wording of the definition of transactional decisions, misleading omissions seem to cover the issue of old debt as well. More importantly, a debt collector might be obliged to provide his full address, the full price (including taxes), performance and complaint handling policy and the existence of a right of withdrawal (providing that is possible—like in the case US consumer debtors who have the possibility to ask not to be contacted by the debt collector). https://webgate.ec.europa.eu/UCPD/public/index.cfm?event=public.guidance.browse&elemID=74#article_62, last visited 09.12.2014.

coercion and undue influence).[16] Due to the broad terms employed by the UCPD,[17] it appears that it could cover most of the occurring abusive debt collection practices, thus establishing a general regime to govern fair debt collection at EU level. The broad definition given to "transactional decisions" also generates significant implications, for it allows the UCPD to extend its application to a wide variety of cases impacting consumer-debtors. The question becomes then, is the UCPD sufficient? And if the answer is positive, then why did the states decide they need additional sector-specific legislation regarding unfair debt collection practices?

The answers lie with the effects of the UCPD. **First** of all, it does not touch upon any conditions of establishment of authorization regimes or on the deontological codes of conduct or other specific rules governing regulated professions. Therefore, states trying to implement a licensing regime of debt collectors are free to do so as they deem fit, because it goes beyond the scope of the UCPD. The situation is similar to that in the US, where the federal FDCPA does not contain a licensing procedure, but such procedures are provided by most mini-FDCPAs. From this point of view, **sector-specific legislation is necessary in order *to complete* the UCPD.**

Second, with respect to both misleading and aggressive practices, the UCPD left it for the national courts and administrative authorities to assess the misleading character of commercial practices[18] or the concept of average[19] or vulnerable[20] consumer. As was emphasized, with respect to aggressive practices, "one of the problems [. . .] is that the term is not a developed concept in most Member States or in European Law."[21] Hence, developing clearer standards and nonexhaustive lists

---

[16] According to Arts 8 and 9 of Directive 2005/29/EC, aggressive practices are those that, by harassment, coercion, including the use of physical force or undue influence, affect the average consumer's freedom of choice or conduct with regard to the product or causes him to take a transactional decision he would not have taken. As factors to be considered in determining whether the practice was unfair or not, the Directive mentions the time, the location, nature or persistence, the use of threatening or abusive language or behavior, the exploitation by the debt collector of specific misfortune or grave circumstances that impair the consumer's judgment or threats with actions that cannot be taken.

[17] On the broad interpretation of the notion "commercial practice," see *Jana Perenicova and Vladislav Perenic v. SOS finance spol. s.r.o.*, Case C-453/10, available at: http://eur-lex.europa.eu/LexUriServ/LexUriServ.do?uri=CELEX:62010CJ0453:EN:HTML, last visited 09.12.2014. Also: Poncibo and Incardona (2005), p. 320. "This definition is broad, ranging from whether to purchase to whether to exercise or not the right arising from the purchase. The unfair practice usually will induce the consumer to make a regrettable decision." It remains unclear what would constitute an induced regrettable decision in the field of debt collection.

[18] https://webgate.ec.europa.eu/UCPD/public/index.cfm?event=public.guidance.browse&elemID=74#article_62, last visited 09.12.2014.

[19] For details on what constitutes "average consumer" at EU level and criticism brought to this standard, see: Poncibo and Incardona (2005), pp. 324–328, Poncibo and Incardona (2007), p. 21 at pp. 26–28; Micklitz et al. (2009), pp. 88–89.

[20] On vulnerable consumers: Poncibo and Incardona (2005), p. 328; and Poncibo and Incardona (2007), pp. 28–29.

[21] Micklitz et al. (2010), p. 139.

of banned debt collection practices remains not only within the powers but also within the responsibilities of member states. Similarly to the situation in the US, where the FDCPA was regarded as a *de minimis* rule, **the UCPD implements only a minimum set of rules,** which are to be further developed by the national legislations where the UCPD specifically allows them to do so.[22]

Third, the UCPD leaves the matter of enforcement to member states, which are to ensure that "adequate and effective means exist to combat unfair commercial practices" and "such means shall include legal provisions under which persons or organizations regarded under national law as having a legitimate interest in combating unfair commercial practices may take legal action [. . .] and/or bring such unfair practices before an administrative authority."[23] Furthermore, states are allowed to impose penalties for infringements of "national provisions adopted in application of this Directive."[24] Thus, member states of the EU must adopt their own enforcement measures, which, based on their procedural laws, may differ from state to state, and their analysis reveals that in what concerns abusive debt collection, they do not suffice for they do not offer appropriate remedies[25] to aggrieved

[22] "In contrast to most other directives in the consumer protection field, the UCPD does not permit Member States to deviate from the standards it specifies, even where this would result in a higher level of protection for consumers." Poncibo and Incardona (2005), p. 317.

[23] Art. 11.1 and the following of Directive 2005/29/EC.

[24] Art 13 of Directive 2005/29/EC.

[25] The enforcement regimes based on the Directive differ significantly from country to country. In France, consumers may use an administrative mechanism of complaints, but the administrative authorities are not obliged to investigate. There is also a possibility to enforce through court action, before civil or criminal courts. The sanctions include imprisonment or fines, as well as court orders of cessation of misleading commercial practices, prohibition on exercising professional activities for a number of years and damages for direct and foreseeable losses. However, the plaintiff must prove that he suffered a loss. https://webgate.ec.europa.eu/UCPD/public/index.cfm?event=public.country.viewEnforcement&countryID=FR, last visited 09.12.2014. In Germany, there is no administrative enforcement against unfair commercial practices through state bodies but through competitors and associations with help of civil law. Enforcement through court action provides for a specific cease-and-desist procedure, and in addition a claim for civil damages can be filed. https://webgate.ec.europa.eu/UCPD/public/index.cfm?event=public.country.viewEnforcement&countryID=DE, last visited 09.12.2014. In the UK, the matter is much more developed. The Directive is implemented by several acts and was enforced by the former OFT and local authorities. However, there is no private right of action against traders by consumers. With respect to enforcement through court action civil actions for injunction orders, criminal proceedings and warrants are available. Again, there is no private right of action against traders by businesses or consumers. The sanctions that may be imposed include orders not to engage or repeat the infringing conduct or statutory fines (which are not higher than £5000). https://webgate.ec.europa.eu/UCPD/public/index.cfm?event=public.country.viewEnforcement&countryID=UK, last visited 09.12.2014. With respect to Romania, the Directive is implemented by Law no 363/2007 on fighting against unfair practices of traders in relation to the consumers and on the harmonization of regulations with the European legislation on consumer protection. The general enforcement of the Romanian legislation on unfair practices is handled by the National Authority for Consumer Protection, a specialized administrative body. Administrative complaints can be filed by any natural person or organization with a legitimate interest. The public authority has a duty to investigate and analyze the complaint within 30 days. With respect to enforcement through courts, the law allows general claims for damages to any person or organization

debtors. Based on the model implemented in the US,[26] additional sector-specific legislation is then required in order to **establish and implement a consistent enforcement regime** based on adequate standards and guidance for judges and administrative bodies and even strengthen the enforcement regime developed under the UCPD.

Last, but not least, **some of the UCPD's provisions might not work in the case of debt collection.** For example, the use of threats or violence in debt collection would qualify it as an unfair commercial practice, but only if it significantly impaired or was likely to significantly impair the average or vulnerable consumer's freedom of choice or conduct with regard to the product or caused him to take a transactional decision that he would not have taken otherwise. If the first part is clear, the second one requires additional qualifications. Does the UCPD mean that only average or vulnerable consumers deserve protection against abusive debt collection practices, or only those average or vulnerable consumers whose behavior was significantly impaired? No matter which one of the two is the answer, the UCPD is too limited,[27] for **there is no justification to differentiate between consumers when they are subjected to abusive debt collection practices**.

Moreover, one may raise questions with respect to the status of the consumer or with respect to the meaning of "influence of consumer's behavior" in the area of debt collection. In what concerns the status of the consumer the Commission obviously felt that the average consumer standard might not always provide a proper parameter for protection,[28] for which reason it made references to vulnerable consumers. This poses additional questions regarding the definition of this other category and the corresponding level of protection it needs.[29] As it will be shown later, the UK has identified some of the categories of vulnerable consumers such as

---

that proves a legitimate interest. Courts can also issue cease and desist orders, prohibit unfair practices. The available sanctions include court orders and fines for administrative offenses, but there is no criminal liability. https://webgate.ec.europa.eu/UCPD/public/index.cfm?event=public.country.viewEnforcement&countryID=RO last visited 09.12.2004.

[26] "The US example might be enlightening for the developing European Union's consumer [. . .] policies. [. . .] The basic consumer protection statute enforced by the FTC is Section 5(a) of the Federal Trade Commission Act. [. . .] **In addition, the FTC enforces a variety of specific consumer protection statutes** that prohibit specifically-defined trade practices and generally specify that violations are to be treated as if they were 'unfair or deceptive' acts or practices under Section 5(a)." Poncibo and Incardona (2005), p. 329.

[27] As emphasized, the UCPD does not consider other categories of consumers, such as those provided with sufficient information but which they cannot fully understand or properly evaluate or those acting under strong emotional factors. Poncibo and Incardona (2007), pp. 31–34. With respect to debt collection, these two categories are extremely important given that most of the unfair collection practices would actually affect consumer debtors emotionally or expose them to information containing a high degree of legal content, which they may not be fully able to comprehend.

[28] "The average consumer [. . .] is however, an overly simplistic concept with little correspondence with the real world [. . .] and should be reinterpreted more flexibly, or even abandoned [. . .]." Poncibo and Incardona (2007), p. 21.

[29] Poncibo and Incardona (2005), p. 327; Poncibo and Incardona (2007), p. 28.

those of low income, unemployed, suffering from long-term illnesses or disabilities or with low levels of education, as well as old or young people.[30] A discussion on whether certain categories deserve special consideration is also under debate in the US for amending the FDCPA. Such survey was not conducted in the EU, although the need for it was raised by European scholars.[31] What is clear though is that these special categories are in fact determined by the sector-specific legislation covering debt collection, based on adequate researches, and not by the legislation implementing the UCPD.

Concerning the influence on consumer's behavior in the matter of debt collection, the broad and vague language employed by the UCPD is problematic. Does it mean that the unfair practice resulted in influencing the consumer to pay his debt? This will not be a problem *per se*, because consumers are expected to pay their debts. Does payment of a debt equal an "economic loss" for the consumer? Obviously, amounts of money are leaving the consumer's patrimony when a debt is paid, but would that be enough to bring debt collection under the coverage of the UCPD? What if the unfair practice resulted solely in the harassment and embarrassment of the consumer, without causing him any economic loss? Should such practice be tolerated? One may argue that undue duress in pressuring the consumer to repay a debt before its due date or under unfair or detrimental conditions qualifies as unfair commercial practice under the UCPD, but cases involving abusive collection practices might not be always as clear-cut.

Another question is, which product does the UCPD refer to—the product from where the debt originated or the actual debt collection service? Obviously, no debtor is going to react positively to debt collection, but on the other side, conditioning protection against abusive debt collection practices on the requirement that it impairs the judgment of the average or vulnerable consumer[32] in relation to the product does not make much sense, for in case of abuse the origin of the debt is irrelevant.[33]

---

[30] Poncibo and Incardona (2005), p. 328.

[31] Poncibo and Incardona (2007), p. 29; and Micklitz et al. (2010), pp. 107–152.

[32] Such issues deriving from the broad wording of the UCPD did not escape the attention of scholars: "Harassment concerns invasion of an individual's private space. [. . .] However, the term harassment is broader and covers many annoying trade practices, such as spam. There is a potential problem of aligning the well-meaning broad scope of this provision with the wording of Article 8 as many of these objectionable practices will not affect the consumer's transactional decision. The average consumer is simply irritated by these practices and ignores them." See: Micklitz et al. (2010), p. 140.

[33] Poncibo and Incardona (2005), p. 329. The authors also criticize the approach taken by the Commission: "[T]he Commercial Practices Directive is plagued by short sightedness and is prudent in considering only the economic interest of consumers." The issues with this approach are even more evident in case of debt collection.

Since the UCPD seeks full harmonization, meaning that states can no longer implement or apply less or restrictive consumer protection measures in the area,[34] it follows that states are not free to establish a larger or clearer degree of protection by implementing the UCPD. It is probably the main reason why most European jurisdictions decided to go for parallel additional legislation. Since the UCPD proves insufficient, **sector-specific legislation appears to be a must in the field of debt collection.** The next question is whether such sector-specific regime should be implemented by substantive law or agency regulation, and it is addressed in the following section.

6.1.2 Substantive Law Versus Regulation

Substantive law and sector-specific regulation operate differently, although their goals are similar and complimentary. But choosing either substantive law or sector-specific regulation will define the main policies pursued by a particular jurisdiction, for each has different objectives. According to Hudson, the general objectives of substantive law are (1) to ensure enforcement (of contracts), (2) to protect property rights for parties and to protect the participants in (financial) markets from harms suffered as a result of civil wrongs and (3) to punish criminal offenses and civil wrongs.[35] Put differently, the *law requires obedience* of statutory or contractual provisions and *seeks to enforce* them. However, substantive law suffers from essential downsizes since it is formulated in an abstract manner, which is meant to cover all cases, and legislators do not consult the market players before exercising their powers. Hence substatinve law does not, usually, assess the theoretical impact on the market as a whole and its enforcement is carried out through courts by aggrieved parties.

The objectives of regulations differ. Their main purpose is to ensure that the regulated sector functions efficiently; to maintain its integrity by *sanctioning, preventing or deterring abuse*; and to protect consumers by *providing* them with *relevant information and education*. However, unlike substantive law, regulations are not adopted in abstract but by direct consultation with the market players and by assessing their effect on the market itself, and they are mainly enforced by governmental agencies, although private causes of action may be available to aggrieved parties.

To summarize, although both law and regulation deal with the allocation of risks between various parties, they operate in their own areas of competence: on the one hand, substantive law is concerned with the establishment of liability and the award of compensation, while on the other hand, regulation has the purpose of fostering a

---

[34] https://webgate.ec.europa.eu/UCPD/public/index.cfm?event=public.directive.browse2&article=article-205&elemID=226#article-205, last visited 09.12.2014.

[35] Hudson (2009), pp. 55–56.

proper, functioning market, in which both consumers and service providers have confidence.[36] Probably nothing exemplifies better these differences than the US and the UK approaches to the issue of abusive debt collection practices, as the following analysis will reveal, given that the US relies also on "hard" regulation (the FDCPAs) while the UK follows the "soft" regulation approach.

6.1.3 The Legal Framework Concerning Abusive Debt Collection in the US

In the US, the legal framework concerning abusive debt collection practices exists on both federal and state levels and consists mainly of substantive law, although the FDCPA has also the declared purpose of preventing, monitoring and sanctioning, in addition to repairing damages incurred and enforcing consumer-debtor rights, which may qualify it also as regulation. Up until now, most US states have implemented their own fair debt collection practices statutes, the mini-FDCPAs,[37] with more advanced and detailed regimes than the one established by the federal act. The reason is that, on the one hand, the federal statute was regarded only as a *de minimis* rule,[38] from which states could derogate by implementing more protective rules to consumers, while on the other hand, the federal statute could not implement measures that fell within the prerogatives of the states, such as a licensing requirement. However, for the purposes of this book, most references are made to the federal statute, while the mini-FDCPAs will be mentioned only where the protection awarded by them differs from or extends the protection offered at federal level.

The FDCPA is limited in scope, covering solely consumers[39] seen as natural persons and excludes any legal persons. From the perspective of secured transactions law, it would seem that any attempt to collect or repossess under UCC Article 9 would escape liability under the FDCPA. However, as mentioned in Chap. 3, since Article 9 does not distinguish between legal and natural persons, in the case a repossession were attempted against a natural person under UCC Article 9, the repossessor might face liability under FDCPA as well,[40] in the case

---

[36] Hudson (2009), p. 57.

[37] A list of states that have implemented their own FDCPAs can be found here: http://www.nolo.com/legal-encyclopedia/state-fair-debt-collection-laws, last visited 3.10.2014. The complete list of mini-FDCPAs, with full text, is available at http://www.fairdebtforconsumers.com/fair-debt-laws.html, last visited 3.10.2014.

[38] FDCPA, 15 USC 1692 (Section 816).

[39] FDCPA, 15 USC 1962 (Section 802)(b), corroborated by 15 USC 1692a (Section 803), (3). The first reference established by declaration of purpose that the idea behind the FDCPA is to redress the injuries of "inadequate" existing laws regarding consumer protection, while the second defines "consumers" as "any natural person obligated or allegedly obligated to pay any debt." In fact, the FDCPA provisions refer only to consumers and not to debtors.

[40] See *infra*, Sect. 6.2.1.1.

his actions amount to any of the abusive practices banned by the act. With respect to the origin of the debt, solely those arising from tax obligations seem to fall outside the coverage of the FDCPA.[41]

The federal FDCPA did not establish a requirement for the licensing of debt collectors presumably because that would have been impossible at a federal level. However, most of the mini-FDCPAs in place have established a requirement for debt collectors to obtain a license[42] for engaging in debt recovery activities within the state, and in some cases the licensing requirement was doubled by the one of setting a bond,[43] which is a measure aiming not only to protect consumer-debtors but also to protect creditors, in case the debt collectors do not pass to them the collected amounts. Such additional protection for creditors makes the bond a highly efficient and valuable tool for ensuring compliance and fair treatment from the debt collectors.

The federal FDCPA declared three main purposes: (1) to eliminate abusive debt collection practices, (2) to ensure that those collectors abiding by the law are not going to be disadvantaged by their competition and (3) to promote consistent state action in protecting consumers against abuses.[44] Therefore, the FDCPA covers a series of debt collection practices deemed to be unethical, such as excessive and unreasonable communications,[45] debtor's harassment,[46] false or misleading misrepresentations,[47] other unfair practices[48] with similar results, most of them adopted by the mini-FDCPAs as well. Any of the mentioned practices (or others causing similar effect) would suffice in establishing liability, which is, according to Hudson, one of the specificities of statutory law.

[41] The exclusion arises from the constructive interpretation of 15 USC 1692a (Section 803) (6) (C), which explicitly excludes tax collectors from the definition of debt collectors.

[42] Among the states that request licensing are Arizona (http://www.nolo.com/legal-encyclopedia/arizona-fair-debt-collection-laws.html), Colorado (http://www.nolo.com/legal-encyclopedia/colorado-fair-debt-collection-laws.html), Connecticut (http://www.nolo.com/legal-encyclopedia/connecticut-fair-debt-collection-laws.html), Florida (http://www.nolo.com/legal-encyclopedia/florida-consumer-collection-practices-act.html), Georgia (http://www.nolo.com/legal-encyclopedia/georgia-fair-debt-collection-laws.html), Idaho (http://www.nolo.com/legal-encyclopedia/idaho-fair-debt-collection-laws.html), Louisiana (http://www.nolo.com/legal-encyclopedia/louisiana-consumer-collection-laws.html), Maryland (http://www.nolo.com/legal-encyclopedia/maryland-fair-debt-collection-laws.html), Massachusetts (http://www.nolo.com/legal-encyclopedia/massachusetts-fair-debt-collection-laws.html), and Washington (http://www.nolo.com/legal-encyclopedia/washington-collection-agencies-law.html). All sites last visited on 02.10.2014.

[43] Among the states asking debt collectors to post bonds are Arizona (http://www.nolo.com/legal-encyclopedia/arizona-fair-debt-collection-laws.html), Colorado (http://www.nolo.com/legal-encyclopedia/colorado-fair-debt-collection-laws.html), and Washington (http://www.nolo.com/legal-encyclopedia/washington-collection-agencies-law.html). All sites last visited on 02.10.2014.

[44] FDCPA, 15 USC 1692 (Section 802) (e). Also: Hector (2011), p. 1606.

[45] FDCPA, 15 USC 1692 (Section 805).

[46] FDCPA, 15 USC 1692 (Section 806).

[47] FDCPA, 15 USC 1692 (Section 807).

[48] FDCPA, 15 USC 1692 (Section 808).

However, what really distinguishes the FDCPA from any other laws or regulations with respect to abusive debt collection is the other characteristic, the award of remedies. The FDCPA provided aggrieved consumer-debtors with a very wide range of remedies from civil damages, civil penalties (for each violation of the act), forming a class action up to the possibility to be awarded punitive damages[49] and even piercing the corporate veil for the sake of enforcing FDCPA damages.[50] Additionally, consumer-debtors are provided with financial and procedural incentives[51] to take action against abusive debt collectors. No other existing law or regulation can match at this point the powerful and numerous remedies and incentives offered by the FDCPA. In fact, the remedies offered in the UK—the European jurisdiction with the most advanced abusive debt collection practices regime—could not be more different.

6.1.4 The Legal Framework Concerning Abusive Debt Collection in the UK

In the UK, the activity of debt collectors is covered mainly by agency regulations (such as the former OFT and the current FCA), the most recent being Chapter 7 of the Consumer Credit Sourcebook (CONC).[52] Hence, the "soft touch approach" taken by the UK is in many important regards different from that adopted by the US, forged on different policies and obviously generating different results.

First of all, it should be mentioned that debt collection was regulated by the Consumer Credit Act 1974 (CCA 1974),[53] with the ensuing amendments,[54] as a type of ancillary credit business[55] that required licensing as a precondition for legal

[49] FDCPA, 15 USC 1962, (Section 813).

[50] The leading case concerning the enforcement of the FDCPA as far as piercing the corporate veil is *West v. Costen*, 558 F. Supp. 564 (W.D. Va. 1983). There the court held that "the FDCPA's purpose "to eliminate abusive debt collection practices by debt collectors," 15 USC 1692a, would be frustrated if MSF's corporate façade was an effective shield against persons seeking their private remedies under the Act to uphold the corporate façade here would illustrate that a corporate collection agency, by operating with a minimum of assets and a fast cash flow, can be effectively judgment proof and yet be a thriving source of income for its owner."

[51] For example, one peculiarity of the abusive debt collection legal framework in the US is the fact that the federal and state laws could be used together by consumers against abusive debt collectors, the sole exception concerning the actual damage incurred by the debtor, which cannot be recovered twice.

[52] Consumer Credit Sourcebook, Chapter 7, Arrears, Default and Recovery (Including Repossessions), http://media.fshandbook.info/content/full/CONC/7.pdf, last visited on 19.12.2014.

[53] http://www.legislation.gov.uk/ukpga/1974/39/contents, last visited on 19.12.2014.

[54] Most important was Consumer Credit Act 2006, http://www.legislation.gov.uk/ukpga/2006/14, last visited on 19.12.2014.

[55] Section 145 (1) (d) of Credit Consumer Act 1974 defined an ancillary credit business as any business so far as it comprises or relates to debt collecting, while subsection (7) defined debt

functioning.[56] Trading in credit activities without a credit license constitutes a criminal offense[57] and is punishable by fine and/or imprisonment.[58] In order to be licensed, applicants are required to pass what is called a "fitness" test.[59] According to UK law, debt collection refers to attempts to procure payments due under consumer credit or consumer hire agreements,[60] whether regulated or exempted, and starting with 2014, it specifically mentions repossession.[61] Hence, it seems that unlike the US, debt collection is more closely tied to enforcement of security interests in personal property and no more distinctions are being made between repossession and other nonjudicial debt collection activities. However, with respect to the passive subject, English law is also concerned solely with consumers, but perceived as individuals (natural persons as well as partnerships of two or three persons not all of whom are bodies corporate or an unincorporated body of persons that does not consist entirely of bodies corporate and is not a partnership).[62] Due to this peculiarity, the protection offered by UK law is obviously wider than that of the US.[63]

---

collection as the taking of steps to procure payment of debts due under consumer agreements or consumer hire agreements, with the exceptions provided by Section 146 (6). http://www.legislation.gov.uk/ukpga/1974/39/section/145, last visited on 19.12.2014.

[56] According to Section 21 (1) of the Credit Consumer Act 1974, a license is required to carry on a consumer credit business or a consumer hire business or an ancillary credit business. http://www.legislation.gov.uk/ukpga/1974/39/section/21, last visited on 19.12.2014. Additionally, Section 24 A (4) (f) specifies that one of the types of business required to apply for a standard license is a business so far as it comprises or relates to debt collecting. Also: Rosenthal (2013), p. 217.

[57] OFT's official website: http://www.oft.gov.uk/OFTwork/credit-licensing/#.UbYnwUAtxp4, last visited on 19.12.2014.

[58] http://www.oft.gov.uk/OFTwork/credit-licensing/penalties-and-requirements/#.UbY2jkAtxp4, last visited on 19.12.2014.

[59] According to Section 25 (1) (a) and (b), an applicant for a standard license must make an application within Section 24 (1) (A) in relation to a type of business and satisfy the OFT that he is a fit person to carry on that type of business with no limitation. Subsection (2) states that in determining whether an applicant for a license is a fit person for the purposes of this section, the OFT shall have regard to any matters appearing to be relevant, including (among other things) c) practices and procedures that the applicant proposes to implement in connection with any such business. http://www.legislation.gov.uk/ukpga/1974/39/section/25, last visited on 19.12.2014.

[60] Rosenthal (2013), p. 218.

[61] CONC, Section 7.13.9.

[62] Rosenthal (2013), p. 17. CCA 1974 did not define the consumer, as the FDCPA did in the US. However, it did define debtor as the individual receiving credit under a consumer credit agreement or the person to whom his rights and duties under the agreement have passed by assignment or operation of law and, in relation to a prospective consumer credit agreement, includes a prospective debtor (p. 19).

[63] Wider coverage may occur in the US as well under state law. However, based on the definition of consumer as provided by the FDCPA, it is clear that the federal statute wanted to exclude any coverage of a legal person, by explicitly referring to natural persons and not to individuals, as the CCA 1974 did in the UK.

In strong connection with the licensing procedure and legal requirements needed to be fulfilled by applicants, in 2003,[64] the OFT issued The Guidance for Businesses Engaged in the Recovery of Consumer Credit Debts (the Guidance).[65] The Guidance established the standards that were expected to be adopted by businesses engaged in debt collection and tried to identify the types of behavior that the OFT considered to be unfair or improper and thus could lead to a withdrawal, suspension or denial of the license.[66] What is interesting is that the Guidance had a much broader application: it caught not only third party "debt collectors" but also original lenders who thus have to follow the same standards contrary to CCA 1974.[67] In this respect, it is also broader than its American counterpart.[68] Most of its provisions were maintained by the 2014 the CONC, issued by the FCA, which replaced the OFT.

Similarly to the US FDCPA, the CONC[69] establishes a series of general *positive* obligations, which it calls *overreaching principles of consumer protection and fair business practice* to be applied to all debt recovery activities. The *first* is the fair treatment of debtors, meaning that debtors should not be subjected to aggressive practices or any kind of deceiving, oppressive, unfair or improper behavior. The *second* is transparency, meaning that the information communicated in relationship with the debt should not be confusing or misleading. The *third* is forbearance and due consideration, meaning that each debtor experiencing financial distress should be treated with understanding and should be helped in his attempt to repay the debt. The *fourth* is proportionality, meaning that measures taken for the recovery should take into account the circumstances and the actions of the debtor. The *fifth* is clarity, effectiveness and appropriateness of policies and procedures when dealing with disputed debts. The *sixth* and last principle is consideration for particularly vulnerable debtors, such as those suffering from mental health issues or with mental capacity limitations.

---

64 Last amendment was in November 2012. http://www.roxburghe.com/OFT664Rev_Debt_collection_g1.pdf, last visited on 19.12.2014.

65 The Guidance, Section 1.4.

66 The Guidance, Purpose, Sections 1.6–1.9. The document mentions that some of the practices that are labled as imporper of unfair may also constitute criminal offenses.

67 The reason is that the Consumer Credit Act 1974 made differences between main and ancillary credit businesses with respect to their types of licenses. As such difference would not be justified in relationship with the debtor, especially as both the creditor and his agents could employ the same tactics in order to recover the debt, the OFT took the right position of imposing same standards for all those dealing with debt collection, personally or via intermediaries. Following the same logic, the guidelines extended the protections offered to debtors to those individuals who are wrongly pursued for a debt, despite the fact that in such case they would not qualify as debtors under the law.

68 By American counterpart here the book refers to the federal FDCPA, for most of the state laws (mini-FDCPAs) include the original creditor in the definition of the debt collector as well.

69 CONC, Sections 7.3–7.4, restating the previous provisions of the Guidance, Overreaching Practices of Fair Business Practice, Sections 2.1 and 2.2.

Other positive obligations are related to the employment of third parties. Collectors (notwithstanding whether they are the original creditors or agents of the original creditors) are advised to make sure that those they employ should act in a way consistent with the fitness to hold a license, under the sanction of risking their own.[70]

The *negative* obligations, on the other hand, are related to several big categories of practices from which collectors should refrain, concerning communication, false representation of authority and/or legal position, physical/psychological harassment, employment of deceptive and/or unfair methods, charging for debt recovery, debt collection visits, statute-barred debt and data accuracy. Similarly to the FDCPA, the list is not exhaustive,[71] allowing for other practices to fall under the coverage of the law as long as their effect is similar to those provided as examples by the statute.

In addition, given the issues encountered in the UK with payday loans, the CONC regulation has maintained the guidance's provisions banning the misuse of a continuous payment authority (CPA)[72] by using the CPA other than setting out in the credit agreement or without the informed consent of the debtor,[73] using the CPA in a manner that is unreasonable or disproportionate or excessive,[74] failing to document or explain the CPA appropriately before entering into the credit agreement[75] or seeking improperly or unfairly to inhibit or discourage the debtor from cancelling the CPA.[76]

---

[70] CONC, Section 7.13.13, restating in more general terms the previous obligation of Section 2.5 of the Guidance. Section 2.5, reads as follows: "Licensed businesses cannot ignore the unfair or improper practices of others instructing them or acting on their behalf. [..] However, we would expect to see that care has been taken in the selection process, complaints about such third parties are properly investigated, and effective action is taken as necessary to ensure that similar problems do not recur."

[71] The Guidance clearly mentioned the nonexhaustive character of its examples in the Forward, while CONC does not make such assertion. However, this cannot be construed in the sense that the examples offered in CONC are exhaustive, the wording of the new regulation suggesting that any practice that causes similar effects would fall under its coverage. In addition, the fact that most of CONC's provisions are restatements of the previous Guidance's provisions is a good indication that the principles behind the Guidance are still valid.

[72] A CPA authorizes the creditor to withdraw sums from the debtor's account, subject to agreed terms, but not through direct debit, standing order or similar payment mechanisms.

[73] CONC, Sections 7.6.1 and 7.6.2, restating and expanding the previous provisions of Section 3.9. m. (i) of the Guidance. Examples of CPA's misuse are debiting higher or lower amounts than agreed, adding default fees or other sums, debiting before or after the due date for payment.

[74] CONC, Sections 7.6.3, 7.6.4., 7.6.5, 7.6.6, 7.6.7, 7.6.8 (1), 7.6.9, 7.6.10 and 7.6.11, restating and expanding the previous provisions of Section 3.9.m. (ii) of the Guidance. Examples of unreasonable use are seeking payment before income or other funds may reasonably be expected to reach the account, seeking payment when there is reason to believe that there are insufficient funds in the account. For details, see the Guidance.

[75] CONC, Section 7.6.1 (1) (a), restating the previous provisions of Section 3.9.m. (iii) of the Guidance. This provision was clearly meant to ensure that consumers entering into payday loan agreements receive sufficient and appropriate *a priori* information in order to be able to give an informed consent. It is doubtful whether such disclosure requirements could really benefit consumers in need for money.

[76] Sections 7.6.16 and 7.6.17 of CONC, restating and expanding the previous provisions of Section 3.9.m. (iv) of the Guidance.

However, since the strategic objective of the FCA—a "conduct regulator"—is to secure an "appropriate degree of protection for consumers," "protect and enhance the integrity" of the UK financial system and promote "effective competition in the interest of consumers,"[77] its regulation in this specific sector has economic, educational and ethical dimensions.[78] The economic perspective is concerned with the health of the UK financial system, specifically with the adverse effects on competition, an aspect similar to the one mentioned by the US Congress at the adoption of the FDCPA, and with creating a suitable environment for financial activity to flourish. The educational perspective is concerned with the education of the population as far as possible with respect to the support available[79] to them, while the ethical perspective tries to ensure that the manner in which the customer is being treated is suitable to each consumer.[80]

The UK debt collection businesses' association itself—the Credit Services Association (CSA)—has also adopted and implemented a code of conduct for the collection practices[81] meant as standards to be followed by its members, under the sanction of disciplinary measures taken within the business association. The document—a self-regulation—is only soft law, "enforced" by the business association[82] and not by a governmental agency; thus, the book will not address it in much detail.[83]

However, interestingly, the same association has produced, together with the OFT, a Guideline for the Usage, Format and Content of Standard Debt Collection Letters (the Standard Letter Guidance)[84] meant to ensure compliance with the standards introduced by the OFT in the area of debt collection. The document was probably meant to be soft law, but it was elaborated together with, and enforced by, the former regulatory body, which means it has to be complied with. It details and develops what might constitute unfair or improper collection practices related to letter communication and can be applied only within the system implemented by

[77] FCA (2014), p. 4.

[78] Hudson (2009), p. 58.

[79] "[M]any people we interviewed had low awareness of the help and support available to them [...] so helping people get the right advice and solution they need [...] is vital." FCA (2014), p. 46.

[80] CONC, Section 7.3.

[81] CSA's Code of Practice, April 2014, http://www.csa-uk.com/assets/documents/compliance-and-guidance/code_of_practice.pdf, last visited 19.12.2014.

[82] The Introduction of the CSA's Code of Practice, April 2014, http://www.csa-uk.com/assets/documents/compliance-and-guidance/code_of_practice.pdf, last visited 19.12.2014, p. 5, states: "Members agree to comply with this Code of Practice by virtue of Membership. We will ensure that Members found to be acting contrary to this Code of Practice will be dealt with in accordance with out disciplinary procedures." However, in the chapter dedicated to "Complaints Procedure" (p. 26), nothing more than "appropriate action" is mentioned in case of breach, without further details concerning what appropriate action would be.

[83] Since no case was reported, one may assume that such document does not play a meaningful role within the general regulatory framework available in the UK.

[84] Use, format and content of standard debt collection communication. Guidance document (December 2013).

the former OFT. However, one must bear in mind that these provisions also help create a clearer image of how debt collectors could mislead consumers during their communication through standard collection letters, which is why some of the forbidden practices will be addressed either in the section referring to communication[85] or in the one dedicated to misleading practices.[86]

Obviously, since the regulation is concerned with objectives other than the substantive law, its remedies will also differ. According to the 2014 Decision Procedure and Penalties Manual (the Procedure), the principal purpose of imposing penalties or issuing a public censure is to "promote high standards of regulatory and/or market conduct by deterring persons who have committed breaches from committing further breaches and demonstrate the benefits of compliant behavior."[87] Hence, the entire procedure is administrative (unless the breach amounts to criminal offense); penalties are imposed with full observance of the principle of proportionality, the highest sanction being the suspension or the restriction of activity. None of these remedies affects the consumer directly, and, for this reason, he is not empowered or encouraged, with any financial or procedural incentives, to take action. This is why, although updated and more detailed than the federal FDCPA, the UK regulation is far less efficient than its American counterpart, as reflected by the small amount of court cases reported.

6.1.5 The Legal Framework Concerning Abusive Debt Collection in France

French legislation[88] with respect to collection agencies refers only to direct communication through mail, strictly bans threats of litigation and, most of the time, requires the hiring of an attorney or process server before any action can be taken by debt collectors.[89] The legal framework is limited in scope and brief, providing for simple, general aspects with respect to who is covered by the applicable provisions, legal requirements for functioning, minimum conditions to be fulfilled in case of amicable recovery attempts, content of recovery standard letters, postpayment obligations of debt collectors and remedies. It does not specify whether it is meant to cover only consumer debt or business debt as well. Due to the silence of

---

[85] *Infra* Sect. 6.2.3.1.

[86] *Infra* Sect. 6.2.3.3.

[87] The Procedure, Section 6.1.2.

[88] Decree No. 96-1112 regulating the activities of persons involved in amicable recovery of debts on behalf of others (in French original: Décret n° 96-1112 du 18 décembre 1996 portant réglementation de l'activité des personnes procédant au recouvrement amiable des créances pour le compte d'autrui.) (1996). It was abrogated in 2012 and inserted without modifications in the Code for Civil Procedure, Chapter 4: Persons responsible for amiable debt collection. See: 783 (2012).

[89] Wise.

the legislator one may be inclined to say that it covers both, for according to general principles of civil law, where the law is expressed in general terms, additional restrictions are forbidden.[90] It also does not contain any provisions with respect to the origin of the debt (the sole notable exception being debts arising from unpaid taxes); hence, a direct connection with secured transactions laws, as in the US or the UK, is hard to establish. Nonetheless, since French law excludes self-help repossessions, any repossession activities fall outside the act's coverage.

Abusive practices are not defined *per se* in French law, but some can be deduced from the positive obligations imposed by the statute. One has to bear in mind though that since the statute does not apply to "those who perform debt collection as part of their professional status or under the regulations of their profession,"[91] such as lawyers or bailiffs or other public officers, the statute is very limited in scope. Leaving attorneys uncovered also constitutes a big gap in the law and a relevant difference from American law.

Abuse may arise from lack of conformity with the functioning requirements such as having a professional liability insurance and an account specially designated for funds collected.[92] Debtors' protection occurs only indirectly, by protecting them from the risk of double payment, in the case the debt collector does not transfer the recovered debt to the creditor: it is deemed abusive to deposit money that resulted from debt recovery in a different account than the one specified above, both to the creditor and to the debtor.

It is also illegal to proceed to debt recovery on behalf of a creditor without having priory concluded with that creditor an agreement to obtain authority thereof and a precise description of the debt's amount and origin,[93] though it is a matter of interpretation whether such a provision could be invoked against the debt collector by the debtor or whether it is only the creditor who would enjoy such right. Given the provisions related to the mandatory content of such an agreement, one may believe that the latter interpretation would be the right one as it tries to protect, on the one side, the interests of the collector (by providing him with rightful and correct information) and, on the other side, the interests of the creditor (who gets insulated from any liability that may arise from the amiable debt collection efforts).

Enforcement is purely administrative and consists in fines imposed in accordance with the classification offered in the Criminal Code. No incentives and no cause for private action are given to the aggrieved debtors, other than the provisions of general tort law, provided by the Civil Code. One may easily conclude that French legal framework on the matter is insufficient for it lacks proper, sector-specific regulation. Judging from the above, a debt collector can take out an insurance, open an escrow account and then proceed to the abuse of debtors, for no adequate remedies are there available to the latter, be it businesses or private parties.

---

[90] According to the Latin maxim used to interpret statutes in France: *Ubi lex non distinguit, nec nos distinguere debemus*. Steiner (2010), p. 80.

[91] 783 (2012), Art. R. 124-1.

[92] 783 (2012), Art. R. 124-2.

[93] 783 (2012), Art. R. 124-3.

6.1.6 *The Legal Framework Concerning Abusive Debt Collection in Germany*

Information in English on German law is scarce. Upon the implementation of the FDCPA in the US, in the late 1970s, a comparison with the judicial system reform adopted by Germany in the matter of debt collection (allowing for default judgments against debtors) led to the conclusion that the latter is so fast and efficient that Germany does not require debt collectors or a legislation to regulate them.[94] The procedure is still in place,[95] but a simple search on the Internet could demonstrate that Germany does have debt collectors,[96] active both on national and international levels. Unfortunately, whether they are regulated and what kind of abuses occur in practice is impossible to determine from the available data, although there are indications[97] that legislative steps are being taken to deal with the new challenges.

The Law on Provision of Non-Judicial Legal Services (RDG)[98] touches upon the issue of nonjudicial debt collection, by qualifying it as a legal service and requiring those involved in providing such services to obtain a license and comply with certain statutory obligations and professional qualifications.[99] According to the doctrine, one of the goals was to protect consumers in the case of collection (*Inkasso*), not only "from incompetent legal advising, but also from untrustworthy debt-collectors."[100] However, despite the statement touching upon the core of the

---

[94] Cohn. Also p. 70: "Thus, in the United States the engagement of collection agencies appears to be an extra-legal step, most commonly used, though fraught with abuse, which is taken before or substituted for, the legal means of a law suit to enforce a duty to pay. The discipline of comparative law often reveals that most diverse methods can be applied for achieving the same goal. In West Germany, for example, the institution of a debt collector is virtually unknown.

The following pages shall describe and evaluate a very simplified procedure, used there, to obtain an enforceable title, the so-called "Reminder Procedure" (Mahnverfahren), which may well be the reason why they have no debt collectors" and pp. 78–79: "Thus, the Mahnverfahren in its new form does appear to be a quick, simple and inexpensive way to obtain an enforceable title. Although venue for it may now lie in a court far away from the adversary's residence, he is still protected by the necessity of being served and by the easy way in which he may force, through contestation, the proceeding to become a full-fledged normal law suit to be dealt with by the court which would have both, jurisdiction and venue if the claim had been pursued, from the start, outside the Mahnverfahren. An American petitioner should keep in mind that though he may have no general venue within the Federal Republic of Germany, he still can avail himself of the Mahnverfahren by petitioning the local court (Amstgericht) Schoneberg in Berlin. The result seems to confirm the assumption made at the end of the Introduction that the Mahnverfahren has eliminated the need for debt collectors in West Germany."

[95] Rainer.

[96] Tajti (2013), pp. 105–106, footnote 308.

[97] Tajti (2013), p. 110.

[98] In German original: Gesetz über außergerichtliche Rechtsdienstleistungen (Rechtsdienstleistungsgesetz—RDG), was adopted on 12th of December 2007 and into force from 1st of July 2008.

[99] http://www.rechtsdienstleistungsregister.de/en/index.php?button=Voraussetzungen&sess_clean=1, last visited 02.10.2014.

[100] Michael Kleine-Cosack, Rechtsdienstleistungsgesetz—RDG—Kommentar (C.F. MüllerVerlag, Heidelberg, 2008) at 143, cited by Tajti (2013), p. 113, footnote 330.

issue of nonjudicial debt collection, the law does not set any banned abusive practices whatsoever.

6.1.7 The Legal Framework Concerning Abusive Debt Collection in Romania

Romania does not have a debt collection law. There is no requirement for the debt collectors to be licensed (as in the case of factoring companies), and the only obligations they have to comply with are those established by the Personal Data Protection Act.[101] A project was adopted in 2010 by the Senate, but the Chamber of Representatives, the deciding forum in this case, rejected it in 2012[102] for legal inconsistencies and also due to the powerful lobby against it of the banking industry. The consumer protection law in force is much too general to provide an appropriate instrument for protecting debtors against the abusive practices employed by debt collectors. Somebody concerned with what defenses might be addressed in battling an abusive collector (misuse of personal data or a blatant invasion in the debtor's privacy area) would have to look for those that might qualify as criminal offenses, similar to the UK or France, but this would hardly be enough.

The only available rules concerning the protection of debtors refer to a legal obligation[103] in cases related to credit agreements for purchase of goods that requires an additional notice of 30 days after failure to pay, before any legal action can be brought. The notice must indicate the reasons for the proposed action and the request for return of the goods. The law also requires the seller to refund to the creditor the equivalent value of the good repossessed. Apart from these provisions—related more to the chapter on repossession—the law is silent on recovery processes and any right consumers would enjoy in this area.[104]

The situation is similar when it comes to credit information sharing. The Romanian Credit Bureau (RCB), a private company owned by the banks, keeps a database of credit information of borrowers of the banking system. The main issue concerning consumers is that information contained cannot be corrected or challenged for inaccuracy directly with the bureau but only with their banks, which can act as debt collectors as well, being in total control over what gets reported. In this

---

[101] Law no. 677/2001 regarding the protection of people with respect to processing personal data and the free circulation of such data (In Romanian original: Legea pentru protectia persoanelor cu privire la prelucrarea datelor cu caracter personal si libera circulatie a acestor date), published in the Official Gazette of Romania, Part I, no. 790/12.12.2001.

[102] Lege privind procedura colectarii debitelor (English translation: "Law Concerning Debt Collection Procedure") (2010).

[103] The World Bank (2009).

[104] The World Bank (2009), p. 7.

regard, the World Bank noticed that it is unclear how many customers actually know that they can dispute the accuracy of the reports in their credit records and how to go about it.[105]

But abuses do exist. Some of them are even denounced by members of the debt-collecting industry;[106] some were experienced by the author of this book during his own practice. In the absence of adequate, sector-specific regulation, Romanian debt collectors resort to phone calls at inappropriate hours (even at midnight), at inappropriate times (Saturdays or Sunday evenings). Calls are being made both on fixed and mobile devices, which exposes the debtor to additional costs when out of the country. Debtors are often threatened that they will not be able to obtain a job, that information about their debt will be made public and they will be subjected to public disgrace. Verbal abuse and threats (with violence) are also common practice, despite the fact that debtors specifically ask not to be contacted again. Threats and personal data of the debtor are also sent via email, to nonsecuritized email accounts and often without reaching the right addressee. Since there is no legal act to enforce, there is no reason for debt collectors to stop. In the US, this would have legal consequences. Not in Romania though.

According to the documents studied, debt collectors also resort to harassing the debtors by dispatching a large number of threatening letters, preprint forms, replicating official bailiff documents and bearing scanned stamps of lawyers or lawyer-like stamps. Debtors are warned that private detectives are now investigating their assets, their personal status and the documents that were used in concluding the credit agreements, where the debt originated from and any other information they could get on them. Audio and video surveillance was mentioned as one of the tools employed thereof, although such surveillance can only be allowed in criminal proceedings, which is not the case. It is sometimes alleged that the results of the investigation would be submitted to the public bailiff and other competent bodies to take measures, despite the fact that the bailiff does not have competences unless a judicial order is presented and there are no other competent bodies to intervene between a debtor and a creditor. Of course, all of the above would cease if debtors would only pay their debt,[107] no matter whether it is time bared or not.

The same letters often bear a red stamp, stating the debt was approved for judicial foreclosure, and a scanned stamp of an attorney, informing debtors that all additional costs related to the recovery will be imposed on them, despite the fact that they represent a fee agreed in a contract for services to which the debtors have not been a part of and cannot be recovered.[108] Other letters ask debtors to pay an amount three times bigger than the alleged debt, without informing them about the nature or the method used to reach such a figure.[109] Obviously, a legally trained

---

[105] The World Bank (2009), p. 8.

[106] Urban.

[107] See the document in Annexes 1.

[108] Annex 2.

[109] Annex 3.

person knows that such documents do not have a real legal value (especially since they do not come with a post receipt, so there is no proof that they have actually reached their addressees), but for those with no legal knowledge, receiving them must have a horrifying effect. Since most business debtors either have or can afford professional legal aid, it is safe to assume that the most affected categories remain consumer-debtors.

The rejected project for a Law Concerning Debt Collection Procedures[110] addressed some of these abusive tactics. Unfortunately, the Code of Conduct adopted by the Association of Commercial Debt Management[111] cannot constitute a valid alternative either, for it simply lacks any complaints or enforcement procedure, even within the Association. Hence, a future legislative proposal concerning banned debt collection practices is needed and, in order for it to be successful, it should consider the proposed building blocks and thoroughly consider the powerful examples provided mainly by the US and the UK.

6.2 The Building Blocks for an Efficient Debt Collection Regime

Proposing a matrix of analysis of statutes regulating debt collection practices is not an easy task to achieve, for several reasons. **First**, and foremost, no such tested formula seems to have been developed yet. **Second**, there are idiosyncratic differences in approach between the chosen jurisdictions that need to be overcome, since the outright adoption of one legal framework or another might be hardly viable in the absence of proper regulatory bodies or governmental institutions. Therefore, the proposed matrix should work beyond systemic differences. **Third**, a mechanical description of the statutes in place (or, in the case of Romania, of statutes proposed) would not be as far-reaching as intended and would not offer as many viable answers and lessons for less-developed systems. **Fourth**, as stated before, a matrix of analysis should help in assessing future statutes or changes in legislation, notwithstanding where, when or how extensive such changes are.

Therefore, the following pages present the **six building blocks** identified by this book for a viable system concerning protection of consumer-debtors against abusive debt collection practices. The identified building blocks, at a minimum, are (1) definition of debt collectors; (2) a licensing system of debt collectors; (3) updated statutory requirements concerning (a) communication with the debtor and third parties; (b) harassment or abuse of the debtor or debtor-related third parties; (c) false, deceptive or misleading forms or representations; (d) validation of

[110] (2010) Chapter IV, Art 9–11.

[111] In Romanian: Asociatia de Management al Creantelor Comerciale. The Code of Conduct is available online, in Romanian on the Association's website: www.amcc.ro/library/files/codul_de_conduita_amcc.pdf, last visited 19.12.2014.

the debt; (e) fees and charges added to the debt; (4) open-end functional definitions, which would allow the statute to be applied by analogy to new abusive practices, by taking into account their effect upon debtors or related third parties; (5) civil liability correlated with incentives for private action; (6) availability of swift and effective state action (administrative enforcement).

It must be emphasized here that the book does not take the position that a regulation of abusive debt collection practices will be automatically successful by simply including the above building blocks. Other circumstances still need to be considered, such as the actual wording of the statutory provisions, correlation with the existent legal framework, the regulatory bodies and consumer protection institutions in place and their powers, the existence of qualified and competent personnel and judges, the level of information to which the debtors have access, regulatory capture and corruption. However, by considering the building blocks proposed and by analyzing current provisions and proposals for reform, one may claim that a system guiding itself by these building blocks has a good chance of becoming efficient.

The following sections address each of the proposed building blocks concerning defining debt collectors, licensing and banned abusive practices, by way of comparative analysis of the five jurisdictions chosen. The building blocks addressing the issue of enforcement—civil liability and available state action, together with the calls for reformation, are analyzed in the following chapter.

6.2.1 Definition of Debt Collectors

In the previous chapter, the book discussed who the *de facto* debt collectors are, starting from the provisions of the FDCPA. Although the topic is similar, this section, however, analyzes only the need for a viable abusive debt collection practices act to clearly define, from its outset, who is covered by its provisions.

6.2.1.1 Identification of Debt Collectors in the US

According to the FDCPA, a debt collector is generally a third party agency that has as a principal and regular scope of business collection of debts,[112] or its agents or employees, as well as attorneys who engage primarily[113] in debt collection. The

[112] *Cirkot v. Diversified Systems Inc.*, 839. Supp. 941 (D.Conn. 1993), where the court held that a third party debt collection agency qualifies as debt collector for the purposes of FDCPA.

[113] *Heintz v. Jenkins*, 514 U.S. 291 (1995) and *Garret v. Derbes*, 1110 F. 3d 317 (5th Cir. 1997). In the latter case, the attorney received 639 debt collection cases, which constituted less than 1 % of the attorney's practice. However, the court held that he qualified as a debt collector for he regularly collected debts due to another. Similarly, in *Scott v. Jones*, 964 F.2d 314, 316 (4th Circ. 1992), where, given that 70–80 % of the attorney's fees were generated from collection cases and the attorney filed around 4000 cases per year, during a 4 year period, the court held the attorney

definition has changed over time, as attorneys were not covered until 1986, and there is potential for affecting a broader range of subjects. For example, the federal FDCPA does not cover original creditors, while the issue of debt buyers remains debatable. But if the original creditor uses a different name,[114] then he will become a debt collector, while courts have held that purchasers of debts after default will qualify as debt collectors as well.[115]

The issue of repossessors is also unclear,[116] for courts have found that neither skip tracers nor repossession agents qualify as debt collectors,[117] unless they also engage in common collection services, such as sending letters, demanding payment, placing telephone calls,[118] although, for example, impersonating police officers for the purposes of repossession constitutes a breach of the peace under UCC Article 9 and would also amount to a violation of the FDCPA. The confusion increases in the case of mini-FDCPAs that consider repossessors as collection agencies.[119]

---

qualified as a debt collector. Since the FDCPA did not define what "regularly" means, the standard applied varies from case to case, based on the analysis of multiple factors (see ruling in *James v. Wadas*, F.3d, 2013 WL 3928631 (10th Cir. 2013). For example, a different outcome was reached in *Mertes v. Devitt*, 734 F. Supp. 872 W.D. Wis., 1990, where the attorney sent a letter to a consumer requesting payment on behalf of his client. The letter did not comply with the requirements of the FDCPA, but since in the past 10 years the attorney was only involved in fifteen collection cases on behalf of the client, out of which only two cases in the past 4 years, the court held he does not qualify as a debt collector. See also the list of cases and discussion in Edelman (2013), pp. 9–15.

[114] *Orenbuch v. North Shore Health Systems, Inc.*, 250 F. Supp. 2d 145 (e.D.N.Y. 2003). In the mentioned case, the collection department of a hospital acted under a different name from that of the hospital, which led the court to consider it a separate entity for the purposes of the FDCPA.

[115] *Munoz v. Pipestone*, 397 F.Supp. 2d 1129, 1133 (D. Minn. 2005). The court held that a debt buyer who never communicated with the consumer qualifies as debt collector, where the debt buyer had an agreement with a collection agency that it would collect the purchased debt and the buyer's principal business was debt collection. For a similar decision: *Olvera v. Blitt & Gaines*, P. C., 431 F.3d 285 (7th Cir. 2005). However, from the reasoning of the courts, it appears that the matter is far from being settled, for example, in case the debt buyer does not have as principal business debt collection but financial investment (like major debt buyers), which might lead to inconsistent or even contradictory outcomes, in the absence of a clear definition. For example: *Scally v. Hilco Receivables, LLC*, 392 F. Supp. 2d 1036, N.D. III. 2005. The case concerned a debt buyer of defaulted credit card debt at high discounts, which hired collection agencies to collect the debt and did not engage in the collection of its debts, although it was accepting direct payments from pursued debtors, if they insisted. The court held Hilco did not qualify as debt collector under FDCPA. On the other hand, assignees (before default), such as car finance companies or mortgage servicing companies, will not qualify as debt collectors. For a detailed list of cases concerning the debt collector status of bad debt buyers, see: Edelman (2013), pp. 7–9.

[116] An exception would be the purposes of 15 USC 1692f(6) (Section 808(6)).

[117] *Goldstein v. Chrysler Financial Co.*, LLC, 276 F. Supp. 2d 687 (E. D. Mich. 2003).

[118] For a list of cases, see: Edelman (2013), pp. 16–17.

[119] The Advisory Opinion "Repossession Companies Acting as Collection Agencies" issued in 2000 by Colorado Attorney General: https://www.coloradoattorneygeneral.gov/sites/default/files/uploads/1-3-00%20Repossession%20Companies%20as%20Collection%20Agencies.pdf, last

State laws, however, adopted a far-reaching approach, by specifically including the original creditors and debt buyers[120] in their definition of debt collectors, to avoid any misunderstandings. Such a decision makes sense, if one considers the purposes of the FDCPA and mini-FDCPAs, which was to prevent and deter abusive collection practices. Basically, there is no justification for which one practice employed by a collection agency is abusive, but the same practice, when employed by an original creditor, is legitimate, when the effect on consumer-debtors is exactly the same.

Hence, when comparing the court's inconsistent outcomes in interpreting the definition adopted by the federal statute and the clear-cut, broader definitions adopted by the mini-FDCPAs, should dedicate more attention to the latter, for they are less known and generally overlooked.

6.2.1.2 Identification of Debt Collectors in the UK

The UK CONC is straightforward when it comes to the identification of those considered debt collectors. The provisions concerning arrears, default and recovery apply to any firm involved in consumer credit lending, consumer hiring, operating an electronic system in relation to lending and debt collecting (unless otherwise provided), including repossessors,[121] as well as to employees, agents or other representatives acting on behalf of the firm.[122] Hence, under the UK regulation, both original creditors and collection agencies are covered. Since the regulation refers to employees, agents and representatives, it might appear that attorneys also

---

visited on 05.10.2014. According to this opinion, "if a repossession company requests the debtor to make payment on the debt, whether to prevent the immediate repossession of the collateral or otherwise, it is collecting or attempting to collect a debt." Hence, "such repossession companies must obtain a Colorado collection agency license." Also: Section 45-1052 of Nebraska FDCPA, which considers self-help repossession to be an abusive collection practice if it happens with breach of peace, as well as Sections 61-18A-3 and 61-18-5 of New Mexico FDCPA, which establish the same licensing and penalties regime and for both collection agencies and repossessors.

[120] For example: Section 1788.2(c) of Rosenthal Fair Debt Collection Practices Act, California Civil Code, Section 1788 et seq.; Sec. 36a-645 (2). (Formerly Sec. 36-243a). Definitions of Connecticut's Creditors' Collection Practices Act (CCPA)—however, this act deals only with creditors, since collection agencies are covered by a separate statute, the Consumer Collection Agencies Act; Section 28-3814(b)(3) of District of Columbia Fair Debt Collection Practices Act; Section 7-101(c) of Maryland Fair Debt Collection Statute, MD Code, Business Regulation; Original creditors collecting their own debts in Colorado, are not included in the Colorado FDCPA but in the Colorado's Uniform Consumer Credit Code (Section 5-5-202.(4)).

[121] CONC, Section 7.1.1.

[122] CONC, Section 7.1.3 (1), requires that firms ensure that their employees and agents comply with CONC and must take reasonable steps to ensure that other persons acting on the firm's behalf act in accordance with the firm. However, the liability for their actions will be primarily with the firm benefitting from their services.

fall under CONC's coverage; however, whether debt buyers do qualify remains unclear, the wording suggesting that they do not.

6.2.1.3 Identification of Debt Collectors in France

Under French law, only third party debt collectors[123] fall under the provisions regarding nonjudicial debt collection from the Code of Civil Enforcement Procedure. Those collecting on their own behalf—original creditors, attorneys or other debt collectors who act under the regulation of their professional status (here the Code refers to both banks and financial institutions (such as factoring companies) or to tax collectors and other state agents such as the huissiers)—are excluded. French law does not distinguish between those collecting debts amicably on a habitual or occasional basis, but since attorneys are not covered, this lack of differentiation is of little importance. It is unclear whether debt buyers would qualify, though the wording of the Code seems to imply that they would not: on the one hand, once the debt is purchased, they no longer collect for another but for themselves, while on the other hand, French law does not distinguish between debts before or after default as the FDCPA does.

6.2.1.4 Identification of Debt Collectors in Germany

As was mentioned already, in Germany the RDG regulates solely the activity of those providing nonjudicial legal services, in which category it also includes debt collection,[124] as long as debt collection is operated as a separate business and on behalf of third parties' assigned claims. It is also specifically stated that assigned claims are not considered foreign to the assignor, meaning that original creditors are not covered, which brings the RDG close to the FDCPA (though only in this narrow aspect). Under German law, only attorneys or firms permanently retaining an attorney for this purpose can operate as nonjudicial debt collectors, a conclusion that derives from the mandatory requirements of the law[125] concerning the licensing of the nonjudicial debt collection business. With respect to debt buyers, a 2014 decision of the Court of Appeals in Munich[126] states that a factoring company that has purchased a debt and is trying to collect it will not qualify as a debt collector for the purposes of RDG (which requires a special license and a mandatory professional insurance for debt collectors) if it is trying to collect the debt on its own.

[123] Art. R. 124-1 of 783 (2012).

[124] RDG, Section 2 (2).

[125] RDG, Sections 11 and 12 concerning the special expertise required and the registration requirements.

[126] Decision 6 U 695/14 of Oberlandesgericht München.

6.2.1.5 Identification of Debt Collectors in Romania

The Romanian project covered both original creditors—through the activity[127] of their own nonjudicial debt collection departments[128] and their personnel[129]—as well as the activity of third party debt collectors, such as collection agencies.[130] Since the law did not distinguish between persons involved in debt collection, attorneys would have been covered, provided they were working for a collection agency or in the internal debt collection department of a banking institution or a commercial enterprise. *Per a contrario*, an attorney would not have been covered if he had engaged in collection activities outside the framework provided by the law—for example, as part of his profession—although there was no logic why an attorney would have been precluded from engaging in abusive practices when working in a collection agency or commercial enterprise but not when acting as an independent provider of legal services.

Another problem was the wrongful qualification made in the definition of debt collector personnel, by inserting the requirement of "habitual" collection, when it came to commercial enterprises or collection agencies. In the absence of any legal standards, the task was left to the courts to define it on a case-by-case basis, which, given the peculiarities of the civilian judicial system (which does not give importance to precedents), would have created inconsistent results and uncertainty.

The issue of debt buyers was left somehow uncovered, for they would not have been caught by the provisions of the law unless they had a collection department of their own and had tried to collect on their own. However, factoring companies would have been considered debt collectors according to the Romanian act, which would have been a peculiar aspect of Romanian law, distinguishing it from its European counterparts, such as in the UK, France or Germany.

6.2.2 *Licensing and Registration of Debt Collectors*

Out of five chosen jurisdictions that have debt collection legislation in place, three agree on one aspect: that debt collectors must be licensed in order to provide their services. In the US, although the FDCPA did not impose such a requirement, most

---

[127] Art 4 of Project Law.

[128] Defined in Art 3 d) of Project Law as a division of a banking institution or commercial enterprise, which acts in the area of debt collection and police the payments to the entities they represent.

[129] Defined in Art 3 e) of Project Law as any person employed by a collection agency, including members of internal debt collection departments, habitually collecting or trying to collect, directly or indirectly, due or allegedly due debts.

[130] Defined in Art 3 c) of Project Law as a specialized enterprise in amicable collection of debts, from both legal and natural person debtors.

of the states[131] have chosen to require debt collectors to obtain a license. In the UK, the requirement is based on CCA 1974,[132] which is basically the only aspect concerning debt collectors that is not dealt with by agency regulation. Registration is required in Germany[133] under the RDG and in France (although there is no provision regarding actual licensing), where they need to file a declaration of interest with the prosecutor or the Tribunal of High Instance in whose jurisdiction they perform their activities.[134] No license or registration is required in Romania, where they only need to abide with the legislation concerning the protection of personal data.

Normally, licenses are granted upon request, provided the applicants satisfy[135] the legal requirements thereof. Compliance with licensing obligations must continue for the duration of the license, together with others that derive from the status of licensee, the power to control belonging to state agencies in the US, FCA in the UK, the competent registry agency in Germany or the prosecutor at the Tribunal of High Instance in whose jurisdiction they registered their activities in France. Nonobservance of these obligations amounts to an offense, which, if it does not qualify for criminal liability,[136] may attract cease and desist

[131] Section 40-12-80 of Alabama Fair Debt Collection Practices Act; Section 32-1021 (A) of Arizona Fair Debt Collection Practices Act; Section 17-240-301 of Arkansas Fair Debt Collection Practices Act; Section 5-2-301 of Colorado Fair Debt Collection Practices Act; Section 36a-801 of Connecticut Fair Debt Collection Practices Act; Section 2301 (11) of Delaware Fair Debt Collection Practices Act; Section 559.553(1) and (2) of Florida Fair Debt Collection Practices Act; Section 7-3-8 of Georgia Fair Debt Collection Practices Act; Section 443B-3.5 of Hawaii Fair Debt Collection Practices Act; Section 26-2223 of Idaho Fair Debt Collection Practices Act; IC 25-11-1-3—Section 3. (a) of Indiana Fair Debt Collection Practices Act; Section 11031 of Maine Fair Debt Collection Practices Act; Section 7-301 of Maryland Fair Debt Collection Practices Act; Chapter 93, Section 24A of Massachusetts Fair Debt Collection Practices Act; Section 904 (1) of Michigan Fair Debt Collection Practices Act; Section 332.33 of Minnesota Fair Debt Collection Practices Act; Section 45-601 of Nebraska Fair Debt Collection Practices Act; NRS 649.075 (1) of Nevada Fair Debt Collection Practices Act; Section 61-18A-5 (A) of New Mexico Fair Debt Collection Practices Act; Section 62-20-15 (a) of Tennessee Fair Debt Collection Practices Act; Section 396.101 of Texas Fair Debt Collection Practices Act; RCW 19.16.110 of Washington Fair Debt Collection Practices Act; Section 47-16-4 (a) of West Virginia Fair Debt Collection Practices Act; Section 33-11-102 of Wyoming Fair Debt Collection Practices Act.

[132] Rosenthal (2013), pp. 319 and 321.

[133] RDG, Section 11 (4).

[134] Section R124-2 (3) of 783 (2012).

[135] In the UK, the obligations to be complied with for obtaining a license is referred to as "fitness test." Rosenthal (2013), p. 326.

[136] Criminal liability may arise under some US state laws such as Section 26-2238 of Idaho FDCPA, for failure to maintain a trust account for depositing the collected amounts; Section 11040 of Maine FDCPA considers a class E crime any debt collection operations without appropriate license; Sec. 28 of Massachusetts FDCPA punishes with imprisonment for up to 3 months any debt collection operations in the absence of license, posted bond; Section 6 of Michigan FDCPA states that any willful violation of the Act may attract imprisonment for not more than a year; Section 61-18A-6 of New Mexico FDCPA considers forth degree felony or misdemeanor any debt collection operations performed without appropriate license. Operating without a license is also a criminal offense in the UK. Finlay (2009), p. 79.

orders,[137] temporary or permanent bar orders,[138] financial penalties,[139] suspension or even revocation[140] of the license.

However, despite its usefulness, the efficiency[141] of the licensing system varies from jurisdiction to jurisdiction, due to issues such as the fact that unfair practices that do not breach specific provisions or are not covered by law escape from the agencies' control or the possibility to implement intermediate and immediate measures to ensure that breaching firms do not continue their unlawful activity during administrative (and court) proceedings.[142] Complementary obligations were also imposed on top of the licensing requirement, in order to increase the protection of the parties involved in debt collection. Several US states require debt collectors to post a bond[143] in order to obtain a license, a measure meant to ensure, among others, that the debt collector will pass the money obtained from the debtor to the

---

[137] For example: Section 36a-807 of Connecticut FDCPA, Section 7-3-23 of Georgia FDCPA, Section 26-2244 of Idaho FDCPA, 445.253, Sec 3 of Michigan FDCPA, Section 649.390 of Nevada FDCPA, or Section 13 (3) of RDG.

[138] For example, the Settlement Agreement between Colorado Attorney General and Out-of-State Attorneys and Debt Collection Law Firms, by which the latter were either permanently banned or temporarily banned from collecting debts in Colorado, together with 200,000 dollars of costs and fees to Colorado, available online at: https://www.coloradoattorneygeneral.gov/sites/default/files/press_releases/2010/03/09/jbc_consent_decree.pdf, last visited 05.10.2014.

[139] Section 39 A of CCA 1974; Section 20 of RDG; Section R124-7 of 783 (2012).

[140] Section 32-1053 of Arizona FDCPA; Sections 17-24-104 (b) and 17-24-307 of Arkansas FDCPA; Section 36a-804 of Connecticut FDCPA; Section 559.730 (1) of Florida FDCPA; Sections 7-3-24 and 7-3-25 of Georgia FDCPA; Section 26-2227 of Idaho FDCPA; Section 11051 of Maine FDCPA; Section 7-308 of Maryland FDCPA; Section 332.40 of Minnesota FDCPA; Section 45-6512 of Nebraska FDCPA; Section 649.395 of Nevada FDCPA; Section 62-20-115 of Tennessee FDCPA; Sections 396.301 and 396.302 of Texas FDCPA; Section 33-11-106 of Wyoming FDCPA; Sections 32 and 33 of CCA 1974 or Section 14 of RDG.

[141] In the US, states fines imposed by the state vary between 500 dollars (93-section 28 of Massachusetts FDCPA and 445.256 Sec. 6 of Michigan FDCPA), 1000 dollars (Section 559.730 (5) of Florida FDCPA; Section 33-11-106 of Wyoming FDCPA), 5000 dollars (Section 7-3-26 of Georgia FDCPA; Sections 26-2227 and 26-2233 of Idaho FDCPA; section 11053 of Maine FDCPA) and 10,000 dollars (445.256 Sec. 6 of Michigan FDCPA) for each violation. However, these administrative fines and penalties do not affect the right of aggrieved consumers to seek compensation through private action as provided by both federal and state FDCPAs. Maximum administrative fines allowed for in the UK (Section 39 A of CCA 1974) and Germany (Section 20 (3) of RDG) are 50,000 pounds, respectively euros, while in France, the maximum will only reach 3000 euros (Section R124-7 of 783 (2012), corroborated by Section 131-13 (5) of the Criminal Code). However, in the UK, financial penalties are imposed in rare cases. See: Rosenthal (2013), p. 336.

[142] This particular legal gap was of concern for the UK where former OFT's powers were increased to allow the suspension of the license with immediate effect in cases where there was an urgent need to protect the interests of consumers. Rosenthal (2013), p. 332.

[143] For example, the wording of the Surety Bond form required by the Consumer Protection Section—Collection Agency Regulation of Colorado Department of Law, stating that "the purposes of this bond are to insure [. . .]that licensee will [. . .]make payment of the proceeds of all collections less charges for collection in accordance with the terms of the agreements made between said licensee and all of its clients [. . .]." http://www.coloradoattorneygeneral.gov/

original creditor, while others, for similar purposes, require debt collectors to open a trust account,[144] a solution adopted also in France. In Germany and France, debt collectors must hold a valid professional insurance.[145]

Notwithstanding any shortcomings, implementation of a licensing system of debt collectors is obviously a useful first step in controlling the activity of debt collectors and an efficient device for administrative enforcement, which is why the book deems it one of the building blocks of an efficient abusive debt collection practices regime. It is surprising that neither France nor Romania considered making nonjudicial debt collection a licensed activity. Both jurisdictions should reconsider their approach and learn from the experiences of the other mentioned jurisdictions, for a licensing system with the appropriate administrative enforcement regime would provide at least the possibility to immediately preclude abusive debt collectors from engaging in unlawful activities.

6.2.3 Abusive Debt Collection Practices

There are many ways in which consumer-debtors may be abused by debt collectors during the collection attempts. Obviously addressing them all, one by one, would go beyond the purposes of this work. Both the FDCPA and the UK regulation have tried to categorize abusive practices on the basis of their effects or purpose: practices that affect *communication* with the debtor and third parties, practices that cause *harassment* and practices that *mislead or deceive* the consumer. However, the length and way in which these abusive practices are addressed differ from jurisdiction to jurisdiction, which is why it is worth having a more detailed look into each of them.

6.2.3.1 Communications with the Debtor and Third Parties

In the light of the FDCPA, communications may occur with the purpose of acquiring information about either the debtor's whereabouts or of his goods, as well as in connection to the actual collection of the debt (debtor's wages or his

departments/consumer_protection/uccc_car/car/licensing_requirements_and_application/surety_bond_form, last visited 05.10.2014.

[144] Section 26-2233 of Idaho FDCPA; Section 909 of Michigan FDCPA; Section 649.355 of Nevada FDCPA; Section 19.16.240 of Washington FDCPA. Without requiring debt collectors to hold a separate account, Section 17-24-104 (b) of Arkansas FDCPA will suspend or revoke their license for not returning the collected amounts to the original creditors, while according to Section 26-2238 of Idaho FDCPA, a person may face 5-year imprisonment for not returning the collected amounts.

[145] For Germany, see: Section 12, Third Paragraph of RDG, requiring a 250,000 euro insurance for each ensured event, and for France see Art R124-2 of 783 (2012).

payment capabilities). Therefore, the restrictions upon communication are twofold: *first*, with respect to direct or indirect communication with the debtor and, *second*, with respect to contacting third parties. The main purpose of regulating communication with either the debtor or related third parties is protection of privacy by limiting the possibilities of its invasion[146] and also protection of the debtor's dignity, by insulating him from public shame. Similar concerns were addressed by the UK legislation, although the abusive practices nominated are much more detailed and cover, unlike the FDCPA, the modern means of communication, such as mobile phones and emails. The potential of abuse connected to communication is emphasized by the fact that French law also felt that it needs to be dealt with, while the failed Romanian project covered it as well.

6.2.3.1.1 Restrictions upon Communication Under FDCPA

The FDCPA established that in order to either enquire for information about the location of the debtor from third parties, or in communicating with the consumer in connection to the debt, the debt collector has to abide by a series of positive[147] and negative[148] obligations. With these positive and negative obligations, the US legislator tried to find a balance between the legitimate right of the debtor not to have his privacy invaded[149] and the legitimate right of the creditor, through the debt

[146] Potach (1978), p. 899.

[147] As positive obligations, the FDCPA states that the debt collector must identify himself, stating his purpose, (confirming or correcting location information concerning the consumer) and, if expressly requested, identify his employer. In addition, the debt collector must contact only the consumer's attorney as soon as he is aware that the consumer is represented by one. This obligation is mitigated though by debt collector's possibility of contacting the consumer when the attorney fails to respond within a reasonable period of time or if the attorney has consented to debt collector's direct communication with the consumer. See Lucas and Harrell (2000), 15 USC 1692 (Section 804) (1) and (6) and (Section 805) (a) (2).

[148] Lucas and Harrell (2000), 15 USC 1692 (Section 804) (2) (3) (4) and (5). Among the negative obligations, the FDCPA mentions the obligation of the debt collector: not to disclose to any third parties that the consumer owes any debt; to refrain from communicating with any person other than the consumer more than once, unless so requested by such person; not to communicate by postcard or resort to any kind of mailing that would suggest that the communication relates to the collection of a debt. The legal provision provides the debt collector with some space by adding a qualification to the negative obligation mentioned. Thus, the debt collector will be entitled to contact the third party more than once if it "reasonably believes" that the response of such person was erroneous or incomplete and that such person now has correct or complete location information. Even so, from the wording of the legal provision it results that such possibility comes with a burden of proof, as in case of a complaint, it is the obligation of the debt consumer to prove the reasonability of his believes. Last but not least, one must mention that the positive obligation of communicating solely to the consumer's attorney is doubled by the negative obligation of not communicating with other persons than the attorney.

[149] Lucas and Harrell (2000), 15 USC 1692 (Section 802) (a). Congressional findings mentioned, among others, "abusive debt collection practices contribute to [...] invasions of individual privacy."

collector, to try to collect the debt and gain information in that respect, as long as the methods used are not unlawful or abusive.[150] The restrictions on communication can be systematized based on a) limitations related to persons, b) limitations related to the time and place and c) limitations related to the method of contacting.

Concerning the **first** category, the statute also imposes restrictions upon the debt collector's contact with the debtor, his spouse, parent (when the consumer is a minor), guardian, executor or administrator.[151] In addition to the negative obligations mentioned, the FDCPA imposed another, by which a debt collector is precluded from communicating with a person other than the consumer, his attorney, the consumer's reporting agency, the creditor, the creditor's attorney and the debt collector's attorney.[152]

To find the logic behind this restriction, one must again refer to the congressional findings,[153] according to which abusive debt collection contributed to marital instability, loss of jobs or invasion of privacy. Obviously, being in debt is a sensitive topic, which can cause distress not only to the debtor but also to those close to him and might also affect his relationship with third parties, which is what the US legislator is trying to prevent. However, similar to the case of gathering information about the debtor's whereabouts, the FDCPA provides the debt collector with some leverage. Thus, the debt collector is entitled to contact third parties in connection with the collection of the debt if he obtained either the prior consent of the consumer, directly from the latter,[154] or the expressed permission of a competent court, or as reasonably necessary to effectuate postjudgment judicial remedy.[155]

Last but not least, the positive obligation of contacting solely the consumer, his attorney or legally allowed third parties, in connection with the collection of the debt, has as corollary a negative obligation of not contacting any other person, with the exceptions already mentioned above.[156] Although this provision has a wide coverage, the logic behind it is simple, for if the debt collector would be permitted

---

[150] Lucas and Harrell (2000), 15 USC 1692 (Section 802) (c). Among the congressional declarations of purpose regarding the implementation of the FDCPA, the US lawmakers stated that "means other than misrepresentation or other abusive debt collection practices are available." Therefore, the FDCPA did not set out to ban debt collection and is not meant to affect the right of debt collectors to collect the debt on behalf of the creditor, but merely to prevent, deter or stop abusive practices.

[151] For the purposes of the section referring to communications, the FDCPA has adopted a broader definition of "consumer," which includes all the enumerated categories. See Lucas and Harrell (2000), 15 USC 1692 (Section 805) (d).

[152] FDCPA, 15 USC 1692 (Section 805) (b).

[153] FDCPA, 15 USC 1692 (Section 802) (a).

[154] The general acceptance is that "prior consent" of the consumer must be expressed voluntarily and directly to the collector. Thus, any contract term that establishes an *a priori* agreement of the consumer to communications concerning debt collection does not qualify as "prior consent" under the FDCPA. In this regard, see H.R. Rep. No. 95-131, 95th Cong., 1st Sess. 5 (1977) quoted by Potach (1978), p. 901, footnote 46.

[155] FDCPA, 15 USC 1692 (Section 805) (b).

[156] FDCPA, 15 USC 1692 (Section 805) (b).

to contact any other person than those specifically mentioned, the entire purpose of the provisions concerning communications would be frustrated.

The **second** category refers to restrictions that concern other aspects, such as the time or place of communication.[157] One positive obligation is the debt collector's obligation to cease all further communications with the consumer upon the consumer's written notification that he either refuses to pay or wishes all communications to stop.[158] However, the FDCPA contains exceptions from this obligation as well. Thus, after receiving such written notification from the consumer, the debt collector is entitled either to advise the consumer that the debt collector's further efforts are being terminated[159] or to notify the consumer that the debt collector or creditor may invoke or intend to invoke specified remedies.[160]

As negative obligations related to communications in connection with the collection of the debt, the FDCPA has precluded the debt collector from contacting the consumer at any unusual time or place known or that should be known to be inconvenient to the consumer.[161] The law deems as inconvenient the period before 8 a.m. and after 9 p.m., local time at the consumer's location, but even this timeframe can suffer changes provided the debt collector has knowledge of circumstances that might make communication problematic within the abovementioned hours.[162] Moreover, this provision becomes problematic nowadays when one can be contacted by mobile phone when not present in his usual location as will be shown in the section related to the increasing need for reform of the FDCPA.

Among inconvenient places for contact, the law has specified expressly the debtor's place of employment, but only if the debt collector has knowledge that the consumer's employer prohibits the consumer from receiving such communication.[163] As the communication concerning debt collection is deemed to be nonpublic by the law, it should not be disclosed to third parties that the communication is in fact an attempt to collect a debt. This provision means that the Congress did not want the debt collector to affect, on the one hand, the activity of the employer who is paying the debtor to perform his work and not waste time (or have its time wasted) with private matters and, on the other hand, to affect the working activity of the employee. The rule is also trying to protect the debtor from becoming liable to his employer for not doing his job during working hours or be subjected to public shame in front of his coworkers.

The **third** category, addressing the method of communication, considers the similar effects that could be achieved by communicating with the debtor through

---

[157] FDCPA, 15 USC 1692 (Section 805) (a) (2).

[158] FDCPA, 15 USC 1692 (Section 805) (c).

[159] FDCPA, 15 USC 1692 (Section 805) (c) (1).

[160] FDCPA, 15 USC 1692 (Section 805) (c) (2) and (3).

[161] FDCPA, 15 USC 1692 (Section 805) (a) (1).

[162] FDCPA, 15 USC 1692 (Section 805) (a) (1) 2nd thesis.

[163] FDCPA, 15 USC 1692 (Section 805) (a) (3).

postcards[164] or by other mailing that would suggest that the enclosed message refers to the collection of a debt.[165] Surprisingly, the US legislator decided to address these practices in the section dedicated to acquisition of location information[166] and also in a separate category of unfair or unconscionable means of collecting debts, although due to their close connection with issues related to communication, it made much more sense to mention them here.

6.2.3.1.2 Restrictions upon Communication in the UK

According to the pre-2014 UK regulation, communication had to be clear, be precise and avoid being misleading,[167] since many of the abuses concerning communication and misleading information were in fact overlapping. The current CONC, however, dropped the aforementioned wording of the provision regarding communications, although in substance the requirements remained the same. The provisions of CONC concerning communication can also be systematized based on (1) whom the communication is addressed to, (2) when and where the communication can take place and (3) how the communication can take place.

First, according to CONC and the Standard Letter Guidance, a firm must not pursue an individual whom the firm knows or believes not to be the debtor,[168] which, by means of interpretation, bans communication with parties who either are not or are believed not to be the actual debtor or his legal or chosen representative. A general ban on contacting third parties with respect to the collection of the debt is stated, but only if disclosure of information concerning the debtor would be "unfair"[169] to him. The regulation does not define what would qualify as unfair, but one may reasonably assume that, as is the case in the US, contacting third parties to inquire about debtor's whereabouts or obtaining information about his capabilities to pay is not prohibited *per se*.

Additionally, the provision refers strictly to the disclosure of information about the debtor to third parties and not to disclosures about the debtor made by third parties. Basically, the regulation tries to achieve a similar purpose to that of FDCPA: to protect the privacy zone of the debtor, by preventing him from public

[164] FDCPA, 15 USC 1692 (Section 808) (7).

[165] FDCPA, 15 USC 1692 (Section 808) (8).

[166] FDCPA, 15 USC 1692 (Section 804) (4) and (5).

[167] Communication through standard debt collection letters was subjected to additional guidance by the CSA and DBSG in association with the OFT, and it is addressed further in this section.

[168] See the general principle provided for in CONC, Section 7.5.2, restated in Section 7.13.4 referring to proceedings meant to validate the debt. A similar ban is specifically mentioned in Section 7.9.11, referring to the case of a firm that would either make contact with the occupier of particular premises (assuming, without further investigation that the occupier is the actual person sought) or send a letter to all persons sharing the same name and date of birth. Also, Chapter B, Section 1.2, 2.3-2.7 and Chapter C, Section 4.1-4.4 of the Standard Letter Guidance.

[169] CONC, Section 7.9.6.

embarrassment and from letting third parties know he is being pursued for a debt.[170] Moreover, unlike the US, which made no such distinction, CONC and Standard Letter Guidance contain rules addressing the issue of vulnerable debtors, such as those with limited mental capacity,[171] who obviously require clear communication and the involvement of a responsible third party acting on their behalf.

While reading the FDCPA, the general view is that communication mainly comes from the debt collector towards the debtor. CONC's perception is that communication should be regarded as a two-way street, with equal rights and obligations. Hence, special provisions are dedicated to the debt collector's obligation to deal with the debtor or his representative (an NGO, attorney, debt counselor or debt adjuster),[172] notwithstanding whether the communication concerns payment, a settlement or a repayment plan. However, the obligation is not absolute, and debt collectors can for objectively justified reasons decline to engage in contact with either the debtor or his representative.[173]

Second, with respect to when and where contact with the debtor can be made, the CONC specifically bans contact at unreasonable times[174] or visits at times when the debtor is vulnerable[175] or in inappropriate locations.[176] As examples of inappropriate locations, CONC mentions the place of work or the hospital where the debtor is a patient, a much more restrictive regime than the one in the US, where visits or contact with the debtor at his work place is not automatically excluded.

Unlike the FDCPA, CONC does not provide for a reasonable period in which communication may be attempted but focuses more on the borderline cases (such as those of debtors working in shifts) and requires debt collectors to pay due regard to the debtor's wishes[177] in respect of when, where and how they can be contacted. Although in appearance the provision is more restrictive than its American counterpart, in reality it provides more flexibility to both the debtor and the debt collector, by eliminating artificial limitations such as fixed working schedule, presence in the same geographical area or in the same time zone.

---

[170] CONC, Section 7.9.7. (1) and (2).

[171] CONC, Section 7.10.3. The Standard Letter Guidance extends the notion of vulnerable debtors to include also debtors who have long-term or terminal illness or other disabilities that impact on their ability to pay. Also, Chapter C, Section 3.1 and 3.2 of the Standard Letter Guidance.

[172] CONC, Section 7.12.2.

[173] Examples of reasons for which the debt collectors are entitled to refuse contact with the debtor or his representative are provided in Section 7.12.3 (2), (3), (4). The list is not exhaustive, and other similar situations could justify the debt collector's refusal, on a case-by-case basis.

[174] CONC, Section 7.9.4.

[175] CONC, Section 7.9.14 (2). The provision was also contained in the previous Guidance, Section 3.13. (b). One situation of particular vulnerability referred to there was when the debtor has proven with a doctor's certificate that he is ill.

[176] CONC, Section 7.9.14 (3). The Section, however, allows such visits in the case the debtor has expressly consented to them.

[177] CONC, Section 7.9.4.

Debt collection visits represent a category of practices that is not specifically mentioned in the FDCPA, but which the UK decided to consider. Examples of improper behavior include but are not limited to not making clear the purpose and intended outcome of any proposed visit,[178] visiting the debtor without providing him with an adequate prior notice of the date and likely time of the visit,[179] not leaving the debtor's property when it becomes apparent that he is unduly distressed or otherwise does not or appears as if he may not have the mental capacity to make an informed repayment,[180] entering the debtor's property without his consent or an appropriate court order,[181] not leaving the debtor's property when reasonably asked to do so[182] or showing up without debtor's prior agreement when the debt is deadlocked or disputed.[183]

The **third** category of prohibited practices related to communication refers to the way in which contact takes place. CONC implements a requirement of immediate disclosure from the debt collector's side, similar to the mini-Miranda developed in the US. Hence, the debt collector must ensure that he first explains who he is working for, his role in or relationship with the firm and the purpose of contact,[184] making sure that there is no misunderstanding with any of the above. Similar to the FDCPA, the CONC prohibits debt collectors from disclosing information related to the debtor that might reveal to third parties that he is pursued for a debt. To make

---

[178] CONC, Section 7.9.12 (1) restating Section 3.13.(a) of the previous Guidance. According to the guidance, it did not suffice to simply inform the debtor about the visit of field agents unless he will also be informed of the intended purpose of the visit.

[179] CONC, Section 7.9.12 (2), restating Section 3.13. (g) of the previous Guidance. The wording of the Guidance, maintained by the CONC, refers to "adequate" notice. OFT's explanation on the meaning of the term "adequate" was that it is going to vary from case to case based on individual circumstances, and there is no reason why such explanation would not be valid under the new regulation. According to CONC, Section 7.9.13, however, the notice requirement may be waived by the debtor provided the debtor is *happy* to speak with the debt collector. Since "happy" is not exactly a legal term, but it implies more than mere agreement—maybe enthusiasm as well—the task of determining the debtor's demeanor is most likely left to the courts.

[180] CONC, Section 7.9.14 (5). This section partially restates the provisions of Section 3.13.(c) of the previous Guidance.

[181] CONC, Section 7.9.14 (4), restating the previous Guidance's Section 3.13(d). This is, evidently, one of the situations that would qualify as a criminal offense as well.

[182] CONC, Section 7.9.14 (6) restating Section 3.13(e) of the previous Guidance. One may find of particular interest the need of "reasonableness" in debtor's request towards the debt collector. Such a standard might implicate not only that the debt collector has a legitimate right to visit the debtor and make himself heard but also that the debtor may not simply cease communication at any point, as it does in its American counterpart. The position adopted by the former OFT and maintained by the current FCA seems to be that as long as it does not impeach the debtor, a debt collector is allowed to do his job and pursue the recovery of the debt. In the search for balance between the creditor's interests and the debtor's interests, it appears that the UK system gives a narrower interpretation to the debtor's right to cease communication.

[183] Office for Fair Trading (2003), Section 3.13. f), p. 44.

[184] CONC, Section 7.9.1. The same requirement is to be found in the Standard Letter Guidance, Chapter A, Section 2.1.

sure there is no indirect risk, deriving, for example, from the debt collector's name, the CONC specifically requires debt collectors to conceal any factor that would lead to the disclosure of debt collection attempts against the debtor and to mark all communication as being private and confidential.[185] For this reason, as in the US, the usage of postcards[186] in contacting the debt collector is forbidden.

However, unlike the FDCPA, and strongly related to the issue of additional charges and fees, the CONC requires debt collectors not to make contact with the debtor on a premium rate or special rate telephone, which would be higher than a standard geographic telephone number.[187] The reference to standard geographic telephone number seems to be referring to fixed telephone charges, although it might include national rates for mobile phones. Whichever interpretation is adopted, it is clear that the usage of mobile phones in contacting debtors should be done cautiously, for the debtor might be abroad and incur roaming charges, which differ from one geographical area to another.

Strongly related to the third category of banned debt collection practices are the provisions contained in the document elaborated together by the CSA and the OFT, concerning the use, format and content of standard debt collection communication. Some of the tactics deemed to be in noncompliance with the guidelines of the OFT, many of them restated in the CONC, are developed in the Standard Letter Guidance, which touches upon modern means of communication such as emails and text messages (SMS), which, as will be shown later, the FDCPA did not address because they simply did not exist at the time when the US act was adopted. Both emails and text messages are deemed unsecure methods of communication,[188] and debt collectors are advised to refrain from using them or to give proper and due consideration to debtor's expressed consent.

Obviously, the core of UK legislation does not differ much from its American counterpart, although in certain details—such as time of contact—it is more flexible and in others—such as place of contact—it is more restrictive. By taking into account modern means of communication, such as emails, text messages or the usage of mobile and smart phones, it is however more modern and more updated than the US FDCPA, which recommends it as a model for any legal reform in the field.

---

[185] CONC, Section 7.9.7, corroborated by Section 7.9.8 (1) and (2). Also: Chapter B, Section 1.3 of the Standard Letter Guidance: "unless the debt collection agency is reasonably certain it is sending letter to the actual customer, it should use correspondence that does not refer to the debt."

[186] Chapter B, Section 1.7 of the Standard Letter Guidance.

[187] CONC, Section 7.9.5.

[188] Chapter G, Sections 1.1 and 2.1 of the Standard Letter Guidance. With respect to text messages, the guidance also takes into account the privacy risk and the possible breach of data protection laws represented by them for users of smart phones, which devices usually display the content of the messages on their screens, even if the phone is locked. However, text messages are deemed proper for encouraging the debtor to make contact, without indicating the nature of the business or demanding payment.

6.2.3.1.3 Restrictions upon Communication in France

Following the systematization used when analyzing the US legislation and the UK regulations, the French law seems to be concerned only with the third category of restrictions, those related to how communication takes place. The only obligation, clearly cut for the protection of the debtor, is the obligation of the debt collector to address to him a letter containing full disclosure about the debt collector's person (including address or registered office) and an indication that he operates as a debt collector, information concerning the initial creditor (including address or registered office), information concerning the debt (the basis and the amount of the principal, interest and other expenses, all distinguished as different elements and excluding expenses that are the responsibility of the creditor), indication of having to pay the amount due and terms for payment and mentioning about the risk of having to pay creditor's costs related to recovery.[189] Additionally the debt collector is obliged to issue a receipt to the debtor for each amount paid[190] but also, in case of partial payment, to inform the creditor thereof and also of any payment proposals coming from the debtor's side, other than immediate and full payment of the debt.[191]

French law does not cover in any way issues such as wrong addressee, time and place of communication or the use modern means of communication, such as emails. These aspects leave the French debtor totally exposed to a wide range of abuses related to communications: the letter can reach related or unrelated third parties, they can be sent both to his home or his place of work, via nonconfidential (such as postcards or envelopes revealing the subject of the content) or unsecure (such as email) mail, which exposes the debtor to the risk of public embarrassment or breach of data protection, most of them hardly quantifiable in civilian systems. In addition to the above, the lack of provisions related to the issue of visits allows basically the debt collector to establish contact anywhere, anyhow, with minor risks of incurring any liability for his actions, other than the general provisions of tort law contained by the Civil Code (grossly unfit for such a task).

6.2.3.1.4 Restrictions upon Communication in Romania

The Romanian project that was not adopted by Parliament also prohibited using any language or symbol, other than the address of the collector, on the communication with the consumer, unless it is the professional name of the collector (but only if it did not indicate the fact that they are involved in debt collection). Despite initial claims that it was inspired by the FDCPA, the legislator's concern only with how contact with the debtor takes place brings the Romanian project closer to the unfit and superficial French law than to the American one.

---

[189] 783 (2012), Art. 124-4.

[190] 783 (2012), Art. 124-6.

[191] 783 (2012), Art 124-5.

Undeniably, since Romanian debt collectors engage in the aforementioned practice, banning such a practice by which personal information is disclosed and the debtor is exposed to public shame would have been a major step forward, even if not sufficient. Issues like those mentioned in the case of France: the time and place of communication, personal visits, employing modern means of communication were left totally unaddressed. Although, generally speaking, having something is better than having nothing, this is not an acceptable principle when it comes to implementing legislation, especially when both the US and the UK could have provided valuable models.

6.2.3.2 Harassment or Abuse of the Debtor or Debtor-Related Third Parties

Debt collectors must refrain from any practices that would harass or oppress the debtor or third parties that are related to him. The logic of extending protection against harassment and abuse to third parties closely connected to the debtor makes sense, given the fact that due to human social relations the debtor might be easily coerced or forced to act in a way contrary to his will, in order to protect others. However, the extent of this protection varies among the chosen jurisdictions.

6.2.3.2.1 Ban of Harassment and Abuse in the US

Closely connected with the prohibitions on communication, the FDCPA also prohibits debt collectors from engaging in any conduct that could cause harassment, oppression or abuse to any person in connection with the collection of the debt.[192] By "any person," the law intended to cover the debtor's family, neighbors, friends and employer.[193] Prohibited practices include threats of violence or injury to the physical person, his property or reputation;[194] use of obscene or profane language;[195] publication of "shame lists" of delinquent debtors;[196] advertising sale of any debt in the attempt of collecting that debt;[197] placing intentional repeated and continuous telephone calls with the intent to harass, abuse or annoy a person;[198] or without meaningful disclosure of the caller's identity as provided by the law.[199]

[192] FDCPA, 15 USC 1692 (Section 806).
[193] Potach (1978), p. 902.
[194] FDCPA, 15 USC 1692 (Section 806) (1).
[195] FDCPA, 15 USC 1692 (Section 806) (2).
[196] FDCPA, 15 USC 1692 (Section 806) (3).
[197] FDCPA, 15 USC 1692 (Section 806) (4).
[198] FDCPA, 15 USC 1692 (Section 806) (5).
[199] FDCPA, 15 USC 1692 (Section 806) (6). The text also established an exception from the abovementioned prohibition consisting in the communications allowed under Section 804.

Although it may be difficult to systematize, the main idea behind these prohibitions is to create a "debtor's zone of privacy"[200] by limiting the scope of communication involved in the collection process.[201] By doing so, the FDCPA has managed to codify various tort theories applicable to debt collection abuses—invasion of privacy, infliction of mental distress, interference with contractual or employment relationships—thus promising to the affected consumer more efficient causes of action, with swifter resolution. Basically, the consumer does not have to go through the lengthy, difficult, expensive and time-costly procedures to prove that the debt collector's act was tortious, for the FDCPA both establishes a legal presumption of wrongful conduct from the debt collector's side and empowers the aggrieved consumer-debtor with incentives to take private action, as it will be detailed later in the next chapter, in the section dedicated to judicial enforcement.[202]

6.2.3.2.2 Ban of Harassment and Abuse in the UK

In the UK, physical as well as psychological harassment[203] was given a substantial coverage in the former Guidance, in a dedicated section, which, surprisingly, was not maintained by the CONC. The current regulation still bans any debt collector behavior that might cause harassment to the debtor, only that now these provisions either are scattered throughout the text or must be deduced from the interpretation of others.[204]

---

[200] For a detailed discussion concerning the "zone of privacy," see footnote 60 in Potach (1978), p. 903.

[201] Potach (1978), p. 903, footnote 59. Potach mentions several constitutional challenges against these restrictions based on the First Amendment during the legislative hearings alleging that the debt collector's communication should be protected as commercial speech. However, the author mentions two court cases contemporary with the enactment of the FDCPA, which seem to reject such objections. On the one hand, in *Millstone v. O'Hanlon Reports*, Inc., 528 F. 2d 829 (8th Circuit, 1976), which concerned similar challenges for restrictions imposed by the Fair Credit Reporting Act, the court rejected them by holding that commercial speech interests must yield to the consumer's right to privacy protected by the statute, while on the other hand, in *Virginia State Bd. Of Pharmacy v. Virginia*, 421 U.S. 809 (1975), the court rejected the debt collector's challenges holding that "the public interest in proscribing harassment of a debtor through contact with his employer about an obligation to a third party simply transcends a finance company's interest in choosing this particular means of collecting a debt." For Potach, the fact that the FDCPA protects the consumer's right to privacy like the Fair Credit Reporting Act, the reasoning of the 8th circuit in Millstone, could only provide additional support for the conclusion that the debt collector's first amendment claims must yield to the debtor's right to privacy.

[202] Chapter 7, Sect. 7.1.1.

[203] A detailed list of what constitutes and does not constitute harassment, explained in a nontechnical language, can be found here: http://www.adviceguide.org.uk/england/debt_e/debt_action_your_creditor_can_take_e/harassment_by_creditors.htm, last visited on 19.12.2014.

[204] To take some examples, according to UK legislation, harassment or abusive behavior consists of putting undue pressure on the debtor or relevant third parties and can occur when contacting

Since harassment is dealt with specifically by CONC, it is hard to assert a downgrading in purpose of the regulation; however, not maintaining a concentrated framework as the previous Guidance did could be construed as a step back, at least in terms of coherence. Interestingly, in a 2009 case,[205] courts have ruled that debt collection can constitute harassment under criminal law as well,[206] which means that under UK law, liability under the Guidance did not replace or substitute but completed general criminal law.

---

debtors at unreasonable times (CONC, Section 7.9.4, restating the previous provision of Section 3.7. a of the Guidance); pressuring the debtor to raise funds by selling his property or by taking on further loans (CONC, Section 7.3.10 (3), restating the previous provision of Section 3.7.b of the Guidance); employing multiple debt collection businesses that are seeking to recover the same debt at the same time (CONC, Section 7.13.10, restating the previous provision of Section 3.7. c of the Guidance); seeking to recover a debt without ensuring that the data is accurate, which results in pursuing the wrong person/an inexistent debt/an incorrect amount (CONC, Section 7.13.4, restating the previous provision of Section 3.7.e of the Guidance); pressuring the debtor to pay more than he can reasonably afford without experiencing undue difficulty or to pay within an unreasonably short period (CONC, Section 7.3.10 (2), restating the previous provision of Section 3.7.i of the Guidance); acting in a threatening manner towards the consumer (CONC, Section 7.9.14 (1); the section partially restates the previous provision of Section 3.7. l of the Guidance); ignoring claims that the debts have been settled or are disputed and continuing to make demands for payment without providing justification and/or evidence as to why the claims are not valid (CONC, Section 7.5.3, restating the previous provision of Section 3.7. o of the Guidance); disclosing or threatening to disclose debt details to third parties (CONC, Section 7.9.6, restating the previous provision of Section 3.7. p of the Guidance); publicly humiliating the debtor (CONC, Section 7.9.7, partially restating the previous provision of Section 3.7. q of the Guidance); either deliberately or negligently (by using postcards or other correspondence, leaving voicemails, asking others to pass messages to debtors, posting messages on social networking sites) (the examples were specifically nominated in the Guidance, and, although not restated in the CONC, there is no reason to consider them invalid, which is why they were mentioned here as well); failing to suspend the pursuit of recovery of a debt under circumstances under which it is clear that the debtor might not have the mental capacity to make relevant decisions regarding the management of the debt and/or engage in the debt recovery process at that time (CONC, Sections 7.2.3 and 7.10.1. (1), restating the previous provision of Section 3.7 r of the Guidance. This particular provision benefited from an extensive comment given by the OFT, in the previous Guidance, pp. 28–30, which comment is still relevant under the CONC as well).

[205] *Ferguson v. British Gas* [2009] EWCA Civ 46 (Court of Appeal).

[206] In the mentioned case, the aggrieved party claimed that British Gas's behavior was unlawful under the Protection from Harassment Act, which created a civil and a criminal offense of harassment. British Gas said that the behavior was not serious enough to amount to harassment and that as a company, rather than an individual, it could not be caught by the legislation. It argued that Ferguson would have to identify an individual directing the activity in order for harassment to be demonstrated. British Gas asked the Court of Appeal to throw the case out before it reached a full hearing because it had no basis. The Court refused and said there was a case to answer. British Gas settled the case. See: OUT-LAW.COM (2009). The case attracted the attention of recent scholarly works as well: Ramsay (2012), pp. 474–476, as an example of "persistent aggressive collection practices," a sign that such practices are finally becoming a concern and a topic for discussion in the European academia.

6.2.3.2.3 Ban of Harassment and Abuse in Romania

In Romania, according to the failed project, a debt collector was precluded from using any techniques that would harass, oppress or abuse the debtors. A nonexhaustive list of behaviors deemed to be a violations of the aforementioned obligation included use of threat of violence or other criminal techniques against a person, its reputation or property; use of obscene or offensive language; advertising the debt's sale in order to force the debtor to pay it; calling the debtor's phone insistently, with the purpose of irritating, constraining or harassing the contacted person; or using telephone calls without a proper or important purpose for the debtor.[207]

The provisions combine certain actions that could also amount to criminal offenses, with several abusive practices Romanian debt collectors resort to, all of them resulting in the harassment of the debtor and subjecting him to fear and mental distress. However, some of the abusive practices mentioned as examples lacked specificity and standards of assessment. The project contained no indication on what either "proper" or "important" purpose of the debtor might be. Since the law would have had a high degree of novelty and Romanian judges are not empowered to create or add to the law, but only to interpret it and apply it, the risk for inconsistent results would have been high. Or having inconsistent results in the application of a law meant to clarify what qualifies as abusive or permissive in debt collection would go against the very purpose of such law and would undermine severely its effect.

6.2.3.3 False, Deceptive or Misleading Forms or Representations

In close relationship with communication is the usage of misleading or false information. A typical example is the one where creditors brand their debt collection departments as different legal entity—with their own letter headings, address and office—giving the impression that the debt has been transmitted to a third party debt collector.[208] In order to systematize the provisions of the FDCPA on this issue, one may categorize them in two groups: usage of false or misleading information with respect to the debt and making false or misleading representations while attempting to collect a debt. Basically, if the restrictions on communications dealt with abusive practices related to the form and means of communication, the practices referred to here deal with the actual content of communication that may be misleading. For the purposes of the book, a twofold systematization was

[207] Art 9, Para. 1 and 2 of Project Law.

[208] By employing this tactic, original creditors try to benefit from two advantages: (1) they send a clear message to the debtor that the collection effort has reached a new phase and will be dealt with in a serious manner by a professional team, and (2) they insulate themselves from the possible negative effects of collection attempts on their image. Finlay (2009), p. 213.

adopted: false or misleading information regarding the debt and false or misleading representations made by the debt collector.

6.2.3.3.1 False, Deceptive or Misleading Debt Collection Methods in the US

The FDCPA extensively prohibits the debt collector from engaging in false, deceptive or misleading methods of collection of any debt.[209] The methods addressed by the statute are only illustrative and do not constitute an exhaustive list,[210] which allows practices having a similar effect to be brought under the coverage of the law.

In the **first** category, usage of false or misleading information with respect to the debt, one may find misrepresenting the amount, character or legal status of a debt;[211] making threats of legal actions that are unlawful or unintended, including the debtor's imprisonment, seizure, garnishment or attachment of property or wages;[212] communicating or threatening to communicate false credit information regarding the debtor;[213] and using forged or misleading documents.[214]

The **second** category covers the usage of false or misleading representations by the debt collector when collecting the debt. The FDCPA mentions, but does not limit to impersonation of a government official, policemen[215] or an attorney;[216] false claims that any individual communication is from an attorney,[217] or misrepresenting a debt collector under a different business name or operation.[218] Under the same category would also fall the use of misleading or deceptive means to collect the debt or data about the consumer;[219] failure to disclose in the initial written or oral communication with the consumer that the debt collector is attempting to collect a debt and that any information will be used for that purpose,

---

[209] FDCPA, 15 USC 1692 (Section 807), pp. 8–9.

[210] Griffith (2012), p. 180. "Because the sixteen examples are not exhaustive, a collector may violate the statute even though its conduct does not fall within any of the specifically enumerated violations."

[211] FDCPA, 15 USC 1692 (Section 807) (2).

[212] FDCPA, 15 USC 1692 (Section 807) (4). Such threats are allowed though, provided that they are lawful and there is the debt collector's actual intent to put them into practice.

[213] FDCPA, 15 USC 1692 (Section 807) (8).

[214] FDCPA, 15 USC 1692 (Section 807) (9).

[215] FDCPA, 15 USC 1692 15 USC 1692 (Section 807) (1).

[216] FDCPA, 15 USC 1692 (Section 807) (3).

[217] FDCPA, 15 USC 1692 (Section 807) (3). This provision has recently attracted more and more attention as consumers complain that they are misled by collection letters printed on law firms' letterheads. These make them believe that an attorney is now involved in the procedure or that litigation is imminent. See Griffith (2012), p. 181.

[218] FDCPA, 15 USC 1692 (Section 807) (14).

[219] FDCPA, 15 USC 1692 (Section 807) (10).

together with failure to disclose in subsequent communications that the communication is from a debt collector;[220] false representation or implication that the accounts have been turned over to innocent purchasers for value[221] or that documents are legal process[222] or, respectively, that they are not legal process and thus do not require action by the consumer[223] or that the debt collector is an employee of a credit recording company.[224]

In strong connection to the practices described above are also those referring to designing, compiling and furnishing the debtor with any kind of form for the purpose of creating a false belief that a person other than the creditor is taking part in the collection or in the attempt to collect the debt, if such a person is not actually participating.[225] The legal provisions of the FDCPA state that any person violating the obligation of refraining from such deceptive means will be assimilated to the debt collector for the purpose of establishing the extent and manner of liability.[226]

To take a recent example, debt collectors have started to include in their collection letter clauses or disclaimer indicating that no attorney has personally reviewed the consumer's case, in order not to be sued for false label representation when using a law firms' letterheads. This raised the additional issue of determining the role of such disclaimers when courts had to say whether the collector is guilty of making false representations or not.[227] In addition, others indulge in usage of ambiguous language, as lack of precision leaves the consumer confused about the collector's future actions or intentions.[228]

Another question that emerged in practice was whether in case the debt collector sends a deceptive of misleading letter to the consumer's attorney, the protections of the FDCPA still apply. And to complicate things even more, courts came up with inconsistent outcomes,[229] though one should agree that a prohibition to refrain from

---

[220] FDCPA, 15 USC 1692 (Section 807) (11). The set of data required to be disclosed by the debt collector is also known as the "Mini Miranda" due to the similarities with the disclosure requirements necessary to be provided by police officers in case of an arrest. Debt collectors are strongly advised to recite it after the initial disclosure. For example, "the 4th Circuit held that the Mini Miranda applies to all communications, including any follow-up correspondence." *Carroll v. Wolpoff & Abramson,* 961 F.2d 459, 461 (4th Cir. 1992) (finding section 1692 e(11) "makes no distinction between initial and subsequent communication. The "Mini-Miranda" Warning, 15 USC Section 1692e(11) (2006), does not apply to a formal pleading made in connection with a legal action and applies solely to communication with consumers, not their attorneys." See Sartip (2012) 5th recommendation, p. 3.

[221] FDCPA, 15 USC 1692 (Section 807) (12).

[222] FDCPA, 15 USC 1692 (Section 807) (13).

[223] FDCPA, 15 USC 1692 (Section 807) (15).

[224] FDCPA, 15 USC 1692 (Section 807) (16).

[225] FDCPA, 15 USC 1692 (Section 812).

[226] FDCPA, 15 USC 1692 (Section 812).

[227] For a detailed discussion and analysis of extensive case law in this regard, see: Griffith (2012), pp. 181–193.

[228] Griffith (2012), pp. 206–211.

[229] "Several circuits agree that the status regulates communications from a collector to a consumer attorney, but the 9th Circuit rejects that approach, ruling instead that the statute does not apply to

false or misleading representations should not stop at the door of a legal office or because the collector now addresses the consumer indirectly, through the services of an intermediary. The reason lies with the fact that, besides being a protection for the debtor, the legal provision is first an obligation of the collector, who must still abide by it.[230] Otherwise, if one accepts the contrary opinion, it would mean that a consumer who is represented by a lawyer is in a worse position than the consumer who is not, as the one being represented would be deprived of the possibility to raise the defense alleging lack of sophistication in order to hold the collector accountable.[231]

Beside the above, the FDCPA also refers to unfair or unconscionable means to collect debts, nominating taking or threatening to take any nonjudicial action to repossess the debtor's property when such action would not be possible, when no such intention exists or when the property in question is legally exempted from such dispossession or disablement.[232] Since the main effect is to mislead the consumer into thinking that he might suffer harsh consequences for not paying his debt, it is not clear why the FDCPA decided to fit it in a different category of abusive practices, similar to the use of postcards or marked mail, which were treated separately from the other abusive practices concerning communication, despite their evident closeness.

In sum, the FDCPA enables the abused consumer to bring action for a broad range of misrepresentative or deceptive practices used in connection with the collection of a debt[233] or to obtain information regarding the consumer. But despite the broad coverage of the act, due to debt collector inventiveness, the statute's lack of clarity or its failure to take the effects of recent technological advancements[234]

---

false representations made to an attorney because the attorney protects the consumer." For details and various cases on the issue, see Griffith (2012), pp. 216–222.

[230] One can only agree with Griffith in this regard, who rightfully underlines the fact that, in case one would adopt the contrary interpretation supported by the 9th Circuit (see supra note 229), the statute would be shifted from its initial purpose and would protect the deceptive collector instead of the consumer, even if the latter is represented. "This limitation on the collector's direct contact does not provide a sanctuary for the collector, but instead insulates the consumer from interaction with the collector." For full opinion, see Griffith (2012), p. 219.

[231] Griffith (2012), p. 221.

[232] FDCPA, 15 USC 1692 (Section 808) (6) (A), (B) and (C).

[233] The doctrine emphasized that in practice it is not really easy to establish such a connection, as usually the question comes down to determine whether the collector would have contacted the debtor in case there was no outstanding debt. In the end, it is the courts' duty to interpret the communication between the debtor and the debt collector. The case law seems to confirm the abovementioned difficulty. For example, in a case in which a mortgage servicer's letter simply reminded the consumers their obligation to make their next payments on time, the court had to find that there was no violation of the FDCPA because the communication did not qualify as being in connection with the collection of a debt under the definition provided by the statute. As there was no default when the servicer sent the letter, the consumers could not prove the connection between the letter received and the debt collection. For details and similar cases, see: Griffith (2012), pp. 193–198.

[234] For abusive debt collection practices that were generated by the employment of technological advancements, see *infra*, Chap. 7, Sect. 7.2.1.6.

into account, many such practices remain uncovered or simply escape being sanctioned. It is one of the main reasons why there has been an increasing call for amendment of the FDCPA.

6.2.3.3.2 False, Deceptive or Misleading Debt Collection Methods in the UK

Based on the current UK regulation, one may also categorize misleading practices in false or deceptive information concerning the debt and false or deceptive representations made by the debt collector while collecting the debt. Unfortunately, similarly to what happened in the case of provisions concerning practices that result in the actual harassment of the debtor, the provisions on false, deceptive or misleading debt collection methods are scattered throughout the regulation and are not grouped in one single place as they were in the Guidance. Hence, although the end result is not much affected, the current regulation decreased in clarity and coherence.

Concerning the **first** category, the CONC refers to actions that might make the debtor believe he owes the costs of recovery, when no such obligation exists,[235] or, when establishing communication with the debtor, might make him misunderstand the reason for making contact.[236] Since the CONC contains special provisions applicable to statute-barred debt, suggesting that the consumer might be subjected to court action for the sum of the statute-barred debt, when the debt collector knows or should know that the limitation period has expired,[237] would also qualify as a misleading information concerning the debt.

Falling under the same category are the practices banned by the Standard Letter Guidance. Hence, a letter sent to the debtor should not use terms that would create a false or misleading impression,[238] should not contain a font size or style that would make it difficult to read[239] and should not contain references to the debt unless there

[235] CONC, Section 7.7.3.

[236] CONC, Section 7.9.2. Section 7.9.3 (1) provides one example of such misleading communication: leaving a calling card to the consumer's address that states or implies that he has missed a delivery and encourages him to make contact.

[237] CONC, Sections 7.15.6 and 7.15.7, restating the previous provisions of Section 3.15 b of the Guidance.

[238] Chapter F, Section 2.1 of the new Standard Letter Guidance. Examples of terms that would overstate the nature of business are the using of terms such as *enforcement, legal, solicitors*, in the trading names, when there is no appropriately qualified staff. Such actions would also qualify as criminal offense.

[239] Chapter E, Section 3.1 of the new Standard Letter Guidance. For example, the font size should not be smaller than 10 and Gothic text should be avoided.

is a reasonable certainty that the addressee is the actual debtor.[240] Any letter making references to legal actions should describe the legal process accurately and completely,[241] should not threaten legal action that cannot be taken[242] and should not be sent to individuals when it is not certain that the address used is the debtor's address.[243] Last but not least, the letters should not be set out in a boxed format that would closely resemble court or official letters,[244] should not display misleading logos[245] or make reference to the debtor's particular sensitive case.[246]

For the second category, concerning false representation of authority or legal position, the CONC specifically bans those practices consisting in any of the following: falsely implying or claiming authority or misrepresenting authority (such as bailiffs, sheriff officers or messengers-at-arm),[247] falsely implying or stating that action can or will be taken when it legally cannot (such as sequestration of goods or bankruptcy in case of debts that are too low to qualify for such proceedings),[248] falsely implying or stating that action has been taken when it has not.[249] Pursuing third parties for debts they are not liable for[250] is also prohibited.

---

[240] Chapter B, Section 1.3 of the new Standard Letter Guidance. In cases of uncertainty, the guidance recommends the usage of "soft letters," which do not contain any references to the debt (Section 1.6).

[241] Chapter D, Sections 1.1 and 2.1 of the new Standard Letter Guidance. The purpose of this requirement is to avoid misleading by omitting steps that would be required before enforcement action can be taken.

[242] Chapter B, Section 2.5 and Chapter D, Section 3.1 of the new Standard Letter Guidance.

[243] Chapter D, Section 1.3 of the new Standard Letter Guidance.

[244] Chapter E, Sections 1.1 and 1.2 of the new Standard Letter Guidance. The position adopted in the UK is that such look-a-like letters are misleading even if they contain disclaimers. The potential misleading effect of such letters, containing disclaimers, is still debated in the US, where courts have taken different approaches on the matter.

[245] Chapter E, Section 2.1 of the new Standard Letter Guidance. Misleading logos could be those falsely implying a connection with a court or a government body.

[246] Chapter C, Section 3.1. This recommendation refers to the cases where the collectors have knowledge of the debtor's mental health problems, long-term or terminal illness or any other disabilities that impact on the debtor's ability to pay.

[247] CONC, Sections 7.11.1 and 7.11.2, restating the previous provisions of Section 3.5.a of the Guidance.

[248] CONC, Sections 7.11. 6 and 7.11.7, restating the previous provisions of Section 3.5.b of the Guidance. However, the CONC has not retained the provisions of Section 3.5. e of the Guidance, according to which it was prohibited to falsely imply or state that failure to pay a debt is a criminal offense and criminal proceedings will be brought. However, such action would qualify under the umbrella of state action that cannot be legally taken.

[249] CONC, Section 7.11.9, restating the previous provisions of Section 3.5.d of the Guidance.

[250] CONC, Section 7.5.2, restating the previous provisions of Section 3.5.f of the Guidance. Unlike the CONC, the Guidance specifically mentioned that the provision covers third parties such as relatives who are not joint parties of the contract.

6.2.3.3.3 False, Deceptive or Misleading Debt Collection Methods in France

The French legislation is not nearly as detailed as the UK or the American and does not expressly touch upon issues like abuse, harassment, deceptiveness, misleading communication or using modern technologies in debt recovery, etc. However, some of the legal provisions concerning debt collection could be construed to refer implicitly to prohibition of misleading information and the positive obligation of debt verification, stemming from the corroborated interpretation of the obligation of the creditor to provide clear information of the debt's origin and amount and the further obligation of the debt collector to provide the debtor with such information.[251]

6.2.3.3.4 False, Deceptive or Misleading Debt Collection Methods in Romania

In Romania, based on the failed project, the debt collector would also have been banned from using false or deceiving identities in the attempt to recover the debt. The examples provided by the project can be grouped based on the same categorization used for the US or the UK in misleading practices concerning information about the debt and misleading practices concerning representations made by the debt collector while attempting to collect the debt.

For the **first** category covering false or misleading information regarding the debt, the project offered only one example, namely, misleading the debtor with respect to the character, amount or legal statute of a debt or any other services or setoffs that could be used by the debt collector in the recovery process. The legislator did not offer any explanation with respect to what the "legal statute of a debt" might mean, but the suggestion seems to refer to those debts that were statute barred. However, such interpretation cannot be asserted with certainty since according to Romanian law, one may attempt to recover a debt even after the limitation period, but without resort to judicial action. The question remains open.

For the **second** category covering false or misleading representations made by the debt collector, the Romanian legislator has mentioned the following: implying the state's involvement in the debt collection or using false uniforms and badges; falsely impersonating an attorney, a bailiff or a bankruptcy liquidator or falsely implying that the communication originates from one of these categories; falsely threatening with imprisonment, confiscation or foreclosure of properties in the case of nonpayment of the debt, when such a legal decision was not yet obtained; threatening an action that cannot be legally executed or that is not intended; falsely informing the debtor that he committed a criminal offense or any other illegality with the purpose of intimidation; using or distributing any written documents that

---

[251] See 783 (2012), Art. R. 124-3, corroborated by Art. R. 124-4.

are falsely presented as official documents, approved by the state or a court; willingly omitting from any written or oral means of communication the fact that such communication refers to debt collection; or providing a false identity according to which the collector works for another type of agency than debt collection.[252]

Interestingly, many of the above represented criminal offenses, which means that the failed act would have provided a swift cause of action to the aggrieved debtors, similar to what the FDCPA had done in the US with the multiple torts. What remained unclear was whether the Romanian act would have been a special criminal act or would have doubled the criminal statutory framework by establishing civil liabilities as well.

6.2.3.4 Validation of the Debt

With the intent of precluding debtors from chasing the wrong person or from trying to collect a debt that was paid, or even as a method of preventing misleading information concerning the debt, fair debt collection practices statutes have provided for procedures meant to ensure the validation of debt. French law can also be construed by way of interpretation to require the debt collector to verify the debt before trying to collect it. Hence, this section discusses not an abusive practice, but rather a positive obligation of debt collectors, upon the consumer-debtor's request or not, to be diligent and make sure that the debt they are trying to collect is both valid and real and that the person subjected to the collection efforts is the one who owes the duty to pay it. Additionally, debt validation addresses the right of the debtor to contest any aspect related to the debt (its existence or its amount). Obviously, the possibility to challenge a debt is an important defense mechanism against debt-collection-related abuses, and no proper fair debt collection practices statute can exist without it.

6.2.3.4.1 Debt Validation in the US

The FDCPA included a positive obligation for the debt collector to comply with a procedure for the verification of debt. Therefore, within 5 days after the initial communication with a consumer in connection with the collection of the debt, the debt collector is obliged to send to the consumer a written notification. The statute specifically mentions what the notice should contain: the amount of the debt; the creditor's name; the debtor's right to challenge within 30 days after receipt,[253]

---

[252] For a complete list, see: Project Law, Art. 10, Para 1 and 2, Letters a)–k).

[253] Debt collectors are advised to wait at least 30 days from the date the debtor received the notice before taking additional action. In *Miller v. Payco-General American Credits, Inc.*, 943 F.2d 482, 484 (4th Cir. 1991), the court held that the Defendant violated the FDCPA where the debt

partially or in full; the validity of the debt under the sanction of assuming the debt to be valid; the debtor's right to obtain verification of the debt or of the disputed portion of the debt; and the right to be provided with the name and contact details of the original creditor, if different from the current creditor.[254]

Additionally, in the case the debtor decides to dispute the debt, the collector is bound to cease any collection attempts until he obtains further verification from the creditor and will be entitled to resume them only after notifying the consumer of the debt's validity or providing him with the data required.[255] It has been construed that this very technical section of the FDCPA represents but another safeguard against any unreasonable intrusions into the debtor's privacy zone.[256] However, the logical suspension of collection efforts during debt validation can turn into a permanent measure in the case the debt collector proves unable to comply with the mandatory information requested by the debtor. This is a highly efficient tool against debts bought and sold multiple times in the absence of proper documents.

In connection with the technical procedure above, the FDCPA states that in the case the debtor fails to dispute the validity of the debt, such failure cannot be interpreted by the courts as an admission of liability by the consumer.[257] In addition, in order to avoid misinterpretations with respect to the abovementioned procedure, the FDCPA clarifies that a communication in the form of a formal pleading in a civil action is not to be treated as an initial communication[258] and neither will the sending or the delivery of any form or notice unrelated to the collection of the debt, but required by other legal statutes or regulations.[259]

From the above it results that the procedure is mandatory and cannot be replaced or substituted by equivalent forms, which would have allowed the debt collectors to circumvent the protections established by the FDCPA. The mandatory content of the notice is also meant as a safeguard for the debtor, for it not only allows him to quickly verify the debt, its amount and provenance, but also it informs him about the right to challenge the information provided, which is extremely useful for most consumers who do not know their rights. Last but not least, the fact that the procedure is technical and mandatory empowers the debtor with a powerful cause of action, for any derogation from the statutory content is considered a violation and will attract the debt collector's liability.

---

collector's letter indicated a demand for immediate full payment of the debt in direct contradiction to the 30-day notice period. The court has labeled this violation "overshadowing." For details, see Sartip (2012) 2nd Recommendation, p. 2.

[254] FDCPA, 15 USC 1692 (Section 809)(a)(1)–(5).

[255] FDCPA, 15 USC 1692 (Section 809)(b).

[256] Potach (1978), p. 908.

[257] FDCPA, 15 USC 1692 (Section 809)(c).

[258] FDCPA, 15 USC 1692 (Section 809)(d).

[259] The FDCPA specifically mentions the Internal Revenue Code of 1986, title V of Gramm-Leach-Bliley Act, or any provision of Federal or State law relating to notice of data security breach or privacy or any regulation prescribed under any such provision of law. See FDCPA, 15 USC 1692 (Section 809)(e).

6.2.3.4.2 Debt Validation in the UK

In the UK, similarly to the US, the CONC provides for obligations regarding the validation of the debt, although similar obligations result from other statutes as well. According to the regulation, a debt collector must offer to the debtor or his representative information vis-à-vis the amount of any arrears and the owed balance.[260] Similarly, a debt collector must make sure, before any collection attempts, that the debtor is pursued for the correct amount.[261] Judging from the wording of these provisions, it appears that in the UK the creditor or the debt collector owes an *a priori*, positive obligation to the debtor, notwithstanding the latter's request, of providing correct and updated information on the status of the debt.

Another positive obligation of the debt collector is to give due regard to the debtor's claim that a debt is either settled, or disputed, and hence suspend or cease any debt collection attempts, at least until there is clear justification or evidence that the debtor's assertion was not valid.[262] Similar obligations are provided and detailed with regard to disputed debts.[263]

As stated before, additional obligations arise from other statutes as well. For example, since debt collectors are processing personal data, they are subjected to the legal obligations stemming out of the Data Protection Act 1998[264] and additional obligations related to the processing of such data for the purposes of debt recovery[265] or verification of such data accuracy[266] in order to avoid the risk of mistaken identity or that one of pursuing the wrong amount of unpaid debt.

With respect to issues related to mistaken identity and disputed debt, the former Guidance mentioned situations that were to be considered by debt collectors, many of them kept by the CONC, but in the same scattered manner mentioned before: inadequate maintenance of accurate and adequate account data, deficiencies in the exchange of accurate and adequate account data, acting on inaccurate or inadequate data in the pursuit of the debt.[267] All these situations should be thoroughly considered by any collector *prior* to seeking recovery of debts,[268] and any consequences arising from failure to do so will constitute unfair or improper practices.[269]

---

[260] CONC, Section 7.4.1.

[261] CONC, Section 7.13.4.

[262] CONC, Section 7.5.3.

[263] CONC, Sections 7.14.1 and 7.14.2.

[264] CONC, Section 7.13.1, restating the previous provisions of Section 3.16 of the Guidance.

[265] Office for Fair Trading (2003), Section 3.17, p. 47. Banned related activities may result in criminal offenses. For example, in one case two private investigators have been fined under Section 55 of Data Protection Act for unlawfully obtaining and selling personal information after tracking down a woman whose partner owed money. The fines amounted to a total of 900£ plus 400£ in costs. See: Williams (2008).

[266] CONC, Section 7.13.2, restating the previous provisions of Section 3.19 of the Guidance.

[267] Section 3.21 of the Guidance.

[268] Section 3.22 of the Guidance.

[269] CONC, Sections 7.13.4–7.13.7, 7.14.6 (1), 7.15.9, restating the previous provisions of Section 3.23. (a), (b), (c), (f), (h) and (i) of the Guidance. However, the CONC did not keep the

On a final note concerning the issue of prior validation, one must mention here the concern of the CONC with the issue of outsourced activities, which are currently acknowledged as a problem in the US. According to CONC, firms resorting to outsourcing owe a duty of care in selecting the third party[270] and must ensure that the third party is in full compliance with the licensing requirements of CCA 1974 and those of the CONC.[271] From the wording of the mentioned provisions, it may be construed that any debt collector resorting to outsourced services is liable for the abusive practices employed by the third party. This is an important difference from the US, where debt collectors are resorting to overseas outsourcing, for they are not liable for the third parties' actions and escape liability for nonconforming practices, which makes the UK legislation better suited in this regard.

6.2.3.4.3 Debt Validation in France

The French legislation does not establish specifically any positive obligation of debt verification. However, the obligation of the creditor to provide clear information of the debt's origin, together with the obligation of the debt collector to provide a letter to the debtor in which detailed explanations concerning the amount of the debt (in principal, interest and other accessories),[272] may be construed in such sense and used in the absence of specific provisions.

6.2.3.5 Fees and Charges Added to the Debt

Strongly related to the debt validation procedure is the issue of extra charges that the debt collectors are trying to impose on consumer-debtors on top of what they really owe. Since inflating the debt is common to all jurisdictions, an efficient fair debt collection practices act must specifically address this issue. The following lines concerning this building block deal with what is currently in place in the chosen jurisdictions in order to determine the most efficient model.

---

entire provisions of Section 3.23 of the Guidance, which offered a much more detailed list of what might constitute unfair or improper practices due to nonobservance of data protection rules.

[270] CONC, Section 7.13.9.

[271] CONC, Sections 7.13.12 and 7.13.13, corroborated by Section 7.12.3 (1).

[272] 783 (2012), Sections R124-3 and R124-4 (as amended by Decret no 2013-109 du 30 janvier 2013).

6.2.3.5.1 The Issue of Extra Charges Added to the Debt in the US

The FDCPA included the issue of extra charges within a wider category of unconscionable means to collect debts. As usual, the act attempted an open-end definition, by providing a nonexhaustive list[273] of examples. Therefore, a debt collector is not allowed to collect amounts in excess of what was expressly provided for in the agreement from which the debt originates or provided by the law,[274] billing telephone calls or telegram fees or any similar charges[275] to any person. In other words, whatever the debtor could not reasonably know or foresee to be added to the debt cannot be recovered.

6.2.3.5.2 The Issue of Extra Charges Added to the Debt in the UK

In the UK, charging for debt recovery is allowed as long as it was provided for in the initial agreement, it is not unfair and the debtor's interests are taken into account.[276] Examples of such levies are misleading the debtor into believing they are legally liable to pay recovery charges when it is not the case,[277] claiming recovery costs in the absence of express contractual provisions,[278] failing to provide clear indication in the credit agreement on the amount to be charged in the case of default[279] or applying unreasonable charges.[280]

---

[273] FDCPA, 15 USC 1692 (Section 808).

[274] FDCPA, 15 USC 1692 (Section 808) (1). For example: in *Stratton v. Portfolio Recovery Associates* No. 13-6574 (6th Cir. 2014), plaintiff alleged that defendant violated the FDCPA by attempting to collect statutory interest on a purchased debt after the original creditor waived the contractual right to collect interest. The district court granted summary judgment in favor of defendant, finding that the statutory interest charge was permitted by state law, and plaintiff appealed. The appellate court reversed, finding that there is no right under state law to collect statutory interest after the contractual interest right is waived and that attempting to collect any interest after waiver is a violation of the FDCPA.—See more at: http://www.sessions-law.com/news-resources/october-27-2014-case-digest/#sthash.fwnHTUXl.dpuf, last visited 10.12.2014. In *Quinteros v. MBI Associates, Inc.*, 2014 WL 793138 (E.D.N.Y. Feb. 28, 2014), the U.S. District Court for the Eastern District of New York denied a debt collector's motion to dismiss an FDCPA case, holding that its $5 surcharge for payments via credit card may have violated the law, for they were not provided in the initial contract. See http://www.insidearm.com/daily/debt-collection-news/debt-collection/fdcpa-case-ruling-on-convenience-fees-having-impact-on-collectors/, last visited 10.12.2014.

[275] FDCPA, 15 USC 1692 (Section 808) (5).

[276] CONC, Section 7.7.1, restating the previous provisions of Section 3.10 of the Guidance.

[277] CONC, Section 7.7.3 restating the previous provisions of Section 3.11.a of the Guidance.

[278] CONC, Section 7.7.2 restating the previous provisions of Section 3.11.b of the Guidance.

[279] CONC, Section 7.7.4 restating the previous provisions of Section 3.11.c of the Guidance.

[280] CONC, Section 7.7.5 restating the previous provisions of Section 3.11.d of the Guidance. In the eyes of the OFT, an unreasonable charge is in this context a charge the level of which is not based on the recovery of actual and necessary costs.

6.2.3.5.3 The Issue of Extra Charges in Romania

In Romania, according to the project, a debt collector would not have been allowed to employ illegal practices in the attempt to collect a debt. The draft offered three examples but left the list open for others with similar results. Among them were the collection of any amounts (including interest, taxes, fees, expenses added to the principal in any way) that did not originate from the agreement between the creditor and the debtor. Other extra charges barred were the charging fees for phone calls, if they were reverse charged or those for delivery couriers to the consumer.

It appears that both the US and the UK have handled the issue of extra charges, with a greater amount of detail and specificity on the UK side. However, it would be hard to speculate which one of them would prove more efficient in practice. What matters is that such extra fees should not be allowed to burden the consumer-debtor even more.

6.2.4 Open-End and Functional Definitions of Abusive Practices

One of the biggest criticisms made of the FDCPA was that it had a largely static nature,[281] which, as will be later shown, did not allow it to keep pace with new technologies or the innovative abusive practices developed by debt collectors. Hence, the law meant to address abusive debt collection has itself become insufficient. One of the identified reasons was the fact that at the moment of the enactment, Congress did not provide any agency with regulatory powers, being under the impression that the act was comprehensive and addressed all possible abuses.[282] Since any amendment had to go through the Congress, amending the FDCPA became a cumbersome task. This issue was partially solved by the 2010 Dodd-Frank Act,[283] which gave the BFCP the authority to prescribe rules with respect to debt collection and issue guidance concerning compliance with the law and undertake research and policy initiatives related to consumer debt collection. Therefore, by way of supplementary agency regulation, the FDCPA can at least try and keep

[281] Hector (2011) p. 1610. For an opinion to the contrary, see: Alderman (2012), p. 586 at pp. 605–606. "The FDCPA was expressly designed for adjustments by the courts to deal with new and unforeseeable acts and practices." However, his opinion is contradicted by the large number of issues that courts have not been able to settle in a satisfactory and consistent manner and by the increased number of calls for reform and amendment of the FDCPA in the recent years, which proves that the act cannot keep up with the new challenges in its current form.

[282] Hector (2011), p. 1610.

[283] 12 US Code, Section 5511—Purpose, Objectives, and Functions, c) (5): "The primary functions of the Bureau are [...] issuing rules, orders, and guidance implementing Federal consumer financial law."

up[284] with abusive debt collection practices. A similar solution has been adopted by the UK, where both the OFT's Guidance and the current FCA's CONC are regulating the nonjudicial debt collection business. Definitions get reviewed and updated regularly, which means that, at least on paper, the regulatory response is quick. Enforcement, on the other hand, is a different issue.

French law does not provide open-end definitions to abusive debt collection practices, since its main concern is more the relationship between creditor and debt collector, while German law makes no reference to abusive debt collection whatsoever, for its provisions refer to licensing only. The Romanian project, inspired by the FDCPA, provided nonexhaustive examples but failed to take into account the usage of modern technologies or innovative practices. Since none of the civilian jurisdictions chosen have a regulatory body with powers similar to those of BFCP or FCA, their answer to new challenges cannot come from state agencies but from the legislators. Since legislators require awareness and time, this building block of an efficient antiabusive debt collection practices law remains of utmost importance and a great challenge for any civilian system.

This concludes the book's analyses of four of the proposed six building blocks for assessing the efficiency of a fair debt collection practices law. If these four were covering the requirements for functioning and proper identification of abusive practices, the next chapter is dedicated to the last two building blocks, concerned with the most important aspect of a fair debt collection law, enforcement and remedies, as well as to the need for reform of debt collection laws.

References

Akina WK (2012) Note: A lie is a lie: The need to define Section 1692e of the FDCPA. Brooklyn J Corporate Financ Commerical Law 7

Alderman RM (2012) The Fair Debt Collection Practices Act meets arbitration: non-parties and arbitration. Loyola Consum Law Rev 24

Cohn SA. A streamlined debt collection procedure in the Federal Republic of Germany Boston College International and Comparative Law Review. http://lawdigitalcommons.bc.edu/cgi/viewcontent.cgi?article=1619&context=iclr

De Boer S (2013) Fair Debt Collection Practices Act. Overview, analyses, and administration. Novinka, New York

Decree No. 96-1112 regulating the activities of persons involved in amicable recovery of debts on behalf of others (in French original:Décret n° 96-1112 du 18 décembre 1996 portant réglementation de l'activité des personnes procédant au recouvrement amiable des créances pour le compte d'autrui.)." France, 1996

Décret n° 2012-783 du 30 mai 2012 relatif à la partie réglementaire du code des procédures civiles d'exécution." France, 2012

[284] The BFCP has already made use of its rule-making and guidance-issuing powers in case of large debt buyers and debt collectors and organized a workshop dedicated to the impact of technology in the debt collection market. For details: De Boer (2013), pp. 6–8.

Edelman DA (2013) Fair Debt Collection Practices Act. http://www.edcombs.com/wp-content/uploads/2013/08/Fair-Debt-Collection-Practices-Act/July/2013.pdf. Last visited 19.12.2014
FCA (2014) Annual Report and Accounts 2013/14. Financial Conduct Authority, London
Finlay S (2009) Consumer credit fundamentals. Palgrave Macmillan, UK
Griffith E (2012) The search for better communication between the debt collector and the consumer under the Fair Debt Collection Practices Act. Univ Kansas Law Rev. http://www.law.ku.edu/sites/law.drupal.ku.edu/files/docs/law_review/v61/04-Griffith_Final.pdf
Hector C (2011) Debt collection in the information age: new technologies and the Fair Debt Collection Practices Act. Calif Law Rev 99
Hudson A (2009) The law of finance. Sweet & Maxwell, London
"Lege privind procedura colectarii debitelor (English translation: Law Concerning Debt Collection Procedure")." Romania, 2010
Lucas LA, Harrell AC (2000) 2000 update on the Federal Fair Debt Collection Practices Act. The Business Lawyer 55
Micklitz H-W et al (2009) Chapter 2: Unfair commercial practices and misleading advertising. Understanding EU Consum Law
Micklitz H-W, Stuyck J, Terryn E (2010) Cases, materials and text on consumer law. Hart, North America
Office for Fair Trading (2003) OFT guidance for businesses engaged in the recovery of consumer credit debts
OUT-LAW.COM (2009) British gas ruling sends warning to all suppliers. The Register
Poncibo C, Incardona R (2005) The EU unfair commercial practices directive: a faltering first step. Lond Law Rev 1
Poncibo C, Incardona R (2007) The average consumer, the unfair commercial practices directive, and the cognitive revolution. J Consum Policy Issue 30
Potach SG (1978) New protection against the unethical bill collector: debtor's remedies under the Fair Debt Collection Practices Act. Creighton Law Rev. https://dspace.creighton.edu/xmlui/bitstream/handle/10504/39039/55_11CreightonLRev895%281977-1978%29.pdf?sequence=1
Rainer (Lawyers/Tax advisers). Debt collection in Germany. Available at http://www.grprainer.com/en/Debt-Collection.html?gclid=CMbo09PS47cCFcSz3godCjsAqg
Ramsay I (2012) Consumer law and policy. Hart, Oxford and Portland
Rosenthal D (2013) Consumer credit law and practice – a guide. Bloomsbury Professional, Great Britain
Sartip MH (2012) Be a confident collection lawyer. South Carolina Lawyer. http://ipubviewer.com/display_article.php?id=1227543#
Steiner E (2010) French law: a comparative approach. Oxford University Press, US
Tajti T (2013) Post-1990 secured transaction law reforms in Central and Eastern Europe. Szegedi Közjegyzői Közlöny
Urban I. Amenintari fizice la adresa unui restantier: "Vezi sa ai si bani in buzunar cand dam de tine" (English translation: Physical Threats against Debtor: "See That You Have Money on You When We Will Reach You"). Available at http://www.urbansiasociatii.ro/manualul_colectorului/HTML/52.html
Williams C (2008) Gumshoes fined for debt collection pretexting blag. The Register
Wise HM. Debt recovery in France. 1–2. Available at http://www.immigration-france-usa.com/gifs/pdf/debtrecoveryinfrance.pdf
World Bank (2009) Romania: diagnostic review of consumer protection and financial literacy, vol 2. Comparison against good practices. World Bank, Washington, DC. License: CC BY 3.0 Unported. https://openknowledge.worldbank.org/handle/10986/12916

Chapter 7
Remedies Against Abusive Practices and Calls for Reform

As the following discussion will point out, the FDCPA has not only indicated which practices will be deemed abusive and banned from the collection process but also stated how they are to be sanctioned. Its uniqueness and greatest accomplishment were to provide aggrieved consumers with **diverse causes of action**[1] **and efficient enforcement mechanisms.** Although its primary target was the abusive independent debt collector, the FDCPA has "crystallized tort theories applicable to debt collection abuses" ... [and has] "extended broad authority to sue for unfair and deceptive collection practices."[2] This chapter will detail the abovementioned remedies and their efficiency and will compare them with their counterparts in the other chosen jurisdictions.

7.1 Remedies

As shown earlier,[3] given the fact that the FDCPA has its own legislative aim, the remedies proposed also generate unique outcomes. The focus is on punishment of civil wrongs and criminal offenses, which should also have a deterrent effect on other debt collectors. The FDCPA demands obedience and produces a sort of negative ethics by strongly emphasizing what is not permitted in the debt collection

[1] Akina (2012), p. 160. The US Congress put at consumers' disposal several causes of action in order to protect their own rights against unfair debt collection practices. By granting the consumers the possibility to act as "private attorneys general," the FDCPA promoted several interests: it rewarded citizens for educating themselves about their rights, forced debt collectors to act more cautiously during the collection procedures and reduced the burden on the FTC (and recently on the BFCP) to monitor minor debt collectors by allowing them to focus on large-scale violations from big debt collectors.

[2] Potach (1978), p. 908.

[3] See *supra* Chap. 6, Sect. 6.1.3.

C.G. Stănescu, *Self-Help, Private Debt Collection and the Concomitant Risks*,
DOI 10.1007/978-3-319-21503-7_7

process and by making available a wide range of remedies.[4] In other words, the FDCPA demands that debt collectors comply or pay compensation. And since the main concern is the consumer, the FDCPA also made sure that **the consumer is properly incentivized to take action on his own, directly against the abusive debt collector**. This feature may be considered the most important peculiarity of the FDCPA[5] unmatched by the administrative enforcement regime available in the UK or by any other enforcement regime available in the other chosen jurisdictions, which is why it is going to be addressed first, as the proper model to follow.

7.1.1 Civil Liability and Incentives for Private Action

Civil liability lies at the center of the debtor's relief under the system implemented by the FDCPA. Each debt collector whose actions are found to be in violation of any of the FDCPA's provisions may be subjected to civil liability, provided the aggrieved consumer decides to bring action against the debt collector. It is irrelevant whether the violation sanctioned was intentional[6] or if the violations were resulting from failure to meet technicalities.[7] In other words, liability is imposed for

[4] The remedies offered by the federal FDCPA were twofold. On the one side, the FDCPA provided for administrative enforcement, which basically allows the consumer to address the FTC with respect to debt collector's noncompliance with the FDCPA's required conduct, while on the other side, the law provided for civil penalties and attorney fees awards, in the attempt to encourage consumers to act on their own. Akina (2012), p. 160. However, since the application of the FDCPA does not affect the application of state laws, the remedies can also arise under criminal law, where the abuse amounts to criminal offense, or under administrative law, where the action of the debt collector would justify the suspension of his activity or the withdrawal of his license.

[5] Despite the benefits given to debtors in order to determine them to act on their own by private action, there has been criticism that these benefits were not enough and that still private actions were not nearly as many as they should have been.

[6] The FDCPA reads: "[. . .] any debt collector who fails to comply with any provision of this title with respect to any person is liable to such person." As the statute does not distinguish between the types of liability, there is no strict liability. See FDCPA, 15 USC 1692 (Section 813)(a). Also Hector (2011), p. 1607.

[7] Initially, such construction was determined by the analogous court decisions regarding the interpretation of the Truth in Landing Act. "Construing the model language of 15 USC 1640 (a), which imposes liability for violations of *any* requirement of the statute, the Fifth Circuit Court of Appeals concluded that "once a court finds a violation, no matter how technical, it has no discretion with respect to the imposition of liability" 539 F.2d at 510. The virtually identical language of the Fair Debt Collection Practices Act, 15 USC 1692 k (a), likewise, would compel the automatic imposition of liability for even technical violations of the Act." See Potach (1978), p. 909, footnote 92. Also in the recent case of *Bicking*, the court held that the failure of the defendant to include the "in writing" requirement could easily deceive the least sophisticated debtor into believing that oral notice is statutorily sufficient, thus violating Section 1692g (a) (4) and (5). In the case at hand, the defendant attempted to collect debt sending demand letters to the plaintiffs. Each letter stated that if the account was not in dispute, the payment was expected. The included verification notice informed the plaintiffs that any notice of dispute or request for

any kind of violation, unless differently provided by the law.[8] With the sole exception of actual damages incurred, no other jurisdiction from those chosen by this work has provided for anything similar to the system introduced by the FDCPA with respect to civil liability. Any court action—where available—would follow the general procedural requirements and the general rules, without any financial or procedural incentives for the debtor to take action in his own hands.

On the contrary, in the UK, as will be shown, the debtor is provided with an alternative to courts; however, he must try to settle the issue with the debt collector, directly and only after may he resort to the service of the Financial Ombudsman (FOS). The reason might be to relieve the courts from unnecessary and expensive trials concerning low-value damages or issues that could be resolved between the parties themselves.[9] A similar logic could easily function in Romania as well; however, consumer-debtors should still have similar incentives as those provided by the FDCPA at their disposal, just in case the administrative procedures or parties' negotiations prove to be unsatisfactory. Additionally, it is clear that the possibility of a lawsuit might have a stronger deterrent effect on debt collectors to refrain from abusive collection practices.

7.1.1.1 Civil Liability and Incentives Under the FDCPA

The American legislators considered that a mere reparation of damages incurred does not have a sufficient deterrent effect against abusive debt collection practices. Hence, it added several incentives to encourage aggrieved debtors to act on their own: the obligation of debtors to pay civil penalties for each violation, the possibility for class action suits and additional monetary awards, the right to receive attorney fees and judicial costs in case of success, together with the right to use multiple venues (federal and state courts) or to choose the best venue at hand.

---

information "must be received within thirty days." Plaintiffs brought a class action alleging that the verification notice failed to inform the consumer that such disputes and requests must be received in writing according to the FDCPA. Defendants tried to argue that the notice was sufficient because "it clearly informed of their right to notify" and in their interpretation a violation of Section 1692g required a more egregious conduct. The court dismissed this interpretation and held that Section 1692g should be read to mean that debtors can trigger the right awarded to them under subsection (a)(4) and (a)(5) *only* through written dispute. Thus, failure to notify them of this requirement, though merely technical, represented a violation of the statute.

[8] The conclusion stems from the corroborated provisions of Section 813 (a), (c) and (e). Letter (a) reads: "except as otherwise provided by this section [. . .]," while letters (c) and (e) state: "A debt collector may not be held liable in any action [. . .] if [he] [. . .] shows by a preponderance of evidence that the violation was not intentional and resulted from bona fide error [. . .]" and "No provision of this section imposing any liability shall apply to any act done or omitted in good faith in conformity with any advisory opinion of the Commission [. . .]." See FDCPA, 15 USC 1692 (Section 813) (a) (c) and (e).

[9] http://www.financial-ombudsman.org.uk/faq/businesses/answers/handle_cases_a3.html, last visited 23.01.2015.

7.1.1.1.1 Civil Penalties for Each Violation

The FDCPA establishes the individual debtor's liability for any actual damages resulting from any violation of the act but also allows for additional damages up to one thousand dollars,[10] at the discretion of the court. Such additional damages may be awarded for each violation committed, despite the fact that it was the same person or against the same person or with respect to the same debt. The additional damages are not punitive but civil penalties, granted in order to increase the deterrent effect of the law,[11] this conclusion being supported also by the fact that in order to receive them there is no need to show the existence of actual damages.[12] Since the enactment of the FDCPA, the doctrine took the position that even in cases where consumers cannot prove an actual harm "courts should award some amount of additional damages in order to properly effectuate the broad remedial intent of the Act."[13] The determination of the damages lies within the attributes of the courts, which should take into account all relevant factors, including the frequency, persistence, nature and intention of the debt collector's noncompliance.[14]

What is more difficult to assess is the category of actual damages. The doctrine took from the very beginning the position that mere out-of-pocket, pecuniary losses would be a too limited concept, inconsistent with the FDCPA's broadly stated intent to redress both pecuniary and nonpecuniary injuries.[15] Otherwise, if one would go for a narrow interpretation, damages for mental distress, just to mention one example, would be excluded, although it is more than obvious that such injuries would be a common and an often result of the abuses related to debt collection,

---

[10] FDCPA, 15 USC 1692 (Section 813) (a) (1) and (2).

[11] At first glance, a civil penalty of five hundred dollars might not have a strong deterrent effect. However, cases in which only one abusive practice occurred are very rare and since the penalty is imposed for each violation, the amount increases considerably. In addition, one should consider the fact of the likelihood that more debtors were subjected to the same abusive practices. Besides the fact that they also have the possibility of constituting a class action and seek punitive damages, each and every one of them will be entitled to seek and receive the civil penalty. In such case, the magnitude of the amounts paid by the debt collector will have the strong deterrent effect sought by the legislator.

[12] FDCPA, 15 USC 1692 (Section 813) (a) (2) (A) and (B) (ii).

[13] Potach (1978), p. 910. In footnote 96, the author offers yet another comparison with the Truth in Lending Act and cites a Supreme Court Decision rendered in *Mourning v. Family Publications Serv Inc.* where, with respect to imposing civil penalties, it was stated: "We cannot conclude that the Congress intended those who failed to comply with regulations to be subject to no penalty or to criminal penalties alone…" 411 US. At 376.

[14] These factors are specifically mentioned by the law. See FDCPA, 15 USC 1692 (Section 813) (b) (1).

[15] Potach (1978), p. 910. The author mentions that the Act addresses also the redress of injuries resulting from the invasion of debtor's privacy, which are normally of a nonmonetary value (footnote 99).

which are banned by the FDCPA.[16] The situation described was seen as a loophole despite the fact that the doctrine stated that nothing precluded the courts from "expanding the statutory concept of "actual damages" in individual cases to redress an abused debtor's non-pecuniary injuries."[17]

7.1.1.1.2 Class Action Suits and Additional Monetary Awards

The FDCPA expressly provided for the possibility of class action suits and authorized an award of additional damages up until one thousand dollars for each named debtor-plaintiff. The courts are empowered to make an aggregate award to all unnamed class members, without taking into consideration a minimum individual recovery, in an amount that does not exceed the lesser of 500,000 dollars or one percent of the net worth of the debt collector.[18] As the latter is not defined by the act, the doctrine took the position that it can be borrowed from the federal income tax regulations.[19] The amount of the aforementioned awards is to be determined by considering the debtor's resources, the number of affected consumers and the extent of the debt collector's intent in committing the violation.[20]

By imposing civil liability on abusive behavior of debt collectors, the FDCPA sought to provide consumers with a relief and a suitable defense against unethical practices. But as it was evident from the very beginning, the statute failed to provide an apparent redress against nonpecuniary injuries, leaving such task at the courts' will and interpretation. Thus, it seems that despite the multiple benefits the FDCPA had from its inception evident loopholes that could affect its effectiveness. Such loopholes became even more evident and grew in numbers, along with the technical developments in the past 30 years, which led to an increase in recent calls for reformation of the FDCPA. These calls will be discussed in Sect. 7.2.[21]

---

[16] Such banned practices were (and still are) harassment by constant telephone calls, threats of physical violence, threats to arrest or seize property. Despite this, the Senate committee seemed to have feared that if they expanded the definition of actual damages to include damages for emotional distress or anguish, a rash of nuisance suits might have overburdened the federal dockets. For more details, see Potach (1978), p. 911, footnotes 100–102.

[17] Such conclusion was based on FDCPA's inception on the analogous interpretation and application of the Fair Credit Reporting Act. Cases were cited in which the courts awarded actual damages for loss of sleep, nervousness, frustration, mental anguish, loss of reputation, embarrassment and humiliation. Potach (1978), pp. 911–912, footnote 103.

[18] See FDCPA, 15 USC 1692 (Section 813) (2) (B).

[19] Potach (1978), p. 912, footnote 105.

[20] FDCPA, 15 USC 1692 (Section 813) (b) (2).

[21] *Infra*, Sect. 7.2.

7.1.1.1.3 Monetary Incentives: Attorney Fees and Costs

As it was mentioned in second chapter, litigation implies costs and expenses. The situation is even harsher for the losing party who will have to cover not only his own costs and attorney's fees but also the winner's. Generally speaking, the principle according to which the loser pays is called the "English Rule"[22] and is applied in four of the book's chosen jurisdiction: the UK, France, Germany and Romania. However, in the US, the general policy is different in the sense that each party, including the winning one, will bear its own attorney's fees. Obviously, this "American Rule"[23] was likely to have a discouraging effect on consumers, especially where the damages resulting from a successful trial against an abusive debt collector would be smaller than the actual attorney's fees.

Hence, in addition to the awarding of damages, the FDCPA has provided an exception from the American Rule and allowed the successful debtors to recover attorney fees and any other related costs.[24] The purpose of such provision was to increase the capability of consumers to sue on their own for any kind of violation, without taking into account the size of the debtor's recovery or if the fees perceived by the attorneys were disproportionate in relationship to the size of such recovery. To make it even harsher for abusive debt collectors, the doctrine issues the opinion that even attorneys representing *pro bono* a successful debtor are entitled to their statutory award.[25] Given the fact that the law does not distinguish between the types of fees, it means they can include those fees paid for the work performed in the original action, on appeal or on remand. The sole condition imposed by the law for awarding the attorney's fees is that the debtor-plaintiff prevails on the merits of the case. The attorney's fees must also be supported by evidence, and the amount of the award is set in accordance with the usual principles used in calculating a reasonable attorney's fees.

On the other hand, if the court finds that the debtor's action was brought in bad faith, then it can award attorney's fees and costs to the debt collector.[26] The explanation is that despite its intent of encouraging aggrieved debtors to take action on themselves, the law does also intend to protect debt collectors from nuisance suits or from suits related to legal and permitted practices under the act. The doctrine emphasized that "courts should presume the good faith validity of a debtor's suit and treat the collector's claim of bad faith harassment with caution.

[22] Garner (2009), p. 609.

[23] Garner (2009), p. 98.

[24] See FDCPA, 15 USC 1692 (Section 813) (a) (3) 1st thesis.

[25] The opinion was at inception based on the analogy with the Truth in Landing Act related case law. For example was mentioned *Seller v. Wollman*, 510, F. 2d 119 (5th Cir. 1975), in which it was held that "in case of success the plaintiffs would not be denied the attorney's fees simply because they were represented by a legal aid society." For details: Potach (1978), p. 914, footnotes 115–116.

[26] FDCPA, 15 USC 1692 (Section 813) (a) (3) 2nd thesis.

Otherwise, this provision could have the unintended effect of discouraging legitimate private actions by abused debtors."[27]

Attorney fees and costs on prevalence on merits, without taking into account the amount awarded for the violation, provide private enforcements with the additional means necessary to obtain compliance with the act. Therefore, such provisions have a two-folded effect: encouragement of victims of collection abuses to seek legal redress and deterrence of debt collectors from engaging in such abuses. Courts have added more substance to these legal provisions by going as far as to pierce the corporate veil, in order to ensure that the FDCPA's purpose of providing aggrieved debtors with private remedies is not frustrated[28] by hiding under the corporate façade.

7.1.1.1.4 Procedural Incentives: Choice of Venue and Multiple Venues

In correlation with the possibility of bringing private action against abusive debt collectors, according to the FDCPA[29] the aggrieved debtors are provided with procedural incentives[30] as well. Hence, they are entitled to sue any federal district court without regard to the amount of controversy or in any other court of competent jurisdiction. All actions arising from the FDCPA must be brought within 1 year from the date of the violation.[31]

Debtors enjoy also the possibility of bringing an action under the act in state courts, considered "other courts of competent jurisdiction" by the law. In addition, in certain cases, even bankruptcy courts might have jurisdiction to hear cases.[32] The reason for allowing multiple competent courts lies with the manifest policy of providing the consumer with the possibility of choosing the **most convenient forum** for him in order to encourage him to take action. Even more, in certain

[27] Potach (1978), pp. 915–916.

[28] *West v. Costen*, cited *supra* footnotes 886 and 1182.

[29] FDCPA, 15 USC 1692 (Section 813) (d).

[30] Another form of abuse that the FDCPA is trying to prevent is related to judicial forums in which the debt collector may bring action. Therefore, in accordance with the legal provisions, the debtor collector is required to use only those venues that are logical or convenient to the debtor, meaning either those in which the real property upon which an interest is secured is located or, in any other cases, those in the judicial district having a very strong connection with the debt (place of signature) or residence of the debtor at the time of the beginning of the action. The purpose was to avoid the situations in which collectors obtain default judgments in distant and inconvenient forums, though such provisions were not able to put a stop to abusive practices involving default judgments in debt collection cases, as mentioned in the previous chapter. A legal disclaimer specifies the fact that the provisions precluding forum abuse are not to be construed in any way as constituting a cause for any legal actions taken by debt collectors against consumers.

[31] FDCPA, 15 USC 1692 (Section 813) (d).

[32] For a more detailed discussion on the possibility of bankruptcy courts or state courts to hear debt collection related cases without remanding them to federal courts: Potach (1978), p. 920, footnotes 146–147.

cases, the two venues would go hand in hand and award cumulative damages.[33] However, as the competence of state courts cannot extend beyond the limits of their territorial jurisdiction, they will not be able to hear cases against debt collectors from another state. In such cases, the jurisdiction will belong naturally to federal courts.[34]

The act also provides with respect to class actions stating that in case one is brought within a single state it may be exempted from the FDCPA's requirements when the abusive practices are also subjected to a substantially similar law.[35] But even in the case of such state exemption, the federal jurisdiction cannot be fully set aside and the debtor shall keep both his statutory claim arising in that state and the remedies provided by the FDCPA's civil liability section, which was eliminated by the abovementioned exemption.[36]

To conclude, the act enables the consumer to seek statutory remedies in any convenient forum, under both state and federal debt collection laws, whichever suits him best. But at the same time, the consumer can never wave under state law his right to pursue the federal remedies authorized by the FDCPA.

7.1.1.2 Civil Liability and Incentives Under UK Law

Unlike the system put into practice by the FDCPA, the one available in the UK allows only for administrative enforcement.[37] Thus, it may be said that although

---

[33] The case law confirmed that damages can be awarded cumulatively under both federal and state laws. In *Gonzales v. Arrow Financial Services, LLC*, 660 F 3d 1055 (9th Cir. 2011), the court reasoned as follows: "The FDCPA explicitly states that it "does not annul, alter, or affect, or exempt any person subject to the provisions of this subchapter from complying with the laws of any State"... a State law is not inconsistent with this subchapter if the protection such law affords any consumer is greater than the protection provided by this subchapter." The court found this language, coupled with the FDCPA's express purpose to "promote consistent State action," as well as deter violations, established that Congress did not intend the FDCPA to preempt consistent state consumer protection laws. Next the court showed that the Rosenthal Act also contemplated dual enforcement: its language states that it should be "cumulative and...in addition to any other... remedies under any other provisions of the law." For details see Journal of Consumer & Commercial Law, Spring, 2012, *71 Debt Collection, 15 JCCOML 71.

[34] One author mentions though that some state courts could retain cases against out-of-state debt collectors on the basis of "minimum contacts" doctrine. See footnote 148 in Potach (1978), p. 920.

[35] FDCPA, 15 USC 1692 (Section 817).

[36] For Potach (1978), p. 921.

[37] None of the UK regulations or statutes related to consumer protection against unfair debt-collecting practices offers the possibility for a civil action or private enforcement system (with incentives and statutory damages) like their American counterparts. Aggrieved debtors can bring action in court based on tort law, but as the latter would go beyond the purposes of this work, it will not go into any details thereof. The current FCA regulation concerning disputes related to abusive debt collection practices is "Dispute Resolution: Complaints" (DISP), which was enacted in September 2014 and covers the powers and responsibilities of the Financial Ombudsman Service (FOS).

updated in terms of abusive practices that may be employed nowadays against debtors, the UK regulation remains far behind the US one by failing to allow and set into practice the possibility for a private enforcement system, similar to the one implemented by the FDCPA. What is even worse is that UK consumers are not even allowed to directly send complaints to the administrative bodies (former OFT, the current FCA or the Financial Ombudsman Service (FOS)). First, they must try to resolve the issue amicably with the creditor/debt collector.[38] Only after are they allowed to either apply to a Consumer Protection Association, which may act as an intermediary in the relationship with the state authority, or, respectively, file a complaint with the Ombudsman, as part of an alternative dispute resolution scheme designed for consumer-credit-related complaints.[39] Therefore, the entire procedure is cumbersome and time consuming, with results that might not make it worthwhile, which is one of the reasons why the US decided to implement a private enforcement system, together with a long tradition and experience gathered in areas such as competition and security laws.

7.1.1.3 Civil Liability and Incentives Under the Proposed Romanian Law

In Romania, in the absence of a special law sanctioning abusing debt collection practices it is clear that there will not be any remedies against such practices either, besides those offered by general tort law or criminal law (in case of actions that would qualify as criminal offenses). Moreover, even if the proposed project would have passed the Parliament's vote, the remedies would have been problematic.

The position adopted by the proposed law was one very concise and lacking any kind of specificity. It simply stated that failure to comply with the provisions of the law will attract disciplinary, misdemeanor (contravention) or criminal liability.[40] The National Authority for Consumer Protection (NACP) would have been empowered to supervise the activity conducted under the law against natural person debtors.[41]

Such provision could not have qualified as a proper remedy against the abuses listed. *First* of all, it provided for no right to private action, despite the fact that the FDCPA was taken as a model, leaving it all for the administrative enforcement, but without any specific criteria to determine the penalties that could have been imposed by the NACP. *Second* of all, there were no procedural or monetary incentives provided for aggrieved consumer-debtors to take action on their own.

[38] http://www.financial-ombudsman.org.uk/publications/consumer-leaflet.htm, last visited 23.01.2015.

[39] http://www.financial-ombudsman.org.uk/consumer/complaints.htm, last 23.01.2015.

[40] Project Law, Chapter V, Art 12.

[41] Project Law, Chapter VI, Art 14.

Probably, in the absence of private causes of actions, the Romanian legislator saw no reason for incentives either.

7.1.2 Administrative Enforcement

Administrative enforcement is an alternative to private enforcement, and it is the solution favored by most of the chosen jurisdictions. However, as the following discussion concerning the US will show, administrative enforcement does not necessarily exclude private enforcement. Their effects are rather complementary, which is why an efficient abusive debt collection practices act should consider including them both.

7.1.2.1 Administrative Enforcement Under the FDCPA

The FDCPA also contains provisions that allow the Federal Trade Commission (FTC) to enforce compliance with the provisions of the act, unless the enforcement of the legal requirement actually falls within the competence of another agency. All powers granted to the Commission by its functioning law are extended by means of the FDCPA to aforementioned enforcement.[42] Interestingly, the Commission is empowered to enforce compliance against any person in violation of the act, irrespective of whether that person is engaged in commerce or corresponds to other jurisdictional tests provided by the Federal Trade Commission Act.[43] The interesting aspect is the fact that, unlike governmental agencies in the UK, for example, the FTC is acting for the benefit of private citizens. No distinction is legally done; thus, the FTC will be able to act in full force.

The purpose of doubling private action with the possibility of seeking administrative enforcement lied with the fact that the Commission was interested in detecting patterns of wrongdoing that could lead to investigations and prosecutions.[44] As the main concerns are the patterns leading to abuses, the FTC does not deal with individual complaints.[45]

However, similar to what the UK is trying to achieve, the FTC is also concerned with providing consumers with better information and educate them about their rights. To ease access to the Commission and in order to facilitate the collection of information, the current website of the Commission is available in both English and

[42] "Because certain practices that violate the FDCPA also violate the FTC Act, the FTC also uses the FTC Act to halt unfair or deceptive debt collection practices." See http://www.ftc.gov/opa/reporter/finance/debtcollection.shtml, last visited 23.01.2015.

[43] FDCPA, 15 USC 1692 (Section 814) (a).

[44] https://www.ftccomplaintassistant.gov/, last visited 23.01.2015.

[45] https://www.ftccomplaintassistant.gov/, last visited 23.01.2015.

Spanish,[46] and those interested in filing a complaint can do that by simply filling up an electronic form specially designed for such purpose.[47]

The powers granted to the FTC in the field of fair debt collection practices proved to be a successful endeavor, as according to the most recent information the "debt collectors generate more complaints to the FTC than any other industry."[48] According to the Commission's website, the FTC has sued over 30 debt collection companies for violating the law, banned some of them from business and made them pay high fines.[49] For example, during 2013 only,[50] the FTC reached a settlement with a debt collector that agreed to stop deceiving consumers and paid nearly 800,000 dollars;[51] shut down a debt collection agency, by additionally freezing all its assets, banning the defendants from engaging in debt collection;[52] and also managed to impose, in another settlement, the largest penalty ever levied on a debt collector, over 3.2 million dollars,[53] after which in 2012 they were able to impose one of over 2 million dollars.[54]

One of the problems that existed with respect to the FTC's powers granted by the FDCPA was the inability to promulgate trade or other regulations in relation to the

---

[46] http://www.consumidor.ftc.gov/, last visited 23.01.2015.

[47] https://www.ftccomplaintassistant.gov/FTC_Wizard.aspx?Lang=en, last visited 23.01.2015.

[48] http://www.ftc.gov/opa/reporter/finance/debtcollection.shtml, last visited 23.01.2015. According to another source, in 2010 complaints jumped over 140,036, the number representing 11 % of all complaints in the commission's database. http://www.nytimes.com/2012/01/31/business/ftc-fines-a-collector-of-debt-2-5-million.html?_r=0, last visited 23.01.2015. Similar information at Hector (2011), p. 1609 and Akina (2012), p. 150. The latter notices a large range of categories but underlines the absence of one to focus explicitly on misrepresentations made to consumers.

[49] http://www.ftc.gov/news-events/media-resources/consumer-finance/debt-collection, last visited 23.01.2015.

[50] For a list of recent cases solved in the recent year: http://www.ftc.gov/opa/2013/02/cfpb.shtm, last visited 23.01.2015.

[51] The complaint referred to alleged misleading practices, which included leading consumers into paying unnecessary fees and falsely threatening them with lawsuits. For details: http://www.ftc.gov/opa/2013/03/securitycredit.shtm, last visited 23.01.2015.

[52] The complaint referred to an operation that allegedly used insults, lies and false threats to collect on payday loans. For details: http://www.ftc.gov/opa/2013/01/goldman.shtm, last visited on 23.01.2015.

[53] The complaint regarded the harassment of consumers and alleged illegal debt collection calls. Basically, the debt collector engaged in calling consumers multiple times per day, calling even after they were asked to stop, at inappropriate times, either early in the morning or late at night, or at consumers' workplaces knowing the employer prohibited such calls. In addition, phone messages were left, disclosing the debtor's name and the existence of the debt to third parties. Last but not least, the company continued collection efforts without verifying the debt, even after consumers disputed the existence of the debt. http://www.ftc.gov/news-events/press-releases/2013/07/worlds-largest-debt-collection-operation-settles-ftc-charges-will last visited 20.09.2014.

[54] The complaint referred to harassment of consumers for money they were not even legally obligated to pay. For details: http://www.nytimes.com/2012/01/31/business/ftc-fines-a-collector-of-debt-2-5-million.html?_r=0, last visited 23.01.2015.

collection of debts by debt collectors.[55] Subjected to a lot of criticism during the years, the problem was solved by the Dodd–Frank Act, which created the Bureau of Consumer Financial Protection (BCFP)[56] and established rule-making powers, including the area of debt collection.[57] Alongside, the Bureau shares now with the FTC[58] the monitoring of the activity of debt collectors.[59] Though it may be too soon to say whether the reform has improved the administrative enforcement effort of the FTC under the FDCPA, it can be reasonably inferred that establishing a new public body with attributes in the field can only be beneficial to the act's purpose.

7.1.2.2 Administrative Enforcement Under UK Law

As mentioned already, the UK allows only for administrative enforcement. Based on the powers granted to it by the Consumer Credit Act 1974 (amended in 2006), the OFT, and now the FCA, required businesses involved in the recovery of debt arising from regulated consumer credit or consumer hire agreements to take all necessary steps to ensure compliance with the former Guidance and the current CONC, and provide proof thereof, under the sanction of being subjected to enforcement actions from OFT's, respectively FCA's, side. Action can be brought upon

[55] FDCPA, 15 USC 1692 (Section 814) (d).

[56] Title X of the Dodd-Frank Act, available online at: http://www.sec.gov/about/laws/wallstreetreform-cpa.pdf, last visited 23.01.2015.

[57] Hector (2011). For a list of regulations adopted by the BCFP, including debt collection, see: http://www.consumerfinance.gov/regulations/, last visited 23.01.2015. Also Akina (2012), pp. 163–164. "[t]he Dodd-Frank Act transferred enforcement and regulatory powers over the FDCPA from the FTC to the BFCP. [. . .] The significance is two-fold. First, the BCFP is a specialized office that represents a consolidation of consumer financial protection authorities that had been originally scattered across several federal agencies. Second, the BFCP has rulemaking authority over federal consumer financial laws, which must be given deferential treatment by the courts."

[58] In 2011, the FTC and CFPB signed a Memorandum of Understanding aiming to prevent duplication of efforts, provide consistency and ensure a vibrant marketplace for financial products or services. In March 2012, the CFPB made a public announcement regarding the sharing of the complaints it received with the FTC's own database. For details, see: Dempsey (2013), p. 34.

[59] http://protectyourfuture.com/consumer-financial-protection-bureau/, last visited 23.01.2015. The reasons for the need of such additional monitoring are the following: "As the economy soured, more people fell behind in paying bills and confronted a diminished ability to repay once the debts moved to collection. That left companies more desperate to recoup losses and led some collectors to be more aggressive in pushing consumers to pay up on a range of debts, including student loan, credit cards, and medical bills. The CFPB said 30 million Americans are currently pursued by debt collectors, for an average debt of 1500 dollars. The bureau estimates that 63 % of the market will fall under its watch." For details, see: Karen Weise—Debt Collectors Face a New Watchdog, BusinessWeek.com, 10/25/2012, available online at: http://www.businessweek.com/articles/2012-10-24/debt-collectors-have-a-new-watchdog, last visited 23.01.2015.

complaints brought by consumer advisors or third party organizations, but investigations are conducted on the FCA's own initiative as well.[60]

The OFT established three principles that would govern enforcement actions, namely, fairness, effectiveness and proportionality.[61] However, the FCA's Enforcement Guide (EG)[62] added to these the principle of open cooperation with those it regulates, the principle of transparent enforcement and the principle of deterrence from illegal conduct.[63] Assessment is to be made by judging each individual case,[64] taking into account factors such as actual and potential harm, scale of frequency and the statutory requirements in force at the time of conduct's occurrence.[65] As result of the assessment, two outcomes are possible: FCA can either require change in conduct or, in serious cases, where the person is deemed unfit to hold a license, it can refuse or revoke the license.[66] Change of conduct can be accomplished by a series of "tools" available to the OFT: a first stage will consist in imposing certain requirements, and only in case of failure to implement them will it resort to financial penalties,[67] which could go as high as 20 % of the relevant revenue.[68] Considering that under the former Guidance a penalty could not go higher than 50,000 £ per breach,[69] the current regulation is obviously a step forward, since the percentage allows for higher penalties, depending on the relevant revenues. However, compared with the million-dollar fines imposed by the FTC, the penalties imposed by FCA can hardly have a similar deterrent effect, especially on big businesses.

Starting with the modifications brought in 2006 to the Consumer Credit Act 1974, a much more important role in the dispute resolution of consumer complaints was assumed by the FOS. Thus, the FOS deals now with complaints about most consumer credit activities, including those dealing with the activities of debt collectors.[70]

---

[60] http://webarchive.nationalarchives.gov.uk/20140402142426/http://www.oft.gov.uk/OFTwork/credit/enforcement-action/ and http://www.fca.org.uk/firms/being-regulated/enforcement, last visited 23.01.2015.

[61] Section 4.8 of the Guidance.

[62] Adopted at 1st of April 2014, available online at: http://media.fshandbook.info/Handbook/EG_FCA_20140401.pdf, last visited 19.12.2014.

[63] EG, Section 2.2.

[64] EG, Section 2.5 (2).

[65] EG, Section 2.10.

[66] EG, Sections 1.1. and 2.35.

[67] EG, Chapter 7 and Chapter 6 of the Procedure (Section 6.5 especially on Determining the Appropriate Level of Financial Penalty).

[68] Section 6.5A.2. (3) of the Procedure.

[69] Section 4.10 of the Guidance. Also: Burridge (2010).

[70] http://www.legislation.gov.uk/ukpga/2006/14/section/59, last visited 09.09.2014. The text reads as follows: 226A (1) "A complaint which relates to an act or omission of a person ("the respondent" is to be dealt with under the ombudsman scheme if the conditions mentioned in subsection (2) are satisfied." Among the conditions specified in subsection (2) of relevance is the one at letter d) "the act or omission occurred in the course of a business being carried on by the respondent which was of a type mentioned in subsection (3)." In its turn, the relevant provision of subsection 3, mentions at letter f) "a business so far as it comprises or relates to debt collecting."

Similarly to cases dealt with directly by the OFT, cases solved by the FOS are subjected to the principles of fairness and reasonableness, as provided in the dispute resolution procedure established by the Financial Conduct Authority's Handbook with respect to complaints.[71] The procedure contains two main phases: the first one is mandatory and takes place prior to the actual application to the FOS solely between the consumer and the business involved (either initial creditor or a third party debt collector). The second one is facultative, and, besides the consumer and the respondent business, it also involves the FOS.

An aggrieved consumer is thus obliged to first try to solve the issue directly with the respondent business. Once a complaint has been received, the respondent has to investigate it; assess it on its merits in a fair, consistent and prompt manner; offer redress or remedial action when appropriate; motivate its decision; and comply with any offer of remedial action or redress accepted by the consumer.[72] A final response must be given in writing to the consumer within 8 weeks from the moment the complaint was received or, alternatively, if a final answer cannot be provided in the statutory 8 weeks, a written response that it should explain why the 8 weeks is not enough and inform the consumer that in this case it can address the FOS immediately.[73] In case a final response is issued, it should resolve the complaint in one of the three manners described by the DISP accepting the complaint and offering redress, offering redress without accepting the complaint or rejecting the complaint. Either way, it should specify that the consumer is free to address the FOS in 6 months from the receipt of the final response.[74]

In case the consumer is unsatisfied with the final response given or is provided with a written response that he is allowed to address the FOS immediately or if he doesn't receive any answer and more than 8 weeks has passed since he filed the complaint with the responding business, then he will be allowed to address the FOS.[75]

But the FOS will not simply analyze the complaint received. According to its procedural rules, it will first verify whether it has substantial[76] and territorial[77] jurisdiction over the consumer and the respondent. If jurisdiction is established, then the FOS will analyze if the complainant is eligible, (meaning if he qualifies as a consumer, micro-enterprise or other legal category),[78] if the

[71] http://media.fshandbook.info/content/FCA/DISP.pdf, last visited, 09.09.2014.

[72] Section 1.4.1 of the FCA's Dispute Resolution: Complaints (DISP), available online at http://media.fshandbook.info/content/FCA/DISP.pdf, last visited 09.09.2014.

[73] DISP, Section 1.6.2 (1) and (2).

[74] DISP, Section 1.6.2 (1) (a)–(e).

[75] DISP, Section 1.6.2 corroborated with 2.8.1 and 2.8.2.

[76] DISP, Section 2.1.1 (2) corroborated with 2.4.1 (1) and (2).

[77] DISP, Section 2.6.3.

[78] DISP, Sections 2.7.1–2.7.3.

complaint is relevant to one or more relationships with the respondent[79] and whether it was referred on time.[80]

If the FOS decides that the complaint is eligible, it has several possibilities. The **first** one is to dismiss it without consideration of the merits, in a motivated written decision.[81] The grounds for such a dismissal are specifically provided by the law and reveal major differences with the situation in the US. Hence, the FOS will dismiss the complaint if the complainant has not suffered any financial loss, material distress or material inconvenience, while in the US no actual loss is required to engage the liability of the debt collector. The FOS will also dismiss the complaint if it is frivolous or vexatious, while in the US, the FDCPA allows its remedies, no matter how small is the damage incurred by the consumer. The same solution will be rendered in case the complaint is obviously lacking any chance of success or the respondent has made an offer of compensation that is deemed as fair, reasonable and still open for acceptance. Since the UK regulatory system is more concerned about the effects on the market, minor abuses seem to be overlooked, tolerated, as long as no actual substantial damage occurred, which in the US would go against the very idea of implementing measures against abusive practices. Under the FDCPA, abuse is abuse, no matter its results.

The complaint will be dismissed if the subject matter of the complaint has been the subject of court proceedings where there has been a decision on the merits or the subject matter of the complaint is the subject of current court proceedings, unless the proceedings have been stayed or suspended in order to have the matter considered by the FOS,[82] which again is a major difference from the US, where the consumer is entitled to multiple venues to incentivize him to take private action. But in the UK, the elective remedies doctrine still functions and no procedural incentives are given. The list includes 17 grounds for dismissal, and the one striking characteristic is the large discretion enjoyed by the FOS in determining which cases can be heard on the merits.

Similar large discretion can be found also in what concerns the determination of the complaint. The Ombudsman is allowed to solve it by reference to what is, in his

[79] DISP, Section 2.7.6 (12) a), which is relevant to debt collection, reads as follows: "the complainant is a person from whom the respondent has sought to recover payment under a regulated consumer credit agreement or regulated hire agreement (whether or not the respondent is a party to the agreement." Any other collection attempts related to bills, rents, trade debts or council taxes will not be covered by the FOS scheme.

[80] DISP, Section 2.8.2. According to the legal provision, the complaint must be referred to the FOS "within 6 months after the date on which the respondent sent the complainant its final response or redress determination or, within either 6 years after the event complained of, or, if later, 3 years from the date on which the complainant became aware (or should have become aware) the he had cause for complaint." The text establishes 3 exceptional situations from the abovementioned rules: in case the delay was the result of exceptional circumstances; the FOS is required to look at the complaint according to its own Transitional Order; or the respondent has not objected on grounds of time limits.

[81] DISP, Sections 3.3.1 and 3.3.2.

[82] DISP, Section 3.3.4. (1)–(4), (9) and (10).

opinion, fair and reasonable in all the circumstances of the case.[83] The determination is not purely discretionary though as the Ombudsman is obliged to take into account, on the one side, the relevant laws, regulations, regulator's rules, guidance and standards and codes of practice and, on the other side, what he considers to have been good industry practice at the relevant time.[84]

Once determination is made, the parties must be provided with a written, motivated statement of it, which will become final and binding provided the complainant accepts it within the specified time.[85] Where the determination was made in favor of the consumer, the Ombudsman may include one or more of the following:[86] a money award (which would include compensation for financial loss (consequential or prospective) or pain and suffering or damage to reputation or distress and inconvenience),[87] an interest award, a costs award (consisting in an amount considered fair to cover some or all the costs reasonably incurred by the complainant in respect of the complaint, plus interest)[88] or a direction to the respondent.[89] The maximum money award, without interest or costs, cannot be, by law, higher than 150,000 £.[90] But in reality, according to the FOS's technical note on Distress and Inconvenience,[91] most compensations will vary between 50£ and 350£,[92] and only in a number of exceptional cases awards would it go beyond

[83] DISP, Section 3.6.1.

[84] DISP, Section 3.6.4 (1) and (2).

[85] DISP, Section 3.6.6 (1)–(3).

[86] DISP, Section 3.7.1.

[87] DISP, Section 3.7.2. For what is meant by "distress," "inconvenience" or "pain and suffering" in the FOS's view, see FOS, *Technical Notes: Distress and Inconvenience*, *available at* http://www.financial-ombudsman.org.uk/publications/technical_notes/distress-and-inconvenience.htm.

[88] DISP, Section 3.7.9.

[89] DISP, Section 3.7.11. Also: FOS) "For example, we will sometimes tell the financial business to make an apology or to provide the consumer with an appropriate service which relates to the original problem."

[90] DISP, Section 3.7.4. If the fair compensation exceeds the statutory maximum amount allowed, the FOS may "recommend" the business to pay the difference as well, but judging from the language used, such recommendation might not be enforceable. See FOS, *Technical Note: Compensation*, *available at* http://www.financial-ombudsman.org.uk/publications/technical_notes/compensation.html.

[91] For a detailed list of compensations awarded based on real-life cases, see FOS) Also: FOS (2011). "Where the degree of distress, inconvenience or other non-financial loss is sufficient to warrant compensation, the amount is generally likely to be modest. Most compensation is for less than 300£ and in only a small number of exceptional cases does it exceed 1000 £. Cases involving pain and suffering are likely to lead to higher compensation than those involving distress and inconvenience."

[92] Extracting from a list of cases that were decided in 2014, the plaintiffs received the following amounts as "fair and reasonable" for their inconveniences: in case DRN 8005761, concerning the collection attempt of a debt without providing the statutory information on the debt's validation, the complainant received "50 pounds for her distress and inconvenience"; in case DRN 9452119, concerning the sale of a debt to two different debt collectors, which resulted in overpayment of the debt, the complainant received "199,12 pounds reimbursement, plus interest of 10, 57 pounds, and

1,000£.[93] Compared to the 1,000 dollars of statutory penalty per breach committed, the scheme proposed by FOS cannot have a real deterring effect on aggrieving businesses. The satisfaction given to consumers is more symbolic than pecuniary.

The FOS alternative dispute resolution scheme is optional, and although similar to court proceedings it is less formal. Its purpose is mainly to put the consumer back in the position in which he would have been if the original problem that led to the complaint had not emerged. Despite its good intentions and being cheap (there are no costs or fees), this alternative dispute resolution system can hardly compete when it comes to efficiency with the private enforcement system implemented by the FDCPA.

7.1.2.3 Administrative Enforcement Under French and German Laws

In France, remedies against debt collectors' breach of their legal obligations are purely administrative and consist of financial penalties. The decree clearly states that noncompliance will be treated as a 5th degree offense, which is the harshest in the French system, including the provisions related to recidivism.[94] The noncompliance sanctioned by the Code refers either to failure to comply with the obligations related to maintaining a professional insurance and a separated account for all recoveries or to any omissions of the mandatory terms of the standard recovery letter.[95] The prosecutors have legal mandate to investigate compliance

a compensation of 300 pounds, together with a written apology"; in a similar case, DRN 5382333, where a bank sold a debt that it previously agreed to write off, which resulted in collection attempts, the complainant received "50 pounds compensation"; in case DRN 9172974, concerning the sale of a debt to a third party, resulting in overstated amounts without proper explanation or documentation, the complainant was "100 pounds compensation"; in case DRN 7783037, where the debt collector wrongfully pursued a consumer for a debt that was not his, the amount of the compensation was 325 pounds; in case DRN 5919254, where the complainant who filed for bankruptcy was still being harassed by the debt collector, the interest and charges to the debt were removed, while the compensation for "distress and inconvenience" was 50 pounds; and in case DRN 7975535, where excessive interest and charges were applied to the account of the consumer, without proper explanation or documentation, the only "compensation" was the removal of the excessive charges.

[93] See case DRN 2396014, where a consumer was pursued for a debt that was not his and the debt collector placed a charging order on his property. The FOS decided to award the complainant 1,000 pounds, plus 8 % interest per year, for the costs he incurred and 250 pounds for the "distress and inconvenience."

[94] 783 (2012), Art. R. 124-7. In French original: "Est puni de l'amende prévue par le 5° de l'article 131-13 du code pénal pour les contraventions de la cinquième classe le fait pour toute personne exerçant l'activité mentionnée à l'article R. 124-1 de: 1° Ne pas se conformer aux obligations prévues à l'article R. 124-2 ; 2° Omettre l'une des mentions prévues à l'article R. 124-4 dans la lettre adressée au débiteur. En cas de récidive, la peine d'amende prévue au même alinéa pour la récidive des contraventions de la cinquième classe est applicable."

[95] 783 (2012), Art. R. 124-7.

at any time,[96] and in the absence of any other specification it may be inferred that they could start an investigation upon a request or complaint from an aggrieved debtor. The fines will vary between 1,500 € and 3,000 € for each subsequent offense when the law so provides.

In Germany, noncompliance with the requirements of RDG would also attract administrative enforcement, consisting in fines. However, the highest amount is 50,000 € and none of these fines would be imposed for actual abusive practices, for the German act covers none.

7.1.2.4 Administrative Enforcement Under the Proposed Romanian Law

In Romania, as mentioned in the previous section, the adopted position was concise and lacking specificity. It merely stated that failure to comply with the provisions of the law will attract disciplinary, misdemeanor or criminal liability.[97] The National Authority for Consumer Protection (NACP) would have been empowered to supervise the activity conducted under the law against natural person debtors,[98] which basically meant administrative enforcement.

Additionally, the project provided for disciplinary liability, which, based on the provisions of the Labor Code, was a purely internal procedure of the debt collector's employer, governed by the provisions of the labor law. But in order to establish the nature of the disciplinary digression, a Code of Good Practices must have been in place with the collector or special provisions thereof should have been inserted in the Labor Code, to make disciplinary liability really possible. Criminal liability would have been an option only in case of a criminal offense, which was the case anyway, even in the absence of a special law regulating debt collection. Last but not least, from the wording of the law it was not really clear if the three types of liabilities mentioned could have gone together, at the same time (where possible), or whether they were only alternative.

Therefore, one can conclude that, although it would have been a step forward in identifying and labeling abusive practices as unlawful, the draft law would have brought no actual improvement in the status of the aggrieved debtor. It gave him with no real power, and it granted him no real remedy. In the absence of remedies and actual enforcement mechanisms, the purpose of regulating abusive practices is simply lacking.

---

[96] 783 (2012), See Art. R. 124-2. In French original: "La justification des conditions requises aux alinéas précédents est assurée par déclaration écrite des intéressés, remise ou adressée, avant tout exercice de l'activité, au procureur de la République près le tribunal de grande instance dans le ressort duquel ils ont le siège de leurs activités. A tout moment, le procureur de la République peut vérifier que les intéressés se conforment aux obligations prescrites par le présent article."

[97] Project Law, Chapter V, Art 12.

[98] Project Law, Chapter VI, Art 14.

7.2 Need for Reform

Despite the efficient enforcement mechanisms, none of the systems above is perfect. The FDCPA is old and outdated, since it was adopted in a time when the Internet and the mobile phones or other similar technological developments did not exist and were not considered. Moreover, the debt collectors proved to be extremely creative, always looking for new collection practices that could circumvent the FDCPA protections and many times succeeding to exploit the gaps and elude the provisions of the law. The UK regulations, despite being updated almost every year, suffer from lack of efficiency, an aspect proven by the ever-increasing number of complaints. Obviously, something is not working and there is room for improvement. France lacks detailed provisions and a proper enforcement mechanism, while Germany and Romania lag behind, although attempts of addressing the stringent issue of abusive debt collection are being made. The following sections address in more detail the reasons why there is a need for reform in the chosen jurisdictions.

7.2.1 Call for Reformation of the FDCPA

The Congress addressed the issue of collection abuse only in 1977, and although it provided some necessary relief to debtors, it became very soon a static legislation, the reason being that the intention behind the law was "only to remedy previous abusive behavior and not to prospectively adapt to a changing industry."[99] Many commentators, despite remarking the Congress's good intentions, have characterized the FDCPA as a "misdirected and poorly drafted statute,"[100] underlining the numerous ambiguities and the fact that courts have failed to interpret the statute in a predictable manner.[101] Other criticism included a failure in creating enough consumer awareness and that even if aware they are unlikely to bring a lawsuit either because it is cheaper to pay the debt than to litigate, they risk having the trial dismissed for being brought in bad faith (which would hold them liable for debt collector's attorney fees and costs) and debt collectors can easily escape liability by showing that the violations were unintentional or were not preventable in an easy manner.[102]

The biggest flaw of the FDCPA seems to be the fact that it is static.[103] In order to have a successful law regime, legislatures need to ensure that the statute they are

[99] Goldberg (2006), p. 718.

[100] Mike Vorhees, cited by Goldberg (2006), p. 723.

[101] Goldberg (2006), p. 723.

[102] For details, see: Goldberg (2006), p. 723.

[103] "Much of the problem lies in the failure to update the Fair Debt Collection Practices Act (FDCPA). Despite the dramatic transformation of the debt collection industry over the last thirty years, the statute has remained largely backward looking [. . .]." See Hector (2011), p. 1601.

implementing is open-ended and well drafted to anticipate and cover future behavior. It is why this work argued that open-ended definitions are one of the building blocks of an effective antiabusive debt collection law. Contrary to such demands, the FDCPA is obviously written to correct only specific issues and thus failed to adapt to changes or to address more subtle forms of disobeying the law. The result was that the debt collection industry learned to adapt to and circumvent the FDCPA by resorting to new abusive ways of getting money from the debtors.[104] As the case law faced difficulties in finding coverage in the old law for these new methods, the necessity of amending the FDCPA became even more stringent.[105]

In the following lines, the book looks into and summarizes some of the most employed tactics by the debt collection agencies in the US in order to circumvent the legal protections offered to debtors. In this way, the weaknesses of the FDCPA are more easily revealed and understood. Where possible, their analysis also refers to suggested solutions by the doctrine or by the case law.

7.2.1.1 Outsourcing Debt Collection Overseas

Upon FDCPA's ban of harassment techniques in order to obtain payment or information, the most obvious solution was to farm out such services to companies that could escape jurisdiction in case of complaint. Thus, the debt collection industry has outsourced or moved called centers to India, Mexico or the Philippines.[106] There are many reasons and advantages: low costs, better returns on capital, lower risk, more flexibility, possibility to employ personnel speaking two or more languages, longer work time, possibility to hire more agents for same costs and increased recovery rate.[107]

But such industry gains come with a price, which is paid by the consumer. Outsourcing implies sending the databases containing debtors' information[108] to other countries, which seriously compromises debtor's privacy rights, especially if those countries do not have laws to protect the debtor's personal information as strictly as the FDCPA does. If one takes into consideration that debtor's privacy rights represent one of the main areas of protection and concern for the FDCPA, it

[104] Goldberg (2006), p. 724.

[105] The need was recognized by the FTC as well, which concluded in its 2009 report that "[t]o provide more certainty to the industry and to protect consumers from harm . . . debt collection law needs to be modernized to take account of today's new communication technologies." See FTC (2009), pt. 1–72; FTC (2009), p. 36.

[106] See Goldberg (2006), p. 731.

[107] Goldberg (2006), pp. 731–732.

[108] Goldberg (2006), p. 732. Usually, these databases include names, addresses, social security numbers and sometimes complete credit histories, which entails that third parties in third countries gain full access to personal information while at the same time escape fully the protective requirements of federal or state laws, which obviously places consumers at huge risk.

becomes evident that by outsourcing debt collectors are able to bypass such protection completely.[109]

The second problem lies with the fact that foreign operators do not only escape the requirements of US laws but may even escape the control of the debt-collecting agencies that employed them, especially if they are not fully owned subsidiaries by separate and independent third parties. Loss of control may pose different threats as such third parties might be driven by the sole desire of increasing profits and retain jobs by reverting to any means possible in order to recover the debts. In such case, debtors might find themselves in the situation of not having any recourse against the foreign collectors, as the FDCPA only allows them to file an action against the debt collector's company. The changing jurisdiction, the high costs that might be employed and the lack of incentives similar with those offered by the FDCPA most likely dissuade debtors from acting against foreign companies, which leads again to the conclusion that such farm-outs enable American companies to escape liability while at the same time foreign companies are free to resort to the abusive and harassing tactics that the FDCPA was actually designed to stop.[110]

Several solutions were suggested to address this issue, although it would be hard to tell which one would be the most effective:[111] banning US companies from outsourcing any services that require passing personal information, limit outsourcing transactions only to countries where reciprocal privacy laws exist, extending the definition of "debt collector" to include foreign agents,[112] prohibiting the sale of databases to overseas companies and replacing it with a lease agreement that would make foreign collectors subcontractors under the law, thus making the US companies liable for any breach of law committed by the overseas companies,[113] a solution close to the one adopted by the UK CONC.[114]

---

[109] Goldberg (2006), p. 732.

[110] Goldberg (2006), pp. 733–734.

[111] For a more detailed discussion of solutions to be employed against outsourcing, see: Goldberg (2006), pp. 734–736.

[112] Such solutions do not resolve the issue of jurisdiction over foreign operators. See Goldberg (2006), p. 735.

[113] Such solution presents itself with multiple advantages: debtors would have an adequate recourse in the US, American companies would be forced to act more cautiously when outsourcing information or when picking up an overseas companies and they would shift the burden of suing overseas to the debt collector. Of course, such a solution would require that the American companies would be held strictly liable, through penalties, for all misconduct related to the use of private data. See Goldberg (2006), p. 736. In practice, it seems to be the solution adopted by the FTC as well. In a case settled in 2012, in which a California citizen was charged of having worked with bogus debt collectors in India, he was charged, among others, for harassing and threatening consumers who, as a result, paid the alleged debts out of fear of being sued or arrested. Consumers have received millions of collection calls from India in a 2-year period, in an operation that made more than 5 million dollars from the victims and resulted in no less than 4,000 complaints to the FTC and the state attorneys general. See: www.ftc.gov/news-events/press-releases/2012/10/us-defendats/who/allegedly-abetted-fake-debt-collector-calls last visited 23.01.2015.

[114] CONC, Section 7.1.3.

7.2.1.2 Targeting Weaker Consumers for Collection

Debt collectors have been accused of implementing and using technology in order to target those consumers that are more likely to pay based on their personal payment or credit history, current employment or income, gender, age and level of education or sophistication.[115] Basically, those targeted are women[116] (considered more likely to pay than men, given that they accrue less savings and engage in more expenses), old individuals (considered easy to confuse, easy to scare and hesitant to engage in lawsuits), low-income individuals (as they are considered less able to engage in lawsuits and less likely to afford hiring an attorney) and less-sophisticated individuals (also considered easy to intimidate and confuse and also hesitant or unlikely to retain an attorney).[117]

If targeting individuals based on income could be justified by the fact that debt-collecting companies are ultimately interested in getting the highest return on their investment and thus it makes sense to direct their efforts in the direction of those who could actually repay the debts, targeting women and older people has little justification, as all delinquent debtors are equally culpable. The problem with the above is that the FDCPA does not expressly prohibit either sex, race or age discrimination, leaving the area totally open for abuse.[118]

Solutions suggested to solve the issue of discrimination include prohibition of any discrimination based on inherent characteristics (such as sex, race and age) or the insertion of a code of ethics in the FDCPA,[119] enactment of a new law preventing discrimination against debtors in connection with collection practices by allowing debtors to file complaints with the FTC[120] and requiring debt-buying companies to disclose raw statistics on the debtors they contact.[121]

---

[115] For details: Goldberg (2006), pp. 737–739.

[116] Women are also targeted in the case of payday loan borrowers. The typical target is a female, who makes around 25,000 dollars a year, is a renter and is more likely a member of a minority than the general population. See Consumer Federation of America (2007), p. 3.

[117] Goldberg (2006), pp. 738–739. See: Strike Debt (2014), p. 147. "Between January 2006 and July 2008 alone, the top twenty-six debt buyers won more than 1 billion in judgments against New York City residents – mostly from low-income communities and communities of color – and only about 1 % of those sued by creditors had legal counsel."

[118] Goldberg (2006), p. 739.

[119] This solution was criticized in its turn due to the fact that in order to sue, consumers should first know that they are victims of discrimination and targeting, which they have no way of knowing. See Goldberg (2006), p. 740.

[120] Under this proposed solution, only the FTC and not the consumer themselves would be able to file suit against debt collection companies for discrimination. See Goldberg (2006), p. 741.

[121] It is deemed that such disclosures would reveal and expose discriminatory patterns, which would enable the FTC to act upon its administrative enforcement powers. Despite that unscrupulous debt collectors could still manipulate the data they would provide, it is believed that increased transparency can only improve the system. See Goldberg (2006), p. 741.

7.2.1.3 Exploiting the Judicial System

As it was mentioned in Chap. 5, judicial collection became a very important tool in the hands of debt buyer companies,[122] which realized that there is a gap to be exploited between the protections offered by the FDCPA[123] in private collections and those offered in judicial collections.[124] For example, small-claim courts have less onerous pleading requirements, which allowed debt collectors to obtain unfair judgments against consumers,[125] without actually providing sufficient proofs. If the claim is not contested,[126] then debt collectors easily obtain a quick judgment against a debtor even when there is no legal merit in it[127] or when the debt was beyond the statute of limitations,[128] discharged in bankruptcy[129] or not owed.[130] At the same time, other recent studies have revealed that debt collectors are able to use the procedural norms of courts of general jurisdiction just as successful as they used small-claim courts.[131]

To increase the confusion even more, the courts could not agree with respect to misrepresentations and false representations performed in front of courts, in relationship to the collection of the debt. The situation refers to cases in which debt collectors have attempted to mislead the court by using as proof documents that appeared to be bank statements but in fact were not, and the contradictory solutions adopted by courts.[132] Thus, while the 6th Circuit adopted a broader interpretation

---

[122] "The growth of the debt buying industry has led to myriad problems, including increased use of the court system to collect the debts in these purchased portfolios. Using automated software, some debt collection agencies have become debt-collection-lawsuit mills, filing thousands of cookie-cutter lawsuits against consumers each month." See Terp (2011), p. 3.

[123] Fox (2012), p. 364 "Unfortunately the FDCPA was written at a time when most collection activity was non-judicial. It has not kept up with the changes in the practice of debt collection and is largely silent when it comes to litigation abuse." Also: The Commercial Law League of America (2007), pp. 21–22.

[124] *Supra* Chap. 5, Sect. 5.2.4.2.

[125] Terp (2011), p. 5.

[126] According to some reports, the vast majority of consumers—80–95 %—do not respond to collection lawsuits, many due to the fact that they receive no notice. See Terp (2011), p. 4.

[127] For details on how small-claim courts are exploited and provide unfair advantages to collectors, see Goldberg (2006), pp. 741–746 and Strike Debt (2014), pp. 146–147.

[128] Fox (2012), p. 384. "A summary judgment granted in error on, for example, a debt that is beyond the statute of limitation, has the effect of laundering the defect from that debt. The debt is now a judgment that can be collected for the next twenty years."

[129] Terp (2011), p. 5.

[130] Consumers alleged attempts to collect impermissible fees, interests or expenses not allowed under the FDCPA. See Terp (2011), p. 5.

[131] Fox (2012), p. 7.

[132] Akina (2012), pp. 152–153. The author mentions two recent cases—*Hartman v. Great Seneca Financial Group* (569 F. 3d606, 613 (6th Cir. 2009) and *O'Rourke v. Palisades Acquisition XVI*, (LLC, 635 F. 3d938, 943 (7th Cir. 2011)—in which the courts took different approaches in interpreting Section 1692e (Section 807) of the FDCPA.

and the opinion that statements made during litigation fall within the scope of Section 1692e,[133] the 7th Circuit took the opposite, narrower approach and held that although a "dubious method," the attempt of the debt collector to mislead the judge is not covered by the wording of Section 1692e.[134] As differences in the interpretation of the FDCPA can benefit neither debtors nor debt collectors, such situations require a legislative solution:[135] "In keeping in line with the FDCPA's purpose of protecting consumers from any misleading representations made in course of collecting a debt, direct and indirect communication would appear equally important."[136]

FDCPA offers no recourse to those debtors who become the victims of unfair judgments issued without sufficient proof. As a solution, it was suggested[137] that the FDCPA should be amended to require debt collectors to deliver to debtors booklets containing information about the functioning of small-claim courts, and their procedures, with an emphasis of the debtor's rights. On the other hand, some states took a different approach and simply banned the debt collectors from taking advantage of the lax procedural requirements of small-claim courts by compelling them to bring actions in conventional courts.[138] Furthermore, some have asked the legislator to take measures to prevent the usage of the court system to turn unsubstantiated claims into default judgments by establishing minimum evidentiary standards to be met by debt collectors before they may obtain a default or a summary judgment in their favor.[139]

Most likely, the best solution would be to enact stricter and more specific pleading rules for stating a cause of action to recover debt in small-claim courts, by requiring debt collectors to provide detailed information about the debt and the

---

[133] Akina (2012), p. 152.

[134] Akina (2012), p. 153.

[135] For a larger discussion on why a broader approach should be adopted by the legislator, see Akina (2012), pp. 154–159. The author rightfully notices that the 6th Circuit took a logical step in recognizing that a consumer's decisions may be affected even after litigation was started. "A consumer is constantly evaluating what decisions to make once a debt collector begins collection attempts. [..] After litigation commences, the consumer must then consider whether she should continue fighting the case or whether she should settle. These later considerations are affected by the perceived strength of the debt collector's case, and if a misleading document that resembles the consumer's outstanding credit card statement attached to the debt collector's complaint, then that may indirectly cause the debt collector's case to appear stronger than in reality." It results that despite the fact that the misleading representation was reaching the debtor only indirectly, it affected him nonetheless.

[136] Akina (2012), p. 159.

[137] The purpose of such amendment is to increase knowledge and awareness, though it is doubtful that such measures would suffice.

[138] Goldberg (2006), pp. 747–748. With respect to the solution adopted by the states, the author takes the view that it would be too harsh to impose a similar ban at federal level because it would infringe the states' autonomy in choosing whether they want to follow this approach or not. Also: Fox (2012), p. 6.

[139] Terp (2011), p. 15.

debtors.[140] In other words, the industry should be forced to fill the holes in its own data by performing a proper account research before filing a suit,[141] in the same way they are obliged to do in case of nonjudicial collection attempts. Such policy would definitely deter debt collectors from bringing suits they are not able to argue in a court of law while at the same time would compensate debtors for their wasted time and money.[142]

7.2.1.4 Collection or Revival of Old Debts

In Chap. 5, the book analyzed the way in which old debt and, especially, its revival became very important for the collection industry because it sells cheap and, if recovered, can generate large profits.[143] Chapter 5 also referred to some of the techniques employed by unscrupulous debt collectors in their attempt to revive such debt. And there are numerous cases in which such attempts are successful.[144]

The real frustration stems from the fact that debtors realize that there is no recourse against pursuing old debt in the FDCPA. The statute merely bans threat of litigation or actual litigation with respect to old debt[145] but otherwise allows debt collectors to follow up on bad debt; as such, debt is actually still valid for nonjudicial collection efforts,[146] at least from the perspective of federal law. Additional problems are created by the debtors' unawareness of these facts, which makes them extremely vulnerable to attempts of revival given that any

[140] "State law, federal law or rules, and court rules should be changed to require a person seeking to collect a debt in court submit basic validation information as part of the complaint. Providing this information up front should increase the likelihood that the amount sued for is the amount owed [...]." See Terp (2011), p. 13. Also see Akina (2012), p. 166. "The BFCP should make debt collection suits simpler by requiring that third party debt collectors procure and maintain all documents necessary to successfully bring a debt collection suit when purchasing debt from an original creditor."

[141] Goldberg (2006), p. 748.

[142] Terp (2011), p. 15.

[143] See *supra* Chap. 5, Sect. 5.3.

[144] For details, see: Goldberg (2006), pp. 749–750 and Strike Debt (2014), pp. 142–143.

[145] See *Huertas v. Galaxy*, in which, as a matter of first impression, the court decided that an FDCPA claim in this regard would require the defendant to have made, explicitly or implicitly, threats of litigation in order to qualify as a violation of the act. In the case at hand, the plaintiff brought action alleging violations of the FDCPA as the defendants sent him a letter regarding a time-barred debt. In deciding the case, the court explained that under New Jersey law, the plaintiff's debt obligation was not extinguished by the expiration of the statute of limitations, as he contended. Thus, although he had a complete legal defense against paying the debt, he still owed it as the statute of limitations merely made the debt unenforceable, without invalidating it. The court took the position though that the FDCPA only allows a debt collector to seek voluntary repayment, without initiating or threatening to initiate a legal suit in connection with the time-barred debt.

[146] Goldberg (2006), p. 750. Also see *Huertas v. Galaxy*, *supra*, footnote 1561.

acknowledgement of the debt or even a minimum repayment has the consequence of causing the debt to reappear in full.[147]

One suggested solution was the amendment of the FDCPA in the sense of completely barring any collection efforts with respect to bad debt,[148] but such a proposal would have overcome the actual purposes of the FDCPA and create unwanted and unreasonable results.[149] Another suggestion was to raise the level of awareness among consumers by forcing the debt-buying industry to inform them about their rights when dealing with collection attempts related to a debt past the statute of limitations.[150] Such solution was already implemented by some states like New York, New Mexico in an attempt to deal with an ever-growing issue.[151] A proposal was also made to forbid or restrict the sale of debts that cannot be brought to court or reported on a credit report anymore,[152] forbid or restrict the revival of debts in the absence of consumers' awareness, impose an obligation on debt collectors to prove that a debt obligation is legally enforceable before taking action,[153] but such proposals are debatable and too far-reaching to match the stated policy of the FDCPA, and hence it is hard to believe they will be implemented.

To take an example from Europe, in the UK, unlike the US federal FDCPA, statute-barred debt is specifically covered by CONC.[154] The text also mentions

---

[147] The rebirth of the debt allows debt collectors to pursue it in full, including through litigation. Also, a resurrected debt may be reported in the consumer's credit report, causing even more significant consequences. For details: Goldberg (2006), pp. 750–751. Also: The 2013 FTC leaflet on time-barred debt, urging consumers to defend themselves in court: www.consumer.ftc.gov/articles/0117-time-barred-debts, last visited 19.12.2014.

[148] Wisconsin and Mississippi have actually adopted this solution and considered extinguished any debt that has passed the statute of limitations. Terp (2011), p. 10.

[149] The flaw of the proposal stems from the fact that such complete bar would obliterate the entire industry, thus damaging the economy. Additionally, it was rightfully emphasized that the purpose of the FDCPA is not to erase consumers' debts but to make sure they are protected against unscrupulous collection practices. The case law took a similar position when in *Walker v. Cash Flow Consultants* the judge held that "a state law that only bars a specific remedy, rather than extinguishing the entire debt, is consistent with the FDCPA." Goldberg (2006), p. 751.

[150] Goldberg (2006), p. 752. It was argued that such a solution would help debtors understand that, although they do not have a legal obligation to pay the debt, collectors are still legally allowed to pursue the old debt. Also: De Boer (2013), p. 11.

[151] State is not uniform in this regard. While most of the state have not yet addressed the issue, New York requires debt collectors to notify in writing if a debt has passed the statute of limitations, while New Mexico requires debt collectors to first make a "good faith" determination of whether a debt is "time-barred" or otherwise unrecoverable by law and, in case the answer is positive, to refrain from collection attempts unless it notifies the consumer about the character of the debt, that there is no legal obligation to pay or to do anything that would waive his legal rights and that any action or partial payment would result in reviving the debt and making it recoverable again. See Terp (2011), pp. 10–11.

[152] Terp (2011), p. 17.

[153] For more such proposals and details Terp (2011), p. 16.

[154] CONC, Section 7.15. The text also mentions that the recommendations with respect to barred debt take into consideration the differences between the laws of the countries forming the UK.

that recommendations with respect to barred debt take into consideration the differences between the laws of the countries forming the UK. Thus, while in England, Wales and Northern Ireland, the debt still exists and is recoverable and debt collection efforts will be permissible, in Scotland, where barred debt is deemed "extinguished" and no longer recoverable, any attempts to collect the debt are banned.[155] Where attempts to collect barred debt are still permissible, unfair or improper practices are: pursuing the debt when the debtor has heard nothing from a creditor during the relevant period; misleading debtors as to their rights or obligations; implying that they could be subjected to court action for the statute-barred debt; continuing to press a debtor for payment after he has stated his refusal to repay a debt because it is statute barred.[156]

7.2.1.5 Use of Voicemails

The delivery of voicemails to answering machines is not covered by the FDCPA, despite the fact that the technology existed at the time of enactment, but was scarcely developed and used in residential homes.[157] The matter was referred to litigation, and the courts had to decide whether voicemails could qualify as communication under the act and implicitly be subjected to FDCPA's disclosure requirements.[158] In their vast majority, courts have decided that voicemails do

[155] CONC, Sections 7.15.2 and 7.15.3.

[156] CONC, Sections 7.15.4–7.15.8, restating the former Section 3.15.b of the Guidance. The last thesis is interesting and takes a stronger approach than the one adopted by courts in the US. There, the view was that as long as the debt is not extinguished, debt collectors may pursue the debt, by complying with the rest of the FDCPA's requirements (including request for cease of communication from the debtor). Here the FCA decided to clearly provide that in such cases, a stated refusal of the debtor that he will not pay a barred debt must result in the cessation of all future collection effort, a solution deemed by this work to be **proper and fair** and a good example to follow.

[157] Hector (2011), p. 1612. Also: see *Zortman*, in which the court found that because the FDCPA is a strict liability statute reading in an intent requirement would defeat the purpose of the statute. In the case at hand, the defendant left multiple messages on the plaintiff's home and cellular voicemail systems. The outgoing messages on the voicemail systems did not identify occupants or potential listeners. Plaintiff brought suit alleging violations of Section 1692c (b) given the fact that the messages left on the voicemail systems were heard by her children. The defendant argued that the plaintiff had no claim for the sole reason that it did not purposefully or deliberately disclose the debt information to a third party. In the analysis of the case, the court determined that the plain language of Section 1692 (c)(b) did not require a purposeful or deliberate intent to make the disclosure of the debt. As the systems used to leave messages did not identify who might actually listen to the messages, the court appreciated that the defendant had a reasonable expectation that someone other than the debtor plaintiff would hear the voicemail messages. In the view of the court, that sufficed in attracting liability, due to the fact that FDCPA is a strict liability statute that explicitly includes an intent element when required.

[158] See *supra* Chap. 6, Sect. 6.2.3.1.

qualify as communication under the FDCPA[159] and thus must comply with its provisions regarding disclosure.[160] The problem is that these courts have employed different reasoning[161] in reaching the same conclusion, while a minority of them have held that voicemails cannot be construed to represent communication under the law.[162] Such differences only emphasize the confusion over determining whether and how to apply the FDCPA to new technologies and create inconsistent results, which is contrary to the purpose of the law. Additional danger was posed by the fact that other people than the intended debtor could hear the message that included personal and confidential information resulting in violations of Section 805 of the FDCPA.[163]

---

[159] Sartip (2012) 8th recommendation, p. 3. The author mentions the federal case *Foti v. NCO Fin Sys. Inc*, 424 F Supp. 2d 643 (S.D.N.Y. 2006), in which it was concluded that a voicemail is a "communication" under the FDCPA and thus had to provide meaningful disclosure of the caller's identity and include the Mini-Miranda disclosure.

[160] Hector (2011), p. 1612.

[161] Despite differences between reasoning, three elements seem to be most important in determining if a voicemail is or not a communication in the eyes of the law: the content of the voicemail message, the practical implications of exempting certain voicemails from the ambit of the FDCPA and, finally, the context in which the voicemail was made. For example, in *Hosseinzadeh v. MRS Associates* (387 F Supp. 2d 1104 (C.D. Cal. 2005), the plaintiff brought suit against the debt collector based on a series of voicemails referring to a "very important matter," which requested the consumer to call back a certain toll-free number and advised him about the consequences of failure to comply with such request. The court held that although the messages did not mention specific information "about a debt or the nature of the call," the indirect references to the debt did suffice in bringing the messages under the communication's definition provided by the FDCPA. In analyzing the practical implications of voicemail communications, courts have noted that exempting voicemails from the FDCPA would in fact allow debt collectors to circumvent statutory requirements. For instance, in *Ramirez v. Apex Financial Management, LLC* (567 F.Supp. 2d 1035, 1042 (N.D. III. 2008), the debt collector kept leaving voice messages on the consumer's answering machine, despite the fact that it already received a letter asking to cease and desist all communication, arguing that the messages could not be construed as communication given that they did not clearly convey information regarding the debt. The court dismissed such interpretation holding that it is in grave conflict with the legislative purpose of the act of protecting consumers from harassing conduct. Similarly with respect to the context in which voicemails were addressed, the courts have held that they will constitute communication under the law, as long as their purpose "was to induce the plaintiff to call the defendant to discuss her outstanding debt." Such was the holding in *Hutton v. C.B. Accounts, Inc.* (No. 10-3052, 2010 WL 3021904 at *2 (N.D. III. Aug. 3, 2010). For details, see: Hector (2011), pp. 1612–1614.

[162] In the cases in which the courts took the position that the voicemails were not communication, the focus was also on the content of the messages, which contained only a name and a request to return the call but did not address the other elements. For instance, in *Biggs v. Credit Collections, Inc*, (No. CIV-07-0053-F, 2007 WL 4034997, at *4 (W.D. Okla. Nov. 15, 2007), it was held that a voicemail that merely identified the name of the caller and asked the debtor to call a provided number was not a communication under the FDCPA. For more details and similar decisions, see: Hector (2011), p. 1615, footnotes 87–89.

[163] Sartip (2012), 8th recommendation, p. 3.

The case law can provide though some useful guidelines on how the issue could be solved:[164] on the one hand, demonstrating that protections offered by the FDCPA should not be diminished because the law makes it difficult or impossible for collectors to use a particular technology[165] and, on the other hand, acknowledging that a consideration of practical effects of any technology should be made when deciding whether to apply the FDCPA or not.[166]

The most obvious solution is to redefine the term "communication" in order to avoid or prevent confusion with respect to contacts containing minimum information[167] and "to shift the definition from its current focus on content towards the role that the contact plays as part of the overall debt collection process."[168]

7.2.1.6 Use of Internet and Mobile Technologies

Debt collectors have quickly adapted to the new technologies and learned how to use them in order to deceive consumers. The Internet and mobile technologies in particular have allowed debt collectors to circumvent the protections of the FDCPA raising at the same time an even more serious concern for debtor's privacy.[169] The range of new abusive practices enabled by technological advancement vary from leaving messages for putative debtors or for third parties through social networks such as Facebook or MySpace[170] to hiding the caller's ID,[171]

[164] Hector (2011), p. 1615.

[165] One argument raised by the debt collectors was that by applying the FDCPA's provisions to voicemails, it would force those to either not use voicemails as a form of communication or pay burdensome litigation costs. This argument has been generally rejected by courts. For details, see Hector (2011), p. 1616, footnotes 91–93.

[166] Hector (2011), pp. 1616–1617.

[167] Hector (2011), p. 1626.

[168] Hector (2011), p. 1627. "Redefining "communication" as "any contact with a debt collector that relates to the *collection of the debt or seeks to induce future action*" would better ensure consumer protection in a manner that does not unduly burden debt collection."

[169] Hector (2011), pp. 1617 and 1620.

[170] Tsotsis (2010). Also: Hector (2011), pp. 1627–1628. "With a social networking website, for example, a consumer would probably not expect a "friend request" from a debt collector. Hence, even if a debt collector used his or her real name, if that name did not adequately represent that the request is from a debt collector, it should be considered a deception."

[171] Hector (2011), pp. 1617–1619. Also see: America (2007), pp. 16–19, containing a discussion of two caller ID cases.

calling the debtor's mobile phone[172] or sending emails.[173] These practices allow debt collectors to infiltrate in the debtor's private circle,[174] obtain information that they would not be otherwise able to obtain[175] and communicate or pressure the consumers in ways that could escape the protections offered by the FDCPA.[176]

Besides the solution recommended *supra* at Sect. 7.2.1.5, regarding the amendment of the definition of "communication," the doctrine had also suggested changes that would put consumers on the same level with debt collectors with respect to the usage of modern communication techniques, the reason being that such platforms would enable consumers to easily and effectively send important messages to collectors and would avoid becoming a one-way street, from debt collector to consumer.[177] Last, but not least, it was inferred that the FDCPA should be modified in order to require mobile and Internet communications from debt collectors to include a disclosure together with an opting-out mechanism. Evidently, in order to make such disclosure and opt-outs effective, consumers should be allowed to respond by using the same technology used by the debt collector in the contact,[178] which is not the case at the moment.

---

[172] Hector (2011), pp. 1622–1623. It was emphasized that unlike residential phone lines and home addresses, the mobile technology means that people might receive communications in a totally different context than the one considered by the FDCPA. Mobile calls can be received at any place and any time (including those deemed unusual by the law) or even on their own expense if called outside their residential state. For a detailed discussion of such issues, see: America (2007), pp. 13–16.

[173] Hector (2011), p. 1622. Also: America (2007), pp. 19–20. The League took the position that emails sent to consumers should not be treated differently than snail mail given the fact that there is a reasonable expectation that they would receive such communications. The League also emphasized that they are free to delete such communication. Thus, it was suggested to amend the FDCPA in the sense of including emails among the permitted ways of communication, provided that such emails are sent with a read receipt request.

[174] Hector (2011), p. 1626. "Consumers have a reasonable expectation to be free from anonymous debt collection contacts that intrude areas they regard as intimate, regardless of whether the contact conveys content regarding a debt."

[175] Hector (2011), p. 1624.

[176] Hector (2011), p. 1623. "Without clearer guidance, courts, consumer, and debt collectors will be left in the unenviable position of drawing imperfect analogies between voicemails and newer communication platforms. This will encourage firms to push the boundaries of the law, disadvantage ethical debt collectors and jeopardize the FDCPA's overreaching goal to safeguard consumers from abuse and harassment."

[177] Hector (2011), pp. 1628–1629. "Notably, although debt collectors are permitted to call consumers in order to request payment of an outstanding debt, in order to dispute the validity of the debt [. . .] consumer must send debt collectors a written notice. New technologies could make it easier for a consumer to dispute a debt, request verification, workout a payment solution, or demand that collectors cease contact." "By ensuring that consumers and collectors alike can take advantage of new technologies, these updates would deter collectors from abusing new communication platforms."

[178] Hector (2011), p. 1629.

A specific issue concerning the use of electronic means was reported with respect to collection of payday loans[179] as multiple electronic attempts to collect resulted in charges that amounted to more than the actual loan.[180] The Federation[181] suggested that in order to avoid such situations, the following practices should be declared unfair by the FTC: basing or securing loans with the borrower's check held for future deposit, holding electronic authorization to access the borrower's bank account as security for payment of a loan and creating demand drafts or remote checks to repay the loans. Since the UK regulation has specifically dealt with this issue already, it might serve as a starting point model for the American legislator.

7.2.1.7 Arbitration in Debt Collection Cases

Starting with 2010, besides debt collectors abusing the judicial system, the FTC noticed an increased number of cases in which both creditors and collectors sought recovery through the use of arbitration. Since neither litigation nor arbitration was providing adequate protection for consumers, the FTC concluded harshly that "the system for resolving disputes about consumer debts is broken"[182] and urged both federal and state governments, together with the debt collection industry and other stakeholders, to make significant reforms. The FTC has made several recommendations concerning arbitration such as providing a meaningful choice about arbitration, eliminating bias by arbitration forums and arbitrators, establishing transparent arbitration procedures that encourage consumers to participate or rendering motivated awards.

The FTC's solutions are somehow unrealistic, for they fail to consider most of the specificities of arbitration proceedings (fast, no jury or right to appeal, more expensive, unpublished or secret opinions, inconsistent and nonbinding solutions, exclusion of class actions, different rules of law or evidence)[183] and especially the fact that these specificities frustrate the Congressional intent behind the FDCPA.

[179] America (2007), p. 11. Payday loans are defined as small cash advances for less than 1,000 dollars, typically in the 300–500 dollar range, based on the borrower's personal check or electronic access for an amount of the loan and the finance charge. To get a payday loan, a borrower should have an open account with a bank, an income source and a valid ID. Loans are due and payable in full on the borrower's next payday and cost 390–780 percent APR for 2-week terms. In theory, on the next payday the borrower could bring in cash and "buy-back" the check or the check can be deposited for payment, but practice shows that most checks are never deposited and are brought back by customers who are encouraged to take another loan. The Federation argues that the essential features of the payday loan described above make them a trap for borrowers and susceptive for collection abuses. America (2007), pp. 3–4.

[180] America (2007), p. 11.

[181] America (2007), p. 12.

[182] FTC (2010), p. i.

[183] Alderman (2012), pp. 589–590 and 603.

They also disregard the strong policy supporting arbitration,[184] even in consumer cases,[185] in the US.

A more realistic opinion was issued by Alderman, who started by emphasizing the fact that a consumer claim under the FDCPA is different from other consumer claims and is supported by different policies,[186] which is why the claims arising under it should not be arbitrable.[187] His proposal is straightforward and requires the amendment of the FAA to exclude FDCPA claims from arbitration or the implementation of an Arbitration Fairness Act, in the sense of prohibiting forced arbitration in all consumer contracts.[188]

The policy considerations raised by Alderman are convincing, and this work takes the position that any solution regarding arbitrability of FDCPA claims must start from them, especially since courts have endorsed these policies going as far as to pierce the corporate veil. It is also debatable whether the minimum protection offered by the federal FDCPA (as a *de minimis* rule) could be waived by those it intends to protect when states do not have the possibility to derogate from its provisions. With respect to the conflict between the FAA and FDCPA, one may notice that they both support powerful public policies. However, while the FAA has a general, broader scope, the FDCPA has a special, narrower one. Therefore, two solutions could be added to Alderman's proposal: either to apply the FAA only with full observance of the FDCPA or, *de lege ferenda*, to amend FDCPA to specifically exclude arbitration.

On a final note, the issue of arbitrability of abusive debt collection cases appears to not be a concern in Europe for the moment, either because of the general ignorance of private businesses offering out-of-court debt collection and related issues[189] or due to the fact that EU legislation and its national versions are considered sufficient. Directive 93/13 ECC, Unfair Terms in Consumer Contracts,[190] deems as generally

---

[184] Alderman (2012), pp. 586–587, including footnote 2, Kaplinsky and Levin (2008), p. 911 and Tajti (2013b), p. 107.

[185] See the Supreme Court's decision in *AT&T LLC v. Conception*, 131 S.Ct. 1740 (2011), holding that the Federal Arbitration Act (FAA) preempts even state unconscionably rules that preclude arbitration provisions that prohibit collective redress or class actions.

[186] Alderman (2012), pp. 587–588.

[187] Alderman (2012), pp. 600–609. Starting from the policies behind the FDCPA, Alderman showed how enforcing arbitration clauses in debt collection cases would actually affect the enforcement and efficiency of the FDCPA: arbitration would deprive the consumer of his substantial enforcement mechanism—the private action through private litigation resulting in binding, public and consistent decisions of courts; would remove availability of class actions in debt collection cases, thus removing one of the powerful deterrent mechanisms of the Act; removes the procedural and financial incentives given to the consumer in order to encourage him to take action. For a contrary opinion, asserting that arbitration of consumer cases respects all standards of fairness (however not addressing the issue of FDCPA cases directly), see: Kaplinsky and Levin (2008), pp. 910–919.

[188] Alderman (2012), pp. 611–612.

[189] Tajti (2013b), p. 107.

[190] Art 3(1) and Article 1 (q) of Annex to Art 3(1) of Directive 93/13 ECC, Unfair Terms in Consumer Contracts.

unfair any contractual term that has not been individually negotiated and would cause a significant imbalance between the parties to the detriment of the consumer by hindering his right to take legal action, specifically mentioning arbitration. Moreover, the chosen European jurisdictions extend the Directive's protection. In the UK, the Arbitration Act 1996[191] declares unfair consumer arbitration clauses that relate to pecuniary remedies, which do not exceed a limit of 5,000 pounds,[192] while the FOS service remains purely voluntary, which might indicate the legislators' concern with the threat of abuse that industry-imposed arbitration[193] could have posed. In France, predispute consumer arbitration clauses are invalid,[194] while in Germany all consumer arbitration clauses should be in a separate document, signed personally by the consumer, unless the whole contract is notarized.[195] Romania was satisfied only with the translation of the Directive's wording.[196] Thus, one may conclude that at least with respect to the issue of arbitrability of abusive debt collection practices, European jurisdictions might not need urgent amendments as the US certainly does. For now, at least.

7.2.2 Need for Reform in the UK

Despite its comprehensive and detailed regulation of banned debt collection practices, this work takes the view that the system is not working efficiently in the UK and the reason can only be the absence of a proper private enforcement system to double the administrative enforcement one. As the legislation is up to date with the modern technologies employed by debt collectors, the issue cannot be, like in the US, an outdated legal text, unable to keep up. On the contrary, the increased number of complaints, referring to the most common forms of abuse from debt collectors,[197] can only be a direct consequence of the lack of deterrent effect of the legislation.

---

[191] Section 91(1) of Arbitration Act 1996 corroborated with the provisions of Order SI 1999/2167.

[192] CIArb), p. 4.

[193] Tajti (2013b), p. 107.

[194] FCC, Article 2061.

[195] ZPO, Art 103(5). German case law also contains instances in which courts have denied enforcement of arbitration clauses where one party was incapable to present its case due to the high costs involved. See the decision III ZR 33/00 from 9 April 2000 of the Bundesgerichtshof.

[196] Annex, Paragraph (1), letter l) of Law 193/2000, republished in the Official Gazette of Romania, Part 1, no 543/03.08.2012.

[197] Media in the UK abounds in news about unfair debt collection practices. See for example: *Call Off the Debt Hounds, The Mirror* (2011), "It is scandalous that ordinary people are being hounded for a few hundred euro. It is also outrageous that hospital are hiring these agencies to go after patients, some who are still recovering from treatment. They have enough worries without getting letters from debt collection agencies threatening court action." Related to intimidating tactics employed by Talk Talk, the broadband and phone company, to chase former customers for debts

A report of the FOS regarding its activity in the year 2012–2013 revealed an increase of consumer credit complaints by 14 %, from 576 to 817 in the number of disputes about debt collectors.[198] As the FOS noticed, consumers' complaints were still about the number of times they have been approached by a debt collector and the way the debt collector had treated them.[199] Others complained about standards of administration, more precise about the debt collector's failure of taking into consideration the payments already made or settlement agreements already in place.[200] Also, debt collectors continue to approach persons who are not the actual debtors.[201]

The same report noticed an even more worrying increase in complaints related to payday lenders, of 83 %, from 296 cases to 542.[202] The vast majority of these complaints were largely related to the way the lenders had made use of the CPA, which allowed the lender to collect payments directly from the consumer's bank account,[203] but included as well lenders trying to take payments unexpectedly or repeatedly attempting to take payments when consumer notified that they do not have sufficient money for the coverage of the debt or simply the recovery methods employed by payday lenders.[204] As shown, the CONC specifically addressed the CPA issue.[205] Results are still to come as the OFT plans to take the battle further to the field of competition law.[206]

---

that they do not owe, see Budworth (2011). Also, referring to a collection agency accused of adding extra costs to debits, cutting corners and aggressively chasing people for money they say they do not owe, see Atherton (2011), Whateley (2012) and Whateley (2011). On the unlawful usage of private data, see: Tighe (2011). Last but not least, with respect to the dubious character of debt collectors in Ireland and calls for reform and legal enforcement, see: Connolly (2010). With respect to complaints received and handled by the FOS, see: FOS (2009), mentioning similar issues like those that reached the media: oppressive and unreasonable collection tactics, attempts to recover from nondebtors, disputed debts or lack of evidence originating from the initial creditor.

[198] FOS (2013), pt. 1-176, p. 62.

[199] FOS (2013), p. 62.

[200] FOS (2013), p. 62.

[201] FOS (2013), p. 62.

[202] FOS (2013), p. 62.

[203] Also: OFT (2013), p. 22: "CPA's have been the subject of a substantial number of consumer complaints such as: the consumer was not aware that they have signed up a CPA or how it would work; lenders taking frequent part payments over several days or weeks, often leaving the consumer facing significant hardship."

[204] FOS (2013), p. 62. Also: OFT (2013), pp. 22–23. "Consumers were being called on their mobile and work phones up to 16 times per day"; "[S]ome lenders were using aggressive collection practices by subjecting customers to repeated and intensive contact over short periods, often in conjunction with the use of CPA"; "Of the 686 complaints received during a 6 month monitoring period, 61 % related to aggressive or unsatisfactory debt collection practices."

[205] Trading (2003), p. 5 and Section 3.9.m., pp. 33–41. Also see OFT's press release addressed to payday lenders: http://webarchive.nationalarchives.gov.uk/20140402142426/http://www.oft.gov.uk/news-and-updates/press/2012/110-12, last visited 19.12.2014.

[206] http://webarchive.nationalarchives.gov.uk/20140402142426/http://www.oft.gov.uk/news-and-updates/press/2013/20-13, last visited 19.12.2014.

7.2.3 Reform in France and Germany

France had a reform of its debt-collection-related legislation in 2012, but it was merely a formal and not a substantive one. By looking at the serious issues from the US—related to outdated legislation—or those from the UK—related to lack of an adequate private enforcement system—one can realize that the simple and concise French legislation cannot be a viable solution. As in Germany the legislation related to nonjudicial debt collection and protection of debtors is just emerging (concerning licensing and registration),[207] the only thing that would require reformation is probably the system and the perception itself. Considering the lack of sources in English, it is hard to say.

The difficulty also regards the discussions or calls for reformation in any of the two countries, though the issues existent in the US and the UK could not have possibly go around France and Germany. The available data,[208] as scarce as it is, indicate that they have not. Moreover, the World Bank[209] has started pushing forward for measures and regulations of this area, using the US and the UK as examples with different approaches for the same issues.

As data protection is pretty much regulated at EU level by the European Data Protection Directive, it is only the implementation that still differs among member states, especially with regard to basic rules (such as legitimacy and proportionality of data processing, purpose of data collection, limitations on data collection) and also the authorized purposes and authorized actors for exchanging credit data.[210] Given the fact that consumer's lives are affected by data collected in the credit registers or in the databases of debt collectors, transparency of the information stored, its accuracy and procedures to access it or correct it should be clearly

---

[207] Tajti (2013b), pp. 110–111 and 113 (footnote 330).

[208] Tajti (2013b), pp. 111 (footnote 322) and 113 (footnote 330).

[209] Rutledge (2010), p. 38: "Consumers should be protected from abusive debt collection practices by credit institutions or third-party debt collectors. This means that rules are required regarding the type of debt that can be collected, the person who can collect debts and the manner in which any debt can be collected. And these rules must then be indicated to the consumer at the time his or her transaction is entered into. There ought to be laws prohibiting debt-collectors from using false statements when collecting a debt, using unfair practices, as well as giving false credit information to others, including a credit bureau."

[210] Rutledge (2010), p. 42. A very telling example is the one of Finland, one of the European countries with a well-developed sector-specific consumer-debtor protection regulation. A collection agency wanted to sell to credit institutions information on customers' credit situation that it had gathered during its debt collection. Since debt collectors need to be licensed, they cannot collect more information than the one essential to their operations, not even with the debtor's consent. Hence, any personal data gathered cannot be used for a different purpose. Given also that the debt collection law stresses the need to protect privacy, the Data Protection Ombudsman denied the right of the debt collector to sell the information gathered on the consumer-debtors. Micklitz et al. (2010), p. 380.

regulated and enforced.[211] Simply licensing or registering third party debt collectors without enforceable codes of conduct will never constitute an adequate solution.

7.2.4 *Call for Reformation in Romania*

There have been some calls for reformation of the nonjudicial debt recovery system in Romania,[212] especially as the World Bank has been asking the Romanian legislator to introduce protections for the customer, against abusive debt collection practices by the banks or third party debt collectors:

> The type of debt that can be collected, the person who can collect the debts and the manner in which debt can be collected must be indicated to the customer at the time the transaction is entered into. The right of debt collectors to contact anyone else about customer's debt must be indicated and the type of information they may see must also be provided. Debt collectors should be prohibited from using false statements during debt-collection, using unfair practices or giving false credit information to others (for example to a credit bureau).[213]

The answer was the draft law adopted by the Senate in 2010 but rejected by the Chamber of Representatives in 2012. Reforming something that does not exist is not an easy task, unless one deems the rejection as a result of an improper proposal. The previous sections dedicated to Romania show that the project was not able to offer any viable remedies against such practices. Although a step forward in identifying and labeling abusive practices, it was but a poor attempt to bring some order in the field.[214] Since it was inspired by the

---

211 Rutledge (2010), p. 43. "Consumers need to be informed about data processing, such as the exact purpose for which their data is processed" [. . .] "Consumers should have the right to contest erroneous data or provide explanations on causes of arrears." "It is recommended that procedures be in place to reduce the risk of identity theft and ensure that technical security of the database prevents unauthorized access." In fact, the European Commission has already launched a proposal for a Regulation on the protection of individuals with regard to the processing of personal data and on the free movement of such data (General Data Protection Regulation) amending the former Directive in place and acknowledging among others that "rapid technological developments have brought new challenges for the protection of personal data. [. . .] technology allows [. . .] private companies [. . .] to make use of personal data on an unprecedented scale in order to pursue their activities." Hence, the Commission concludes: "it is time to build a stronger and more coherent data protection framework in the EU, backed by a strong enforcement [. . .]" See: http://ec.europa.eu/justice/data-protection/document/review2012/com_2012_11_en.pdf, pp. 1–2, last visited 19.12.2014.

212 Urban (2007). Also: Tudoriu (2011), *at* http://www.juridice.ro/168991/probleme-legale-privind-activitatea-de-phone-collection.html.

213 Rutledge (2010), p. 42.

214 Alternative explanations for the rejection of the project could be found in its pro-debt collector's approach, given the fact that the proposal came from a senator owing one of the biggest collection agencies in Romania, while another explanation could be political. In 2010, when the

FDCPA,[215] the draft totally disregarded abusive practices related to usage of mobiles, emails, voicemails or social network platforms in recovery attempts; exploiting court procedures; time-barred debt or house visits. Just because they were not mentioned in the statute, one cannot simply assume that they would have been banned by courts using analogies or the fact that the list of statutory examples was not exhaustive. Obviously, the UK regulatory body felt the need to mention them. A Romanian viable model should mention them too in order to provide the courts and consumers with a clear guide.

The project law had a lot of inadvertences, and the fact that the Senate adopted it in its initial form may come as a surprise if one considers the negative recommendations of the Senate's Legislative Council.[216] To mention only a few examples, the law defined the debtor only as the natural person who owes payment for a debt,[217] despite the fact that further the act mentioned that the procedure of collection applies to all collections, either against natural persons or against legal persons.[218] Therefore, either the debtor's definition should have included legal persons as well or the following provisions should have excluded any misunderstanding with respect to legal persons. The project made reference to personal bankruptcy, although such procedure is not yet established in Romanian law; thus, any reference to it were inapplicable.[219] A provision that stated that all debts handled through the procedure for debt collection would gain priority over debts whose recovery is sought through other type of proceedings (thus securing unsecured debts)[220] was also criticized for being against the principles established by the Civil Code and the Bankruptcy Law.[221]

The Legislative Council of the Senate has also observed and asked for modification of the project, correctly noticing that in its form the statute would be totally inapplicable with respect to disciplinary or misdemeanor liability because it lacks an active subject. The text was also deemed to be incomplete, because it did not identify the examining competent body, the procedure for examination, the

---

Senate approved the project, the majority belonged to the Liberal Democratic Party and the abovementioned senator was a member of that party. In 2012, the majority switched to the opposition, namely the Liberal-Socialist Union, so the project lost its parliamentary support.

[215] Initially, the proponent, Senator Iulian Urban, has advertised the idea by translating and commenting the FDCPA for the Romanian public, arguing the implementation of a law similar to the US model. That proposal included even the reference to civil penalties for each breach of law and the right to private enforcement. Unfortunately, the project that was submitted to the Parliament's approval lost many of the initial ideas. Urban (2008), *available at* http://www.urbaniulian.ro/2008/07/01/legea-privind-colectarea-amiabila-a-debitelor-propunere-legislativa-facuta-de-urban-iulian/.

[216] Senate's Legislative Council (2010), available in Romanian only.

[217] Project Law, Art 3, a).

[218] Project Law, Art 5, a) and b).

[219] Legislative Council (2010), point 5, p. 3.

[220] Project Law, Art 3. f).

[221] Legislative Council (2010), point 5, p. 3.

sanctions or the body authorized to impose them. The recommendation was to entirely reformulate the article.[222]

A better idea would have been to follow the initial plan, of implementing an FDCPA-type of act, but an adapted and modernized version (here the UK regulation would have been useful), and provide for civil, administrative and even criminal liabilities in case of abuse. The initial public proposal contained requirements with respect to licensing of debt-collecting agency in order to bring them under the authority of financial supervisory bodies. Repeated or grave breaches of the law would have led to the withdrawal of the license. It included provisions on validation of debt and suspension of recovery attempts until the debt was verified.[223] Despite that all chosen jurisdictions agree that debt collection should be at least a licensed activity, none of these important clauses made it to the project that was submitted to the Parliament.

However, the book contends that even such a project would have been far from an appropriate legal regime. It contained no appropriate incentives for the consumer in terms of territorial or substantive jurisdiction or attorney fees, judicial fees and related court expenses or reversed burden of proof. It said nothing about the procedure, which should be deemed as urgent in order to minimize the damages done to the consumers. It did not provide any solutions for an administrative body with the force and powers of the FTC or BFCP or at least with the attributes of the UK FOS. It had no guidelines for courts or consumers. It did not allow for class actions nor specified any policies that needed to be enforced to have a strong deterrent effect on abusive collectors. It basically failed on all proposed building blocks.

What is obvious is that Romania needs a debt collection law. Both the industry and the consumers are asking for it, and so do international financial institutions. The reasons are legion: the industry of debt collection is in full expansion due to the increase of consumer credit and the economic crisis, which both led to an increase of unpaid debts.[224] In order to control and supervise this industry, a sector-specific legal framework is needed.[225] Protection of interests, personal data and confidentiality of information must be also considered, together with the private zone of the consumer.[226] And an end to abuses must be set in place.

---

[222] Legislative Council (2010), point 13, p. 5.

[223] Urban (2008).

[224] Urban (2007).

[225] Tajti (2013a), p. 13.

[226] Urban (2007), p. 1.

7.3 Conclusions

The US FDCPA and the UK CONC clearly represent the recognition of the fact that the rights of debtors (be it natural persons or even SMEs under UK legislation) deserve a larger degree of attention.[227] The general layer of protection available for consumer protection appears as unfit to deal with all the issues posed by nonjudicial debt collection Hence, an additional layer of protection is needed, in the form of sector-specific regulation, as the US and the UK have already implemented. Their counterparts from France and Germany, as well as the failed attempt from Romania, point into the same direction.

The FDCPA has tried to secure the debtor's rights to privacy and to not be subjected to any abusive or unethical debt collection practices. It also tried to level up ineffective or lacking state regulations and to overcome inadequate traditional tort theories, by providing specific and tailor-made statutory actions to fit the context. Encouragement of meaningful state regulation of abusive debt collection practices, the acquired uniformity and comprehensiveness of state laws may be considered one of the greatest achievements of the FDCPA.[228] Despite recent heavy criticism—mostly due to the act's inability to keep up with technological developments—the FDCPA managed to provide the debtor with civil remedies and effective incentives to encourage him to take private action. Combined with additional state legislation and powerful administrative enforcement mechanisms, it is a viable and successful model of efficiency.

On the other hand, reform was called by both the debt collection industry's representatives and consumers' advocates, under the motivation that necessary clarifications and adequate mechanisms that would enable the act to respond to a rapid changing society and technologies, could only benefit all those involved.[229] The steps taken by the Dodd–Frank Act to provide the BFCP with regulatory powers to double the substantive law's provisions are a solid acknowledgment of the issues and an attempt to correct them.

Reform is needed in the European jurisdictions too. As shown, despite being updated and comprehensive, the UK CONC fails to provide an effective enforcement tool to consumers and the issue of abuse is far from being solved. France's approach, drawing only general lines regarding communication and the debt collector's fiduciary duties, can hardly be construed as appropriate tool for courts or consumers. Germany focuses just on licensing and registration,[230] while Romania

[227] For answers to criticism that such an act would only increase debt delinquency, see Potach (1978), pp. 922–923, footnote 156.

[228] Potach (1978), p. 923.

[229] America (2007), pp. 26–27. The League's call for reformation consisting in providing FTC with the power to write and enforce regulations implementing the FDCPA was answered positively by the Dodd–Frank Act, which granted such powers to the newly created Bureau for Financial Consumer Protection.

[230] Tajti (2013b), p. 113, footnote 330.

struggles with finding a project to implement. The law adopted by the Senate, but rejected by the Chamber of Representatives, was rightfully dismissed. It failed to establish a proper framework or to provide for appropriate means of enforcement. In fact, it basically lacked any. Implementation for the sake of implementation is of no use. Thus, it is this work's opinion that looking at the policies behind the FDCPA, the way they were implemented by the legislator and interpreted by courts and the way the FCA's CONC approached the large categories of abuses related to the use of modern technologies would provide a good starting point for a proper draft.

References

Akina WK (2012) Note: A Lie Is A Lie: the need to define Section 1692e of the FDCPA. Brooklyn J Corp Financ Commer Law 7:145
Alderman RM (2012) The fair debt collection practices act meets arbitration: non-parties and arbitration. Loyola Consum Law Rev 24:586
Atherton M (2011) Debt collector's tactics exposed. The Times, London
Budworth D (2011) Anger grows over talk talk 'bully' calls. The Times, London
Burridge N (2010) Debt collectors pursued wrong people. The Independent
Call off the debt hounds. In: The mirror, 2011
Connolly P (2010) Fear and owing. The Sunday Times, London
Consumer Federation of America (2007) Collecting consumer debts: the challenges of change. In: Comments to the federal trade commission regarding the fair debt collection practices act
Décret n° 2012-783 du 30 mai 2012 relatif à la partie réglementaire du code des procédures civiles d'exécution. France, 2012
De Boer S (2013) Fair debt collection practices act. Overview, analyses, and administration. Novinka, New York
Dempsey L (2013) The FTC and FDCPA. Collector (0010082X) 78
FOS (2009) Recent complaints involving debt collection businesses. Financial Ombudsman Service, UK
FOS (2011) Ombudsman News
FOS (2013) Annual review of consumer complaints about: insurance, credit, banking, savings and investments. Financial Ombudsman Service, UK
FOS, Technical note: compensation. Available at http://www.financial-ombudsman.org.uk/publications/technical_notes/compensation.html
FOS, Technical notes: distress and inconvenience. Available at http://www.financial-ombudsman.org.uk/publications/technical_notes/distress-and-inconvenience.htm
Fox JL (2012) Do we have a debt collection crisis? Some cautionary tales of debt collection in Indiana. Loyola Consum Law Rev
FTC (2009) Collecting consumer debts: the challenges of change. Federal Trade Commission
FTC (2010) Repairing a broken system. Protecting consumers in debt collection litigation and arbitration. Federal Trade Commission
Garner BA (2009) Black's law dictionary. WEST, US
Goldberg L (2006) Dealing in debt: the high-stakes world of debt collection after FDCPA. South Calif Law Rev 79:711
Hector C (2011) Debt collection in the information age: new technologies and the fair debt collection practices act. Calif Law Rev 99:1601
Kaplinsky AS, Levin MJ (2008) Consumer arbitration: if the FAA "Ain't Broke", don't fix it. Bus Lawyer 63:907

Micklitz H-W, Stuyck J, Terryn E (2010) Cases, materials and text on consumer law. Hart Publishing, North America
Office for Fair Trading (2003) OFT guidance for businesses engaged in the recovery of consumer credit debts
OFT (2013) Payday Lending. Compliance Review Final Report. Office for Fair Trading
Potach SG (1978) New protection against the unethical bill collector: debtor's remedies under the fair debt collection practices act. Creighton Law Rev
Rutledge SL (2010) Consumer protection and financial literacy: lessons from nine country studies. The World Bank
Sartip MH (2012) Be a confident collection lawyer. South Carolina Lawyer
Senate's Legislative Council (2010) Approval of the legislative proposal concerning the procedure for debt collection
Strike Debt (2014) The debt resisters' operations manual. PM Press, Oakland
Tajti T (2013a) Post-1990 secured transaction law reforms in Central and Eastern Europe. Szegedi Közjegyzői Közlöny
Tajti T (2013b) Systemic and topical mapping of the relationship of the draft common frame of reference and arbitration. Kazimieras Simonavicius University, Vilnius
Terp R (2011) PAST DUE: why debt collection practices and the debt buying industry need reform now. Consumer Union of United States, Inc
The Commercial Law League of America (2007) Fair debt collection practices act. White Paper
Tighe M (2011) Data leak companies may face prosecution. The Sunday Times, London
Tsotsis A (2010) Facebook debt collection case is definitely a first. TECHCRUNCH, Nov. 19, 2010
Tudoriu F (2011) Probleme legale privind activitatea de Phone Collection (English translation: "Legal issues concerning the phone collection activity")
Urban I (2007) De ce avem nevoie de o lege destinata colectarii debitelor (English translation: "Why do we need a law on debt collection")
Urban I (2008) Legea privind colectarea amiabila a debitelor – propunere legislativa facuta de Urban Iulian
Whateley L (2011) Unreasonable demands. The Times, London
Whateley L (2012) Troubleshooter. The Times, London

Chapter 8
Conclusions

As the book shows, self-help and debt collection go back as far as the beginning of trade. They are not a new phenomenon, and they will continue to be with us in the future. It is beyond doubt that self-help repossession and private debt collection methods are rampant in practice today in most legal systems, even if not necessarily recognized by positive law or scholarship. However, the lack of recognition raises concomitant risks, for any self-help method has a potential for abuse and this work argued that only by acknowledging the problem can one find a solution.

The second chapter pointed out that rediscovery of self-help by sophisticated legal systems does not necessarily mean a return to primitivism, but a response to the inability of the states to provide adequate, speedy and less-costly methods needed for the development of credit and business in modern-day economies. By recognizing and incorporating an increasing number of nonviolent self-help actions into its legal framework as rational and effective solutions to disputes,[1] common law systems seem to have found an answer to the aforementioned needs. There are indications that civilian systems will follow, a trend that is also apparent in the DCFR. Its drafters clearly stated that the rules concerning enforcement "essentially focus on [. . .] extra-judicial enforcement."[2]

However, as the book revealed, different perceptions on self-help arise from the different takes on secured transactions laws, different levels of reform, different concepts of ownership and different public policies (such as extensive protection to both debtors and consumers). Therefore, harmonization efforts came with a compromise at the expense of self-help devices and the DCFR, despite its good intentions, makes no exception.

The third chapter emphasized another aspect that went unnoticed, namely that self-help remedies are and have been for a long time an integral part of contract law in all selected jurisdictions. The only difference is that, while in the US or the UK

[1] Taylor (1998), p. 845. Also McCall (1973), pp. 72–74.

[2] von Bar and Clive (2010), p. 5614.

C.G. Stănescu, *Self-Help, Private Debt Collection and the Concomitant Risks*,
DOI 10.1007/978-3-319-21503-7_8

they are recognized and referred to as self-help means, the civilian systems fail to acknowledge them as such.[3] The most important consequence is that the self-help remedies hidden in civilian systems' contract law are in fact available to unsecured creditors, which are free to resort to them as they see fit. However, when it comes to enforcement of security interests, traditional civilian systems, such as France and Germany, ban access of secured creditors to self-help remedies on grounds of public policy.

The book took the view that this factual contradiction present in civilian systems cannot be justified. By proving that self-help remedies are neither incompatible with civilian systems nor unknown to them, the second chapter argued that self-help remedies should be made available also to secured creditors, for they have been more careful when granting credit and hence deserve more protection. Obviously, since it would be an exception from the civil law principle of judicial enforcement, any form of nonjudicial self-help requires special legislation, with additional protection for debtors in order to prevent and deter abuse.

The fourth chapter focused on specific self-help remedies such as self-help repossession and administrative receivership and proved that they are compatible with civilian systems too. The book analyzed the mechanisms behind private enforcement and tried to point out both similarities and peculiarities between the chosen jurisdictions that recognize it as a useful legal tool in the realization of secured interests. The analysis revealed that in the US, the focus is on the balance between the aggrieved creditor's rights to recover his debts and the debtor's rights not to be subjected to any abuse in the process. For this purpose, standards such as the prohibition of breach of peace during self-help repossession and commercial reasonableness of any private sale of the collateral were implemented and developed by the UCC. Additional rules, such as the 60 % rule, protect consumers, mainly those who built up a considerable equity in the collateral, and insulate them from any arbitrary decisions the creditor might take during foreclosure procedures.

The UK, influenced by the EU legislation, focused more on educating the consumer instead of providing him with a handful of remedies and incentives to sue, taking the view that an informed consumer is a protected consumer. In the case of regulated agreements, the legislator took a paternalistic approach and precluded creditors from using self-help means against consumers, by imposing restrictions of repossession. However, the UK appears to have failed in finding the balance sought by the UCC, for once default was not cured and repossession has occurred, the debtor is left entirely defenseless, at creditor's will.

With the implementation of the RNCC, Romanian law has chosen a hybrid system that combines the private enforcement means of the UCC with limited judicial control. On paper, the solution seems to have found a middle way between

[3] A Romanian scholar distinguished between what he calls *passive self-help* (where parties simply refuse to perform an action), which remedies are remnant in any system's contract law, and *active self-help* (which implies an active involvement of the party exercising it, the most famous example being self-help repossession), which are to be found mostly in jurisdictions that follow UCC Article 9. Rizoiu (2011), p. 581.

the two, thus establishing a balance between the different needs and interests of creditors and debtors. However, the RNCC did not establish any special rules for consumer protection. The lack of relevant court cases raises the question whether debtors (either professional or consumers) are equally protected or in fact equally exposed. The provisions with respect to judicial control suggest the former, but reality might support the latter. The current RNCC regime is too new to have generated a practice. It is hard to believe that private enforcements do not occur, but due to absence of court cases one could only speculate on their effects.

As already mentioned, creditors are skeptical about the efficacy of the judicial process when it comes to collection of debts, given the lengthy procedures, high expenses incurred, inherent risks and uncertainties.[4] Creditors rarely resort to litigation until all self-help remedies (where available) and nonjudicial collection efforts have been exhausted without result. Since self-help repossession and administrative receivership are not the only nonjudicial remedies available, the book turned to factoring and nonjudicial debt collection by debt collection agencies.

As emphasized, the problem with nonjudicial debt collection is the need to also consider the concomitant risks involved. Romania, for example, does not have a law against abusive debt collection practices or a licensing system of debt collectors. This allowed nonfinancial business organizations to engage in debt collection under the cover of factoring operations against consumers (pseudo- or quasi-factoring), thus escaping supervision of financial regulatory bodies. This phenomenon created additional risks. On the one hand, collecting consumer debt in the absence of any kind of sector-specific consumer protection regulation, from unlicensed and unsupervised business entities, puts consumers in great danger to incur unsanctioned abuse. On the other hand, tolerating unsupervised nonfinancial business entities to conduct specialized services in a wider area than that of supervised financial entities exposes the latter to unfair competition.

These are the very reasons that led to the enactment of the Fair Debt Collection Practices Act (FDCPA) in the US, as sector-specific regulation and consumer protection against unfair debt collection practices. The natural conclusion is that Romania must become aware and grasp the practical risks of tolerating pseudo-factoring and its consequences and, following the US and the UK models, address these issues and the need for sector-specific consumer protection.

The FDCPA thus provides a solid starting point, despite the emergence of ever newer types of abuses and the repeated calls for reform,[5] which were addressed in the final chapter. In Europe, however, though similar issues have risen, the analysis reveals that the response is not as strong and adequate as in the US (with the UK being a notable exception). The explanation might be that the dimension of abuses related to debt collection in Europe is significantly lower than in the US, but in the absence of concrete statistics one may only speculate.

[4] King and Cook (1996), p. 7.

[5] "The recent increase in reported debt collection complaints is proof enough that the FDCPA is still a necessary shield for consumers." Akina (2012), p. 150.

The book also proposed six building blocks for a viable system concerning protection of consumer debtors against abusive debt collection practices. The identified building blocks are (1) definition of debt collectors; (2) a licensing system of debt collectors; (3) updated statutory requirements concerning (a) communication with the debtor and third parties; (b) harassment or abuse of the debtor or debtor-related third parties; (c) false, deceptive or misleading forms or representations; (d) validation of the debt; (e) fees and charges added to the debt; (4) open-end functional definitions, which would allow the statute to be applied by analogy to new abusive practices, by taking into account their effect upon debtors or related third parties; (5) civil liability correlated with incentives for private action; and (6) availability of swift and effective state action (administrative enforcement).

However, it must be reemphasized here that this work does not take the position that a regulation of abusive debt collection practices will be automatically successful by simply including the above building blocks. The only contention is that a system guiding itself by these building blocks has a good chance of becoming efficient.

The US FDCPA and the UK CONC clearly represent the recognition of the fact that the rights of debtors (be it natural persons or even SMEs under UK legislation) deserve a larger degree of attention.[6] The general layer of protection available for consumer protection appears as unfit to deal with all the issues posed by nonjudicial debt collection. Hence, an additional layer of protection is needed, in the form of sector-specific regulation, as the US and the UK have already implemented. Their counterparts from France and Germany, as well as the failed attempt from Romania, point into the same direction.

The FDCPA has tried to secure the debtor's rights to privacy and to not be subjected to any abusive or unethical debt collection practices. It also tried to level up ineffective or lacking state regulations and to overcome inadequate traditional tort theories, by providing specific and tailor-made statutory actions to fit the context. Encouragement of meaningful state regulation of abusive debt collection practices, the acquired uniformity and comprehensiveness of state laws may be considered one of the greatest achievements of the FDCPA.[7] Despite recent heavy criticism—mostly due to the act's inability to keep up with technological developments—the FDCPA managed to provide the debtor with civil remedies and effective incentives to determine him to take private action. Combined with additional state legislation and powerful administrative enforcement mechanisms, it is a viable and successful model of efficiency.

On the other hand, reform was called by both the debt collection industry's representatives and consumers' advocates, under the motivation that necessary clarifications and adequate mechanisms that would enable the act to respond to a

[6] For answers to criticism that such an act would only increase debt delinquency, see Potach (1978), pp. 922–923, footnote 156.

[7] Potach (1978), p. 923.

rapid changing society and technologies could only benefit all those involved.[8] The steps taken by the Dodd–Frank Act to provide the BFCP with regulatory powers to double the substantive law's provisions are a solid acknowledgment of the issues and an attempt to correct them.

The conducted analysis revealed that reform is also needed in the European jurisdictions. Despite being updated and comprehensive, the UK CONC falls short of providing an effective enforcement tool to consumers and the issue of abuse is far from being solved. France's approach, drawing only general lines regarding communication and the debt collector's fiduciary duties, is insufficient. So is Germany's focus on licensing and registration.[9] Romania still struggles with finding a project to implement. The proposal that was analyzed in the final chapters was rightfully dismissed, for it failed to establish a proper framework or to provide for appropriate means of enforcement. Thus, it is this book's final conclusion that only by looking at the policies behind the FDCPA, the way they were implemented by the legislator and interpreted by courts and the way the FCA's CONC approached the large categories of abuses related to the use of modern technologies will the legislators find a good starting point for a proper draft.

References

Akina WK (2012) Note: A Lie Is A Lie: the need to define Section 1692e of the FDCPA. Brooklyn J Corp Financ Commer Law 7:145

Consumer Federation of America (2007) Collecting consumer debts: the challenges of change. In: Comments to the federal trade commission regarding the fair debt collection practices act

King LP, Cook ML (1996) Creditors' rights, debtors' protection, and bankruptcy. Mathew Bender, New York

McCall JR (1973) The past as prologue: a history of the right to repossess. South Calif Law Rev 47

Potach SG (1978) New protection against the unethical bill collector: debtor's remedies under the fair debt collection practices act. Creighton Law Rev

Rizoiu R (2011) Garantiile reale imobiliare. O abordare functionala – Analiza economica a dreptului garantiilor reale – Introducere in regimul juridic al ipotecilor mobiliare. Universul Juridic, Bucharest

Tajti T (2013a) Post-1990 secured transaction law reforms in Central and Eastern Europe. Szegedi Közjegyzői Közlöny

Tajti T (2013b) Systemic and topical mapping of the relationship of the draft common frame of reference and arbitration. Kazimieras Simonavicius University, Vilnius

Taylor CR (1998) Self-help in contract law: an exploration and proposal. Wake Forest Law Rev 33:839

von Bar C, Clive E (2010) Principles, definitions and model rules of European private law. Draft Common Frame of Reference (DCFR). Oxford University Press, Oxford

[8] America (2007), pp. 26–27. The League's call for reformation consisting in providing FTC with the power to write and enforce regulations implementing the FDCPA was answered positively by the Dodd–Frank Act, which granted such powers to the newly created Bureau for Financial Consumer Protection.

[9] Tajti (2013a, b), p. 113, footnote 330.

Annexes

Annex 1

TOP
Investigatii

> The current document is allegedly signed by a private detective, although the heading belongs to the debt collecting company. Among others, the letter informs the debtor that he may be audio and video surveyed in the conditions of the law. However, according to Romanian legislation, surveillance is allowed only by court order or prosecutor's order, which is probably meant to infer that the debtor is criminally prosecuted.

[redacted]

AVERTISMENT

CU PRIVIRE LA INCEPEREA PROCEDURII DE INVESTIGARE

Subsemnatul [redacted] detectiv particular atestat de Directia Generala de Politie a Municipiului Bucuresti sub nr. G0[illegible]194, desfasurandu-mi activitatea in cadrul **Top Investigatii SRL**, va instiintez prin prezenta cu privire la faptul ca **investigatia privind obtinerea de informatii cu privire la persoana si solvabilitatea Dvs., precum si cu privire la circumstantele in care ati incheiat contractul de credit 7307397 cu Raiffeisen Bank SA a inceput.**

Ca urmare, in temeiul legii 329/2003 republicata si HG 1666/2004, urmeaza ca in dosarul Dvs. sa se desfasoare urmatoarele activitati:

- **verificarea solvabilitatii** prin identificarea bunurilor si surselor Dvs. de venit;
- **verificarea calitatii de asociat sau administrator** al unei societati comerciale, sau de **persoana fizica autorizata**;
- **verificarea actelor ce au precedat incheierea contractelor** de credit;
- culegerea de **informatii despre persoana Dvs.**.

In realizarea activitatilor amintite, **se vor utiliza toate mijloacele legale prevazute de legislatia in vigoare**, inclusiv ***inregistrarea de imagini si sunete in conditiile legii***.

Informatiile rezultate in urma anchetei vor fi prelucrate si ~~furnizate clientului, care le va transmite~~ **executorului judecatoresc** si **organelor abilitate sa ia masuri** in situatia existentei de nereguli la incheierea contractului de credit.

> This paragraph contends that the data obtained about the debtor will be transmitted to the bailiff and to other authorized bodies. However, since judicial enforcement is performed through the bailiff system, there are no other "authorized bodies." Here the letter tries to suggest again that the debtor might be criminally liable.

Investigatia initiata poate inceta **in situatia in care se primesc instructiuni de la SC TOP FACTORING SRL pentru inchiderea dosarului** ca urmare a achitarii debitului.

Contactati **SC TOP FACTORING SRL** la numarul de telefon **021 365 31 16** pentru a obtine informatii suplimentare despre dosarul Dvs..

Detectiv Particular [redacted]

SOCIETATEA COMERCIALA TOP INVESTIGATII S.R.L. BUCURESTI-ROMANIA

C.G. Stănescu, *Self-Help, Private Debt Collection and the Concomitant Risks*,
DOI 10.1007/978-3-319-21503-7

Annex 2

This stamp resembles the stamp used by bailiffs in Romania. The text literally means: "Approved for judicial enforcement." However, the letter only speaks of a warning concerning the possibility of having the debt judicially enforced. Hence the stamp is misleading.

Note that there is no indication on how the alleged owed amount was calculated, or how it could be challenged.

Str. Tudor Arghezi nr.21, et.5
Sector 2 Bucuresti

topfactoring

CUI:18496757
J40/4569/2006

AVIZAT
PENTRU
EXECUTARE SILITĂ

[redacted]

AVERTIZARE
PRIVIND POSIBILITATEA INCEPERII
PROCEDURII DE EXECUTARE SILITA

Subscrisa **SC TOP FACTORING SRL**, vă aducem la cunoştinţă faptul că s-a finalizat analiza dosarului având ca obiect debitul Dvs. provenit din contractul de credit Raiffeisen Bank nr. **7307397**, cesionat către **Glasro Holdings LTD**, **în vederea adoptării măsurilor de recuperare prin executare silita.**

Vă informăm că incepând cu data de 30.08.2012 se va putea inainta organelor competente cererea formulată de către Cabinetul de Avocatură al SC TOP FACTORING SRL, cu privire la recuperarea prin intermediul executarii silite a creanţei deţinută împotriva Dvs..

Vă aducem la cunoştinţă că toate costurile ocazionate de procedura executarii silite vor fi suportate de Dvs., în conformitate cu dispoziţiile art.371[7] alin. 2 Cod Procedură Civilă. Aceste costuri pot consta în (fără a se limita la):

I. **TAXĂ DE TIMBRU;**
II. **ONORARIU EXECUTOR JUDECĂTORESC;**
III. **ALTE CHELTUIELI DE EXECUTARE, DUPĂ CAZ.**

Prin urmare, pentru a evita consecinţele legale expuse, achitaţi suma de 382.24 RON până la data de 30.08.2012.
Platile se pot efectua la orice sucursala Raiffeisen Bank, in contul RO70RZBR0000060013869357, deschis la agentia Dorobanti, sau la orice punct de lucru PayPoint, utilizand codul de bare de mai jos:

1230401499310169164000382230001

Pentru informaţii suplimentare, ne puteţi contacta de luni până vineri între orele 08:00-21:00, sâmbăta între orele 09:00-15:30 sau duminica între orele 10:00-14:00, la nummărul de telefon: **021 365 31 16** (tarif normal).

SC TOP FACTORING SRL,
prin avocat Magdalena Cristescu

Uniunea Naţională a Barourilor din România
CRISTESCU MAGDALENA
Cabinet de Avocat
Baroul Bucureşti

Referitor la prelucrarea datelor cu caracter personal, va informam ca societatea SC TOP FACTORING SRL este autorizata ca operator de date cu caracter personal, cu nr. 3164 si prelucreaza datele dumneavoastra cu caracter personal furnizate la incheierea contractelor de prestari servicii, precum si obtinute din baze de date publice. Va aducem la cunostinta ca aveti drepturile prevazute de art.12-18 din Legea 677/2001, in special dreptul de acces, de interventie si de opozitie, pe care vi le puteti exercita printr-o cerere scrisa, semnata si datata, trimisa la adresa societatii noastre.

Annex 3

Str. Tudor Arghezi nr.21, et.5
Sector 2 Bucuresti

topfactoring

CUI:18496757
J40/4569/2006

This letter refers to a statutory barred debt. The debtor is "encouraged" to make a minimum payment (which would basically revive the debt) under the threat that in case of judicial enforcement, more expenses will be added to the initial amount. The debtor is not informed in any way that no judicial proceedings are available against him.

[redacted]

Costurile executarii silite vor majora datoria!

SC TOP FACTORING SRL, mandatar al cesionarului **Glasro Holdings LTD** va reaminteste ca debitul restant, provenit din relatia contractuala pe care ati avut-o cu **Raiffeisen Bank SA** este de **390.28 RON**.

Va instiintam ca pe dosarul Dvs. se adauga lunar dobanzi penalizatoare sau legale pana la plata integrala a debitului.

Totodata, pe langa acestea, in urma executarii silite se vor cumula costuri suplimentare ce pot ajunge la 239.03 RON, constand in onorarii executor, onorarii avocat, cheltuieli de executare, taxe de timbru etc., suma care va va fi imputata.

Va recomandam sa alegeti rezolvarea amiabila si sa achitati pana pe **25.09.2012** suma de **75.00 RON** utilizand detaliile de mai jos:

Suma totala de plata actualizata la data de 14.09.2012	**390.28 RON**
Suma minima de plata pana la data de 25.09.2012	**75.00 RON**
Modalitati de plata:	
1. La orice sucursala **Raiffeisen Bank** in contul **RO70RZBR0000060013869357** (deschis la agentia Dorobanti), mentionand referinta unica **7307397** si beneficiar **SC TOP FACTORING SRL.**	
2. La orice punct de lucru PayPoint utilizand codul de bare imprimat mai jos: 12304014993104023280003902700 1	
Dupa ce achitati, contactati un consultant **SC TOP FACTORING SRL** la **021 365 31 16** pentru a stabili detaliile achitarii diferentei!	

In cazul in care nu sunteti de acord cu propunerea noastra va somam sa achitati suma de **390.28 RON** in maxim 5 zile de la data primirii notificarii!

Confirmati plata la nr. de fax **021 301 29 29** sau la adresa de e-mail **arhiva@topfactoring.ro**. Pentru informatii suplimentare ne puteti contacta de luni pana vineri intre orele 08:00-21:00, sambata intre orele 09:00-15:30 sau duminica intre orele 10:00-14:00, la numarul de telefon: **021 365 31 16.**

Manager Departament Colectare Debite
[redacted]
SC TOP FACTORING SRL

DEPARTAMENTUL RECUPERARE DEBITE

SC TOP FACTORING - RECUPERARE DEBITE
EXECUTARE SILITA
ACTIUNI IN JUSTITIE
AMIABIL

Referitor la prelucrarea datelor cu caracter personal, va informam ca societatea SC TOP FACTORING SRL este autorizata ca operator de date cu caracter personal, cu nr. 3164 si prelucreaza datele dumneavoastra cu caracter personal furnizate la incheierea contractelor de prestari servicii, precum si obtinute din baze de date publice. Va aducem la cunostinta ca aveti drepturile prevazute de art.12-18 din Legea 677/2001, in special dreptul de acces, de interventie si de opozitie, pe care vi le puteti exercita printr-o cerere scrisa, semnata si datata, trimisa la adresa societatii noastre.

The manufacturer's authorised representative in the EU is Springer
ature Customer Service Centre GmbH, Europaplatz 3, 69115 Heidelberg,
rmany. If you have any concerns regarding our products, please
act ProductSafety@springernature.com

d and bound by CPI Group (UK) Ltd, Croydon, CR0 4YY
06/10/2026
02229006-0003